Tocqueville and the Two Democracies

Tocqueville and the Two Democracies

JEAN-CLAUDE LAMBERTI

Translated by Arthur Goldhammer

HARVARD UNIVERSITY PRESS
Cambridge, Massachusetts
London, England
1989

321.8
L 171 T

Copyright © 1989 by the President and Fellows of Harvard College
All rights reserved
Printed in the United States of America
10 9 8 7 6 5 4 3 2 1

First published as *Tocqueville et les deux démocraties,* © Presses
universitaires de France, 1983

This book is printed on acid-free paper, and its binding materials
have been chosen for strength and durability.

Library of Congress Cataloging-in-Publication Data
Lamberti, Jean-Claude.
  [Tocqueville et les deux démocraties. English]
  Tocqueville and the two democracies / Jean-Claude Lamberti :
translated by Arthur Goldhammer.
     p.   cm.
  Translation of: Tocqueville et les deux démocraties.
  Bibliography: p.
  Includes index.
  ISBN 0-674-89435-9 (alk. paper)
  1. Tocqueville, Alexis de, 1805–1859—Contributions in
political science.   2. Democracy.   3. France—Politics and government.
  4. United States—Politics and government.   I. Title.
JC229.T8L35313   1989   88-18758
321.8—dc19   CIP

$50.00

✖ *Contents*

✖ *Foreword*

by François Bourricaud

IN TOCQUEVILLE'S WORK several projects
and several ambitions are mingled. Clever people, more impressed
perhaps than they should be by academic titles, find it difficult to
overcome a cruel prejudice: Was Tocqueville a *real* sociologist? To be
sure, Raymond Aron included the author of *Democracy in America* in
the pantheon of "founders of sociology." But it must be conceded that
Tocqueville was not a professional sociologist like Emile Durkheim or
Max Weber, nor even like his contemporary François Guizot, who,
before serving King Louis-Philippe as a minister, taught the comparative history of European institutions at the Collège de France.

With Tocqueville, intellectual ambition and political ambition were
intertwined, at least until Napoleon III's coup d'état of 2 December 1851
prevented him from exercising the responsibilities for which he had
diligently prepared himself from youth. But his two ambitions, that of
the politician and that of the author, did not merely coexist; each was
implicit in the other. To master such divergent impulses obviously
required exceptional virtuosity. It is no easier for kings to be philosophers than for philosophers to be kings. Tocqueville was perhaps less
susceptible than most of his contemporaries to utopian delusions. He
had too much sense and too much taste to see himself as a magus or
prophet. His shock and distress at the sight of the wild men brought
to the fore by the disturbances of February 1848—so apparent in his

Souvenirs—indicate how repellent he found the romantic conception of the historical process.

Tocqueville's career in parliament and as a minister offers a good illustration of what Max Weber calls the "ethics of responsibility." Despite his opposition to Guizot, he never joined the petty intrigues against that minister of the king. And his contemptuous attitude toward Lamartine reveals his distrust of that poet-politician's effusive lyricism and his aversion to demagogues who count on Providence to repair the consequences of their hastily improvised schemes.

A man of responsibility, Tocqueville was nevertheless also a man of conviction (to borrow another phrase from Weber). In his case, however, it is wrong to think that conviction meant holding to a set of "principles" or a "doctrine." Guizot, not Tocqueville, was the doctrinaire, who, it has been said, mistook the Charter of 1830 for holy writ. Tocqueville was more flexible. He understood the relativity and mutability of institutions. For him, political problems, even if they were more than merely topical and involved what we would call value judgments, could not be treated as pure ideal objects without historical and circumstantial references. *Democracy in America* is not a book of the same genre as the *Social Contract*. Nor is it a book of current affairs; it is, rather, a work of commitment. Tocqueville subscribed—unhesitatingly, unflaggingly, and I am tempted to say passionately—to certain fundamental values, but over the course of time he entertained different views as to how those values could be embodied. As his thought progressed and his experience grew, he even came to doubt that those values could be realized at all in a country like France. Charles X said that he and Lafayette shared the quality of not having changed since their youth. Even if, in fragments written for the second volume of *The Old Regime and the French Revolution* and published after his death, Tocqueville showed himself to be a severe judge of the political capabilities of the leading revolutionaries; and even if it seemed to him that the "magnificent sunrise" of 1789 had turned all too quickly into the nightmare of the Terror, Tocqueville kept faith with the inspiration and the values of the Constituent Assembly. He was, as François Furet might say in *Penser la Révolution française,* a man of the national party.

The reader of Tocqueville confronts a major obstacle, for he was an author who attempted to respond to certain problems of his day. Yet he believed that the questions he posed and answers he gave to them would retain their meaning long after the circumstances that gave rise to them had disappeared.

A second difficulty in reading Tocqueville has to do with his method. With many writers, methodological preliminaries serve simply as precaution and camouflage; with some, methodology even obscures the meaning of the work. Durkheim is a case in point: his strict profession of the positivist faith, his claim to treat "social facts as things," his peremptory remarks on social constraint aggravated the difficulties which in any case would have derived from his overly broad conception of "Society." Not being a professor, Tocqueville was fortunate in not having to take positions in a variety of scholastic disputes. But his methodological parsimony is not always exempt from obscurity.

One snare that political "theory" does not always manage to avoid is that of *essentialism*. The theorist's weakness for classifications and abstractions dates perhaps from the Greeks. The regime types that Plato lists in the *Republic* and defines by systems of attributes constitute a hierarchy. So implacable is the logic of these systems that the observer feels he can explain the actual behavior of rulers and ruled and predict the downfall of one regime and its replacement by another. Understood in this way, regime types are not mere conventions that help us comprehend the diversity of events and circumstances, not mere types or forms in the sense of Weber or Simmel, but Platonic Ideas, with the power to compel phenomena to conform to their image or, more radically, to produce or engender those phenomena.

Political philosophy is as spontaneously essentialist as the old biological philosophy, which saw every species as defined by a set of enduring traits that rigorously determined once and for all the behavior of individual members. One of Tocqueville's most invaluable contributions was to teach political philosophers how to remove their essentialist blinders. The success of the first volume of *Democracy in America* was due, in part at least, to the interest that the French of 1835 took in the United States. The comparative lack of success of the second volume, published in 1840, was due to the difficulty of a work which asked not just about the future of American democracy but about the future of democracy in modern society generally. Nevertheless, it is superficial to see the first volume as a monograph on American institutions and the second as a sequel composed of timeless and moralizing reflections on the "essence" of democracy.

From his very first book Tocqueville was able to see through the illusory unity of the essence or "concept" because he had discovered a fundamental *paradox*. If democracy is defined as the sovereignty of the people, it is easy to see that, as Benjamin Constant taught, the sovereignty of the majority is potentially just as tyrannical as the sovereignty of the monarch. Tocqueville's contemporaries, memories of the Terror still fresh in their minds, were quite naturally inclined to accept this thesis. To the objection that some countries had experienced and were still experiencing democracy without enduring the terrible tribulations that had marked the Revolution, they had a ready response: Switzerland was a small country, and the United States was still too young to permit any conclusions to be drawn. Democracy was condemned by its very essence to succumb to despotism and terror; these were a part of its being, as Aristotle might have said: *ti ēn einai.*

Tocqueville does not lapse into such tautologies. Why did the French version of the democratic regime produce the crimes of the Jacobins whereas the American version had shown itself prudent and peaceful? That is the question that runs through the two volumes of Tocqueville's first great book. But Tocqueville's comparisons are not haphazard. The societies whose resemblances and differences he seeks to elucidate are kindred societies. In the case of England and the United States, that kinship is evident. Tocqueville himself calls attention to the direct filiation. The relationship between France and England and the United States is more complex. But all three societies shared what I have called in the *Tocqueville Review* (1980) a "cotradition." This cotradition does not of course coincide with the sum of the three national traditions; rather, it is defined by elements common to all and exerts a controlling and regulating influence over the functioning and development of each.

Tocqueville avoided the pitfalls of conceptual realism: he did not mistake words for things or treat regimes as essences. But he also sidestepped the danger of empiricist nominalism: he never believed that social processes are singular and hence incomparable. He was wary of abstractions which envisioned democracy "in general." He distinguished varieties of democracy, French and American in particular. But he was alert to "family resemblances," to the constants that remained when the differences had been shorn away.

Tocqueville's analysis did not stop at distinguishing two or even several types of democracy; it was not simply a refinement of one "essence" into a range of variants but a fleshing out of the notion of democracy itself. Tocqueville discerned three aspects of the democratic phenomenon: political, socioeconomic, and cultural. Everyone knows that democracy is a way of organizing the relationship between rulers and ruled. But what people too often forget is that the form of government depends on the way in which scarce goods such as honor, prestige, money, and power are distributed among the members of the society. The socioeconomic aspect of democracy involves what sociologists call social stratification. The interrelationship of political regime and social stratification is highly complex. Finally, democratic societies are distinguished by the relative importance of various ideologies compounded of "general and dominant passions" and "dogmatic beliefs." Here, Tocqueville had to deal with what sociologists call the "value problem," which in modern democratic societies centers on the blending of libertarian with egalitarian values.

Democracy is a composite phenomenon. It is a compromise among often divergent requirements and principles. As a result, democratic societies experience tensions that can be resolved only by a combination of fortune and political skill. American democracy is unique because its cultural ideals, distribution of resources and status, and form of government have remained compatible over a long period of time. But this compatibility is far from perfect; what is more, it is largely fortuitous. Although the absence of a nobility spared the English colonies of the New World from the contamination of a feudal past, American democracy was far from "pure." For one thing, the "peculiar institution," slavery, contradicted the credo set forth in the Declaration of Independence. For another, aristocratic and patrician elements survived, especially in the judiciary, which had a considerable impact on the operation of local and federal government. Finally, American democracy was fortunate in that it was rooted in a pious, austere, and hardworking people. It created itself, as it were, and did so more or less peacefully. The glorious episode to which Americans refer as the Revolution was in fact a war of independence waged by a free people against their relatives across the sea.

Nothing could be farther from Tocqueville's mind than the notion of historical necessity. It would be silly to enlist Tocqueville in the tiresome disputes between historians and sociologists. He was unquestionably a man interested in history as much as in social analysis and saw no reason to establish insuperable barriers between the two. Two examples of social processes which Tocqueville analyzes in a quite modern spirit stand out with particular clarity. The final chapter of the first volume of *Democracy in America* contains an analysis of the forces tending to exacerbate the hostility between the North and the South over the question of slavery to such a degree that preservation of the union appeared problematic. All the pertinent variables are identified:

demographic, economic, cultural, juridical, and political. Tocqueville considers the incentives for southern planters to increase their slave holdings as the English demand for cotton increased; he examines the segregation of the races in the South and the consequent conflict between slave and free states in Congress; and he notes the increasingly radical debate over slavery, which had already shifted from political to constitutional grounds. All of these things led him to foresee the likelihood of the civil war that did in fact break out twenty-five years after the publication of his book.

In the second volume of *Democracy in America,* Tocqueville considers the growth of government intervention. Again, he uses a hypothetico-deductive model. Assume a population of isolated individuals, who cannot or do not wish to organize themselves. Suppose, further, that these individuals place a very high value on certain goods that can be produced only by collective effort (what today would be called "public goods"). Now, suppose that politicians or government officials offer such goods to individuals eager to acquire them and incapable of producing them by their own effort. If this should happen, either because the individuals in question are unable to work effectively in concert or because the politicians or bureaucrats are in the best position to offer such goods "on the most favorable terms" (that is, at the lowest possible cost), the result could well be the subjugation of the individuals receiving the goods to those who purvey them. "The overwhelming and protective despotism" of the welfare state would be all the more difficult to resist if its first harmful effects were scarcely perceptible; by the time the need for resistance became apparent, it would be too late.

Tocqueville never maintained, however, that bureaucratic despotism was an inevitable consequence of democracy or that the slavery question would inevitably spell the end of the American Republic. He sought, rather, to specify the conditions under which such outcomes would be more or less likely. For the answer, however, one must await the verdict of history, often long in coming and almost always shrouded in obscurity. Furthermore, just as hypothetico-deductive models are subject to historical verification, historical processes themselves can only be analyzed with the help of well-chosen sociological hypotheses. The French Revolution is a historical fact. But history is no more a matter of pure contingency than sociology is of pure necessity. As soon as we try to explain why certain events followed one course rather than another, we are forced to invoke hypotheses whose scope transcends the particular events studied by the historian. Thus, for Tocqueville, revolutions are more likely at the end of periods of expansion and enrichment, as the pace of growth slackens and stalls, than in prolonged periods of decline or stagnation. In the final book of *The Old Regime and the French Revolution* he traces the cumulative enthusiasms that destabilized the monarchy and ultimately swept away the Parlements and the privileged orders, which proved unable to foresee the consequences of their obstructionism.

Was Tocqueville guilty of cultural fatalism? So careful not to invoke the "essence" of democratic regimes to explain the workings of democracy in America, did he not succumb to the temptation to "reify" the national character? Tocqueville conceived of the national character in much the same way that Montesquieu understood "the general spirit of a nation," yet he did not explain it in terms of experience or heritage or adaptation. Can one say that democratic values were "functional" in the natural and social environment that existed in the United States? I do not think that Tocqueville would have answered this question in the affirmative. Did he believe that Americans were impervious to historical experience? His answer is not explicit. But in considering France and England, he was so acutely aware of the transition (or sudden shift) from aristocratic to democratic values that it seems unlikely that he believed in the unalterability of cultural phenomena. When he alludes to "general and dominant passions" and "dogmatic beliefs," he obviously means to imply that these enjoy some measure of stability beyond the preferences of individuals and the fashions and enthusiasms of successive generations. But he does not regard the national character, any more than the political regime, as an "essence" or self-subsistent Platonic "form." (The only point on which I find him in error concerns his view, based on a tendentious interpretation of French history, that France is fated to be governed by a bureaucracy.)

Tocqueville: historian, sociologist, or philosopher? The question is not a very interesting one. In introducing Jean-Claude Lamberti's fine book, I have attempted to say quite simply that, however subject to criticism Tocqueville's work may be in certain respects, it remains a model for all who are wary of abstractions and "essences" and yet wish to bring intelligibility and comprehension to the analysis of social processes.

Tocqueville and the Two Democracies

Introduction:
The Man and
His History

Is Tocqueville in the process of being adopted as an American writer? It might seem so, given that he is better known to educated readers in the United States than in France, and comparing the scant work devoted to him in France with the abundance and quality of American Tocqueville scholarship in recent years.[1] The working manuscript, rough drafts, and preparatory notes for *Democracy in America* reside in Yale University's Beinecke Library,[2] and the study of Tocqueville has been an American university tradition for years, ever since George Wilson Pierson devoted a magisterial work to tracing the journey of Alexis de Tocqueville and Gustave de Beaumont through the United States.[3] Only rarely are we informed about every stage in the development of a masterpiece in the literature of politics, and we are fortunate indeed that we do possess such knowledge about the greatest political work of the nineteenth century, *Democracy in America*. Although the work is French, its interpretation and above all the study of its creation are primarily the work of what I shall call the Yale School, by which I mean all those scholars who, like Pierson, have based their work on the Yale archives.

The Paris School, insofar as it exists, is interested more in *The Old Regime and the French Revolution*[4] than in *Democracy in America*. The latter, notwithstanding Raymond Aron's pioneering work, has attracted little attention from French philosophers and sociologists,[5] the philosophers deeming it perhaps insufficiently speculative and the sociologists insufficiently scientific—to say nothing of those who simply find it too American. Nevertheless, French historians regard *The Old Regime* as a book of the first importance, as may be gathered from Georges Lefebvre's introduction to a recent edition;[6] the scholarly research of André Jardin, thanks to which we can now read Tocqueville's "unpublished fragments and notes on the Revolution";[7] and the brilliant work of François Furet, *Penser la Révolution française*, more than half of which is devoted to Tocqueville.

This division of labor is unfortunate, for it tends to divide Tocqueville's work into two parts, one American and one French, whereas in his first work he is constantly making at least implicit comparisons between American democracy and the French Revolution, and he wrote *The Old Regime* after the failure of the Second Republic, whose constitution he had hoped to write in a manner reflecting the lessons learned from his study of the American Republic. It is misleading to say that Tocqueville ceased to reflect on America after his youth, because the Revolution of 1848 rekindled French interest in what was then called the "American School." And it is just as misleading to say that *The Old Regime and the French Revolution* contains all of Tocqueville's thinking on the Revolution, when in fact he had meditated constantly upon the subject ever since 1836, when he wrote an article about it at the behest of John Stuart Mill.[8] In the second volume of *Democracy in America*, published in 1840, Tocqueville attempts to distinguish between democracy and revolution; indeed, as we shall see, the structure of the work is determined by the difficulties he encountered in doing so.

With Tocquevillean scholarship specialized in this way on either side of the Atlantic, the inevitable result has been to introduce an artificial cleavage in a body of work which from beginning to end is based on comparison of France and the United States.[9] The consequences of this are considerable. Severed from knowledge of the suffering and failure of revolution in Europe, reflection upon American democracy is likely to degenerate into utopian mythmaking, singing the praises of the "blessed republic." To argue that the lessons of *Democracy in America* are relevant only to the United States is to encourage belief in American exceptionalism while discouraging the use of comparative methods in political science. It is also to neglect the fact that the unique features of democratic liberalism in the United States are due to the absence of a great revolution at its origin.[10]

But to treat the French Revolution without considering, in a comparative light, the history of the American Republic is to overlook a needed corrective to an illusion quite widespread in France, namely, that the Revolution necessarily had to follow the course that it did, in all its aspects and characteristic phases. Democracy and revolution are not the same thing, hence the democratic idea should not be confounded with the ideals of 1793. Indeed, democracy was in fact jeopardized—and is still jeopardized today—by a revolutionary tradition that destroys democracy while invoking its name.

In this book I shall consider the two central themes of Tocqueville's work: democracy and revolution. The relation between the two is fundamental to an understanding of Tocqueville's thought. Throughout his life he considered both themes together, just as he had done in his youth, in the earliest stages of his vocation. His comparative method enabled him to render both faces of democracy with remarkable fidelity.[11]

The Man and His Vocation

Alexis de Tocqueville was born on 29 July 1805 to a family of the old Norman nobility whose history can be traced (as is rarely the case) all the way back to the twelfth century. His ancestors, who used the patronymic Clerel, settled at Tocqueville around 1590 and acquired the estate and seigneurie bearing that name in 1661. Among the companions of William the Conqueror who distinguished themselves at the Battle of Hastings was a Norman gentleman by the name of Clerel, and although there was no certain proof of the filiation, Alexis de Tocqueville considered himself a descendant of that warrior.[12] This family, which counted among its ancestors not only Saint Louis but also Cesare Borgia and Vauban, rose in stature in the eighteenth century through inheritances, services rendered to the military, and marriages, especially marriage to the family of Damas-Crux. "The nobility of Cotentin," Tocqueville said, "was accustomed to see us marching at its head."[13]

Alexis's father, Count Hervé de Tocqueville, was born in 1772 to Bernard de Tocqueville and Antoinette de Damas-Crux; he married Louise Le Peletier de Rosanbo, the granddaughter of Malesherbes.[14] Of all his ancestors, Alexis de Tocqueville most resembled, I think, this courageous defender of Louis XVI, whose curiosity and intellectual independence, civic feeling, and passion for justice he shared.

At the age of sixteen he discovered in his father's library Descartes and the eighteenth-century philosophes, and his Catholic beliefs would throughout his life be shaken by this early reading. Never again, save perhaps in his final days, was he free from doubt: "I believe," he wrote his tutor, the abbé Lesueur, "but I can no longer practice."[15] But the crisis was more profound than this letter would indicate, and all his life Tocqueville struggled to regain his faith and win the children of Descartes over to Christianity. He aspired to reconcile the "spirit of religion" with the "spirit of liberty." It was in this form that his vocation first revealed itself.

Though he suffered from lifelong contradictions and doubts, Alexis de Tocqueville nevertheless clung to a few simple but powerful ideas. His political and intellectual life was shaped in essence by two convictions first acquired in childhood and confirmed in early adolescence: love of liberty and hatred of revolution. He never doubted that the human soul is free and immortal, and in his last major published speech he recalled that liberty had always been his primary value: "I regard and have always regarded liberty as the first of goods. I still see it as one of the most fertile sources of male virtues and great actions. I should not relinquish it for any amount of tranquillity or well-being."[16] Family memories and education impressed upon his mind an ineradicable horror of the revolutionary spirit.

Tocqueville's melancholy was not that of an aristocrat forced to endure the triumph of democracy, but that of a liberal as devoted as any to the spirit of 1789 and unable—in either his work or his political life—to make a clear distinction between democracy and revolution, although for a time he did believe (and it was one of the happiest times of his life) that he had found in America a democracy pure of any contamination by revolution. But this was a brief respite, and by the time the second volume of *Democracy in America* was published in 1840 Tocqueville had devoted a good deal of space to consideration of the doubt that is central to his political thinking: Is there not an inherent tendency in democratic society to create, if nothing is done to prevent it, situations as dangerous to liberty as revolution is? Already we can detect adumbrations of a question that Tocqueville would not treat in full rigor until the *Souvenirs* and *The Old Regime and the French Revolution*: Was the Revolution of 1789 a peculiar accident of French history, or were its most dangerous aspects typical of the risks faced by every democratic society?[17]

This, I think, is the question that Tocqueville took most to heart and that animates all his work and illuminates his political behavior. If I am right, the most common interpretation of Tocqueville is, if not exactly mistaken, in any case insufficient: it is vague and superficial to say that Tocqueville, an aristocrat, always had doubts about democracy, and the statement is simply wrong if by democracy one means the sort of liberal democracy that Tocqueville admired in New England and in the United States Constitution. It is true, however, that he always feared that democracy would succumb to its flaws and lead to excesses similar to those that marred the French Revolution. In Tocqueville the concept of democracy is ambivalent: it can refer to political realities as different as France and the United States, and it can be used as both an antonym and a synonym of revolution.

But given the seductiveness of psychological interpretations and the widespread taste for black-and-white solutions, Tocqueville's work will no doubt continue to be seen as that of an "aristocratic democrat," one a little more democratic than his peers but still a true son of his class, with each commentator free to choose precisely how much of the aristocrat and how much of the democrat to include in the final mix. Without a genuine political analysis, the boldness of Tocqueville's project is missed. Tocqueville hoped to outflank the French Revolution: for him, the best counterrevolution was the perfect democracy.

Intellectual and Political Apprenticeship

Tocqueville's principal ideas were formed quite early and by his own admission changed little over the course of his life.[18] He was not so much a great reader as a great investigator,[19] and Sainte-Beuve said of him that "he had begun to think before having learned anything." Not much is known with certainty about Tocqueville's early reading, but his correspondence[20] during the years he was writing volume two of *Democracy in America* tells us about his favorite authors. To his friend and cousin, Louis de Kergorlay, he wrote: "There are three men with whom I spend a little time each day; they are Pascal, Montesquieu, and Rousseau."[21] Although drawn from youth to works of political philosophy and history, he seldom cited the authors he had read, for he was keen to express his own views and probably liked to flaunt his originality.[22]

It would be absurd, however, to conclude that he did not read the young liberals of his day: some of the political writings of Benjamin Constant, Madame de Staël's *Considerations on the French Revolution*, and the *Essay on Revolutions* written by his relative Chateaubriand in 1826.

Tocqueville was closer to the so-called Doctrinaires than to Madame de Staël and her friends.[23] Of all the men he met, by his own admission Pierre-Paul Royer-Collard was the one who had the greatest influence on him. But he did not meet him until after the publication of *Democracy* in 1835, and before that date he knew nothing of Royer-Collard's writings apart from a few speeches delivered in the Chamber. Royer-Collard was closer to Chateaubriand than Benjamin Constant could have been; he was the most monarchist of the liberals, just as Chateaubriand was the most liberal of the monarchists. Before leaving for America Tocqueville had met Guizot, and from 11 April 1829 until 29 May 1830 he attended Guizot's lectures in the company of his friend Gustave de Beaumont.[24] Long afterward, during their service as deputies, the two friends were almost always opposed to Guizot, who broke with Royer-Collard during the debate over the laws of September 1835. But as a historian Guizot taught the two young men a great deal.

Guizot's course in modern history[25] dealt in 1828 with the general history of civilization in Europe from the fall of the Roman Empire to the French Revolution and in 1829 and 1830 more specifically with the history of civilization in France. The word "civilization," at the time quite new, was of great significance, implying ideas of progress, social development, and individualism.[26] Guizot held that the growth of the Third Estate was "the most active and decisive element in French civilization." In this the two young aristocrats found much food for thought, especially since Guizot portrayed French feudalism as an anarchic, oppressive regime incapable of constructing an aristocratic polity. In England, according to Guizot, monarchy and feudalism had developed together, and the struggle between them had given rise to free institutions, whereas in France the failure of feudalism to create aristocratic institutions and the inability of the communes to construct a democracy had led to absolute monarchy. By contrast, Tocqueville would always think of the French aristocracy as a local government that protected liberty against the encroachments of the central government, and he would never concede that the reign of the middle classes could be the culmination of civilization.[27] His myth of the aristocracy was not undermined by historical argument, and his intuition saw through the bourgeois prejudices of Guizot, who was less capable than Tocqueville of conceiving of democracy.

After completing preparatory school Tocqueville had read Thiers's *Histoire de la Révolution*, which he says occasioned in him "a singular horror and the most violent antipathy against its author."[28] He found Thiers's justification of the Terror to be the height of political immorality. During the July Monarchy there was a growing tendency to transform the French Revolution into a Jacobin myth. Revolutionary orthodoxy inspired by Robespierre and Saint-Just took hold of the imagination of many members of the republican opposition. The *Histoire parlementaire de la Révolution*, published by Philippe Buchez from 1834 to 1840, excused the crimes of the Terror and confusingly mingled long excerpts from the *Moniteur* with philosophical reflections in which Jacobinism was portrayed as an attempt to realize Christian morality. Tocqueville witnessed the development of the revolutionary myth under the July Monarchy from Buchez to Louis Blanc.[29] He watched as the liberal tendencies of the democratic and socialist left were gradually supplanted by a confused ideological mix in which egalitarian passions predominated. For Tocqueville, the chief vices of the Revolution were its contempt for the individual and his rights and its crimes against liberty, whereas the democratic-socialist school, enamored of equality above all else, saw the quest for liberty as nothing more than a symptom of individualism.[30]

The Irresistible Progress of Democracy

In the introduction to *Democracy in America* we find both of Tocqueville's major themes, democracy and revolution, at times linked, at other times set in opposition. In the first four pages, the "great democratic revolution" is confounded with the irresistible progress of democracy. Later, however, Tocqueville introduces a distinction between the confused, transitional situation of France (pp. 8–10),* which after the Revolution finds itself in a state between the Old Regime (pp. 6–7)[31] and the ideal Democracy (pp. 7–8), and the finished Democracy of the United States, where one can see "the results of the democratic revolution which is taking place among us, without having experienced the revolution itself" (p. 11). In France it is almost impossible to distinguish what is democratic from what is revolutionary, whereas in America representative democracy can be seen in its unalloyed form, in

---

*DA, I, introduction, pp. 8–10. For an explanation of this citation, see headnote to the Notes.

all its novelty and purity. Is the "great democratic revolution" simply another name for progress, or is it irresistible only because riots and battles make it so? Was the revolutionary crisis inevitable? More generally, does history unfold according to necessary laws? Even before he has an opportunity to set forth the broad outlines of his political philosophy, Tocqueville touches on these fundamental questions, about which the work itself remains oddly reserved, since the analysis of *Democracy in America* leaves little room for excursuses on history and revolution.

Tocqueville's expository technique and uncertain vocabulary are responsible for innumerable misunderstandings.[32] For example, his assertion that the progress of democracy is irresistible has been seen not as an impartial scientific judgment but as the profession of a political creed. Yet there is a major flaw in this interpretation of the introduction, which radically divides the author's philosophy from his sociology, much as the first book of Montesquieu's *Esprit des lois* is sometimes read in isolation from the rest of the work; that flaw is to ignore the organic unity between the introduction and the body of the book. In Tocqueville the architecture is essential, and the introduction to volume one of *Democracy* should be reread along with the conclusion to volume two and the chapter that forms the true conclusion of volume one: "The Main Causes Tending to Maintain a Democratic Republic in the United States."[33]

In this chapter Tocqueville asserts that "laws do more than physical causes to maintain the democratic republic in the United States, and mores do more than laws."[34] He ends the section with these words: "If I have not in the course of this work succeeded in making the reader feel what importance I ascribe to the practical experience of Americans, to their habits, their opinions, and in a word to their mores, in the maintenance of their laws, then I have failed in the principal aim which I set myself in writing."[35]

Tocqueville's diaries of his travels in America show that from his arrival he used categories borrowed from Montesquieu: physical causes, laws, mores.[36] All his American research is based on these, and the observations accumulated during the journey served as the basis for the conclusions just quoted.

At the end of this chapter, Tocqueville turns again to an analysis of the French situation, noting (pp. 326–330) that a long series of revolutions has combated the influence of religion, destroyed respect for the leaders of government, and diminished the spirit of individual resistance to power that is the hard core of the love of liberty. In France there are no more "free mores," that is, mores capable of contributing to the defense of liberty against possible erosion by authority. Revolution after revolution has exacerbated the contradictions inherent in these free mores, artificially opposing one to another. The best proof that such effects are not necessary products of either democracy or the natural movement of history is to be found by comparing France with the United States. Correct use of the comparative method thus makes it possible to distinguish in this crucial respect between the effects of democracy and those of revolution.

To substantiate this thesis, stated in the very introduction to the book, required a prodigious labor of comparison and induction; only then could the role of institutions and above all of mores in maintaining the democratic republic be stated with any precision. In my view, it is this conclusion of the work that makes possible a correct interpretation of the introduction, refuting the numerous criticisms that have been leveled at Tocqueville for his alleged belief in providential intervention in history or in the irresistible ascent of democracy. In a letter to his friend Kergorlay, Tocqueville defends his introduction and then adds: "It is now almost ten years since I first conceived of some of the ideas that I have just set forth." Are we to believe that at the time of Charles X's accession to the throne, while Tocqueville was still a law student and well before he attended Guizot's lectures, he had already formed his fundamental ideas and come to believe in an irresistible movement toward equality of condition?[37] The idea, at first sight surprising, stands up to scrutiny. Tocqueville knew men who did not hesitate to formulate bold hypotheses about the future, Chateaubriand among them.[38] He had conceived of the notion of an irresistible movement toward equality by observing, both within himself and in the world around him, that behind the facade of aristocratic laws and manners characteristic of the Restoration, French mores, ideas, and attitudes were undergoing a far-reaching process of evolution.[39]

Tocqueville found that the new society had left its mark on crucial ideas as well as customs, and, harking back to the tradition of the Enlightenment aristocracy and the patriotic nobility of the Constituent Assembly, he found himself wedded to the spirit of '89 and highly critical of the Ancien Régime. His initial ideas were not the product of lengthy reasoning; they were born of a penetrating intuition which saw the radical tendencies inherent in established structures. He first examined the mores of his time by means of that "subtle spirit" of which

Pascal said: "From the eyes it goes straight to the heart; and by the movement of the outside it knows what is going on within."[40] He excelled at interpreting human relations by such intuitive means and at attaining that knowledge which Pascal attributes to the "heart,"[41] at uncovering the most stable foundations of human mores, what Tocqueville liked to call "mother ideas" or "engendering facts." Tocqueville's intuitive genius resides in such knowledge, which penetrates to the source of ideas and feelings and which perceives, beneath what he called "mores," all the contrary currents, both superficial and profound.

The idea of an ineluctable triumph of democratic society and mores was originally—and from early youth—the fruit of Tocqueville's profound insight into his own day. The study of the past, the lessons of Guizot incorporated into the Introduction to *Democracy in America*, came later, adding seemingly objective justification to this original intuition and helping Tocqueville find the means to express his political aim, which was to diminish the excesses of terror and enthusiasm to which the progress of equality can give rise.[42] In essence, the idea of irresistible progress toward a democratic society is based on an intuitive grasp of contemporary mores and on the reasoned conviction, justified in the conclusion to *Democracy*, that the stability and longevity of a regime depend above all on its adaptation to those mores and on the conflict or harmony that exists among their constitutive ideas, beliefs, and attitudes.[43] Certain political, social, and economic conditions made lasting contributions to the progress of equality, but Tocqueville was a long way from believing in any necessary, immanent law of historical development or ineluctable progress of mankind.[44] History cannot teach us precisely when a long-term trend will suddenly reverse itself: tomorrow or ten centuries from now? To answer such a question one must appeal to wisdom as much as to history: "Would it be wise to believe that a social movement that has come so far can be halted by the efforts of a generation?" Political wisdom consists in judging not so much by laws as by mores, and the wise man knows from history that "mores" evolve only very slowly. That is why it is reasonable to conclude that the democratic movement, which is still in the ascendancy, will continue to dominate for a long time to come. Morally and politically, however, the affirmation of the right to equality can take very different forms, depending on whether or not it is coupled with an affirmation of liberty.

PART ONE

Freedom and Equality

1 ❧ *Aristocracy and Democracy*

The American National Character
and Democratic State

Near the end of volume one of *Democracy in America*, Tocqueville points out the need to "distinguish carefully between the institutions of the United States and democratic institutions in general"[1] so that proper conclusions may be drawn from the American experience. He was no doubt aware, however, of the difficulty of following his own advice, because five years later, in the preface to volume two, he recognized that many factors other than democracy had exerted "an immense influence" on the way Americans thought and acted. Nevertheless, he deliberately limits his goal to describing the influence of equality on the ideas and inclinations of citizens in democratic societies. The brevity of this pronouncement may strike the reader as an imposition. But with the help of manuscripts in the Yale archives, we can reconstruct what the preface to volume two was originally supposed to look like and understand how between 1836 and 1838 Tocqueville gradually abandoned the idea of justifying his intentions in a lengthy introduction. In one draft, for instance, he proposes to identify "what is American or English without being democratic." It is very difficult, he adds, "to separate out what is democratic, commercial, English, and Puritan. To be set forth in preface."[2]

Another difficulty for the reader stems from Tocqueville's silence as to the American national character. He simply alludes to what is "American or English without being democratic" or to what stems from "commercial, English, and Puritan" factors. Tocqueville's travel diaries contain his earliest reflections on this subject: the American, he writes, is "the Englishman delivered unto himself."[3] The very obvious differences between the two can easily be interpreted in terms of the contrast between aristocratic society and democratic society. What is more, the true nature of the English character can be seen more clearly in America, where it stands revealed in pure form, whereas in England its peculiar features are mixed with others stemming from long years of aristocratic domination. "All that is illustrious, generous, proud, and given to luxury in the British character is aristocratic and not English."[4] This view carries special weight because it is that of a Norman gentleman who considered himself honored to be a descendant of a companion of William the Conqueror who had distinguished himself at the Battle of Hastings.[5] It suggests the importance that Tocqueville attached to the concept of national character, which he no doubt derived from Montesquieu's concept of "the general spirit of a nation."[6] In reworking Montesquieu's idea, however, Tocqueville modified it profoundly, and enriched it by discriminating between aristocratic and democratic societies.

The national character is not defined by commonality of race or language. Tocqueville always rejected the simplistic views of those who worshiped the idea of necessity; he was opposed, in particular, to the reductionist theories of his friend Gobineau.[7] In analyzing societies he was more concerned with the evolution of what we would nowadays call mental structures or *mentalités* than with purely physical factors such as race or climate. Tocqueville appears to have gone even further in this respect than his master, Montesquieu. Still, just as the "general spirit of a nation" was for Montesquieu a synthetic concept, so, too, was the national character for Tocqueville a particularly stable synthetic structure, capable of evolving only very slowly and formed by the habits of centuries, habits shaped by both physical and political factors.

If the French Canadians remain "absolutely similar to their former compatriots in France,"[8] and if the colonies of Germans settled in Pennsylvania "preserve intact the spirit and mores of their country,"[9] then the English character must also have been preserved on the other side of the Atlantic. Yet between the first settlements in the seventeenth century and Tocqueville's arrival on American shores, society's slow evolution had created a new situation, a democratic social state (*état social*). At times Tocqueville seems unsure of the relation between national character and social state. For example, in his diary for 26

December 1831 he writes: "I suppose that what is called the character of a people is often nothing but the character inherent in its social state. That is why the English character might be nothing other than the aristocratic character. What suggests that this is the case is the immense difference that exists between the English and their descendants in America."[10] Tocqueville is right to point out the confusion of many previous travelers, but he is in no danger of repeating their mistake; in this note, written solely for his own use, the "English character" refers to the character of the English in England, as shaped by aristocratic domination. If the character of their descendants in America is different, it can only be because the social state of the Americans is democratic.[11] Nevertheless, the notion of national character is not therefore devoid of interest; its full meaning does not become apparent, however, until one has grasped its precise relation to the social state. What Tocqueville is doing, really, is testing Montesquieu's basic concepts; we can follow the progress of this testing by reading his travel diaries, and we can see the results in the early pages of *Democracy in America*, particularly chapters two and three, in which he draws two new concepts out of Montesquieu's "general spirit of a nation": the national character and the social state. These are based on the opposition between aristocratic and democratic societies, fleshed out by constant comparison of England with the United States.

American Democratic Society

Readers and—even more often—commentators on Tocqueville frequently complain about his imprecise terminology, noting that the term "democracy" is never rigorously defined, despite its central place in the work. Analysts[12] have identified at least half a dozen distinct meanings, and in a remarkable recent work James T. Schleifer has established a list with no fewer than eleven different definitions of the word.[13]

In truth, there are numerous (though sometimes unclear) relations among the different meanings. Although I cannot claim to have eliminated all the ambiguities, I believe that Tocqueville's various uses of the word "democracy" cluster around two principal definitions: (1) democracy is a type of political regime characterized by a government of the people; (2) more commonly, democracy is a "social state" characterized by a tendency toward equality.[14] The reality of the "democratic social state" can be observed in America more readily than anywhere else,[15] but in theoretical terms the democratic social state can be understood as an irresistible tendency, an inevitable outgrowth of equality. At times Tocqueville treats this tendency itself as a fact, as in a letter to his friend Kergorlay written a few weeks after his arrival in the United States: "We are headed toward unlimited democracy. I do not say that this is a good thing. What I am seeing in this country persuades me on the contrary that France will adapt to it badly. But we are driven there by an irresistible force. Whatever may be done to arrest the movement will result only in brief pauses . . . In a word, democracy now seems to me to be a fact, which a government may seek to regulate but not to halt."[16] Four years later, when he published *Democracy in America*, Tocqueville exalted this tendency even more, calling it a "providential fact" revealed "under the impulse of a kind of religious dread,"[17] the "most continuous, ancient, and permanent tendency known to history."[18] In America the democratic social state is a fact, whereas in Europe, where it is still mingled with the legacy of the past, it takes the form of a historical tendency as undeniable as a fact, a "social revolution,"[19] a "great democratic revolution."[20]

Sometimes the author defines democracy or the democratic social state in terms of its essential characteristic: objectively, equality of "condition" or its correlate, social mobility, or, subjectively, the feeling of equality. All these meanings are closely linked; they can readily be distinguished from the strictly political senses of the term "democracy" simply by following the advice that Tocqueville himself recorded in the margin of his manuscript: "Note that in this chapter the social state must never be confused with the political laws that flow from it. Equality and inequality of condition are social facts and should never be confused with democracy or aristocracy, which are laws."[21] After considerable effort, of which traces remain in drafts written between 1833 and 1835,[22] Tocqueville arrived at a distinction that exactly fitted the American situation; for other societies he was obliged to consider mixed (that is, less exclusively democratic) social states in which the "dogma of popular sovereignty" or the "majority principle" was less fully realized.[23] From the beginning of *Democracy in America* Tocqueville distinguished between the democratic social state and the political democracy embodied in the principle of popular sovereignty.[24] In European countries the social and political situation was less simple; the social states and political regimes found there would have to be described as mixed, composed of both aristocratic and democratic elements. The distinction needed to describe Tocqueville's model, the

United States, and its various approximations led to a new definition of the word "democracy": "Popular sovereignty and democracy are perfectly correlative words; one sets forth a theoretical idea, the other its practical realization."[25] Thus the same word, "democracy," in its political sense, can refer in one context to the principle of popular sovereignty or its ideal embodiment and in another context to a practical approximation to that ideal markedly different from the American model.

Although Tocqueville is not very systematic in his use of terminology, his intuition of the essential is so powerful that the variety of uses of the term "democracy" rarely creates a serious ambiguity for the attentive reader;[26] it seems rather to contribute to the richness and vigor of Tocqueville's thought.[27]

MONTESQUIEU EXTENDED THE classical theory of political regimes by carefully delineating the nature and principle of each type of government. Though still fairly traditional in his definition of the "nature" of a government, he was innovative in his thinking about the "principle" that "makes it act" and "the human passions that make it move."[28] A relation between type of government and type of society was thus established essentially in terms of ruling passions. Montesquieu also sketched out an analysis of the fit between a form of government and a form of society, but he did not carry this line of thinking very far, contenting himself with observing the natural concordance between republican government and states of limited geographic size, whereas states of middling size accorded best with monarchy and vast empires ran the risk of falling into despotism.[29] Tocqueville, who had the example of a large and successful modern republic before his eyes, was able to avoid contradicting the *Esprit des lois* by invoking,[30] as Hamilton had done before him,[31] Montesquieu's remarks concerning the virtues of the federal republic, "which has all the internal advantages of republican government and all the external strength of monarchy."[32] For Tocqueville, however, physical dimensions alone were not sufficient to characterize a social state; he sought to identify the essential social characteristics of democracy, supplementing the moral characteristics to which Montesquieu had given the name "principle." Like Montesquieu's moral analysis, Tocqueville's sociological analysis led to the discovery of a dominant character which formed or modified all the others: equality of conditions, which in the final analysis is the social principle of democracy, just as love of equality is its moral principle.

Sociological and moral reflection both hinge on equality, understood in the one case objectively as a legal structure and in the other subjectively as a dominant passion.

Although Tocqueville defined the "principle" of democracy differently from Montesquieu, he nevertheless remained profoundly faithful to Montesquieu's thought. Both men believed that between forms of society and forms of government there is an intelligible relation whose basis lies in the nature of reality, whereas neither accepted the view that social organization by itself can wholly determine the mode of government. The concept of the democratic social state not only shows how far Tocqueville's sociological analysis had progressed beyond Montesquieu's but also attests to the originality of his historical vision. Both thinkers had pursued the same goal, namely, to define the conditions of freedom, but, unlike Montesquieu, Tocqueville could no longer believe in aristocratic solutions. While keeping faith with the spirit of Montesquieu, his liberal disciple broke with the aristocratic tradition of which Montesquieu was the heir.

TOCQUEVILLE WAS NOT content simply to borrow Montesquieu's comparative method and liberal inspiration. He made a notable contribution to perfecting the instruments of comparative study. Melvin Richter has given an admirable analysis of Tocqueville's borrowings from Montesquieu.[33] It should be said, however, that Tocqueville added new concepts and refined old ones as required for a work of sociological synthesis. He was obliged to develop the concept of social state precisely because he was unable to give a satisfactory analysis of the American national character. At the end of *Carnet alphabétique A*,[34] in a note written on 29 May 1831, he wrote: "Up to now it cannot be said that there is an American character, unless it is that of not having one."[35] In the same notebook we find a two-page analysis of the American national character: "A characteristic restlessness seems to me one of the distinctive features of this people. The American is consumed by the desire to amass a fortune; it is the unique passion of his life."[36] The author then shows how this anxiety about wealth is combined with the "confidence of a gambler who risks only his winnings." For the reader of *Democracy in America* it is not difficult to recognize in this fragment, written in the summer of 1831, the first draft of part two, chapter thirteen, of volume two: "Why the Americans Are Often So Restless in the Midst of Their Prosperity."[37] But it is also easy to see that in the first text the emphasis is on the national character, and

American social mobility is not explicitly related to the democratic social state, whereas in the final text both the desire for material prosperity and the democratic social state figure in the explanation. The chapter ends with an observation apt to draw the attention of a sociologist: "Americans do not kill themselves, however distressed they may be."[38] Thus, American restlessness, understood at first as an expression of the national character, is ultimately shown to be a product of a social state, indeed a product in perfect harmony with the norms of the society and posing no obstacle to the integration of individuals into the group. To see just how far Tocqueville has come, compare this analysis with that of Montesquieu, who, having noted that the English availed themselves of suicide quite easily, examined their restlessness and ultimately attributed it to the climate.[39] Analysis of the democratic social state increasingly supplanted the quest for the national character; such analysis could be pursued independent of purely political reflection on the nature of regimes. In observing democracy in America, Tocqueville attempted to maintain a careful distinction between democracy in the political sense and the democratic social state: "Democracy constitutes the social state, the dogma of popular sovereignty constitutes political law. The two things are not analogous. Democracy is a way of being for society. The sovereignty of the people is a form of government."[40]

Tocqueville's originality lies in his having examined in a single work both American society and its institutions, starting with an analysis of what he called America's democratic social state. He writes: "The social state is commonly the product of circumstances, sometimes of laws, but most often of a combination of the two. But once it exists, it can itself be considered the first cause of most of the laws, customs, and ideas that govern the conduct of nations; what it does not produce, it modifies."[41]

Thus, early in his work, Tocqueville developed the concept on which almost all his analyses would be based, generally in the form of a contrast between two ideal types: aristocratic and democratic. These ideal types consisted essentially of two elements: the social state in the strict sense and what Tocqueville called "mores." As we have seen, the idea of a democratic social state was born of a comparison between England and the United States; or, to put it another way, it was derived from the apparent differences in the English character when observed in two different social states. Tocqueville's thinking is stated even more clearly in a passage of his travel diaries entitled "Causes of the social state and the present government of America."[42] Only half a page long, this passage contains a list of ten "causes," and Pierson has shown that it summarizes what Tocqueville considered the most important ideas to be gleaned from his conversations and research in New England. The central tenets of his book had already taken shape; so much is clear from the first seven "causes" in Tocqueville's list, which concern the social state: origin, geographical location, commercial and industrial activity, material prosperity, religious spirit, enlightenment, and mores.[43] What he says about origins deserves particular attention: "Excellent starting point. Intimate mix of religion and spirit of freedom. A cold and calculating race."[44] In this we see the seeds of chapter two of *Democracy in America*: "Concerning their point of departure and its importance for the future of the Anglo-Americans."[45] In a sense, the idea is that the English national character, a synthesis of diverse physical, moral, and political causes, underwent a kind of disintegration when transplanted to the United States, contributing some of its elements to the new social state that developed there. The "cold and calculating" nature of the "Anglo-American race" remained unchanged. Religious feeling and free spirit, also elements of the English national character, turned out to be particularly important in defining the nature of the American social state because they proved incompatible with the dominant ethos of the mother country. "Puritanism was not only a religious doctrine," Tocqueville notes, "but was in several respects identified with the most absolute democratic and republican theories. That was the element that aroused its most dangerous adversaries."[46]

These passages show that Tocqueville based his distinction between aristocracy and democracy on an analysis of the classical features of the English national character. Initially, as Seymour Drescher has shown, his models were England and the United States.[47] Examination of Tocqueville's travel notes reveals that between the spring and autumn of 1831 he became increasingly conscious of the divergence between the Old World and the New, where the system of "maximal local initiative" had made the Americans different from the English. In his diary for 26 December 1831 Tocqueville noted "an immense difference between the English and their American descendants."[48]

Drescher observes that at this point Tocqueville had yet to set foot in England. But he knew his Montesquieu. Such astute American observers as Pierson and especially Drescher have shown themselves adept at revealing Tocqueville's American sources and demonstrating the importance of his discovery of local democracy in New England, but they neglect Tocqueville's roots in France.[49] The point of the preceding pages has been to show that the Tocquevillean concept of a social state was based on the notion of national character, on the "general spirit of a nation," which Tocqueville inherited from Montesquieu. "America offers the most perfect image, for better and for worse, of the special character of the English race."[50]

I NOW WANT to add to what the American commentators have said a remark about Tocqueville's notion of the "point of departure." Recall that, among the causes of the social state, Tocqueville includes what he calls its "origins,"[51] because he is convinced that "no one can free himself entirely from the past."[52] Now, among the elements characteristic of the origin of the social state of the Americans, Tocqueville lists in the first place their "excellent point of departure."[53] He refers again to the point of departure in the title of chapter two of *Democracy in America*, in the body of which we find the following statement: "There is not an opinion, custom, or law, nor, I might add, an event, which the point of departure does not easily explain. Readers of this book will therefore find that this chapter is the germ of all that follows and the key to almost the whole work."[54] Furthermore, in concluding this same chapter, the author adds more about the nature of the point of departure, which he says must be "kept constantly in mind": "Anglo-American civilization is the product . . . of two quite distinct elements, which in other countries have often been at war with each other but which the Americans have somehow managed to incorporate one within the other, forming a marvelous combination. I refer to the spirit of religion and the spirit of liberty."[55] This summary is in some ways surprising, given that Tocqueville, in his most elaborately developed travel notes, treated "the intimate mixture of religion and the spirit of liberty" as an element of the origin of the American social state distinct from its "excellent point of departure."[56] Is it possible that what was distinguished in an early draft was confounded in the final text?

In order to answer this question we must look at chapter nine, which is the true concluding chapter of volume one, since chapter ten, devoted to the future of the three races in America, was, as Schleifer has shown, a late addition to the text.[57] In chapter nine Tocqueville achieves the principal aim of the first volume, which, he tells us, is to explain "the principal factors that tend to maintain the democratic Republic in the United States."[58] Furthermore, this chapter seems to develop the ten-point analysis mentioned in the notebooks.[59] The same factors figure in both places, but in the final analysis they are ordered in such a way as to show that "laws contribute more to the maintenance of the democratic Republic in the United States than physical factors, and mores contribute more than laws."[60] More clearly than chapter two, the concluding text shows how Tocqueville distinguished between what he called, in his travel diaries, "the excellence of the point of departure" and "the intimate mixture of religion and the spirit of liberty." Here, in fact, he treats the point of departure as one of the "accidental or providential causes that contribute to the maintenance of the democratic Republic in the United States,"[61] while deferring consideration of the political influence of religion to another part of the chapter. "The Americans had in their favor the accident of birth: their fathers had previously imported to the land on which they settled equality of conditions and intelligences, from which the democratic Republic would one day spring as from its natural source. And that is not all. Along with a republican social state they bequeathed to their descendants the habits, ideas, and mores most apt to enable the Republic to flourish. When I think about what this original circumstance produced, it seems to me that the destiny of America was contained in the first Puritan who approached these shores as surely as that of the human race was contained in the first man."[62] This text echoes the splendid exordium of the first chapter, in which Tocqueville, following the inspiration of Bossuet, depicted the vast American continent as the "still empty cradle of a great nation,"[63] and described the Indians in their savage liberty as pagan precursors of the Puritans who would come to fulfill the design of Providence, bringing to the New World a sort of second creation, the "seed of a great people which God dropped from his hands onto a predestined earth."[64] Tocqueville was most likely neither entirely committed nor entirely indifferent to these images, which he employs with undeniable art.

What most interested him was surely the political originality of the American people from the inception of the United States. "The social state of the Americans is eminently democratic. It has had this character since the inception of the colonies; it has it to an even greater degree today."[65] For the historian and sociologist this is certainly a fact of the utmost importance. Tocqueville, who was convinced that the first form of social organization in history was aristocratic, here contemplates an unprecedented historical anomaly: Americans are born equal. From this fact flowed many consequences. "America," Tocqueville writes, "is the only country in which it has been possible to observe the natural and tranquil development of a society, and in which it has been possible to specify the influence exerted by the point of departure upon the future of the state."[66] Earlier, in his travel diaries, Tocqueville had noted that certain characteristics of American history made the country easier to know than some others. For the sociologist this was a rare opportunity: American institutions form "a perfectly logical chain."[67] Indeed, all of them derive from a single governing idea: equality. Since, moreover, the Americans were not obliged to combat a powerful local aristocracy, this equality was able to develop naturally, peacefully, and logically. There were few observable exceptions to this rule, all of them residues of aristocratic institutions inherited from English law.[68] Otherwise American institutions were highly uniform and intelligible to a rare degree. "The fact is that there are relatively few nations that can be understood fully. If the Americans are in this position, the reason is that they built their social edifice upon a blank slate."[69]

This society was not built around an aristocracy,[70] and therefore it did not have to win its political independence from an aristocracy. Instead, those aristocratic elements that existed in the colonial era, especially south of the Hudson, provided the principal military leaders for the war against the English; Tocqueville observes that the American Revolution owed "its greatest men" to the class of wealthy southern landowners.[71] Although he wants to show that the democratic element in the United States had become "not only preponderant but in a sense unique,"[72] he is nonetheless careful to indicate the country's historical and geographical diversity. In his analysis of the American social state in chapter three, he distinguishes social forms along two axes: north-south[73] and east-west.[74] Even greater diversity is recorded in his travel notes, which occasionally shed new light on the distinction between aristocracy and democracy. When, for instance, Tocqueville writes that "the ultimate form of democracy can be observed in the West,"[75] his explanation hinges primarily on equality in education, but his notes on his travels in Ohio include an interesting further analysis in which he shows that three waves of immigration were necessary to completely erase the influence of English law.[76]

It is often possible, and sometimes quite useful, to indicate degrees of difference between aristocracy and democracy; in particular, this can be done by measuring the distance from the initial English model. I maintain, however, that Tocqueville made a further, radical distinction between American democracy and French democracy, a distinction that was absolute rather than a question of degree; although less visible than the preceding one, this distinction was nevertheless a cornerstone of Tocqueville's work. The primary reason why the Americans had useful lessons to teach a French political philosopher imbued with the comparative method was that they had been spared the need to destroy a powerful aristocracy in order to create their democracy. Democratic society in France had come into being in the wake of a terrible revolution, whereas American democratic society had been born without revolution. What is called the American Revolution is only a way of referring to the war by which the Americans won their independence. On the American side of the Atlantic, democracy was not born of civil war as it was in France; it was not born of the destruction of an aristocracy. Tocqueville, who never ceased to ponder the consequences of the destruction of the French aristocracy, saw American society in terms of two comparisons: he compared England and America in order to understand the difference between aristocracy and democracy in the absence of any internal revolutionary crisis; and he compared France and America in order to understand the effects of the Revolution on French democratic society. By using the comparative method in the study of French society, Tocqueville hoped to be able to distinguish the results of the equalization of conditions from the consequences of the revolutionary crisis.

At the time he wrote *Democracy*, Tocqueville believed that this method would enable him to distinguish between the effects of the French Revolution on the generation or two that followed it and the longer-term effects of the trend toward greater equality. Although the contrast between aristocracy and democracy is not fully revealed until one has compared America with both England and France, it is nevertheless useful for understanding America itself. The diametrical opposition between the two social states is analyzed throughout *Democracy in America*, few of whose chapters do not touch on it in some way. No American reader found this excessive; but was this not rather surprising for a work published between 1835 and 1840, that is, in an era when this dichotomy, of which Jefferson had been so fond, must have seemed rather outmoded in the American political lexicon?[77] In reality, Tocqueville's work is still as enlightening for American readers today as it was for readers in the Age of Jackson, for it shows how fortunate the country was that it never had to endure a lethal contest between aristocracy and democracy. Tocqueville's apparent anachronism is in fact a sign of his historical intuition and the secret of his work's longevity. Louis Hartz, in his *Liberal Tradition in America*,[78] paid homage to Tocqueville not only for having shown clearly that America represented the European liberal ideal functioning without European social antagonisms but also for having realized that the Americans themselves could not understand the uniqueness of their own brand of liberalism without examining the conflicts and revolutions that had attended the coming of liberalism in Europe.

The Aristocratic and Democratic Social States

The recurrence of the contrast between democracy and aristocracy throughout *Democracy in America* is not simply a rhetorical device but a veritable theoretical instrument that furthers comparative study in a variety of ways. It is mentioned more than a hundred times,[79] not out of clumsiness or inelegance of style but deliberately, in order to focus the analysis on this fundamental contrast between two types of society and, ultimately, on two types of human being.

In order to grasp fully how Tocqueville goes about comparing aristocracy and democracy and identifying areas in which they are similar or different, I think it best to concentrate attention initially on the comparison of social states. Hence the rest of this chapter will be concerned with that topic, and the problems of governing a democracy will be deferred to chapter four.

FOR THE SAKE of clarity, Tocqueville ultimately chose to define two pure social states, whose key features he describes. It would not be misleading to borrow a term from Max Weber and call these two pure forms "ideal types." Social types are defined in terms of both social characteristics and moral qualities. The dominant moral and social characteristics of actual societies are not always in accord and may in some respects be contradictory. In a text originally intended for the preface to volume two of *Democracy*, Tocqueville explained his method: "In order to make myself understood, I am constantly obliged to consider extreme states: aristocracy unalloyed with democracy, democracy unalloyed with aristocracy. At times I attribute to one or the other of these two principles effects more far-reaching than they generally produce, because in general they do not exist in isolation. The reader must judge for himself how much of what I say is my true opinion and how much is said in order to make myself understood."[80] America, however, embodies a democratic society almost devoid of any residue of aristocratic society and undamaged by any form of democratic revolution; it therefore offers an excellent approximation to the pure democratic state, whereas in Europe the principles of aristocracy and democracy are always at war.[81]

In fact, the American case is more complex than it appears at first sight. At the root of American society is an extreme form of the democratic social state coupled with mores inherited in part from the English aristocracy. In Tocqueville's view, no pure form—whether democratic or aristocratic—would have been viable. With this caveat in mind, I shall nevertheless adopt, for convenience, the convention of referring to both the ideal type and its American approximation as "pure forms." By contrast, the European countries exemplify "mixed forms," that is, social states combining to a significant degree features of both aristocracy and democracy. In America, surviving aristocratic elements have neither economic power nor direct political influence; they are almost entirely sublimated. Thus, it is easy to distinguish between America, a society that is mixed yet quite close to a pure democracy, and Europe, whose mixed societies are neither aristocratic nor democratic.

Tocqueville faced greater difficulty in defining what he meant by the aristocratic social state; in fact, he did not give a full definition prior to the article he wrote in 1836 at the behest of John Stuart Mill. There he defined first what he called the "aristocratic elements": scarce goods, which by nature "can only be the property of a few," such as birth, wealth, and knowledge. These "aristocratic elements" are found in all nations. A social state is aristocratic to the extent that these goods tend to become concentrated in the same hands. Such a social state cannot acquire stability without an aristocratic political regime: "When all who are blessed with these exceptional advantages work in concert at government, the aristocracy is powerful and durable."[82] By contrast, the more democratic a society is, the more its elites are divided.[83]

Inequalities are thus inevitable and universal; hence their existence cannot serve as a criterion for distinguishing a democratic from an aristocratic society. But inequalities can be distributed in different societies in very different ways. In traditional agrarian societies, privileges tend to accumulate in certain families, whereas in the America that Tocqueville visited they were already widely dispersed, as Tocqueville noted in his constant comparisons of New England with aristocratic England and prerevolutionary France. The accumulation of social goods—birth, wealth, knowledge—defines the aristocratic social state, and the exercise of power by the social elite constitutes aristocracy in the full sense of the word. Surely it is unnecessary to point out the modernity of this conception,[84] which is based on such current notions as the concentration of political resources[85] and the relative unity of the elite.[86]

With such a definition it is clear that actual social states can be either more or less aristocratic or democratic but never purely one or the other; the pure forms are ideal types. In every democratic society there are aristocratic elements, and every aristocracy is obliged to limit itself, to exemplify what Montesquieu called "moderation," in order to avoid cutting itself off completely from the people and thus quickly falling into impotence and ruin.[87] Observable types are necessarily mixed, even if their dominant characteristics leave them indelibly marked with the stamp of aristocracy or democracy. Once again, the imprecision of Tocqueville's vocabulary compounds the difficulties: referring sometimes to a political form, sometimes to a social type, the term "aristocracy" is also used "in its vulgar sense" to denote "the upper classes as a whole"[88] or as a metonymy for an aristocratic institution (*corps*).

Nevertheless, the reader of *Democracy in America* has no difficulty comprehending the contrast between aristocracy and democracy. As Tocqueville constructs the pair, he simultaneously achieves a major simplification: aristocracy is relegated to the distant past, and America is held up as a model for the European democracy of the future. No doubt the French Revolution prepared Tocqueville's readers for viewing aristocracy in such a light. In a dramatic change, a simple new scheme was substituted for the previous complex system of noble corps and orders. In writing *Democracy in America* Tocqueville fell in with this manner of stylization while correcting whatever distortions may have resulted from the political passions of the day. Later, in writing *The Old Regime*, he would return to analyses first sketched in 1836 and study relations among the French elites prior to 1789. The two approaches—ideal-typical and historical—do not correspond to successive stages in Tocqueville's thinking; instead they reflect above all the different kinds of problems with which he had to contend. In both volumes of *Democracy in America* attention is focused on democracy. In order to bring out the need for new solutions to new problems, Tocqueville contrasts aristocracy and democracy as two very different types of society belonging to two distinct periods of history (as far as the pure forms are concerned). On the other hand, in both his 1836 article and *The Old Regime*, he is interested in analyzing the crisis of the Old Regime, and hence in examining the period of transition from aristocracy to democracy; he therefore investigates those who played leading roles in the crisis, namely the ruling elites.

IF WE EXAMINE history from a great height and take in with a single glance eras remote from one another in time, we discover that democratic society and aristocratic society have been in conflict for a very long time indeed; this observation is the cornerstone of Tocqueville's first masterpiece, as Jean-Jacques Chevallier has shown in a brief and elegant paper, remarkable for its accuracy and insight.[89] There is no need to recount here in full detail Chevallier's systematic examination. I shall instead follow a somewhat different course in showing how the whole of the work seems to flow from the fundamental opposition between aristocracy and democracy. Aristocratic and democratic societies differ sharply in spirit and structure: the former is characterized by inequality, hierarchy, and organic structure; the latter by equality, hatred of hierarchy, and inorganic structure.

Although it is hardly surprising that equality and inequality figure in such a comparison, Tocqueville deserves credit for having contrasted equality not only with inequality but also with hierarchy; aristocratic societies, he argues, are both inegalitarian and organic in their structure: "Aristocracy accorded to each citizen a place in a long chain that stretched from the peasant to the king; democracy breaks the chain and separates the links."[90] The consequences of this were numerous: in particular, ideas of liberty and equality were born of the notion of man as individual. In the celebrated chapter in which he shows that individualism originates with democracy,[91] Tocqueville clearly reveals his disapproval of individualism, which he blames on "erroneous judgment."[92] Like traditional thinkers before him and like all great sociologists after him, from Durkheim to Louis Dumont, he understands that the individual must be seen as a creation, indeed a fairly recent creation, of society; he rejects the contrary view, that society is born of individuals. His theory of the democratic origins of individualism runs counter to the philosophy of the *Social Contract*. Throughout the second volume of *Democracy* he analyzes the philosophical, moral, and political consequences of egalitarian individualism with an anxiety that culminates in the discovery of a secret link between modern individualism and a new form of despotism.

Here, however, I want to raise a point that has also been noticed by

Louis Dumont.[93] Although Tocqueville clearly demonstrated the organic nature of aristocratic societies, he made no attempt to show how the values implicit in the social order could have been based on knowledge of reality, that is, on a natural hierarchy of value. A brilliant sociologist, he was also a philosopher (at least during the summer of 1836, when he read Plato, pen in hand),[94] but the sociologist silenced the philosopher. Tocqueville repudiated metaphysics, as his reading of Plato clearly shows. From that philosopher's work he retained, not the dependence of the art of politics on a science of being, but the subordination of politics to morality.[95]

Because aristocratic societies are highly cohesive and organic in nature, they are also stable. Tocqueville makes two observations on this point: the fixed connection between a family and a piece of land gives a kind of visible, geographical immortality to the great names; and as a consequence of these roots in the land, ideas and mores tend to remain stable. Early in *Democracy* he notes: "Aristocracy takes to the land. It attaches itself to the soil, from which it draws its support. It is created not by privileges but by the hereditary transmission of property in land."[96] The stability of ideas, beliefs, and mores reflects the order that exists in aristocratic societies and is in no way incompatible with dynamic passions, great ambitions, and violent crises. When all is said and done, however, "nothing in the world is more settled in its views than an aristocracy."[97]

Improvement is not foreign to the conception of man characteristic of aristocratic eras, yet the tendency is to confine progress "within certain unbreachable boundaries."[98] By contrast, in a more fluid democratic society, "the image of an ideal and always fugitive perfection offers itself to the human spirit."[99] Laws providing for the equal division of inheritances put an end to the age-old connection between family and land and introduce a fluidity which to Tocqueville's mind has as many advantages as disadvantages. Equality of conditions encourages social mobility, which in turn makes it possible to tolerate de facto inequalities; situations in which inequality exists but changes over time do not prevent the feeling of equality from flourishing. Fragmented and unstable, democratic society fosters "a nervous activity, an outpouring of energy."[100] For Tocqueville stability is not the same thing as strength, nor is grandeur the same as duration;[101] hence the opposition between aristocracy and democracy can achieve a kind of equilibrium. Every society requires a minimum of stability, however, and Tocqueville hopes that democratic societies, by nature unstable with respect to family property, individual structures, and laws, will nevertheless prove capable of preserving mores, religious beliefs, and constitutional principles to the greatest possible extent.

Mobility is characteristic of democratic society just as fixity and stability are essential traits of the ideal-typical aristocratic society. Take social relations. In an aristocracy people are ranked from birth, whereas in a perfect democracy they acquire status solely through their own efforts. The first chapters of the second volume of *Democracy*, which deal with mores, frequently contrast the mobility of democratic man, always in search of a better situation, with the stability of aristocratic man, whose role is prescribed or established at birth. Particularly significant in this respect are the chapters devoted to the ease and simplicity of social relations in America,[102] and to relations between master and servant.[103]

Furthermore, social relations in democratic societies are more specific, those in aristocratic societies more comprehensive (or, as a Parsonian sociologist might put it, more diffuse). For example: "In aristocracies rents are not paid solely in money but in respect, affection, and services. In democratic countries they are paid only in cash."[104] This is even more true when inequalities of wealth, knowledge, and birth reinforce one another, as they do in the typical aristocracy. Social relations of such a diffuse, comprehensive nature are all too likely to become relations of superior to inferior, whereas the well-defined, specific relations characteristic of democracy make it possible to reconcile functional obedience with equality. Recall Montesquieu's assertion that the true spirit of equality "does not consist in seeing to it that everyone commands, or that no one obeys, but in obeying and commanding one's equals."[105] Montesquieu was thinking primarily of political life; in America Tocqueville saw obedience and equality reconciled in social life, even in the relations between master and servant: "Within the limits of this contract, the one is servant and the other master; outside it, both are citizens, both men."[106] He must have surprised many Europeans of his day by concluding that American servants "are in a sense the equals of their masters."[107]

The Decline of Aristocracy

The comparison of Great Britain with France was intended to point up the differing behavior of two aristocracies in the face of revolution or the danger of revolution. Like the Genevan J. L. de Lolme,[108]

Tocqueville thought that the chief differences between the history of England and that of France could be explained in terms of such behavior, or, more precisely, in terms of the contrasting evolution of the English aristocracy and the French nobility.[109]

Thanks to its relative willingness to accept new members, the English aristocracy was able to incorporate both the old families and the new aristocracy of wealth, whereas in France nobility became a caste. The English revolutions therefore caused no break in the aristocratic tradition; in the nineteenth century, moreover, the aristocracy defused revolutionary tensions by opportunely adopting laws of a democratic tenor. The historian Ernest Labrousse praised the English for incorporating in their politics "an extraordinary bomb-disposal technology." Tocqueville was probably the first to recognize this in the contrast he drew between England's comparatively peaceful history and France's record of revolutionary explosions. He was fascinated by the English aristocracy's aptitude for preserving its political liberties, for which he expressed his admiration in his 1836 article and many times thereafter: "The masterstroke of the English aristocracy was its ability for a long time to convince the democratic classes of society that the common enemy was the prince, and to become the representative of those classes rather than their principal adversary."[110] But there is nothing Machiavellian about Tocqueville's liking for this ability to "convince" the "democratic classes"; he is no less admiring of the common folk. "There is no better proof of the grandeur of the English people than its willingness to accept liberty without equality."[111] Accordingly, in the great democratic revolution that began in the twelfth century and was still proceeding throughout Europe, England had fared much better than France, as Tocqueville noted nostalgically in a draft of volume two of *Democracy*: "Some nations come to democracy through liberal institutions, as the English will do; others come through absolute power, as we have done."[112] For Tocqueville, the decline of aristocracy was both inevitable and just; despite his admiration for the English aristocracy, he knew that it was destined to give way to democracy, and in the first instance to the middle classes, but he believed that it would prove capable of defending liberty and averting major revolutionary crises.[113]

TOCQUEVILLE'S JOURNEY TO England in 1835 had a decisive influence on his perception of the differences between the French and English middle classes. In England these classes sought to ally themselves with the aristocracy and adopt its values, whereas in France, nearly a half-century after the Revolution, they still defined themselves primarily in opposition to the aristocracy. From the diaries he kept on this trip, one can gather how surprised he was by the stability of English society and by its capacity to absorb powerful thrusts of democratization without revolution.[114] In Restoration France greater power for the middle classes was favored by the disciples of the Idéologues as well as by former habitués of Madame de Staël's Coppet circle. Destutt de Tracy had developed a theory of society according to which upper and lower classes would tend to equalize around the middle, and in 1819 Benjamin Constant wrote in *La Minerve* that "the great benefit of the Revolution was that it introduced the intermediate class into the affairs of state." The Doctrinaires, who in many ways picked up where the Idéologues left off, went further still. During the Restoration, Royer-Collard, bolder than Benjamin Constant, maintained that the middle class was the natural representative of the interests of all; and Guizot, in his course on the history of civilization, showed that the middle classes were playing a growing role in the development of civilization and the exercise of power. French history since 1789 was, he said, characterized by the ascendancy of the middle classes, and later, in his *Memoirs*, he explained why he had based his policy on them: "The policy that we supported and followed was thus based primarily on the preponderance of middle-class influence, an influence acknowledged and recognized to be in the general interest of the country."[115] Clearly, Guizot was no longer satisfied with the mere participation in affairs of state that had so delighted Benjamin Constant; for Guizot, nothing less than middle-class domination of politics would do, and in reading him one sometimes gets the impression that he speaks as the representative of a government that aspires to control the throne itself. For example, in a pamphlet published just after the Revolution of 1848, he says of the middle classes that "not only have they achieved their ascendancy, they have justified it." He then adds: "When they were led to establish a new monarchy in 1830, the middle classes embarked upon this difficult undertaking with a spirit of justice and political sincerity, thereby reaping honor of which no event can deprive them."[116]

About the same time Tocqueville reached quite a different conclusion, as is clear to anyone who has read the celebrated opening passages of his *Souvenirs*.[117] Here, however, I shall cite instead, as the perfect counterpoint to the passage from Guizot, an excerpt from an unpublished letter written in May 1848 to the English historian Grote: "The flaw in the 1830 charter and the still greater flaws in those who applied it probably made a thorough reform necessary. The nation could no longer breathe in the close atmosphere of a bourgeois and shopkeeper's aristocracy, whose selfishness and corruption equaled its benightedness . . . In several respects this revolution has left deep and indelible marks. Its most prominent accomplishment is the overthrow of the middle classes and the advent of political influence on the part of those who may properly be called the people."[118] At the beginning of his *Souvenirs*, Tocqueville recalled the gist of a speech he had delivered on 27 January 1848 in which he had predicted the February revolution. In fact, however, he had expressed his contempt for the government of the middle classes much earlier. On 25 August 1847, for instance, he wrote to his friend Nassau Senior: "This [middle] class is gradually becoming, for the rest of the nation, a corrupt and vulgar little aristocracy, to whose rule it seems shameful to submit. If such feelings are accentuated among the masses, it could lead to great misfortunes later on."[119] Was this really the same man who in America had noted in his travel diary for 30 November 1831: "There is one thing which America demonstrates invincibly and which I had doubted until now: that the middle classes can govern a state"?[120]

FOR TOCQUEVILLE, HOWEVER, America was a country almost entirely populated by the middle classes, and the high level of social mobility, the great number of property owners, and the absence of serious social conflict were features without equivalent in Europe. In France the so-called middle classes were only a small minority, and perusal of the drafts of volume two of *Democracy* leaves no doubt as to the author's opinion of their government. In a democratic era he believed that it was impossible for liberty to be based on aristocracy or, indeed, on any privileged class by whatever name one chose to call it. He added this note in the margin: "It would be perhaps less shrewd but surely more forthright to say that one intends the upper classes to govern."[121] Still more clearly, another text denounces "the impossibility and peril of middle-class government. The need is to move toward government of all by all."[122] The political difference between Tocqueville and Guizot is evident in this brief note: "I do not believe in the ultimate organization of government for the sake of the middle classes, and if I did believe it possible, I would oppose it."[123] Throughout his career as a legislator, Tocqueville was indeed opposed to Guizot's policy, and it is perhaps regrettable that he never kept the promise he made to himself while pondering the contents of his final chapter: "To express some sort of view on the question of the middle classes raised by M. Guizot [illegible word] and so many other things."[124]

In fact, the final text of *Democracy in America* contains none of the further developments that its author had planned. Had Tocqueville been less discreet in his criticisms, had he expressed his thoughts more directly, he would not have been understood any better by a political class almost entirely won over to the "political formula"[125] of "government by the middle classes." And had he been widely understood, he might have undermined the fragile basis of the government's legitimacy. Had he gone any further than he did, he would have stepped outside the "dynastic opposition," and his criticism would have seemed to reflect either aristocratic prejudice or republican passion. Thus, the future deputy, who was destined to sit between the center-left and the left, to some extent censored the author of *Democracy in America*.

It WAS NOT until after the Revolution of 1848, in his posthumously published *Souvenirs*,[126] that Tocqueville was able to express openly what he had often said to friends or noted in his drafts. The reign of the middle classes and the political errors of its leaders had triggered a new revolutionary explosion, whereas in England the same revolutionary tendencies had been channeled into reform. Why were the middle classes able to govern successfully in America and to participate in government in England, while in France their rule led to disaster?

For America, the answer was simple, comprising three parts. First, America was almost entirely populated by a vast middle class from which no one felt permanently excluded. Or, to put it another way, America was, compared with Europe, a classless society, and what Americans referred to as government of the middle classes was in fact democracy. Second, and less commonly cited, Americans had never known aristocratic domination in the European sense: "The great advantage of the Americans is to have come to democracy without having to suffer democratic revolutions and to have been born equals rather than becoming so."[127] Hence, as Louis Hartz has so ably demonstrated, the American middle classes preserved some of the sobriety of the spirit of '76 along with a belief in the self-evident nature of American values.[128] They shared none of the messianism of European liberalism. Third, we come to a point that is generally forgotten today but that, I believe, was as important to Tocqueville as the other two: by granting political freedom to all, or almost all, citizens, the Americans limited the dangers inherent in the democratic social state and, in particular, succeeded in preventing the development of antagonistic classes. On each of these three points, France and the United States were diametrically opposed.

Hardly less striking was the contrast between the manifestation of democratic tendencies in England and in France. Tocqueville was especially interested in extreme, radical expressions of democracy. In his 1835 notebooks he compared the French and English radicals and concluded: "In sum, I can now conceive of how an enlightened man of good sense and good intentions could become a radical in England. I have never been able to conceive of the conjunction of those three qualities in a French radical."[129] English liberals formed a continuous spectrum from extremists to moderates, whereas in France liberals had to be careful to refrain from joining their voices with those of extremists who fomented revolution. In England the middle classes, though less numerous than in America, were nevertheless broader than the narrow French electorate under the July Monarchy and sought to imitate the aristocracy rather than combat it. By contrast, in France, nearly half a century after 1789, the middle classes still sought to distinguish themselves from the aristocracy and remained wedded to attitudes that had marked the early phases of the Revolution.[130] French mores were not so much liberal as marked by the experience of 1789. In the United States and England, on the other hand, freedom rested more on mores than on laws.[131]

In 1835 and again in 1840 John Stuart Mill published important articles on *Democracy in America* in the *London and Westminster Review*.[132] Royer-Collard considered these pieces to be not only a good review but "an original work of great profundity and considerable value."[133] As for Tocqueville himself, after receiving the first article he wrote to Mill: "Of all those who have been kind enough to attempt to interest the public in me, you are the only one who has fully understood me."[134] I shall be citing frequently from Mill's reflections. For now, I want to note one criticism: all the moral and social effects of democracy described in volume two of *Democracy in America* were at work, according to Mill, in aristocratic England; they were related to the growth of the middle class and did not necessarily imply destruction of the aristocracy.[135] In the absence of a detailed response from Tocqueville, we are reduced to conjecture. Fortunate England, he may have thought, and unfortunate criticism. It may indeed have been possible that the effects of democracy mingled with the heritage of aristocracy without destroying it: such was England's good fortune. But that does not prove that the account of the ideal types in *Democracy in America* is incorrect. Mill treats Tocqueville's typology as though it were a blueprint for historical development, which as Mill understands it tends in one direction only, toward greater equality and civilization, where "greater" is taken in almost a quantitative sense. In short, Mill is reading Tocqueville in terms of a model borrowed from Condorcet. In fact, however, Tocqueville's typology is essentially a tool for comparative analysis, capable of revealing the way in which tendencies associated with one type of society can reinforce or oppose tendencies associated with another type of society. The English middle classes blended democratic and aristocratic tendencies fairly harmoniously. In France, however, the middle classes characteristically rejected the aristocratic heritage.[136]

How can these differences be explained? *Democracy*'s young author may have thought that they were consequences of the Revolution. Later, having become a historian, he looked for more remote causes in the different evolutionary patterns of the two aristocracies.[137] Yet, if Tocqueville's thoughts on this point developed and changed over time, two ideas recur constantly in his writings, even if, for political reasons, he abstained for a time from expressing them publicly: first, that the decline of aristocracy is inevitable and just; and second, that the nature of the transition from aristocracy to democracy depends in large part on whether or not such intermediate social forms as may develop accept or reject the legacy of aristocratic values, most notably that of political liberty. Tocqueville's outline of the reasons for the greatness of aristocracies is superficial, but his account of the laws governing their decadence is powerful. For him, England offered the best model, France the worst. His aristocrat's instinctive distaste for the bourgeois estranged him almost as much from the English as from the French, but his pondering of politics made him see in his compatriots' errors a threat to liberty. He felt that in France the hybrid of "aristocratic liberalism" had quickly compromised itself and that therefore democracy could take hold only by means of revolution and class war. This distressed him all the more because he felt that it was not inevitable. The classes, he believed, had in essence been destroyed in 1789 when the old "orders" were eliminated; they survived only in the transitional period between a society of orders and a society of individuals, between aristocracy and democracy.

The Necessity and Justice of Democracy

In Tocqueville's work the opposition between aristocracy and democracy has, I think, three kinds of significance: sociological, political, and moral.

While the vocabulary may be borrowed from classical political philosophy, the dichotomy envisioned coincides with the distinction between traditional and modern societies in contemporary sociology: on the one hand, a society of orders; on the other, a society of individuals. The contrast was so striking that Tocqueville reached the following conclusion: "They are like two distinct branches of mankind, each of which has its own peculiar advantages and disadvantages, its goods and its evils."[138]

Two branches of mankind, two worlds, or, as we would now say, two social systems: it is a merit of Tocqueville's method that the unity of the different aspects of each type of society stands revealed. Montesquieu had led the way with the first analysis of what sociologists nowadays call social systems in his *Esprit des lois*.[139] Because of the radical difference between the aristocratic and democratic systems, Tocqueville warns the reader that caution is in order: "One must take care not to judge newly born societies according to ideas drawn from societies that no longer exist. To do so would be unjust, for the differences between these societies are so great that they cannot be compared."[140]

The principal political interest of Tocqueville's typology is related to his distinction between the democratic social state and democratic government. He points out that it would be much more dangerous to allow society to be dominated by an exclusively democratic principle than to entrust its rule to a democratic government. In working notes for volume two of *Democracy* he wrote: "Danger of allowing a single social principle to assume unchallenged supremacy in a society. General idea that I wished to bring out in this work."[141] If a democratic society were to reject all aristocratic values, it would not be viable.[142] Democracy would be destroyed in the name of democracy. By rejecting all tradition and renouncing individual rights, local liberties, and the disinterested search for excellence and the Good, it would perish by its own hand. For a moderate aristocrat like Montesquieu, the best aristocracy was not the most aristocratic but the most moderate: "The closer aristocracy is to democracy, the more perfect it is."[143] Also a moderate, Tocqueville had similar feelings about the democratic social state: the best democracy is not the most extreme.

Finally, the contrast between democracy and aristocracy, coupled with the distinction between democracy as a social state and a democratic form of government, is morally instructive, for it teaches men to distinguish between what must be and what is susceptible of alteration through exercise of their responsibility as free men. On the final page of volume two of *Democracy in America* Tocqueville indicated more clearly than he had done in the introduction how he conceived of the relation between Providence and human freedom: "Providence did not make mankind either entirely free or completely enslaved. Around each man Providence has in truth drawn an ultimate circle beyond which that individual cannot venture; but within broad limits man is strong and free, and so are peoples."[144] Tocqueville was a steadfast opponent of fatalist doctrines according to which man's freely chosen actions are invariably foredoomed to ineffectiveness, as his correspondence with Gobineau confirms.[145] He criticized historians of the era of democracy for their irritating tendency to make nations subject "either to an inflexible Providence or a blind Fate."[146] Although he rejected fatalism with violent indignation, he was willing to entertain deterministic theories. He did not deny that historical facts make sense, that they are governed by what Montesquieu liked to call "the nature of things," and he tried to understand the laws of history. But there is a tremendous, if often neglected, difference between the determinist, who argues that if event A takes place then event B must necessarily follow, and the fatalist who flatly declares that event B must ineluctably occur. Tocqueville, who never failed to observe the distinction, congratulated Mill for having expounded it so clearly in his *Logic*.[147] Determinism in some form is as indispensable in the social sciences as it is in physics, but fatalism implies a metaphysical commitment that Tocqueville was unwilling to make. He did not claim to make history predictable, but only to render it intelligible so as to clarify the choices open to men of action. He was interested not in constructing a philosophy of history but in creating a "new political science."[148]

Some readers of Tocqueville object, however, that freedom in political action can only be illusory once it is assumed that the tendency toward democracy is irresistible, that is, fatal.[149] In fact, the apparent contradictions in Tocqueville's work result from a failure to distinguish between the democratic social state and the moral and political forms that democracy may take. It is true that Tocqueville believed that

Providence had dictated the advent of the democratic social state,[150] but he repeats throughout *Democracy in America* a point that is most clearly stated, perhaps, in the conclusion to the chapter "The Social State of the Anglo-Americans":[151] namely, that different peoples can create very different consequences from the same social state. Depending on how they use their freedom, they can construct either a liberal democracy or a new form of servitude. In other words, men are called to cooperate in the divine act of creation.[152]

In Tocqueville's writing, Providence refers not to Nature or to the Catholic dogma of Providence, in which by 1835 he no longer believed, but to a justice that transcends history.[153] It is to be found both in historical necessity and in mankind's vocation to complete in the moral realm what is already prescribed by the laws of history. Tocqueville's historical vision was not confined within a system like the visions of Comte, Hegel, and Marx; it remained open to the plurality of possibilities. But in order to choose among those possibilities one had to determine not only what was necessary but also what was just.

In the conclusion to *Democracy in America*, Tocqueville overcame both doubts and private preferences to assert that equality was more just than aristocratic hierachy; "justice," he added, "is the source of [democracy's] grandeur and beauty."[154] For him, the just notion of freedom was the democratic notion.

2 ✖ *Liberty and Equality*

Liberty and Equality under the July Monarchy

Tocqueville's contemporaries were apt to distinguish between liberty and equality. This cleavage in the values of 1789, already apparent during the Restoration, took new forms under the July Monarchy, among both liberals, who became increasingly conservative after the failures of Jacques Laffitte and Casimir Périer, and democrats, who by 1832 had been relegated to the opposition, with dismal prospects of coming to power. The former believed that liberty in the new society could be based on an ersatz bourgeois aristocracy, while the latter, increasingly persuaded by the Jacobin mythology developed by historians like Buchez and Roux,[1] ignored the political value of liberty and believed that equality would suffice to produce it. Tocqueville opposed both camps; he believed that within democratic society a firm basis would have to be established in order for liberty to flourish, and he had no illusions as to the government of the middle classes. In the future, liberty could not be based on aristocracy; it was dangerous, moreover, to attempt to limit access to government to a single class. "Liberty will never be established among these [democratic] peoples except by respecting equality. Anyone who, in the centuries upon which we are about to embark, attempts to base liberty upon aristocracy is doomed to failure . . . Anyone who attempts to retain power within a single class, by whatever name it may be called, is doomed to failure."[2] Against the dogmatic champions of democracy, on the other hand, he used an argument inspired by Montesquieu: freedom does not always grow in proportion to equality; beyond a certain threshold, the principal of equality is not enough to ensure the political vitality of democracy, and equality turns into its opposite; it then becomes a principle of corruption and death, destroying freedom.

Tocqueville was actually pursuing two goals simultaneously. He was attacking those confused individuals who, out of hatred for the Old Regime, confounded equality with freedom and believed that eliminating privileges was enough to ensure liberty. At the same time, he wished to show that, in the future, liberty could have no firm foundation other than equality. Although the two values of 1789 were not easy to reconcile, he sought ways to make them compatible and hoped to make others see the need for doing so. Although he lacked, to put it mildly, Condorcet's optimism, he agreed with Condorcet that liberty and equality were closely intertwined. He hoped to revive the spirit of the Constituent Assembly, the spirit of "that first period of '89 when love of equality and love of liberty" rivaled each other in the hearts of every Frenchman, a "time of youthfulness, enthusiasm, pride, and generous and sincere passions, which despite its errors will live forever in human memory."[3] Tocqueville's contemporaries noticed chiefly those aspects of his work that corresponded to their own concerns and neglected those parts that ruffled their settled habits of mind or ran counter to their interests. As a result, and most unjustly, Tocqueville has become an author who is constantly cited to illustrate the conflict between liberty and equality. Though not entirely wrong, this reading is based on a one-sided interpretation of the work. The result of oversimplifying the differences between Montesquieu and Rousseau and between the Constituent Assembly and the Convention is to obscure the significance of the spirit of '89 and the new society's need for both liberty *and* equality. Tocqueville was indeed a disciple of Montesquieu, but he was also a man of his time, yet less forgetful of Rousseau, Constantin de Volney, and Condorcet than many of his contemporaries.

To dispel any impression of paradox, it should be noted that the distinctions so often invoked by Tocqueville between liberty and liberal sentiments as well as between equality and egalitarian sentiments can be applied to his own personality. Tocqueville had an aristocrat's liking of and feeling for liberty, yet he championed a theory of democratic liberty. There is a divorce in him between, on the one hand, his heart and mind, his tastes and sentiments, and, on the other hand, the conclusions to which he was led by his lucidity in political matters and his sense of justice. Whatever he thinks, writes, or does, he always exhibits an ardent love of liberty, of "human liberty, the source of all moral grandeur."[4] Therein resides his certainty, his singleness of purpose: "I continue as I have always done to regard liberty as the primary good. I still see it as one of the most fertile sources of the male virtues and of great actions. There is no tranquillity or prosperity for which I would forsake it."[5]

Tocqueville has left no precise or complete account of what he meant by liberty, a fact deplored by his commentators, some of whom, including Antoine Redier and Jack Lively, have attempted to reconstruct the complete doctrine from brief notes scattered throughout the master's work.[6] I shall also make such an attempt, but in doing so I shall follow a different course, yet one that remains, I think, faithful to Tocqueville's manner of thinking. He had no taste whatsoever for pure speculation. Whatever the question, he always begins with comparative research. Only afterward does he attempt to define the essence of, say, liberty or freedom. He insists, moreover, on the need to distinguish clearly between a phenomenon and the sentiments associated with it. Tocqueville's thought, in my view, proceeds generally from comparison of social, moral, or political forms to reflection on political values and finally to an analysis of the forces that contend within men's minds. I shall therefore adopt this method in analyzing first equality, then liberty, and finally the relations between the two.

Democratic Equality and Revolutionary Equality

During his travels in the United States, Tocqueville recorded in his notebooks what seemed to him the peculiar features of equality in America, features that were difficult for a European to apprehend. Americans considered themselves equals but lived in a variety of situations. Despite the existence of numerous, easily identifiable, de facto inequalities, equality of a sort unknown in France did indeed prevail throughout the United States. For Tocqueville, equality in America was in the first place a matter of social equality, which went well beyond simple equality before the law: "I am speaking of equality in the relations of social life, an equality in view of which certain individuals gather in the same places, share ideas and pleasures, and join their families together."[7] In this respect France and America were quite different. Tocqueville concludes: "In sum, in America as in France, people are classified into various groups in the course of social life. Shared habits, education, and above all wealth establish these categories. But the rules are neither absolute, nor inflexible, nor permanent. They establish temporary distinctions and do not create classes in the proper sense of the word."[8]

Equality before the law was conceived in the same way on both sides of the Atlantic, but in America there were no fixed social distinctions and men considered themselves equals, whereas in France under the July Monarchy the mores and sentiments remained those associated with an inegalitarian society. France lacked that disposition to which the Greeks had given the name *isotimia*, equality of respect, a disposition that Tocqueville was astonished to discover in America. In 1900 Bryce also noted that in the United States equality meant first and foremost "equal esteem."[9]

For a liberal, equality means essentially equality in law and not equality in fact. But in France equality did not go beyond mere civil equality.[10] In America, what Tocqueville called "equality of conditions" encompassed legal equality, social equality, and equality of respect.[11] But the fullest and strongest sense of the term is apparent in the first sentence of *Democracy in America*: "No novelty in the United States struck me more vividly during my stay there than the equality of conditions." If this was a "novelty" for Tocqueville, clearly it cannot be confounded with equality as it existed in France—mere equality before the law combined with inequality in social relations. Equality of conditions is the "principal idea" in Tocqueville's masterpiece, the foundation of the new science which he successfully sought to establish once he had overcome his initial astonishment.

In August 1835 Tocqueville wrote Count Molé: "In America all laws derive, in a sense, from a single thought. All society is as it were founded on a single fact; everything stems from a single principle. America is like a great forest crossed by a number of straight highways, all of which lead to the same place. It is simply a matter of discovering the point at which they all converge, and everything becomes apparent all at once."[12] For Tocqueville, this point was clear: "The more I studied American society, the more clearly I saw equality of conditions as the creative element from which each particular fact derived, and all my observations constantly returned to this central point."[13] In Europe the picture was less simple, because laws and mores were not in harmony.

Tocqueville was well aware that, of the various forms of inequality prevalent in 1789, the Revolution had destroyed primarily inequality of estate.[14] It had done away with the orders that existed under the Old Regime and established the principle of equal rights for all, but it was a long way from having eliminated the boundaries between the upper and lower classes. At best it had only shifted those boundaries, and the July Monarchy had to some extent concealed them behind the fiction of a government of the middle classes. Because equality before the civil laws was the Revolution's great conquest, the French tended to consider such equality the essential element of what Tocqueville called equality of conditions. But nonegalitarian mores and sentiments persisted in French society. Why, then, did he believe that civil equality would eventually bring to France first equality of esteem and finally political equality?

For two reasons, apparently, one sociological, the other psychological. Tocqueville believed that the new postrevolutionary laws of inheritance would profoundly alter French society and foster greater social mobility. Furthermore, he thought that egalitarian sentiment, which had originated in hatred of the Old Regime, remained a powerful force in France. Its influence was visible in contemporary thought and even in constitutional texts.

For proponents of natural law, equality among men exists only in a moral sense, while for exponents of positive jurisprudence, equality exists only in a juridical sense. The famous sentence with which the 1789 Declaration of the Rights of Man begins[15] ceases to be vague only if it assumes a revolutionary meaning; it expresses the desire, characteristic of the French revolutionaries, to translate natural law into positive law and to destroy the orders of the Old Regime. In America, neither the Constitution nor the Bill of Rights makes a declaration of equality, but equality prevailed in the mores of the society to a sufficient degree that Americans enjoyed a feeling of equality. In France, the very notion of equality before the law could not be understood except in terms of the revolutionary break with the past; in society and culture inequality remained a potent and visible force.

THERE WAS NO small gap, then, between the democratic equality of the Americans and the revolutionary equality of the French. Nevertheless,

Tocqueville believed that the dynamics of equality would diminish that gap, provided that social mobility in France proved comparable to social mobility in America. Did he not in fact overestimate the effectiveness of the Revolution's laws regulating inheritance? And was he not mistaken about social mobility in his own day, which may have been quite different from that of the revolutionary period? Tocqueville did indeed believe that social mobility in a society of civil equality gives men a sense of equality. Social mobility exists where there are no fixed and permanent barriers between groups and where everyone enjoys the opportunity to acquire wealth or pursue goals of his or her own choosing. The young author of *Democracy in America* no doubt knew America in 1835 more objectively than he knew France, and he probably did overestimate both the effect of the laws on inheritance and the degree of social mobility in his own country. A scion of one of the leading families of the Cotentin, born into a segment of society that supported the legitimate monarchy, he had been taught that France had undergone profound social change both during the Revolution and Empire and since. He was in a position to observe the differences between the Old Regime bourgeoisie, which had suffered from the Revolution almost as much as the nobility, and the new bourgeoisie, born of the Revolution and made wealthy by the purchase of nationalized property and the sale of arms and provisions to the army and the imperial government. Did Tocqueville believe that the kind of individual social mobility typical of industrial and commercial societies could extend or even rival the powerful changes that had come in the wake of the Revolution? Did he not see that the new bourgeoisie was in the process of stabilizing itself? It may indeed be necessary to concede that the young author who published the first volume of *Democracy in America* in 1835 did harbor illusions of this kind; but the second volume, published in 1840, is much more realistic and is impervious to this sort of criticism.

Nevertheless, in 1835 Tocqueville believed that the dynamics of equality could enable the French to traverse the same ground that the Americans had already crossed. He neglected, however, to point out some major obstacles that the French might encounter, including not only its lower social mobility but also its lower level of prosperity compared with the United States. Since the eighteenth century, America in general had fared considerably better than Europe. As William Penn put it, America was "a good poor Man's country," and in the circumstances it is not hard to understand how Jefferson could have spoken of "lovely equality."[16]

These reservations about Tocqueville's vision of French society in his own time bear only indirectly on his main theme, for they concern the possibility of applying to France the lessons of his American experience. What was new in America—radically new, in Tocqueville's eyes— was not the degree of social mobility or the existence of de facto inequality, but the fact that under certain conditions men in America who lived unequally in unequal situations nevertheless considered themselves to be equals. Tocqueville was intelligent enough to be astonished by this observation. For him, human similarity was neither the objective basis of equality nor a valid political goal but a product of the imagination of the democratic social state; nevertheless, its importance could not be overstated. Similarly, the notion that there is a human nature in which all men share equally could not, in Tocqueville's view, serve as the sole logical basis for the construction or reconstruction of society, because human nature is at once a revealed fact of creation and a product of increasing equality, equality being the historical form in which the designs of Providence manifest themselves. Tocqueville's theory not only expands on Rousseau's but also puts it in perspective; indeed, Tocqueville transcends Rousseau in two respects, harking back to Bossuet's view of history-as-Providence while at the same time proposing the first sociological theory of human nature.

If the crux of his thought is as I have described it, then it is of little importance whether or not he exaggerated the egalitarian character of the Age of Jackson.[17] The equality to which Tocqueville refers is not to be found in economic comparisons or even in an equal distribution of power but chiefly in the ability to give a new meaning to human relations. In the second volume of *Democracy* Tocqueville sought to characterize precisely how the ideas, feelings, and mores associated with equality acquire this transforming capacity once men begin to believe that they are in fact equals. Rousseau had written: "He who undertakes to institute a people must feel capable of, as it were, changing human nature."[18] In the United States, however, human nature had been changed not by the legislature and not by the democratic philosophy of Rousseau but by the effects of egalitarian sentiments. In Tocqueville's view, those effects went beyond merely altering the style of human relations and resulted in the creation of veritable new men. No chapter of *Democracy in America* better illustrates this creative power of equality than that devoted to relations between masters and servants in volume two, where Tocqueville makes the following extraordinary statement: "Equality of conditions makes servant and master new beings and establishes new relations between them."[19]

Are we obliged to discount this idea simply because it is explicitly concerned only with masters and servants? To do so would, I think, be to mistake not only the meaning of the statement but also that of the chapter itself, which despite its title is one of the most general in the whole book, one of Tocqueville's finest statements on equality.[20] His real subject is even more difficult than that of reconciling liberty and equality; it is the question of authority and obedience among equals. "Why does one man have the right to command, and what compels another man to obey? A momentary and free accord of their two wills. By nature neither is inferior to the other; one becomes inferior temporarily as a result of the contract. Within the limits of this contract, one is the servant, the other the master. Outside it, both are citizens, both men."[21] The author goes on to show that civil society can be founded upon such contractual relations, yielding a social order that is obviously quite different from that prevalent in aristocratic societies. In the democratic order, the superior does not offer protection in exchange for devotion; there is neither respect nor servility, and there are none of those subtle relations whereby servant identifies with master. The master has no influence over the opinions or mores of his subordinates. The relation between master and servant is limited to scrupulous execution of the contract between them, and the two men "remain strangers to each other."[22] Tocqueville refuses to say whether he thinks such social relations are better or worse than those found in older societies; he simply concludes that social order can be based on relations between equals. "What is most necessary among men," he says, "is not a certain order; it is order."[23]

It is rather remarkable that the gist of this chapter on master-servant relations can be described without mentioning all that Tocqueville has to say about the specific problem of domestic servants. But I want to make two further points before I leave this chapter. First, Tocqueville says: "No matter how wealth or poverty, power or obedience, accidentally puts great distances between two men, public opinion, based on the normal way of things, puts them near the common level and creates a sort of fancied equality between them, in spite of the actual inequality in their lives."[24] In other words, wherever equality of conditions prevails, a powerful collective image of equality can make people forget about de facto inequalities, even those of considerable magnitude. Thus, equality of conditions does not mean equality in fact; indeed, it is what causes people to forget about real inequalities. This idea of equality stands in sharp contrast to that based on similarity; to confound two such different ideas, says Tocqueville, is to "comprehend in a most crude and tyrannical form the equality that is born of democracy."[25] If, in the final analysis, all concepts of democracy come down to a choice between similarity and moral equality, Tocqueville's choice is clear.[26] He does not invoke either natural law or the fiction of a fundamental pact, and he did not agree with Rousseau's dictum that "rather than destroy natural equality, the fundamental pact substitutes a legitimate moral equality for any physical inequalities that nature might have created among men."[27] Nevertheless, Tocqueville is close to Rousseau when he notes that full equality of conditions encourages, and if necessary creates, a new and powerful feeling of equality, which transforms man's perception of his relations with his fellow man. Why, then, is Tocqueville considered an original thinker and one of the founders of modern sociology? Because he showed the extent to which the discovery of a natural community among men is a product of the democratic social state but not a product of either nature or political democracy. To be more precise, Tocqueville held that the democratic social state produced an ambiguous moral notion of equality which could quickly be corrupted into egalitarian passion and envy if it was not elevated above social relations and given a transcendent basis in the equality of men before God. Tocqueville developed his ideas in a Jansenist climate, and there are attenuated echoes of the doctrine of the Fall in the Augustinian idea that the earthly City is vulnerable as long as it has not been united with the City of God.

The chapter's second conclusion quite obviously concerns France, even though the country is not mentioned by name; the text merely contrasts in general terms a democratic state of affairs with a revolutionary one. "But what am I to say of those sad and troubled times when equality comes into its own in the midst of revolutionary tumult, when democracy, after it has been established in the social system, still fights painfully against prejudice and mores?"[28] In societies where equality of conditions is incomplete, reduced to little more than equality before the law, and where equality is embodied in civil law but not yet in social mores, there is no firm basis for obedience and command, and "obedience then loses its moral basis in the eyes of him who obeys;

he no longer considers it as some sort of divinely appointed duty, and he does not yet see its purely human aspect; in his eyes it is neither sacred nor just, and he submits to it as a degrading though useful fact." The final consequence, which Tocqueville formulates only in the case of master-servant relations, is phrased in such a way as to suggest to the reader how it might be extended to society as a whole: "There is covert, intestine conflict between permanently suspicious rival powers."[29] This transitory state, revolutionary rather than democratic, results in confusion of what is with what is right, obscuring each to the point where "no one knows exactly what he is, what he can do, and what he ought to do."[30] But where Plato blamed this confusion, this disorder, this collapse of obedience, on democracy,[31] Tocqueville blames it solely on the nature of the transitional period—not on democratic equality but on revolutionary equality. For him as for Montesquieu, democracy is not incompatible with obedience: "He seeks not to have no masters but to have only equals for masters."[32] Just as Montesquieu distinguished between "orderly democracy and democracy which is not," Tocqueville distinguishes between democratic equality and revolutionary equality. For him, revolution is a corrupt form of democracy, corresponding to what Montesquieu called "the extreme spirit of equality."

Up to now I have considered equality only in ideas, sentiments, and civil society. Yet it is also a political value, which makes itself felt more or less quickly once equality has triumphed in the realm of civil laws and mores: "It is impossible to believe that equality will not ultimately penetrate the political realm as it has penetrated elsewhere. It is impossible to conceive of men eternally unequal in one respect but equal in all others; eventually they will therefore be equal in all respects."[33] Hence democratic equality in the full sense of the word consists of both political equality *and* equality of conditions, where the latter term covers not only equality before the law but also equality of opportunity (assured by social mobility) and equality of consideration. Tocqueville believed that democratic society created and sustained a dynamic of equality so powerful that it would inevitably lead to political equality in one of two possible forms: "Rights must be given either to every citizen or to none."[34] Society's moral state is not strictly determined by its social state. A democratic social state is compatible with several different states of mind, depending on the form taken by the spirit of equality. "There is in fact a legitimate and masculine passion for equality, which spurs all men to wish to be powerful and highly esteemed.

This passion tends to elevate the small to the rank of the great. But one also finds in the human heart a depraved craving for equality, which causes the weak to wish to drag the strong down to their level and which reduces men to a preference for equality in servitude over inequality in freedom."[35]

This perversion of equality, which stems from envy and can lead to servitude, is a possible concomitant of the development of political democracy.[36] Only by recognizing the rights of the individual can such a danger be averted. With this proviso, political democracy is possible, but in a liberal rather than Rousseauan form. Thus, Tocqueville is calling for a liberal solution to the problem of democracy rather than a democratic solution as such. He was always wary[37] of the possibility that egalitarian sentiments would degenerate into passions whose very satisfaction would increase man's woe: "The desire for equality becomes more and more insatiable as equality becomes greater."[38]

In any case, no matter what precautions were taken against the degeneration of egalitarian sentiments, love of equality was destined to become the dominant sentiment in democratic societies, or, as Montesquieu might have said, their "principle." Love of liberty can exist in a democracy, or it can be sacrificed to the dominant passion. "I believe that democratic peoples have a natural appetite for liberty; left to themselves, they would seek it out; they love liberty and suffer when anyone tries to deprive them of it. But they have an ardent, insatiable, eternal, and invincible passion for equality; they want equality in liberty, and if they cannot have it they also want it in slavery."[39] This passage from the second volume of *Democracy* elaborates upon ideas stated in the first volume in the course of an examination of the "political consequences of the social state of the Anglo-Americans."[40]

If the Americans had managed to combine liberty with equality, they owed their good fortune to the wisdom of their legislators, to their own lights, and above all to their mores. At intervals Tocqueville reminds the reader of America's great luck in not having had to endure the disruption of a major revolution. But what about the French, whose inegalitarian mores were still at odds with their new laws? What sort of democracy were they likely to arrive at, and by what course? That question, which always lies just below the surface of volume two of *Democracy in America*, is scarcely touched on in volume one, except in the introduction and at the end of the chapter that forms the true conclusion of the work.[41] In both instances the special role of revolution in France is stressed, along with the importance of mores in the success of the Americans. In volume two, references to France, though often implicit, are quite numerous; they take the form either of an analysis of a transitional state between aristocracy and democracy or, more characteristically, of allusions to a revolutionary social state. Revolutions stir up egalitarian passions, which quickly assume an extreme form: "Democratic peoples love equality at all times, but in certain periods they carry their passion for equality to the point of madness. This happens when the old, long-threatened social hierarchy is finally destroyed after a final, intestine battle, and the barriers that once separated citizens are finally overturned. Men then hurl themselves upon equality as upon some item of conquered booty and clutch it to them as though it were a precious good that someone might wish to steal."[42] In France, where equality was achieved in revolution, the democratic principle was tainted from the very start by corruption in the form of extremist egalitarian passions—pushed to "the point of madness."

It is reasonable to assume that, as Tocqueville mulled over these matters, he had in mind the well-known chapter three of book eight of Montesquieu's *Esprit des lois*, on the extreme egalitarian spirit, but it is probable that his thoughts also turned to the chapter, less often cited today,[43] that immediately follows it: "Great successes to which the public contributes greatly give it such pride that it is no longer possible to govern." The examples that Montesquieu chose from ancient history no doubt paled before that which contemporary history had impressed upon the mind of Tocqueville: the successes of the French people in their struggle first against aristocracy and later against Europe had permanently altered their political sensibilities.[44]

THE INTRODUCTION TO volume one of *Democracy in America* cites equality of conditions as the crucial factor in the development of a democratic society in America, and the rest of the volume confirms this assertion. But volume two takes a less simple view of the matter. As Tocqueville proceeds, he makes increasing use of comparisons between France and the United States, and these take him a long way from the simplicity of his original conception. In fact, there are two different frameworks for the book, or, if you prefer, two different factors that contribute to the development of democracy: equality of conditions and revolution. This duality carries through all the parts of volume two.

The structure of the book is complex. Each part begins with a chapter devoted to the influence of equality, and perhaps the most prominent line of argument links these introductory chapters from section to section, reflecting the author's overall conception. But within each part, there is also a somewhat less prominent line of argument, whose importance varies but is always quite significant; here Tocqueville obviously concerns himself with France, even when that country is not named, and he emphasizes the influence of revolution rather than that of equality. From this comparison it emerges that revolution is responsible for the ills generally attributed to equality by Tocqueville's contemporaries. One of the more subtle beauties of his work is that, at the conclusion of reflections that can only be called aristocratic by virtue of both their tone and their elevated vantage point, equality emerges exonerated on all counts.

Stunning as this paradox is,[45] the question remains whether the 1840 text accords with the theory of equality as the "crucial factor" as set forth in the introduction to volume one, published in 1835. Any possible contradiction is immediately blunted insofar as the French Revolution was itself caused by the need for equality.

Inequality can cause revolution if it stands in the way of social mobility and the circulation of elites. Hence the chapters in volume two that seem to make revolution the crucial factor in the development of certain democratic societies, in particular the French, do not contradict the main idea of the work. Rather, they examine a special case of the rule in question, studying the specific path followed by countries in which egalitarian passions, exacerbated by impediments to social mobility, precipitate a revolution, which in turn results in lasting exaltation of those very passions, perpetuating them in an extreme form. Any difficulty in reconciling Tocqueville's various statements on the subject vanishes as soon as we cease to confuse the notion of "crucial factor" with that of "point of departure." In both France and America equality is the crucial factor, but in each case the point of departure is different.

In these circumstances, Tocqueville asked, what future could France expect? Either there would be a series of periodic revolutions and sudden changes of regime, or else an American-style equilibrium would be attained. For the latter, Tocqueville believed that France would need to achieve greater social mobility, gradual transformation of social mores, and political liberty, but not necessarily to adopt American-style institutions.[46]

All commentators on Tocqueville have pointed to the originality of his crucial-factor theory and his powerful, systematic approach; but few have noted the dual nature of the analysis, which, following Montesquieu, always distinguishes between simple love of equality and extreme egalitarianism. Furthermore, Tocqueville brings out the force of this distinction by constantly comparing the United States with France, that is, the American norm with that modern form of excess unknown to Montesquieu, the French First Republic.

Liberty

Better than any of his contemporaries Tocqueville understood the nature of democratic equality, yet he was persuaded that he must accept it because he lived in an era in which liberty could no longer find a basis in inequality, that is, in aristocracy, and in which "there is no legislator wise enough and powerful enough to maintain free institutions without taking equality for his first principle and symbol . . . Thus it is not a question of reconstructing an aristocratic society but of engendering liberty within the democratic society in which God has made us live."[47] Tocqueville's hierarchy of political values is quite clear: he accepted equality because there was no other possible foundation for liberty; he was a democrat because he was a liberal—a democrat by reason but a liberal by passion. Antoine Redier, in the course of his research in the Tocqueville family archives, discovered an unpublished fragment, apparently a page of a diary that Tocqueville wrote for himself and entitled "My instinct, my opinions." Here is the text of Tocqueville's profession of faith:

> Experience has taught me that most men, and surely myself, always come back in the end to more or less their fundamental instincts, and that they do well only those things that are compatible with their instincts. Let me therefore consider in all sincerity what my fundamental instincts and earnest principles are.
>
> For democratic institutions I have an intellectual preference, but I am by instinct an aristocrat, which is to say that I despise and fear the mob.[48] I passionately love liberty, legality, respect for rights, but not democracy: that is my innermost feeling . . . Liberty is the first of my passions: that is the plain truth.[49]

On the basis of this text, it is tempting to trace Tocqueville's feelings about liberty back to aristocratic tradition and the religious idea of the free and responsible soul. No doubt his experiences in the United

States, as well as his reading of Pascal, Montesquieu, and Rousseau between 1835 and 1840, added depth to his views and enabled him to elaborate a theory of democratic liberty. But fundamentally his views on liberty stem from his family tradition and his religious education. Later he would compare his opinions to those of his contemporaries and be obliged to employ the terms of discourse current among them. All were acutely aware of living in a new age and inclined to distinguish between modern and ancient notions of liberty, between democratic and aristocratic ideas of freedom. Tocqueville's thinking combines reflections of this type with others derived from his tireless comparison of French with American forms of liberty. Briefly, let us examine how these reflections were understood by Tocqueville's contemporaries, as a prelude to investigating how Tocqueville reacted to the liberal views of his day and how much of those views he incorporated into his work.

It is not certain that Tocqueville read Benjamin Constant; his disciple Edouard Laboulaye deplored his not having done so.[50] Nevertheless, it is tempting to compare Tocqueville's ideas with those set forth in Constant's famous speech to the Paris Athenaeum in 1819, the subject of which was "The Liberty of the Ancients as Compared with That of the Moderns." "The goal of the ancients was the sharing of social power by all citizens. That was what they called liberty. The goal of the moderns is security in private enjoyment, and they call liberty the guarantees that institutions afford to those enjoyments."[51] In an 1814 pamphlet entitled *On the Spirit of Conquest and Usurpation* (chapters 6–8), Constant had described the absurd attempts by revolutionaries inspired by Rousseau and Mably to impose the liberty of the ancients upon the moderns. This foolishness, which resulted in despotism, was rooted in neglect of individual liberties. Respect for the individual as such was unknown to the Greeks. The individual was recognized only as a citizen, and the only guarantee he enjoyed was that stemming from his share of sovereignty. The idea, Christian in origin, of according rights to the individual as such, as a man and not merely as a citizen, was reaffirmed by Renaissance individualists and by the modern school of natural law theorists; ultimately it led to the Declaration of the Rights of Man and of the Citizen of 1789 and to the individualist doctrine of that era, perhaps best expressed by Sieyès: "The final cause of the whole social world must be individual liberty."[52]

It is indeed surprising that Tocqueville never cited Constant, but he may have refrained from doing so in order not to be compelled to spell out their areas of disagreement, which in my view were as extensive as their areas of agreement.[53] In any case, Tocqueville has a modern, that is to say, an individualistic, conception of liberty, but this did not satisfy him as it did Constant, for he also attempted to preserve what Constant was apparently willing to relinquish without undue regret, namely, the pleasure of public action. Tocqueville discovered very early that there was pleasure to be had in political activity. By family tradition as well as temperament he was equipped to assume the point of view of those who govern. At age twenty-four he wrote to his friend Beaumont: "It hardly needs saying that we must make ourselves political men."[54] For him as for Aristotle, political life was a means of human fulfillment. His work shows that he wanted to distribute the benefits of that life as widely as possible, for he believed that political liberty was essential if certain human defects encouraged by equality were to be corrected. *Democracy in America* is the last great theoretical expression of civic humanism, as Tocqueville's English translator, Henry Reeve, was well aware: "You have made the book of the people for France as Machiavelli made the Book of the Prince for Cesare Borgia."[55]

Now, the two final historical manifestations of civic humanism were the founding of the American Republic and the French Revolution, and Tocqueville indefatigably asked himself why the French enterprise, for all its grandeur, had failed to create a free and stable republic whereas the Americans had succeeded. As he pursued this question, he discovered the contrast between French liberty and American liberty. For Tocqueville, a crucial feature of American liberty was that it was based on age-old habits and customs as well as on laws, and not, like French liberty, on proclamations made in the name of abstract principles. Americans cherished not the liberty of natural law but, as Burke said in his famous address to the House of Commons on 22 March 1775, their historical freedoms. Burke was pleading for compromise with the rebellious colonies: "They are therefore not only devoted to liberty, not to liberty according to English ideas, and on English principles."

Burke touches on a point that all who accord political value to a continuous tradition like to emphasize. Thibaudet said that liberty is a good that ripens with age. What was miraculous about the American experience was that the transition from an aristocratic to a democratic form of liberty occurred without crisis. From the standpoint of those who possess "liberties, there is no difference between liberties and privileges; from the standpoint of equality things are quite different."

Tocqueville speaks of liberty, not liberties, which is already an indication of his choice; his vocabulary alone is enough to distinguish him from the counterrevolutionaries. Unlike some revolutionaries, however, he clearly enumerated the essential ingredients of what he called liberty: freedom of thought, recognition of individual rights and guarantees of those rights, and political freedom. Yet he was also firmly attached to independence and to individual pride, hallmarks of aristocratic liberty.

Unlike Chateaubriand, Tocqueville rejected the aristocratic notion of honor. But both men had to struggle to free themselves from the idea that liberty consists of concessions and privileges, and both clung to the hope that an intimate alliance could be established between the spirit of liberty and dignity. In 1850 Tocqueville wrote his friend Kergorlay: "I have no traditions, I have no party, I have no cause other than that of liberty and human dignity. Of that I am sure."[56] Had he really broken as thoroughly as he maintained with the traditions of his class? His entire work represents an immense effort to transfer aristocratic values to a democratic society, and for the benefit of that society; those values began with appreciation of human excellence, mutual respect, and proud affirmation of individual independence. For both Tocqueville and Chateaubriand these constituted the heart of aristocratic liberty.

Jean-Jacques Chevallier has called attention to a curious passage in Guizot's 1828 lectures on the history of European civilization.[57] Guizot pays homage to the German barbarians for having introduced into European civilization "the sentiment of personality, of human individuality in its free development . . . a sentiment unknown to virtually all previous civilizations." Chevallier observes:

> Guizot had more to say about the nature of this sentiment, which he praised despite its 'evil side': it was the sentiment of independence for independence' sake, an appetite for freedom which in any event revealed itself for no other purpose than to satisfy its craving. This was something entirely different from the civic liberty of the ancients or from liberty in its Christian sense, which depends on man's transforming himself inwardly (lecture 2, p. 33). If, as seems likely, Tocqueville attended Guizot's lectures in 1828, he must have found confirmation of some of his own inclinations. Listen, for instance, to what he says about liberty: "In all ages some men have been passionately attached to [liberty] for its inherent attractions, its peculiar charm, independent of its benefits, simply for the pleasure of being

able to speak, act, and breathe without constraint, under the sole government of God and the laws. Anyone who seeks in liberty something other than itself is made to serve . . . Do not ask me to analyze this sublime appetite; you must feel it for yourself. Of its own accord it enters those great hearts that God has prepared to receive it. It fills them, inflames them. There is no hope of explaining this to mediocre souls who have never felt it."[58] The emphasis is on independence for its own sake. This is the Germanic idea of liberty, of which modern liberty, liberty in the English mold, is the remote heir. As Montesquieu said, "This admirable system was found in the woods."[59]

It is easy to see why Chevallier sees Tocqueville as "a liberal aristocrat . . . a direct heir of Montesquieu."[60]

Nevertheless, Tocqueville is also aware of the negative aspects: "This aristocratic notion of liberty produces among those who have received it an exalted sense of their individual worth, a passionate zeal for independence. It gives to selfishness a singular energy and power."[61] Aristocratic liberty may imply selfishness, but it exalts the individual and precludes his harboring any servile sentiments. "However subservient the subjects of the Old Regime may have been to the will of the king, one sort of obedience was unknown to them: they did not know what it was to bow down before an illegitimate, contested power, little honored and often despised, yet to which people willingly subjected themselves because it served or might harm their interests. That form of servitude was always foreign to them."[62]

DESPITE THE FORCE of his aristocratic attitude toward liberty, Tocqueville deemed democratic liberty better suited to his time, and in his "Essay on the Social and Political State of France Before and After 1789" he even declared that it was just: "According to the modern, democratic, and I daresay just notion of liberty, every man is presumed to have received from nature such lights as he needs to guide his conduct and is therefore endowed at birth with an equal and inalienable right to live independent of his fellowman in all respects concerning himself alone, and to govern his destiny as he sees fit."[63] Here, the moral content lies in the idea of equal rights for all, but as Raymond Aron points out, the definition is still both negative and indeterminate: negative because expressed in terms of independence and "indeterminate in that it remains unclear just what 'concerns oneself alone.'" Aron adds that from other passages it is clear that for Tocqueville liberty can be "realized authentically only in liberty in the specifically political sense, that is, through citizen participation in the administration of local affairs and government."[64] Ultimately, Tocqueville's "just, democratic" idea of liberty contains three ingredients: an idea of independence, inherited from Germanic ancestors via the aristocracy;[65] an idea of political participation, inherited from the ancients; and an idea of equality before the law, inherited from Christian moral teachings.

The Germanic idea of liberty includes a notion of obligation: independence must be preferred to all other goods. Nevertheless, Germanic liberty is not liberty for the good, but liberty for itself; it does not lead to a moral end but is an end unto itself. It is a value because it gives the man of pride a sense of his own worth. It entails obligation but only in regard to oneself.

For the ancients, liberty was more than a right; it was a duty. The citizen owed everything to the city and placed such a value on his freedom to participate in its government that he could not even conceive of individual freedom in any other sense. Thus freedom was just another name for civic obligation.

With Christianity appeared the notion that all human beings have equal rights because all have equal moral responsibilities. Hence it is the duty of every man to recognize that others enjoy equal rights. Christianity provided the moral strength necessary, first, to moderate the Germanic idea of freedom and then to extend aristocratic liberties to all.

Combine these three ingredients and you have what Tocqueville called democratic liberty: liberty that is not only a right but a duty in the fullest sense of the word, an obligation to oneself, to others, to one's city, and to God.

What if people forget that liberty is a duty—civic as well as moral? What if they simply take advantage of the right to be free and neglect their civic duties? Tocqueville's answer would be that the French aristocracy was swept away because it forgot its civic duties. In fact, aristocratic liberty, like democratic liberty, is not viable without the exercise of political freedom; participation in government is a duty as well as a right. When the French aristocrats allowed themselves to be stripped of their political freedom, they may have believed that they would continue to be able to enjoy the privilege of independence; in reality they were digging their own graves, as Tocqueville is frequently at pains to point out in *The Old Regime and the French Revolution*. Did the French aristocracy perish simply because privileges were destined to disappear from the face of the earth? No. The English aristocracy, more open than the French and above all more attentive to its civic duties, was able to preserve both its liberty and its privileges. To be sure, it was condemned to decline, as are all aristocracies, but the process of decline would be continuous and gradual. Democratic liberty is the normal product of aristocratic liberty, and, as civilization and enlightenment progress, no violent crisis is necessary to extend the rights of a few to ever greater numbers.

It remains to be seen how Tocqueville reached this conclusion while meditating, in the terms set by contemporary debate, upon the various forms of liberty. How did he come to reject the notion that aristocratic liberty and democratic liberty are by nature fundamentally different?

Three aspects of his thought contributed to this conclusion. First, his lifelong interest in the political life of England and the United States made him sensitive to the role played by habit and custom and taught him to apply the corrective of Anglo-Saxon empiricism to what he believed to be the overly rationalist tendencies of the Physiocrats, Condorcet and his disciples the Idéologues, and, more generally, much of eighteenth-century political philosophy.[66] Perhaps he agreed with Joseph de Maistre that no people can give itself liberty that does not already possess it. But he knew the answer to this offered by Madame de Staël in her *Considerations of the French Revolution*: in France liberty was ancient and despotism new. The liberty demanded by the French in 1789 was not only their natural right but their historical right. Of course. But the French had long since lost the habit of liberty by the time they rediscovered the idea. This, too, was one difference between Europe and America: "Among the Americans it is thus liberty that is ancient; equality is comparatively new. The contrary is true in Europe, where equality, introduced by absolute power and under the gaze of kings, had already entered into the habits of nations long before liberty entered into their ideas."[67] Once again Tocqueville is elucidating an idea of Montesquieu's, who had observed that people tend to define liberty in terms of whatever political values they are used to: "Those who savored republican government placed it in that government; those who had rejoiced in monarchical government placed it in monarchy. In the end, every man called liberty that government which conformed best to his customs and inclinations."[68] Hence it is hardly surprising that so many Frenchmen confounded liberty with equality.

Second, Tocqueville found that, different as aristocratic liberty was from the liberty of the Americans, however democratic, the two had one point in common: both were intimately associated with religion. Anglo-American civilization is "the product (and one should continually bear in mind this point of departure) of two perfectly distinct elements which elsewhere have often been at war with each other but which in America it was somehow possible to incorporate, forming a marvelous combination. I mean the *spirit of religion* and the *spirit of freedom*."[69] In France, where these two elements were "at war," Christianity was combated not as a religious doctrine but as a political institution associated with the aristocratic system: such was Tocqueville's thesis, set forth twenty years after *Democracy in America* in the first chapter of *The Old Regime*.[70] Tocqueville concludes: "It is a great mistake to believe that democratic societies are naturally hostile to religion. Nothing in Christianity or even Catholicism is absolutely contrary to the spirit of these societies, and several things are quite favorable."[71] The interpenetration of Church and State had been a cause of conflict. As long as the two were kept separate, democratic liberty could not only coexist with religion but even draw moral strength from it. "When any religion has struck profound roots in a democracy, do not disturb it but rather preserve it as the most precious heritage of the aristocratic centuries."[72] Note that Tocqueville is speaking here not about Christianity but about religion in general, and recall that when he wrote these lines he was not a believer.[73] Clearly, therefore, his view is not the same as that set forth by Chateaubriand in his *Génie du Christianisme*. Tocqueville is concerned primarily with the conditions under which the transition from aristocratic to democratic liberty can be made without disruption.

Finally, note that the distinction between ancient and modern forms of liberty was not so clear to Tocqueville as it had been to Benjamin Constant, because Tocqueville had found both forms in America, the former in the township, the latter in the states and the federal government.[74] Besides Greece and England, cases with which Constant had dealt, it was therefore necessary to consider America as the place where the two were combined. France, the home of revolutionary liberty, was by contrast the place where they were most sharply distinguished, first in the tragic attempt to recreate the ancient form of liberty and later in the hope that the Restoration would found a new form of liberty, which increasingly resembled its English model. For both Tocqueville and Constant, representative democracy was a child of the modern spirit.[75] But Tocqueville was not satisfied merely to read in America the future of Europe; he admired the continuity of the thread that led from one form of liberty to the other and observed that in the United States the ancient form still played an indispensable educational role.[76] As for the opposition analyzed by Constant, it was neither so clear nor so absolute as it might seem at first sight, for it concerned both the remote history of civilization and more recent events in France.[77] The suggestion is that the two forms of liberty are, in a radical sense, mutually exclusive, whereas the American example shows that this need not be the case. Influenced by lingering memories of the Revolution, Constant tended to draw a sharp distinction between democracy and liberalism. Though no less attentive to this distinction, Tocqueville, from his more serene vantage point, brought his American experience to bear in attempting to reconcile the two.

ULTIMATELY, HOWEVER, ONE MUST ASK whether Tocqueville's conception of liberty was a liberal one, based upon a negative idea of freedom, upon an absence of constraint, or a democratic one, in which liberty is identified with participation in government.[78] The answer is easy, encompassing both the author's personal preferences and his judgments concerning the objective conditions of his time: Tocqueville was a liberal, and he was a democrat only because he was a liberal convinced that in the modern age liberty could not be based upon inequality. In the drafts of volume two of *Democracy in America* we read: "I believe that if those who live in the democratic centuries were deprived of liberty, they would readily fall beneath the ordinary level of humanity. Liberty is therefore more precious in these centuries than in all the others. I also think that liberty can never be established in a nation without respect for equality. Anyone who in centuries to come attempts to establish and found liberty upon aristocracy will fail."[79]

Henceforth, liberty is possible only if it is a right shared equally by all, but in its essence it is negative liberty, as is evident from the text (previously cited) in which Tocqueville proclaimed his acceptance of the concept of equal liberty for all.[80] Liberty is based on the absence of constraints, and insofar as political liberty is concerned, on the absence of arbitrary action by the government. In this sense liberty therefore presupposes some measure of independence, but as Montesquieu had noted, it is more than that: "One must keep in mind what independence is and what liberty is. Liberty is the right to do what the laws permit, and if a citizen could do what the laws prohibit, he would no longer possess liberty, because others would have the same power."[81] Nevertheless, instructed by the French Revolution and by the surprising implications in Rousseau's work that the Revolution revealed, Tocqueville did not look upon law as the sole guarantee of liberty, because he knew that the popular will could prove harmful to such fundamental liberties as freedom of thought and freedom of association. Instead, he placed his confidence in the idea of rights guaranteed by both political liberty itself and a constitution of some sort. Furthermore, he held that there is no liberty unless man has the right to exercise moral responsibility. "Liberty is in truth a sacred thing. Only one other thing is more worthy of the name: virtue. And what is virtue, if not the free choice of what is good?"[82]

Negative liberty founded upon a moral base: such was Tocqueville's primary political value as well as the first value in his personal hierarchy. Relatively indifferent to the nature of the political regime in the narrow sense, he sought to foster a love of political liberty in his contemporaries.

In order to avoid seeing contradictions where none exist, it is useful to distinguish between liberty itself and an individual's or society's attitude toward liberty. Doing so helps us to understand how Tocqueville's aristocratic attitudes could coexist with his favorable judgment of the principle of equal liberty for all. As he wrote to Mill in 1835: "I love liberty out of taste, equality out of instinct and reason. These two passions, which so many people pretend to have, I believe I really feel within myself, and I am ready to make great sacrifices for them. Those are the only advantages I grant myself. They have more to do with the absence of certain common vices than with the possession of rare qualities."[83] Tocqueville always experienced liberty as a need for responsibility and dignity, but he knew that many of his contemporaries demanded it only as a means to an end. He ascribed to himself no particular moral superiority, but he knew that if liberty was sought solely as a means to equality or prosperity it would quickly degenerate.

For Tocqueville, the chief danger was not the abuse of power but the weakening of liberal sentiments,[84] which would leave life confined within the private sphere and thus, as a consequence of individualism, abandon man to what Tocqueville called "a sort of respectable materialism,"[85] preparing the way for a new form of despotism. The most pernicious effect of democracy might well be to diminish the energy of liberal sentiments to the point where men satisfied with their prosperous tranquillity would no longer even notice the absence of freedom, whereupon a new Leviathan might establish itself without recourse to violence, even respecting certain of the outward forms of liberty.[86]

Tocqueville, like Chateaubriand, believed that liberty consisted first of all in human dignity.[87] Chateaubriand was fond of criticizing Constant, and in his letters to Madame Récamier he displays all his haughty contempt for bourgeois liberals who sought liberty through the maximization of pleasure and viewed it as no more than a means to happiness conceived in materialistic terms. Tocqueville's sentiments were quite similar, but rather than condemn he sought to correct, to elevate the liberalism of the new society. For him, the principal danger was the very thing that Constant praised as the "proud and jealous isolation of the individual in the fortress of his right" and the resulting conception of political freedom as a mere guarantee of private rights. In contrast, Tocqueville believed that the primary need was to reawaken the public spirit of the citizenry, to cause men to look beyond their own interests in public affairs, and through exercise of political liberty to overcome the pettiness of the passions that democratic society all too often engendered.

Liberty and Equality

At the time Tocqueville wrote, the conjunction of liberty with equality was an ideal achieved in no country except the United States. There was no difficulty reconciling the two from a moral standpoint, but problems arose as soon as the question was formulated in psychological or political terms. The democratic social state accorded to individuals both equality of conditions and independence, but, as Montesquieu had noted, independence was not the same thing as liberty, which requires a further notion of the rights possessed by every responsible individual. Such a notion is not a necessary consequence of the democratic social state. When everyone enjoys an equal right to be free, then freedom can be reconciled with equality defined in terms of equal rights rather than natural similarity. Once the principle of civil equality is accepted, the dynamics of equality tends to introduce political equality as well; there is no guarantee that a proper balance will be struck between popular sovereignty and liberty in the sense of individual rights. For Tocqueville, America was interesting precisely because it showed how a balance could be struck between liberty and equality, thereby bringing some measure of justice to political affairs— no easy task.

In the notes he made prior to writing the first volume of *Democracy in America* Tocqueville wrote: "Love of liberty is a nobler and fuller sentiment than love of equality . . . Democracy [is] more favorable to the spirit of equality than to that of liberty." The same ideas figure in the title of one of the best-known chapters of volume two: "Why Democratic Peoples Show a More Ardent and Enduring Love for Equality than for Liberty."[88] But the content of the chapter is quite different, in part because it ranges well beyond what the title promises, in part because it extends the argument of volume one by attempting to correct misinterpretations by an overly conservative readership. Hence from the beginning Tocqueville seeks both to set forth his views as clearly as he can and to reassure a public worried about the thought that democratic society will soon come to France. "Equality can be established in civil society yet not prevail in politics." This formulation, of course, recalls the situation existing under the July Monarchy. Tocqueville is content simply to note that this is an incomplete form of democracy, but he does not say that it is necessarily a transitional stage, even though all his work would tend to suggest such a conclusion. At the same time, he maintains that democratic values form an indissoluble whole fully embodied in democracy in its mature form, which he defines not by reference to American society but only as a distant point in the imagination, an ideal that he discusses in the future tense: "Men will be perfectly free because they will all be entirely equal; and they will all be perfectly equal because they will be entirely free. The democratic peoples are moving toward this ideal." Never in Tocqueville's work do we encounter a thought closer than this to Rousseau and Condorcet. Nevertheless, Tocqueville is careful to distinguish between the ideal and the reality, and he immediately adds that various combinations of liberty and equality are practicable in actually existing societies. Hence it is important to distinguish between the two, even if in their most extreme form they are one, for that extreme remains a mere hypothetical possibility. "I suppose," Tocqueville said at the beginning, "that all citizens cooperate in the government and that each one has an equal right to do so." In any other situation there are grounds, as Rousseau himself would have acknowledged, for distinguishing between liberty and equality, since the acts of the sovereign would no longer be expressions of the general will.

Apart from the introduction, the contents of this chapter do not fulfill the promise made in the title, except for a scant half page (p. 102), where the author points out that the principal passion of the democratic centuries is love of equality. This is a truth he is as tired of hearing as of repeating: "It has been said a hundred times that our contemporaries are more ardent and tenacious in their love of equality than in their love of liberty." I would wager that the commonplace was particularly irritating to Tocqueville when stated, as Chateaubriand liked to do, in its most sweeping form, contrasting democracy, enamored of equality, with aristocracy, supposedly based on the principle of liberty.[89] In reality, Tocqueville says, men have always preferred equality to liberty; he devotes a good third of the chapter to a demonstration of this universally valid proposition. Having thus digressed from the subject announced in the chapter title, he continues in the same vein by devoting the end of the chapter to the effect of revolution on the love of equality and to the consequences of the comparative length of time for which liberty, on the one hand, and equality, on the other, have been recognized by the society as important values.

Tocqueville wants to go further than Montesquieu, to explain why the spirit of equality assumes an extreme form. In one respect, however, his explanation is more an application of *L'Esprit des lois* than an innovation: Montesquieu (book 8, chapter 4) had written that the "extreme spirit of equality" could originate in great popular victories. Tocqueville casts the democratic revolution in this light. With his contrast between the consequences of liberty and those of equality, he can be read as an intermediary between Montesquieu and Weber: "The goods that liberty secures reveal themselves only at length"; hence they are not yet clearly perceived in France, where equality preceded liberty (pp. 103–104).

To conclude these comments, I shall cite, as is often done, the superb closing passages of this chapter; unfortunately, few who cite them note that they are at odds with the logic of the chapter and that their rhetorical beauty contributes to the false impression already created by the title: "I think democratic peoples have a natural taste for liberty; left to themselves, they will seek it, cherish it, and be sad if it is taken from them. But their passion for equality is ardent, insatiable, eternal, and invincible. They want equality in freedom, and if they cannot have that, they still want equality in slavery. They will put up with poverty, servitude, and barbarism, but they will not endure aristocracy." What no one ever cites is the following sentence, which conforms much better to the content of the chapter: "This is true at all times, but especially in our own." Our own? For the reader impressed by the title and rhetoric of the chapter and by prevailing opinion, our time is the "age of democracy," which has seen liberty ranked below equality in the hierarchy of values; but for the reader attentive to Tocqueville's argument, it is clear that equality is always preferred to liberty by the majority, and that "our time" refers to the time of the French Revolution.

Revolutionary violence and disorder arouse such a desire for order and tranquillity, however, that liberty is also threatened from that angle: "Desire for public tranquillity then becomes a blind passion, and citizens are apt to succumb to a very disorderly love for order."[90]

The weak and intermittent concern for liberty on the part of the majority is threatened by more powerful political passions, especially in the aftermath of revolution. Nevertheless, on the basis of his knowledge of the United States and his love of liberty, Tocqueville believes that a balance can be struck between liberty and equality.

WHILE WORKING ON what he called his final chapter (which in fact became part four of volume two of *Democracy in America*), Tocqueville wondered "how to go about combining the spirit of equality with the spirit of liberty in a leveled society. For me that part is the most important."[91] His concern about this chapter is evident in another note: "General idea of final chapter: How the ideas and mores I have just described facilitate despotism."[92] Volume one had shown how the democratic social state can lead to either servitude or freedom, depending on the nature of a people's feelings about equality. Volume two again stresses the ambiguous consequences of equality, but here Tocqueville embarks upon a new line of argument: "Equality produces two tendencies: one leads men directly to independence and may even thrust them suddenly into anarchy; the other leads them along a longer, more obscure, but more certain path into servitude."[93] The emphasis is no longer on the psychology of the egalitarian passions but on the notion of unforeseen consequences, on the "obscurity" of the path. A political order can be established without having been anticipated or willed by anyone, simply as an objective consequence of certain ideas and emotions. This view does not contradict the one set forth in volume one. That early view had already changed as the work progressed and Tocqueville came to consider the possible weakening of liberal sentiments and the complications introduced by revolution. In the final text the effects of revolution are stressed even more: "They had wanted to be free in order to become equal, and, as equality took hold with the aid of liberty, liberty became increasingly difficult to maintain."[94]

Comparing texts chronologically, we can see how far Tocqueville had come from Montesquieu. Initially inclined to view the corruption of democracy as a consequence of extreme egalitarianism, Tocqueville elaborated in a very original way upon an idea of Montesquieu's by showing how this followed from revolution. In the end he put forth an entirely new theory, closer to Weber than to his mentor, Montesquieu.

All of Tocqueville's work is a meditation on the relations between liberty and equality. His most original thoughts on the question are found in the final part of *Democracy in America*, which I shall analyze later. But we have already touched on the central question of Tocqueville's work: Is political freedom sufficient to dispel the ambiguity of equality and its consequences? Or, to put it in a more acute way: Will liberty survive equality? Can we place our hope in the belief that the evils of equality will be overcome as the consequences of revolution recede into the past? The revolutionary wants liberty in order to achieve equality, whereas the liberal accepts equality in order to save liberty: "We liberals," said Rémusat, "were born in the midst of revolution."

PART TWO

Democracy in America and in France

3 🙰 The Primacy of Law

The Limits of Sovereignty

"I regard as impious and detestable this maxim, that in matters of government the majority of a people has the right to do anything, yet I place the origin of all powers in the wills of the majority. Am I in contradiction with myself? There is one general law which has been made, or at least adopted, not only by the majority of this or that people but by the majority of all men. That law is Justice. Justice therefore defines the limit of each people's right."[1] This statement alone is enough to place Tocqueville alongside Sieyès, Benjamin Constant, and Royer-Collard in the ranks of classical liberalism, among those who rejected the notion of unlimited sovereignty, and, in a broader and more venerable sense, among those who placed justice ahead of law.

Before Benjamin Constant, Sieyès had (on 2 Thermidor in the Year III of the revolutionary calendar) raised his voice in protest against unlimited sovereignty, using a curious expression that makes us conscious of the link that exists between the classical doctrine of absolute sovereignty and what we nowadays call totalitarianism: "And I say this, that as people become more enlightened, as they move farther from the time when they mistook their will for wisdom, the notion of sovereignty will once again be trimmed to its proper limits; for I repeat, the sovereignty of the people is not unlimited, and many systems approved and honored today, including the one to which people are still persuaded they owe a great debt, will be seen to be mere monkish conceptions, poor schemes for Re-total [*sic*] rather than Republic, and all harmful to liberty and ruinous of the public as well as the private good."[2] This argument is developed further by Benjamin Constant in the first chapter of his *Principles of Politics*, which traces the philosophical origins of the doctrine in question: "Rousseau misunderstood this truth, and because of this error his *Social Contract*, so often invoked in favor of liberty, has become the most terrifying weapon in the arsenal of all forms of despotism."[3]

This idea, which forms the basis of postrevolutionary liberalism, can also be found in the writings of Tocqueville, who does not state it any more clearly than Constant. The latter wrote that "in a society based on the sovereignty of the people, certainly no individual or class has the right to subject the rest to his or its private will; but it is false to say that society as a whole possesses unlimited sovereignty over its members."[4] Furthermore, in certain circumstances citizens have a duty not to obey the law: "A positive, general, unrestricted duty, whenever a law appears unjust, is not to obey it. This inertial force does not lead to upheaval, revolution, or disorder."[5] Tocqueville adopted this doctrine, adding to it nothing but the connection between justice and reason deduced by the Doctrinaires and especially Royer-Collard: "When I refuse to obey an unjust law, I am not denying the majority's right to command; I am simply appealing, beyond the sovereignty of the people, to the sovereignty of the human race. There are some who are not afraid to say that in matters which concern only itself a nation cannot go completely beyond the bounds of justice and reason and that there is therefore no need to fear giving total power to the majority representing it. But that is the language of a slave."[6]

It is unfortunate that Tocqueville, in keeping with his rule never to engage in doctrinal debate or even to refer to the work of others, never spelled out his critique of Rousseau. In this respect Constant's words are more pointed and elegant: "The error of those who, with good faith in their love of liberty, have granted unlimited sovereignty to the people stems from the manner in which their political ideas were formed. They saw in history a small number of people, or even a single man, in possession of an immense power, and who did a great deal of harm; but their wrath was directed against the possessors of power and not against power itself. Rather than destroy power, they thought only of replacing it."[7] Constant traces the philosophical root of this flaw beyond Rousseau to Hobbes.[8]

Constant, for his part, preferred to speak of authority rather than sovereignty. Like Tocqueville, he believed in certain rights, which in his mind had nothing to do with any hypothetical state of nature; and he defined what those rights were far more carefully than Tocqueville. Listen to what he says: "Citizens possess individual rights independent of all social or political authority, and any authority that violates those rights becomes illegitimate. The rights of the citizen are individual liberty, religious liberty, and liberty of opinion, including the freedom to publicize that opinion, enjoyment of property, and guarantee against all arbitrary exercise of power. No authority can infringe those rights without shredding its own charter."[9] Note that there is no question here of hypothetical natural rights; it is not an issue of human rights but, as Constant explicitly states, of the rights of citizens. These are independent of authority in that any infringement of them is contrary to the purpose for which that authority was instituted in the first place, namely, to safeguard the liberty of individuals. Like most men of his generation, Constant subscribed to the declaration made by Sieyès on 18 Thermidor in the Year III: "The final cause of the whole social order must be individual liberty."[10]

Possibly Tocqueville never set forth a theory of sovereignty precisely because he felt that Constant's views were generally accepted. But why, then, did he never say so, and why did he adopt the language of the Doctrinaires, who rejected any sovereignty not founded on justice and reason? The few passages on sovereignty in *Democracy in America* seem to contain a confusing blend of ideas drawn from the Doctrinaires and from the notion of popular sovereignty. The Doctrinaires did not recognize any sovereignty inherent in the body politic as a whole; they held that politics is subsidiary to morality and justice.[11] Although their solution is not very satisfactory, it is not contradictory. Constant acknowledges the principle of popular sovereignty but insists upon a guarantee of individual rights as a limitation upon that sovereignty; for him, political freedom is essentially a guarantee of individual liberties. The doctrine is not without coherence. But it is logically inconsistent to hold, as Tocqueville does, that popular sovereignty is compatible with the supremacy of political liberty over individual liberties and with limitations on sovereignty, because the subordination of politics to justice means little if political liberty is the supreme good and popular sovereignty has been proclaimed.

It must be admitted, then, that the theory of sovereignty is not the best part of Tocqueville's work. Yet he has a very keen appreciation of justice coupled with an original conception of rights. His concept of the rule of law is an interesting contribution to liberal theory, and from his study of the United States he was able to draw certain conclusions about the importance of judicial guarantees of liberty.

Rights

Tocqueville is not a theorist; he is suspicious of political speculation. He is well aware that limitations on sovereignty and guarantees of individual rights cannot be obtained by appeals to evidence or pure reason. He hopes, rather, to be instructed by the study of institutions and mores using the comparative method. He sets forth his ideas on the subject of rights only briefly, in passages of *Democracy in America* devoted to rights in the United States,[12] and in still more succinct meditations on natural rights in *The Old Regime*.[13]

Without respect for rights, human relations would be reduced to relations of power. The existence of rights is the sign of a properly human society, a society worthy of intelligent, responsible beings: "After the general idea of virtue, I know none more beautiful than that of rights, and indeed the two are mingled. The idea of rights is nothing but the idea of virtue applied to the world of politics."[14] Here Tocqueville means political virtue, which he (as well as Montesquieu) distinguished from moral virtue; unlike Montesquieu, however, he did not define political virtue in terms of the renunciation of private goods for the sake of the general welfare. American democracy is distinguished by its notion of rights for all, a notion ignored by the European elites prior to 1789.[15]

Tocqueville then distinguishes three different ideas of rights: the divine and the moral, which come first, and the political, which in more recent times has increasingly been linked with private interests. "Do you not see that the divine notion of rights is disappearing? Do you not recognize that mores are changing and that with them the moral notion of rights is vanishing? Do you not notice how on all sides belief is giving way to reason and sentiment to calculation? If, in the midst of this universal upheaval, you do not succeed in linking the idea of rights to private interest, which stands out as the only fixed point in the human heart, what will you have left to govern with other than fear?"[16] This is an impressive passage, perhaps the most anxious in all of *Democracy in America*. The author sees despotism as an imminent prospect unless the concept of rights, sapped by the decline of its ancient props, morality and religion, can somehow be strengthened in an era when political rights are shored up solely by the uncertain support of private interest.

Commentators like to compare Chateaubriand, who resigned himself to ending his political career in the camp of legitimate monarchy, with Tocqueville, who, they say, was better able to envision the future. Comparison of the passage just cited with the following text from Chateaubriand's *Mémoires d'outre-tombe* may leave a different impression: "Christianity is the most philosophical, most rational appreciation of God and creation. It subsumes the three great laws of the Universe: divine law, moral law, and political law. Divine law is the unity of God in three essences; moral law is charity; political law is liberty, equality, fraternity. The first two principles are mature; the third, political law, is not yet complete, because it could not flourish so long as intelligent belief in an infinite being and universal morality were not firmly established."[17] Chateaubriand is made optimistic by faith, whereas Tocqueville accumulates reasons to doubt. But Tocqueville's doubt is not about America, as his subject, rights in America, might seem to indicate; it is about France, as the conclusion of the passage clearly shows: "There can be no doubt that the moment when political rights are granted to a people hitherto deprived of them is a moment of crisis—a crisis often necessary but always dangerous."[18] Once again we encounter the idea that the danger inherent in all evolution toward democracy is particularly acute in France. Accordingly, Tocqueville is all the more firmly committed to a policy concerned with maintaining, as far as possible, an unbroken continuity of rights.

Note, finally, that Tocqueville's thinking about rights is quite traditional. There is no mention of "natural" rights, although the idea of a natural law, divine in origin and known both through revelation and moral effort, is presented in sketchy fashion without further development. Nevertheless, justification of rights on utilitarian grounds is not ruled out. We know, moreover, that Tocqueville believed that the utilitarian theory of morality best described the democratic age.[19] Oddly enough, in a historical vision dominated by the principle of continuity, the theory of natural rights is neglected, overshadowed on the one hand by the reference to natural law and on the other by the embrace of utilitarian ideas.

THOMAS HOBBES HAD revivified political philosophy by making an explicit, and nontraditional, distinction between the "right of nature" and the "law of nature."[20] Subsequently, the method of geometrical reasoning applied to questions of politics quickly destroyed the natural law school, a task finally completed by the work of Rousseau.[21] The period in question corresponds to what Tocqueville's contemporary Auguste Comte called the age of metaphysics, intermediate between the age of theology and the age of sociology. Although Tocqueville's terminology is different, he, too, believed that natural law theories were intermediate stages of thought which appeared when people could no longer perceive the source of rights in the divine and which gained favor thanks to the social and political circumstances analyzed in *The Old Regime and the French Revolution*.

The French Revolution, Tocqueville observes, "considered the citizen abstractly, outside of any particular society, just as religions consider man in general, independent of country and time. It did not seek to know simply what were the particular rights of the French citizen, but rather what were the general rights of men in political matters."[22] Thus it became a "sort of new religion," which, though "imperfect," possessed great propaganda value. Theories of natural rights had existed previously but had never produced a revolution. Hence in the moral climate prevailing in France in 1789, there must have been a particular receptivity to demands based on "natural rights." Tocqueville writes: "There are times when men are so different from one another that the idea of the same law being applied to all is incomprehensible to them. There are other times when it is enough to show them the vague, remote image of such a law for them to recognize it at once and hasten toward it."[23]

When the political differences between men are no longer marked, society is already obeying certain of the characteristic laws of democracy, even if formally it remains a monarchy or society of orders. It is not surprising that some of the ideas set forth in the first section of volume two of *Democracy in America* recur here: democratic peoples are inclined to use and abuse general ideas in politics, especially if the people themselves are excluded from political practice.[24]

No American legislative body experienced such passion for general ideas in politics as did the Constituent Assembly and Convention in France.[25] This shows, once again, that revolutionary passions are democratic passions carried to an extreme. The *Old Regime* contributes something that was not present in Tocqueville's 1840 writings, namely, an analysis of the special role of the philosophes: "How was it that around the middle of the eighteenth century the men of letters became the country's principal politicians, and what were the consequences?" In a society politically leveled by the weight of the bureaucratic monarchy, the complete absence of political liberty for both the philosophes and the great nobles who protected them meant that they knew nothing of "that great science of government which teaches one to understand the general movement of society, to judge what is happening in the mind of the masses, and to foresee from this what will ensue."[26] Under such conditions, freedom of thought, the only liberty that continued to flourish in those times, was not enough to permit men to conceive and plan joint actions. Hence reform was justified in terms of natural equality and abstract moral principles, ideas totally opposed to those on which the society had been built. Tocqueville thinks he can sum up the political thought of the philosophes by saying that they believed it "appropriate to substitute simple and elementary laws, drawn from reason and natural law, for the complicated, traditional customs that governed the society of their time."[27]

The Americans, having always had charge of their own political affairs, were less apt to make general ideas their guiding light in politics.[28] True, the Declaration of Independence was the first affirmation of the rights of man: "We hold these truths to be self-evident: that all men are created equal, that they have been endowed by their creator with certain inalienable rights, among them life, liberty, and the pursuit of happiness." This was the doctrine of the good Dr. Locke as interpreted by a religious people: natural law, divine in origin, is the source of the rights of man.[29] The French Declaration of the Rights of Man (1789) was quite different. The revolutionary implications of the declaration of 1776 were far more limited than those of the declaration of 1789. In France, Tocqueville believed, the effects of political inexperience were combined with those of political leveling as well as with a deliberately subversive spirit unknown in America; apparently, freedom of thought was obliged to become revolutionary to the extent that other forms of liberty were denied.[30]

Burke had denounced the zeal for abstract ideas so prevalent among the French revolutionaries, and Madame de Staël had called attention to the political inexperience of the members of the Constituent Assembly. By linking these two characteristics in an intelligible way, Tocqueville developed a sociological theory to counter the metaphysical theory of rights.[31] Assertion of natural rights, he argued, is characteristic of a democratic age; but such an assertion can take two forms—and did in fact take two forms in America and France. In

America, where political and religious freedom prevailed, the doctrine of natural rights represented no sharp break with either the divine or the moral conception of rights; it served effectively to limit power without unleashing a violent revolution. In France, where political and religious freedom were unknown, the doctrine of the rights of man proved to be a formidable instrument of revolution, breaking all ties to the divine and moral conceptions of rights and distorting the way in which people conceived of the relation between the man and the citizen.

In reality, the rights of man are really only rights of the citizen.[32] The contractualist view is unmasked as an illusion: the political state does not grow out of the state of nature; rather, that state of nature is a product of the imagination, typical of a certain type of political state. The very idea of human nature that ultimately results from the divine conception of rights is, similarly, the product of a process of equalization. Only certain very specific social and political conditions can account for the fact that citizens long deprived of their rights could have affirmed the rights of man. The eighteenth-century philosophes reasoned from the rights of man to those of the citizen; Tocqueville's sociology reasons from the rights of the citizen to the rights of man.

NEVERTHELESS, THE CONTENT of Tocqueville's doctrine of rights was indeed inspired by the spirit of '89, although it makes significant additions to the celebrated second article of the Declaration of the Rights of Man, which had included in its list of "natural and imprescriptible rights of man" only liberty, property, security, and resistance to oppression. Tocqueville added this gloss, which to date has been published only in Roland Pierre-Marcel's *Essai politique sur Alexis de Tocqueville*:

> a. Individual liberty: inadequate procedural guarantees, preventive arrest, home searches, responsibility of government agents to the proper authorities.
> b. Religious liberty.
> c. Freedom of association: vital liberty, destroyed by the Revolution, incomplete under the Restoration, finally extended to include religious association.
> d. Freedom of the press: still more vital, it made the July Revolution, yet does not really exist.
> e. Freedom of elections: limited jury, means of corruption, centralization.

I wish that my country were as convinced of these truths as I am.[33]

Tocqueville not only lists the fundamental freedoms but states his reservations concerning their insufficient realization and guarantees. Neither in this note nor anywhere else in his work does he distinguish between civil liberties and public liberties as contemporary authors did, most notably Rossi in his *Course on Constitutional Law*. Tocqueville's brief remarks on individual liberties relate to what the 1789 text calls "liberty and security," leaving the reader to imagine a state of affairs far less satisfactory than that existing in Britain, with its doctrine of habeas corpus. Resistance to oppression is not mentioned, but some of the most effective forms of resistance are, including religious freedom, which did not figure in the 1789 texts but did appear in the Charter of 1830. Hasty and incomplete, this list is nevertheless revealing of Tocqueville's ideas and their originality.[34]

Thus Tocqueville remained faithful to the spirit of '89 but was critical of the Revolution for having destroyed freedom of association and of the July Monarchy for having curtailed freedom of the press, failing to guarantee the "security" of its citizens, and refusing to allow its agents to be answerable to the regular courts. His liberalism was essentially political, concerned with outcomes and means as much as with principles. This just about sums up Tocqueville's doctrine of rights, which, as Pierre-Marcel has rightly pointed out, owes much to Benjamin Constant.[35]

Pierre-Marcel devotes a hundred pages of his book to Tocqueville's doctrine of individual rights and their guarantees, and he has, I think, incontrovertibly shown that the liberal tradition was continuous from Constant to the founding of the Third Republic and that Tocqueville occupied a key position in a long line of political thinkers from Constant to Rossi, Charles Rémusat, Léonce-Victor de Broglie, and Lucien Anatole Prévost-Paradol, culminating in Adhémar Esmein and Etienne Vacherot.[36] Laboulaye suggested but did not actually state that Tocqueville had not read Constant: "How much toil and fatigue that noble mind might have spared itself had he read the liberal publicist. In all his pamphlets, of which he *probably* knew nothing, would he not have found his own thoughts expressed with as much finesse as force?" Pierre-Marcel, who cites this text,[37] challenges the assertion and in my view succeeds in showing a striking parallelism in the two men's ideas, even if he cannot conclusively prove his case, since Tocqueville left no direct evidence of having read Constant, whom he never cites.

NEVERTHELESS, TOCQUEVILLE'S WISH to be original does not explain everything. Although I agree with Pierre-Marcel that Tocqueville was familiar with Constant's thought, I do not think it is enough merely to say that Tocqueville belonged to the liberal tradition, without explaining why he wished to be seen as a "new breed of liberal."[38] Pierre-Marcel's analysis is firmly based on objective comparison of the rights doctrines of the leading French liberals of the nineteenth century. His method is valuable in that it brings out a juridical doctrine in Tocqueville's work that he himself never bothered to systematize, but it suffers from the drawback of not showing what is truly original in Tocqueville's writing, except on one quite crucial point (which it brings to light), namely, his views on freedom of association.

Throughout his work, including the brief note already cited, Tocqueville stressed the "vital" character of this freedom, which he said had been "destroyed by the revolution." Although not unaware of the dangers of permitting free association in France, Tocqueville in volume one of *Democracy in America* maintained that it was nevertheless a fundamental liberty in both its civil and political aspects: "Next to the freedom to act alone, man's most natural freedom is that of combining his efforts with those of his fellows to act in common. The right of association therefore seems to me by its very nature almost as inalienable as individual liberty. The legislator cannot will its destruction without attacking society itself."[39] Nevertheless, the author notes that this freedom, while "beneficial and fecund" in America, may be dangerous and even destructive in France (or, more precisely, "in Europe"). His point is clear, however, and once again he is contrasting a democratic situation with a revolutionary one.[40] By 1840 the risks of violent revolution had vanished, and Tocqueville had been scandalized by the laws of September 1835; in volume two of *Democracy* he therefore insisted on greater freedom of association (and of the press) while acknowledging that, like any public liberty, the right to associate must be regulated in practice: "I do not believe that a nation should always allow its citizens the absolute right to associate in political matters, and I even doubt that it was ever wise in any country and at any time not to impose limits on the freedom of association."[41] But in France the resistance party had erred in locating those limits; in Tocqueville's view it was wrong to curtail the right to associate even more than had been done in 1830.[42] "This leads me to think that freedom of association in political matters is not so dangerous for public tranquillity as has been assumed; it may well be that, after shaking the structure of the state for a time, ultimately it firms it up."[43]

The second volume of *Democracy in America* contributed much more than a program of moderate opposition to the party of resistance, however. It presented a veritable theory of the unity of freedom, particularly in chapters five, six, and seven of part two, which were devoted, respectively, to freedom of civil association, freedom of the press,[44] and freedom of political association. Freedom of association, about which Constant was silent, occupies, along with individual liberty and political liberty, a central place in Tocqueville's thought, because it is useful in combating the illusions of individualism and in overcoming the relative weakness of individuals compared with the power of government in an atomized society. "Civil associations facilitate political associations; but at the same time political association develops and singularly perfects civil association."

"In civil life, every man can, if need be, imagine that he is capable of meeting his own needs. In politics he could never conceive of such a thing."[45] Industrial and commercial partnerships, political organizations, and moral, religious, and intellectual institutions serve an educational purpose; they correct the erroneous belief in self-sufficiency that arises from the individualism inherent in the democratic age.[46] That is why the "science of association" is described as the "mother science"[47] and political associations are considered to be "like great free schools"[48] to which citizens come to learn.

PIERRE-MARCEL IS WELL aware of Tocqueville's contribution to the political thought of his time, and he points out not only his originality as compared with Constant but also his fertile influence on other writers.[49] His widely echoed political views are summed up in the final section of volume two of *Democracy*: "I firmly believe that no new aristocracy can be established in the world. But I believe that ordinary citizens, by associating with one another, can become prosperous, influential, and strong—in a word, aristocrats. In this manner one might obtain several of the greatest political advantages of aristocracy without its injustices and dangers. A political, industrial, commercial, or even scientific or literary association is an enlightened and powerful citizen, which cannot be made to bow down at will and cannot be subjected in obscurity to the heel of oppression, and which, by defending its private rights against the exigencies of power, preserves the liberties of all."[50]

Isolated and weak, individual citizens in democratic societies would be incapable of resisting power by themselves; they might well become so estranged from one another that they would no longer understand the common interest or the need for limiting the power of the state. The theory of associations is a response to a political necessity, that is, to the need to protect against these twin dangers of democratic society. But it is more than that, even if most commentators look no further. For Tocqueville, the political order is not the ultimate end; it is worthwhile only insofar as it allows human beings to make the most of the freedom and spiritual greatness that is theirs by right. Thus it is man's humanity itself that is threatened by misguided democratic individualism with its constricted moral view. Political liberty is not the ultimate goal—not an end, but a means of saving mankind. Thus we discover the true significance of free association:

> The moral and intellectual fiber of a democratic people would be subject to no less danger than its trade and industry if the government everywhere took the place of private associations. Feelings and ideas are renewed, the heart expands, and the human spirit develops only through the reciprocal action of men upon one another. I have shown that this action is virtually nonexistent in the democratic countries. Hence it must be created artificially. Only associations can do this.[51]

Few commentators call attention to this moral and spiritual dimension of Tocqueville's humanism, which stretches beyond politics.[52] In this perspective, the distance from Constant to Tocqueville is greater than Pierre-Marcel suggests. The latter rejects and combats the individualism upon which the former constructed his political philosophy and which also served as the foundation of bourgeois liberalism, a school of thought whose views should be carefully distinguished from Tocqueville's.

Tocqueville borrowed from Constant and Royer-Collard the notion of "freedom to resist," but his attitude toward freedom is closer to Chateaubriand's than to Constant's. It is a mistake to think that Chateaubriand's hostility to Constant was based solely on their rivalry over Madame Récamier; the two men had very different conceptions of life and liberty. Chateaubriand's aristocratic liberalism was a long way from Constant's bourgeois liberalism—bourgeois because it was individualist. Tocqueville attacks the illusions of individualism throughout his work, and his theory of rights cannot be fully understood if it is presented as an extension of Constant's theory, which incorporates the right of association. This, however, is what Pierre-Marcel does, in an effort to show the historical development of the theory of rights in the French liberal context. But to confuse Tocqueville's liberalism with the individualist liberalism of Constant and his followers is to obscure Tocqueville's most original contribution. He is both too noble at heart and too democratic-minded to be mistaken for a bourgeois liberal. For him, individual liberties are important not as ends in themselves but as means. It is worth noting that the brief unpublished note cited earlier deals mainly with what we would now call public liberties. For Tocqueville, political liberty was not, as it was for Constant, a mere guarantee of individual liberties; it was desirable for itself, because man cannot fulfill himself except through association, and association requires political liberty. Political association, Tocqueville believed, is the highest form that human association can take, with the possible exception of churches.

Individualism, a democratic ill, is aggravated by revolution, according to Tocqueville,[53] who no doubt thought that Benjamin Constant himself had been afflicted by the malady when he preached "the proud and jealous isolation of the individual in the fortress of his right" and formulated what Emile Faguet, a century later, called "the boldest and most extreme system of individualism ever conceived by an intelligent man."[54] Unfortunately, Faguet also tried to persuade his reader that Constant deserved credit "for having separated liberalism from other elements to which it had been attached."[55] Constant, we are told, was the "inventor" of liberalism, the man who gave the doctrine the sharp outline and supreme distinction of a drawing by Ingres.[56] Tocqueville probably believed that Constant's liberalism was still sullied by defensive reactions against the excesses of the Revolution and contaminated by revolutionary individualism. No doubt he also felt that the pure liberal doctrine was to be found elsewhere than in the *Principles of Politics*, a book written during the Hundred Days while its author was negotiating with Napoleon over the draft of the "additional act."[57] He believed that liberalism had bungled its comeback in France under the Restoration, yet he did not on that account look for it in the final attempt to maintain the despotism of the Empire. Thus Tocqueville had good reason never to mention Benjamin Constant, seeking instead to establish liberalism on a new foundation by going all the way back to Montesquieu and attempting to adapt his teaching to modern democratic society.

The Rule of Law

Tocqueville belongs to a long tradition of philosophers who wanted both liberty and legality, believing that the best way to obtain the former was by means of the latter. Their political philosophy can be characterized as a quest for procedures for limiting power by making it impersonal. Long ago Cicero wrote: "We serve the law, that we may be free."[58] Tocqueville shared this conviction to such a degree that when he treats of liberty he often feels the need to qualify it with an adjective such as "regulated" or "regular." In his last writings he again alludes to "the desire to feel that one is in the power not of a man but of God and the law."[59] For both Tocqueville and Montesquieu liberty consists in obeying just laws and only just laws.

Governmental coercion is justified only insofar as it enforces respect for general rules of conduct considered to be just, which is the best way of protecting the liberty of all. Tocqueville noticed the respectful attitude of Americans toward the law,[60] and he attempted to explain why such an attitude was unknown in France: "People often complain that the French despise the law; alas, when would they have learned to respect it? With the men of the Old Regime, the place that the notion of law should have occupied in the human mind was vacant."[61] Liberty flourished in psychology and mores, but it was absent from the law and found only irregular and intermittent expression in public life. "Yet if unruly and unhealthy liberty of this sort prepared the French to overthrow despotism, it made them less apt, perhaps, than any other people to replace despotism with the peaceful and liberal rule of law."[62]

WHAT CONDITIONS ARE required to ensure the rule of law? This question arises in a particularly acute form when liberty is taken to be both the principle and the end of society, for then the only justifiable sovereignty is that of law. It is not, as is often said in France, a question of weakening the principle of authority by depriving society of the right or faculty to defend itself; division of power is preferable.[63] It is easier to agree about the minimum than about the ideal conditions necessary for the rule of law. When Locke, in chapter nine of his *Second Treatise on Civil Government*, lists the criteria that distinguish the civil state from what he calls the state of nature, he is simultaneously stating the

minimal conditions for the rule of law: first, the existence of permanent, established laws, known to everyone; second, an impartial judiciary; and third, a collective authority to enforce the laws and protect
the community from outsiders.

The law protects liberty by prohibiting arbitrariness, which necessarily implies a limitation of power, as is clearly stated in article five of
the 1789 Declaration of Rights: "The law has the right to prohibit only
those actions which are harmful to society. Whatever is not prohibited
by law cannot be prevented, and no one can be compelled to do what
the law does not command."[64] Article nine of the Declaration of the
Rights of Man and of the Citizen of 24 June 1793 is clearer still: "The
law must protect public and individual liberty against the oppression of
those who govern."

After reading article five of the Declaration of 1789, one can only feel
perplexed upon discovering that article six states that "the law is the
expression of the general will." Two philosophies of law are juxtaposed
without regard to the question of their compatibility. In fact, liberty
and legality require limitation of power, even if it happens to be the
power of all. Liberal logic and democratic logic can be reconciled, but
in order to do so one must first recognize that they are distinct. No
doubt the members of the Constituent Assembly underestimated the
difficulty of the problem.

Rousseau, who is often blamed for the confusion apparent in the
Declaration of Rights, to say nothing of the woes of the Revolution,
had in fact clearly perceived the difficulty of placing "the law above
man,"[65] and there can be no doubt about his liberal intentions. No one
has better expressed the ideal of liberty and legality: "A free people
obeys the law, but it obeys only the law, and it is thanks to the power
of the law that it obeys no man."[66] But he wanted both to affirm the
sovereignty of law and to make the law the expression of the general
will. He drew a distinction between the general will and the will of
all.[67] It would be unfair to forget the strict conditions that he placed on
the expression of the general will and wrong to think that he believed
every trend in public opinion must become law.

Most criticism of Rousseau reflects opposition to his democratic
philosophy rather than a true apprehension of the dangers implicit in
his philosophy of rights. Rousseau admits no constitutional guarantee
of individual rights; the general will is always the sole arbiter of its
proper limits. But the idea of unlimited sovereignty is incompatible
with the idea of guaranteed individual rights. On this point Benjamin

Constant was not mistaken, and his critique goes to the heart of Rousseau's system.

A philosophy that seeks to reconcile liberty and the law can only conceive of a relative and limited sovereignty, and only on such terms can it be reconciled with democratic philosophy. The law must, moreover, respect the norms of justice recognized by all: this idea was still current in Tocqueville's day, especially in America, where no sharp break was acknowledged between the divine conception of rights and the moral and political conceptions. Today, of course, most authorities in jurisprudence hold that the law is the law solely because it has been established as such according to constitutional rules and by the authorities designated for the purpose.[68] Such a complete divorce between the idea of law and the search for transcendent justice was still unknown in Tocqueville's America, though he had already been able to detect signs of the weakening of the divine and even of the moral concept of rights. For him, the extreme situation in which the law is nothing but the will of the legislator occurred only in revolution and was incompatible with ordinary liberty. "When a nation within a brief period of time has several times changed leaders, opinions, and laws, the men who compose it eventually acquire a taste for change and become accustomed to the idea that all change occurs rapidly with the aid of force. They then naturally acquire a contempt for forms, whose impotence they witness every day, and they are impatient with the empire of rules, which they have seen overturned so often."[69] More than ten years later, Tocqueville was—alas!—just as pessimistic about the chances for "ordinary liberty" in France: "I knew," he wrote at the beginning of his *Souvenirs*, "that, while a great revolution can establish liberty in a country, several successive revolutions make all ordinary liberty impossible for a very long time."[70]

THE CENTRAL QUESTION of any liberal doctrine of law is how to ensure that the law will respect individual rights. For the sake of both analytic clarity and historical accuracy, I shall consider separately three distinct answers to this question. First, the law can be made subject to intangible principles of justice, conceived in terms of either reason or revelation. Second, a concept or criterion of the just law can be derived from the notion of harmony between the law and a people's mores. Finally, in order to secure the rule of law the executive power must be made subject to its authority. Each of these three aspects of the question corresponds in a rough way to one of Tocqueville's three concepts of right: the divine, the moral, and the political. Tocqueville was fully convinced that the law ought to conform to universal standards of justice which men could know in at least a negative sense, through their refusal of injustice. Furthermore, he was convinced that the law acquires authority only when the fundamental laws are accepted by everyone. But how could the authority of the law be established, or reestablished, in an age when the supernatural idea of divine justice was disappearing and the moral conception of rights was losing its force?[71]

The idea of subordinating positive laws to divine law, of making the lawgiver subject to divine revelation, had lost nearly all its political force even in America, as Tocqueville was well aware. Although he declared himself a nonbeliever,[72] he nevertheless believed in "a general, unwritten law that is above all the particular laws the sovereign may make and to which obedience is due before all other laws."[73] This conception of law as the expression of a natural order or transcendent law seems as essential to democratic liberalism as does the idea of law as the expression of the will and interests of the majority. When only the latter idea remains, liberal democracy degenerates, setting the stage for its own destruction. Above all law Tocqueville recognized what he, following Royer-Collard, called the sovereignty of justice and reason.[74] The only objective criterion he gives is that of universality, and it seems that its principal use is to denounce injustice, because direct, positive knowledge of what is just is beyond human understanding except in the most formal sense.[75] The idea of natural law survives here only in its secularized, rationalized form, reduced to the requirement of equality and reciprocity, liberty and human dignity.

Once again, Tocqueville is following Montesquieu: "The law, in general, is human reason, inasmuch as it governs all the peoples of the earth; and the political and civil laws of each nation should be nothing other than special cases to which human reason is applied."[76] Like Montesquieu, Tocqueville believed that the legislator was bound by considerations of justice and that the law was something other than "a pure act of power."[77] Tocqueville was especially close to Montesquieu when he sought to establish a link between laws and mores in keeping with what he called the "moral conception of rights," or harmony between laws and mores.

EVER SINCE ANTIQUITY there have been two ways of understanding natural rights: Aristotle observed physical nature in the hope of finding the right solutions to more or less general problems, whereas the Stoics imagined a universal law of reason.[78] The latter tradition culminated in Condorcet and Destutt de Tracy, while Montesquieu and Tocqueville, who were more attached to the comparative than to the deductive method and attentive to the concrete rather than the abstract, belong to the first. In *L'Esprit des lois* (book 19, chapter 4) Montesquieu defines the "general spirit" of a nation as a composite of all the factors that govern men, including religion, laws, and mores, and Tocqueville's two great works can be read as studies of the American and French national characters. Now, Montesquieu says that "to the extent that one of these causes is stronger than the others in any given nature, the others will give way before it."[79] Montesquieu's lesson should be strictly applied to Tocqueville's three conceptions of rights. Tocqueville believed that, as the divine conception of rights disappeared and the moral conception weakened, the laws of a nation would exert greater and greater force on its national character.

Between Tocqueville and Montesquieu, however, lay a century of revolution. France was no longer entirely as Montesquieu had described it (at the beginning of book 19, chapter 5), and Tocqueville could no longer believe that "most of the peoples of Europe are still governed by mores."[80] It was no longer true, for instance, of France, although it was perhaps still true of the America that he had visited. The oft-repeated adage that the United States offered Europe a vision of the future frequently obscures traditional and even archaic features of American society that had survived its brief and untroubled history. Condorcet, for one, had maintained that the United States pointed the way to Europe's political future, but Tocqueville, though he expands on this idea at considerable length, sensed the air of "antiquity" mingled with the "biblical fragrance" of Puritanism in the beginnings of the American Republic.[81] What is more, he noted that continuity among the three "ages of right" had been preserved better in America than in Europe. France had been so transformed by the Revolution that it was cut off from its past; a danger existed, moreover, that through promulgation of laws at odds with the nation's enduring characteristics, the rule of law would be reduced to nothing more than the rule of the legislator.[82]

How much of Montesquieu's teaching was Tocqueville able to accept? Rereading book nineteen of the *Esprit des lois* with this question in mind, that is, attempting to read the text as Tocqueville might have read it between 1835 and 1840, we can answer this question in many ways. It is clear that *Democracy in America* is informed throughout by the lessons of Montesquieu. It would be an easy exercise to comment on book nineteen in such a way as to bring out both Tocqueville's debt to Montesquieu and his own great originality. For now, let me note simply that the method set forth in Montesquieu's first chapter is the same as Tocqueville's, that is, more attentive "to the order of things than to the things themselves." In his third chapter we find a sentence that might well be used to sum up *The Old Regime and the French Revolution*: "Liberty itself seemed unbearable to peoples not accustomed to its enjoyment." For the time being let me skip over chapters five through eight, to which I shall return when the time comes to discuss individualism, and proceed directly to chapter twenty-seven, the second of the great "English" chapters in *Esprit des lois*. This is where Tocqueville found the idea of a need for an "education in liberty" through political freedom and a free constitution, in order to develop the mores required by a free society. In comparing the United States with France he kept this lesson in mind, and on it he based his political program: "In America, free mores created free political institutions; in France, it is up to free political institutions to create free mores."[83]

Nowadays we tend almost automatically to identify the law with legislation, and it requires an effort of mind to understand how our voluntarist, formalist conception of law gradually emerged from the idea of law as something in conformity with divine justice and mores as well as defined by decisions of the courts.[84] Although Locke considered the legislative power to be supreme, he condemned the faculty to legislate in an absolute and arbitrary manner,[85] and in Tocqueville's time the English lawmaker still had to take account, if not of natural law, which figured only in theory, then at least of common law, the compendium of customs and laws that had been the arm of Parliament against absolute monarchy. The same common law had been used by the American colonists in the struggle for independence, and it took root in America thanks to such great jurists as Kent and Story, whom Tocqueville studied closely.[86] The strength of common law derived from experience and tradition, whereas the law that grew out of the French Revolution was supposed to derive from reason and remake the world, starting with a clean slate.[87] Tocqueville emphasized the difference between legislated law, law literally made by the legislator, and law based on precedent; his analysis of the American legal mind shows that he did not underestimate its political significance.[88]

*   *   *

WITH RESPECT TO PRINCIPLES, Tocqueville conceived of law as an expression of human reason; with respect to specific ordinances, he sought the teaching of experience and held that the law must be adapted to mores and customs.[89] He rather envied the Americans and the English for the guarantees against legislative omnipotence offered them by the tradition of common law and the political power of magistrates. Of American law he wrote: "The popular origins of legislation often sap its goodness and wisdom but contribute singularly to its power."[90]

The idea, cherished by liberals, of the rule of law is in the final analysis rather ambiguous: the question is, what law will rule? If it is natural law, the reflection of transcendental justice or reason, its rule is assured, in a vague and uncertain way, only by a people's adherence to a set of religious and moral beliefs constituting its idea of what is right. History shows that modern legislators freed themselves from such norms when religious beliefs and opinions became increasingly diverse. As "mores" became less and less unified and lost their power to constrain, the will of the legislator increasingly became the only communal norm; the only remaining guarantee against arbitrary rule was the constitution and, under its authority, the systems of formal legislative and procedural rules and constitutional (including judicial) guarantees.

Justice and Judicial Guarantees

If men are to consent to the decisions of the law, they must have confidence in the way in which that law is elaborated, in its content, and in the judges who will hear their grievances. Among the guarantees of individual rights necessary to a good constitution, Tocqueville attached the utmost importance to judicial guarantees; he always regarded strong judicial institutions and independent magistrates as an essential element of the rule of law.

"The great purpose of justice is to substitute the idea of law for the idea of violence, to place intermediaries between the government and the use of physical force."[91] From this definition it is clear that any confusion of the judicial with the executive power would prevent the former from achieving its aim. It also follows that in any society that enjoys lawful liberty, the role of justice is primary. Tocqueville's ideal is to replace, wherever possible, administrative bureaucracy with courts of law. In a draft of volume one of *Democracy* we read: "A society is well governed and firmly established to the extent that the judicial power is paramount."[92] The judiciary guarantees liberties in two ways.

First, it cannot, by the very nature of its power, constitute a threat to liberty, for it cannot compel private individuals to behave in a particular way: "Confined within its limits, the judicial power is the weakest of the three powers; it has only a power of opinion, hence it limits itself to preventing rather than doing. Owing to its nature, liberty has nothing to fear from it."[93] Second, the judiciary is the best guarantee of individual rights, the surest safeguard against infringement of those rights by society: "The power of the courts," Tocqueville points out at the end of volume two of *Democracy*, "has always offered the greatest possible guarantee of individual independence, and this is especially true in the democratic era."[94] Heavily influenced by classical liberalism,[95] these conclusions are the result of Tocqueville's study of the judiciary in volume one, where he stated the three essential characteristics of the judicial power: that it make no pronouncement except in contested matters, deal only with individual cases, and intervene only when called upon to do so.[96]

Tocqueville's originality emerges only when we move from legal analysis to political analysis and apply his own comparative method, which as always contrasts American democracy with the French Revolution. In a democracy, he says, the judiciary is "both a barrier and the people's safeguard."[97] It is a safeguard insofar as it guarantees the rights of individuals, and a barrier insofar as it teaches individuals to respect the rights of others and, in the political realm, provides a counterweight to the power of the majority.

Tocqueville admired the political power of the American courts and showed how it flowed logically from the existence of elected administrative bodies.[98] The Americans had, moreover, made the judiciary extraordinarily powerful by giving judges the right to base their decisions on the Constitution rather than on law, and not to enforce any law they deemed unconstitutional. Indeed, the Supreme Court became a sort of aristocracy in which considerable authority was vested; it sat perched at the summit of the American democratic order. Tocqueville saw only benefits in this arrangement, which he believed posed no threat to democracy: "Thus the Americans have bestowed enormous political power upon their courts, but by obliging them to attack laws only by judicial means they have greatly diminished the dangers of that power."[99] Mill, less suspect than Tocqueville of harboring aristocratic sympathies, agreed with him on this point and noted in his review of the first volume of *Democracy in America* that the power of judges in a democracy is not so dangerous as it would be in an aristocracy or monarchy.[100] When the power of the people is incontrovertibly dominant, the best counterweight is the power of the judiciary to protect the rights of individuals.

It would be contradictory to give judges this power and at the same time to affirm the unlimited sovereignty of the people. Nevertheless, the Constitution clearly affirms the absolute sovereignty of the people. Hence judicial guarantees are revocable. With judicial oversight of legislation the Americans provided a novel solution to the problem of the place of the courts in a democracy.[101] Madison saw it as "America's unique contribution to political science."[102] At a deeper level, Americans, thanks to their veneration of the Constitution, succeeded in separating authority from power, preserving in the face of popular power an authority vested, not in a senate as with the Romans, but in the judiciary.[103]

Yet this admirable solution depended on peculiarly American conditions and was not readily adaptable to other countries. Respect for the Constitution and its amendments was the first of these conditions,[104] and nothing like it existed in France or even in England, as Bryce observed in his *American Commonwealth*: "The most powerful supreme court could obtain nothing in England as long as Parliament retains the power to change any part of the law."[105] The United States is unusual in that it is a country with a written but not an inflexible Constitution, where the law is not simply the will of the lawmaker because the legislature is circumscribed by both precedent and the Constitution. The principle of continuity, so important to Tocqueville, thus plays a crucial role; as a result, the law as expression of the popular will coexists with other sources of law. Politically this is reflected in the power of the lawyer, whom Tocqueville presents explicitly as the only type of aristocrat compatible with democracy.[106] Lawyers are men who like order and legality and precedent, who assure the continuity of law and thus constitute an effective counterweight to the enthusiasms of the majority and, if need be, to what Tocqueville calls the "tyranny of the majority."[107]

THE SITUATION IS quite different in France, where "lawyers" helped to overthrow the monarchy in 1789. Tocqueville adds: "It remains to be seen whether they acted because they had studied law or because they were unable to contribute to the making of it."[108] Lack of political liberty was the great flaw of the Old Regime and the primary cause of its ruin, but Malesherbes's great-grandson noted in his book on the subject that the judicial institutions of prerevolutionary France were free and fostered a taste for freedom in all citizens: "We had become a country of absolute government in our political and administrative institutions, but we had remained a free people in our judicial institutions . . . Magistrates often called the proceedings of the government frankly despotic and arbitrary acts. Judicial habits had in many respects become national habits. It was from the courts that people took the idea that every question is subject to debate and every decision subject to appeal, along with the use of publicity and the love of forms, all of which are inimical to servitude. This was the only portion of a free people's education that the Old Regime gave us."[109] True, the Parlements had attempted to take part in policymaking and administration, tasks for which they were unsuited and in which they hindered the government without protecting the citizenry. In the constitution of the Old Regime they did indeed constitute counterweights, as Montesquieu maintained, but in Tocqueville's view "the counterweights were misplaced . . . The Parlements were poorly constructed as instruments of liberty and not well suited to the use that people wished to make of them. But they were better than no instrument at all."[110] To have provided a firm guarantee of liberty, magistrates should have contented themselves with "examining specific cases in detail and obliging the administration and the government to observe all the laws, that is, with serving as mediators between the sovereign and private individuals."[111]

The French Revolution (that is, the Constituent Assembly, the Legislative Assembly, the Convention, the Thermidorians, and on down to Bonaparte) claimed to honor and uphold the rights of individuals, including the right to an independent judiciary, but history shows that it actually increased the powers of government and diminished the guarantees that it wished to establish. The Constituent Assembly, in opting for popular election of judges (Law of 16 August 1790), drew its inspiration from Montesquieu;[112] but Danton, as Minister of Justice, criticized the elected judges for insufficient "patriotism," and, indeed, elections for new judges were often held before the old ones' terms of office had expired. Under the Terror even this abuse of power proved insufficient, and revolutionary tribunals were set up on the model of the one in Paris. Under the Consulate, rather than overturn the results of popular elections, as had been done so frequently under the Directory, the government chose to assume control of the nomination and promotion of judges, who were appointed for life. Of Montesquieu's ideas only the jury of the court of assizes remained; the essence of his teaching was all but forgotten, namely, that the worst hands in which to place the power to judge were those of the executive,[113] which was literally where that power lay in cases involving the administration.[114]

BENJAMIN CONSTANT CAPTURED perfectly the liberals' weariness of so many unkept constitutional promises and declarations: "During nearly all the Revolution, courts, judges, judgments—none were free."[115] "All the constitutions that have been given to France guaranteed individual liberty, yet under each of them individual liberty was constantly violated. The reason is that a mere declaration is not enough; positive safeguards are needed."[116] Tocqueville thought the same thing, and the safeguards he recommended are the same as those recommended by Constant in his *Principles of Politics* (chapters 18 and 19). Both men stressed the need for a powerful and independent judiciary, and both expressed confidence in the forms and procedures of justice. Both held that judges should be appointed for life and afforded independence and respect. During his travels in the United States in 1831–32, Tocqueville found that election of judges was rare in the United States, and that where it was practiced it was found not to be very satisfactory; he never believed that it was a necessary consequence of democracy. Like Montesquieu and Constant, he believed in trial by jury and praised the educational value of jury duty.[117]

Law and the Sociology of Knowledge

Pierre-Marcel has written that since Tocqueville was not an expert on the law, he was inferior in this respect to Constant.[118] Undeniably this is true, but it is just as true to say that despite his errors (and his errors on administrative law are not the least of them)[119] he proved himself capable of situating the problem of justice in a historical and political perspective much more comprehensive than Constant's constricted and defensive individualism. Influenced far more by Montesquieu's relativism than by any of his specific precepts, Tocqueville never forgets that the significance of a legal institution in a democratic situation can be entirely different from its significance in a revolutionary one, and he senses that Constant's view is still unduly influenced by reaction against the Revolution. Though scattered, brief, and unsystematic, his views on law are coherent and original and lead to reflections far in advance of their time. Underlying the descriptive parts of *Democracy in America* is the constant contrast that Tocqueville draws between the continuity so evident in the English and American empirical legal tradition and the claim of the French revolutionaries to have eradicated the past and made the law anew on a rational rather than an empirical basis. In developing certain insights contained in volume two of *Democracy in America*, *The Old Regime and the French Revolution* proposes an ingenious sociological explanation for the theory of the rights of man, anticipating later developments in the sociology of knowledge.

4 ✖ *Democratic Government*

THERE ARE TWO concepts of republic,[1] and Tocqueville analyzes them at the end of volume one of *Democracy in America* with greater precision than in the better-known introduction, where the tranquil reign of democracy in America is contrasted with a French democracy "whose progress has ever been amid the disorders and agitations of conflict."[2]

"What is meant by 'republic' in the United States," Tocqueville wrote,

> is the slow and quiet action of society upon itself. It is an orderly state really founded on the enlightened will of the people. It is a conciliatory government under which resolutions have time to ripen, being discussed with deliberation and executed only when mature. In the United States, republicans value mores, respect beliefs, and recognize rights. They hold the view that a nation must be moral, religious, and moderate all the more because it is free. In the United States "republic" means the tranquil reign of the majority. The majority, when it has had time to examine itself and to prove its standing, is the common source of every power. But even then the majority is not all-powerful. Humanity, justice, and reason stand above it in the moral order; and in the world of politics, acquired rights take precedence over it. The majority recognizes these limits, and if it does break through them, that is because, like any man, it has its passions and, like him, may do evil knowing what is good.

But we in Europe have made some strange discoveries. According to some among us, a republic does not mean the reign of the majority, as conceived hitherto, but the rule of its strenuous partisans. In governments of this type it is not the people who control affairs, but those who know what is best for the people: a happy distinction which allows rulers to act in the nation's name without consulting it and to claim its gratitude while trampling it underfoot. Moreover, a republican government is the only one whose right must be recognized to do whatever it chooses and which is allowed to scorn everything that men have hitherto respected, from the highest moral laws to the common conventions of accepted opinion. Until our day it had been thought that despotism was odious, whatever form it took. But now it has been discovered that there are legitimate tyrannies in this world and holy injustices, provided that it is all done in the people's name.[3]

This stirring passage depicts the destruction of republican freedom in democracy's name and denounces that modern technique of oppression which deprives the people of all real power while granting it the appearance of absolute sovereignty.

The Sovereignty of the People

Let us follow Tocqueville's argument: "If one wishes to discuss the political laws of the United States, it is with the dogma of popular sovereignty that one must begin."[4] For the sake of clarity, let me state at once a definition which Tocqueville does not in fact give until four chapters later: "Strictly speaking, one can define sovereignty as the right to make the laws."[5] This is a classical definition, borrowed from Jean Bodin, Hobbes, and Rousseau. In a democracy this right belongs to the people, but, Tocqueville adds, in a modern democracy this sovereignty is not absolute and the people exercises its right to make the laws through intermediaries, its chosen representatives.

Like Benjamin Constant, Tocqueville rejected the notion of absolute sovereignty, as we saw earlier. I now want to reconsider this point in a new light. "Sovereignty," Tocqueville notes in a draft of volume one, "is nothing other than right of free choice applied to a society rather than to an individual."[6] There is no reason to think that this free choice will accord with reason, in which respect society is no different from the individual.[7] " 'The people are always right': that is the dogma of the republic, just as 'The king is never wrong' is the religion of monarchy. It is a large question whether one is more false than the other; what is certain, however, is that neither is true."[8] This brief note shows how steadfastly Tocqueville refused to enter into metaphysical disputes about politics, stubbornly sticking to the simple assertion that a majority, like an individual, can be wrong. "I would like someone to explain to me what is meant by the common saying that an entire people can never wholly trespass beyond the bounds of reason. No doubt it is rare for a nation to stray so far. But what does the will of the people generally express? A majority, and what is a majority taken collectively if not an individual with opinions, and usually interests, in contradiction with those of another individual called the minority. Now, if you are willing to admit that an individual in whom all power is vested can abuse that power against his adversaries, why won't you admit the same thing for the majority? As for myself, I believe that only God can be granted omnipotence without creating difficulties."[9]

In truth, very few of Tocqueville's French contemporaries would still have affirmed the absolute sovereignty of the people and the infallibility of the general will in the manner of Rousseau. With respect to sovereignty, the most salient difference between America and France had to do with the federal nature of the United States and the existence of more or less independent public entities standing between the citizen and the federal government. In the complexity of American political life Tocqueville discovered the principles of federalism at every level.[10] Communities were treated as free individuals in matters that concerned only themselves, and the state with jurisdiction over them intervened only in matters of common interest to several communities within its borders; it had the right to intervene because the communities voluntarily gave up a part of their independence to the state, just as the states gave up part of theirs to the federal government.[11] This method of establishing sovereignty, from the bottom up rather than, as in France, from the top down, strongly influenced the way in which sovereignty was conceived, as well as the sovereign's powers and rights,[12] so much so that the federal principle could be seen as both the most perfect expression of popular sovereignty and the surest limitation upon it.

Everyone is familiar with the marvelous pages at the beginning of *Democracy in America* on communal freedoms, valuable both for their detailed analysis of townships in New England,[13] and for the support they have lent to generations of French liberals and democrats in their struggles for decentralization:

> The strength of free peoples resides in the local community. Local institutions are to liberty what primary schools are to science; they put it within the people's reach; they teach people to appreciate its peaceful enjoyment and accustom them to make use of it. Without local institutions a nation may give itself a free government, but it has not got the spirit of liberty . . . If you take power and independence from local government, you may have docile subjects but you will not have citizens.[14]

Tocqueville apparently drew his inspiration from a book that enjoyed a considerable reputation during the Restoration: Henrion de Pansey's *Du pouvoir municipal*, which from its opening lines emphasized the mixed nature of municipal affairs, part public, part private: "Below the legislative, executive, and judicial authorities lies a fourth power, at once public and private, which combines the authority of the magistrate with that of the head of a family; this is municipal government." Without local freedoms, the author goes on to show, there can never be a public spirit, for "no one would support an order in which he would be an alien."[15] It is not impossible that Tocqueville knew, through family tradition, of the ideas of his great-grandfather Malesherbes and was aware of the terms in which the latter denounced the centralization of government effected under Louis XVI: "These, Sire, are the means by which they are working to stifle the municipal spirit in France, to extinguish if possible even the feelings of the citizens; they have, as it were, proscribed the entire nation and placed it in receivership."[16]

IN THE FINAL analysis, however, apart from active participation in local politics, does the sovereignty of the people consist in choosing its representatives or in taking a direct role in government? "I see an important difference," Tocqueville wrote in a draft of volume one, "between a people's right to choose its government and the supposed right of each individual to take part in government. The first proposition seems to me to contain an incontestable truth, the second a manifest error."[17] He makes a seemingly contradictory assertion, however, in the chapter on popular sovereignty, where he says that in the United States "it takes on every possible form as the exigencies of the case require. Sometimes the body of the people makes the laws, as at

Athens; sometimes deputies, elected by universal suffrage, represent it and act in its name under its almost immediate supervision."[18] In reality, however, direct democracy is limited to local government, and then only when the local municipality or township does not exceed a certain size.[19] Otherwise, American democracy is representative democracy. Except in small communities, Tocqueville firmly believed that modern democracy can only be indirect.

In France after 1830, such theorists of constitutional monarchy as Guillaume de Barante, Berriat Saint-Prix, Rossi, and Pinheira-Ferreira[20] saw the source of all powers in the sovereignty of the people, but they used the term in a negative manner, that is, to exclude any other principle of sovereignty. The sovereignty of the people was implicitly recognized in the Charter, but this sovereignty, unlike sovereignty in times past, could not be delegated. Popular sovereignty always exists, they argued, no matter what the form of government,[21] but it is exercised only in revolution.[22] At the very least these theorists of the July Monarchy had to recognize the direct assertion of popular sovereignty: if the law and the general interest were neglected, the will of the people could establish a new authority. The July Monarchy was in fact a concrete example of this theoretical possibility, a fact about which moderate theorists had little to say; but the *Gazette de France* and other legitimist newspapers commonly referred to Louis-Philippe's regime as a "revolutionary government," while the *National*, the *Tribune*, and other republican publications were compelled to identify the cause of revolution with that of popular sovereignty.

The theories of the moderates led to a conclusion as paradoxical as it was dangerous: the people are sovereign, but in the course of ordinary, peaceful political life there is no way for them to exercise their sovereignty. Tocqueville never really spelled out a theory of sovereignty because he sensed the inadequacy of contemporary doctrines to explain the fragility of power and the deeper historical trends. It was impossible for him to deny the gap that existed between the source of sovereignty and its practical exercise, but he refused to concede that the only possible basis for representative democracy was an absolute separation of the two. In America he saw an example of a complex political system with extensive popular participation, owing not only to the extensive right to vote but also to the influence of public opinion and the role of local government.

Tocqueville believed that in a representative democracy the highest political offices could not be properly discharged by the average citizen, but that it was not a good idea to limit the handling of public affairs at all levels to a particular kind of citizen, whether defined in terms of property or competence. If participation was limited in either of these ways, it was no longer proper to speak of "public" affairs.[23] In a free system of government, public life is by definition open to all citizens, but that does not mean that every citizen has the aptitude to govern; at different levels of government, different skills are required and different interests are at stake.

Local democracy responds to the immediate need for self-government. It deals with questions that concern each citizen in an immediate way and requires no special competence. At the state and, even more, at the federal level, however, decisions concerning major public works, economic and fiscal policy, defense, and foreign relations cannot be entrusted to all; every citizen has sense enough to understand that at this level popular sovereignty exerts itself only through election of representatives and through the reaction of the public to decisions taken by the government, or in any case to the most visible consequences of those decisions. In France, where a long tradition of centralization had left citizens to confront the state directly, the absence of intermediate levels of public life was reflected in theories of sovereignty in terms of a rigid opposition between the popular source of sovereign power and its limited exercise. In the United States, the proliferation of local governments and the hierarchy of laws, all subordinate in the last instance to the Constitution, made it possible to uphold the principle of popular sovereignty while at the same time allowing various forms of participation in public life and genuine exercise of that sovereignty. Once again, Tocqueville opposes to the clear distinctions of Cartesian thought the actual experience of the Americans, finding yet another application of what I have called the principle of continuity.

"It is the principle of representation," Tocqueville noted as he began work on volume one of *Democracy in America*, "which eminently distinguishes modern republicans from ancient ones."[24] Mill in his *Autobiography* expresses his gratitude to Tocqueville for having made him understand this. Yet it should be noted that, according to *Democracy in America*, it is possible for a form of direct democracy to coexist in local communities with more modern forms of democracy and, further, that even in America there remained a danger that representation would devolve into mere delegation, which Mill feared as much as Tocqueville.[25] Demagogic representatives pandering to tyrannical opinion may abdicate their responsibilites and plunge the republic into the most archaic forms of democracy, reminiscent of Athens in its worst moments. Only political education of the people can diminish this danger, and the principal reason for the success of the American Republic is that the American people are "the most advanced in their practical political education."[26] Tocqueville was not one of those liberals who placed boundless hopes in the value of education and enlightenment. He understood the danger of applying abstract theories or semiscientific reasoning to politics and knew that educated but politically inexperienced people are fatally drawn to such theories. He therefore believed that, at a time when scientific and technological progress would in any case require wider education, particular attention should be paid to offering all citizens improved instruction in concrete, practical politics. He states his pedagogical as well as scientific intentions at the beginning of *Democracy in America*,[27] and the work is filled with scholastic metaphors: local governments, juries, and political associations are all described as great free schools, open to all, from which the public mind receives its education.[28]

Montesquieu distinguished three different kinds of education, which we receive, respectively, "from our fathers, from our teachers, and from the world," and he suggested that each kind might yield different political effects.[29] But Condorcet and his disciples, the Idéologues, with their simplistically optimistic outlook, had believed that everything could be accomplished by educating the educators. Ignoring them and looking all the way back to Montesquieu, Tocqueville rediscovered the idea that the political effects of different kinds of education may be different; in politics he believed above all in the particular form of "education by the world" that he called political education. This was the source to which he looked for what Montesquieu expected education to accomplish under a republican government: namely, to inculcate "love of the laws and the fatherland," or what Montesquieu called political virtue.[30] In this respect, local government is the primary school of democracy. For Tocqueville as for Mill,[31] local government was the primary source of political education. In fact, Mill praises Tocqueville for his account of the educational virtues of New England township government, but he is less enthusiastic about the applicability of these ideas in England,[32] and he places a higher value on elections than on direct participation. This is because, in Mill's view, rational democracy is defined not as direct government of the people by the people but in terms of the control exerted by the people on their rulers, this being the best guarantee, according to Mill, of good government.[33] Mill understood Tocqueville and his concept of political education remarkably well, but being more of a rationalist and a remote heir of the Ideological tradition, he held somewhat different views, as is evident here. Mill wanted people to be taught to understand what reasonable choices were and to study the procedures which in his view offered the best guarantee of liberty. Tocqueville's goals were the same, but for him political life had a value in itself, for it involved knowledge of the world and transformed those who participated in it.

Democratic Government

Tocqueville never believed that the France of 1830 ought to adopt American-style institutions. Like Montesquieu, he thought that the value of political institutions was not absolute but relative to each nation's state of moral and social development. "I am witnessing here [that is, in the United States] the success of institutions that would inevitably cause an upheaval in France," he wrote to his father in June 1831.[34] He clearly did not belong to the "American School" as Armand Carrel understood it,[35] though he was not very far from it. Just as clearly, however, his journey to America, to say nothing of volume one of *Democracy*, was in large part motivated by the interest that he and other Frenchmen of the late Restoration and early July Monarchy took in American institutions.[36]

Tocqueville's work can be read in two ways. One would stress the fact that America's success was unique, as Tocqueville pointed out in a letter to his father written shortly after his arrival in the United States: "Two thoughts have preoccupied me to this point: first, that this is one of the most fortunate nations in the world; and second, that it owes its enormous prosperity far less to its own peculiar virtues or to a form of government superior in itself than to the particular conditions in which it finds itself, which are unique and ensure that its political constitution is perfectly in harmony with its needs and its social state."[37] Yet this argument, that America is somehow exceptional, is scarcely mentioned in the first volume of *Democracy in America*, and then only at the end.[38]

A second possible reading of Tocqueville would emphasize the lessons that he thought France might draw from the American experience. This is the reading that Tocqueville encourages in the introduction to *Democracy in America*, and even more in his prefatory note to the twelfth edition (1848): "Let us look to America not in order to copy in a servile way the institutions that it has created for itself but rather in order to gain a better understanding of what institutions might be suited to us, not to borrow examples but to draw lessons."[39] True, by this time French interest in American institutions had revived after a long eclipse. But even after the July Monarchy seemed to have achieved stability, there were lessons to be drawn from the American experience, and, in Tocqueville's view, for the direct benefit of the regime. Mill was not mistaken when he noted that part two of volume one of *Democracy in America* contains a systematic comparison of aristocracy and democracy along with its analysis of American democracy; hence Tocqueville's reflections on the evolution of democracy begin in volume one and not, as is often believed, in volume two. Mill neglects, however, to point out that volume one treats democracy only in a political sense, whereas the first three sections of volume two treat it as a social state.[40]

THE MOST DELICATE question, the one that caused the greatest misunderstandings and aroused the most passionate reactions, was that of institutions. When he began his investigation of democratic government in the United States, Tocqueville knew this perfectly well: "I am well aware that I am treading on live cinders. Every word in this chapter must in some respect offend the various parties that divide my country. Nevertheless, I shall say all that I think. In Europe we find it difficult to judge the true character and enduring instincts of democracy because in Europe two contrary principles are at war and we cannot say precisely what should be ascribed to the principles themselves and what to the passions to which the conflict gives rise."[41] By contrast, in America it is possible to contemplate democracy in its pure form and to observe "its natural complexion," for there a democratic government rules a society more democratic than any other. Tocqueville nearly entitled his first volume *On the Rule of Democracy in the United States.*[42]

In France (or, as Tocqueville prefers to say, in Europe), it is difficult to distinguish between what is revolutionary and what is democratic, and Tocqueville's purpose is none other than to overcome this difficulty by means of a realistic and impartial description of what democracy is. Politically, this was the purpose of his first work, as is evident from the letter he wrote on 21 February 1835 to his friend Eugène Stoffels, a document important enough to warrant quoting from it here at length:

To those who had created for themselves an ideal democracy, a luminous dream which they think it would be easy to translate into reality, I have attempted to show that they have filled their canvas with false colors; that the democratic government they recommend, even if it procures real benefits for those who are able to tolerate it, does not have the noble features with which their imaginations endow it; and, further, that this government can sustain itself only under certain conditions of enlightenment, private morality, and belief which do not exist among us and which we must work to obtain before drawing political conclusions.

To those for whom the word "democracy" is synonymous with upheaval, anarchy, spoliation, and murder, I have tried to show that democracy could manage to govern society while respecting fortunes, recognizing rights, sparing liberty, and honoring religion; that if democratic government was less apt than others to develop certain noble faculties of the human soul, it had its fine and great qualities; and that perhaps, after all, the will of God was to extend a mediocre happiness to all men rather than to concentrate a great sum of felicity in a few and foster something like perfection in a small number. I believe I have shown that, whatever their views in this regard, the time for deliberation is over; that society moves on and each day impels them ever closer to equality of conditions; that they had no further option but to choose between two inevitable evils, that the question was not whether one could have aristocracy or democracy but whether one would have a disorderly and depraved democratic society delivered up to passionate frenzy or bowed down under the weight of a yoke heavier than any man has had to bear since the fall of the Roman Empire.

I hoped to diminish the ardor of the former and, without discouraging them, to show them the only path to follow.

I sought to diminish the terror of the latter and to bend their will to the idea of an inevitable future, in such a way that, the enthusiasm of the former having been quelled along with the resistance of the latter, society might advance more tranquilly toward the necessary fulfillment of its destiny. That is the central idea of the work, the one from which all the others derive . . . Up to now, moreover, very few men understand it. Many people whose opinions are opposed to mine like what I say, not because they understand me but because they find, by looking at only one side of my work, arguments to support their passion of the moment. But I have confidence in the future, and I hope that a day will come when everyone sees clearly what a few perceive today.[43]

In a dark age when democracy and revolution are confounded, Tocqueville is resigned to the idea that his work will be misunderstood. Nevertheless, he believes that in the future thoughtful readers will be able to distinguish between what is American, what is democratic, and what is revolutionary.

TWO READERS, TOCQUEVILLE thought, had understood his work particularly well: Royer-Collard and John Stuart Mill. On 3 October 1835 he wrote the latter: "Of all those who have tried to arouse the public's interest in me, you are the only one who has entirely understood me, the only one who has been able to grasp from an overview the full range of my ideas and the ultimate inclination of my mind, and who has at the same time maintained a clear perception of the details."[44] He praises Mill especially for having brought out, in his *London and Westminster Review* article, the very important distinction between delegation and representation,[45] a distinction whose ultimate political significance was still little understood by the general public. Tocqueville concludes: "For the friends of democracy, it is not so much a matter of finding ways to make the people govern as it is of finding ways to make the people choose those most capable of governing, and then to give them enough power to direct affairs in their broad outline but not in detail and not as to the means of execution."[46] In essence, the democracy of the future is representative democracy.[47] The French revolutionaries ignored this, subjecting representatives to intolerable pressures. As for direct democracy, still practiced in certain New England towns, its value was more pedagogical than political, and it owed more to the special circumstances of New England than to the notion of pure democracy. To see that this was indeed Tocqueville's view, it is enough to compare his attitude toward local government in New England with his strictures on pure, direct democracy as practiced in Switzerland.[48] He recommended that terms of office in the legislature not be unduly curtailed and that elections be held in two stages,[49] in order to strengthen both the power and the competence of legislators; in these respects he indicated his disagreement with American practices, which he considered to be dangerous.

Mill regarded *Democracy in America* as the first philosophical analysis of representative democracy. He saw clearly that Tocqueville was attempting to treat democracy in general as well as democracy in America and, hence, that in order to follow his argument from part two of volume one on, it was essential to distinguish between what was specific to American government and what was characteristic of democracy in general. Tocqueville put his readers clearly on notice: "The political constitution of the United States is, it seems to me, one of the forms that democracy can give to its government, but I do not believe that the American institutions are the only ones or the best ones that a democratic people can adopt."[50] To see this as a mere formal caveat would be a mistake. Tocqueville was asking his readers to exercise powers of discrimination that few of them were willing to use. Let us turn now to the text of *Democracy in America*, making use as necessary of the comments of Mill, who is here a particularly useful guide, not only for the glosses on the text which he provides and whose value Tocqueville recognized but also for his criticisms, to which Tocqueville never responded.

Although Mill did not challenge Tocqueville's analysis of the weaknesses of democratic government, he maintained that aristocratic governments were scarcely superior and, in any case, that the opinion of the English ruling class was as fluctuating, impulsive, and incompetent as that of the people.[51] Hence one of Tocqueville's central arguments was called into question: that democracy is less skillful than aristocracy in selecting, organizing, and controlling means of action.[52] This is the central idea of the chapter on democratic government, and Tocqueville was careful to consider it from every possible angle: the flawed and changing nature of democratic laws, the instability and incompetence of administrators, the propensity of democratic government to spend excessively, corruption in government, relative weakness in times of crisis, and inability to conduct a wide-ranging foreign policy.[53] Far from believing, as Montesquieu put it, that the people are "admirable for choosing," Tocqueville held that universal suffrage in the United States discouraged the ablest men from seeking office.[54]

Tocqueville makes it quite clear that for a European country to choose so democratic a government would be suicidal.[55] Democratic institutions aggravate certain inevitable defects of the democratic social state, particularly envy, with the result that the ablest people either shun or are excluded from public office.[56] If Jackson's America was no longer so admirable as Washington's, most Frenchmen in 1835 believed that part of the blame lay with the rapid extension of the right to vote.[57] Tocqueville therefore did not need to state this explicitly; it was enough to suggest it. Given his severe criticism of American democracy, why were Americans not unsympathetic to Tocqueville's work, which indeed has been admired by many of them for more than a century and a half? The reason is that he shows that Americans were able to tolerate democracy only because of their exceptional qualities of enlightenment, mores, and political education. By disclosing both the dangers of democratic government and the successes of that form of government in America, Tocqueville cast the people of the United States in the role of the new chosen people.

WOULD DEMOCRATIC GOVERNMENT be possible in other countries? *Democracy in America* never says that it would, nor does it answer the fundamental question of democratic theory: How can democracy be reconciled with a wise and powerful central government? It does, however, point out that America enjoyed a continent placed at its disposal by Providence, had vast resources, no dangerous neighbors, and at bottom had almost no need of government. In such conditions the most tragic defects of the democratic system could be avoided: "The great privilege of the Americans is their ability to commit reparable errors."[58] The political drawbacks of democratic government were not so extreme in America as to render that government insupportable. For instance, the instability of laws deplored by Hamilton, Madison, and even Jefferson[59] did not affect the fundamental laws. Montesquieu, speaking of the English, had noted that the attitudes of the parties were very different depending on whether the debate concerned ordinary laws or fundamental laws.[60] In his travel diary for 8 January 1832, Tocqueville, applying the same distinction, again pointed out the contrast between American democracy and the political disorder of revolutionary France: "In regard to political institutions, there are two kinds of instability, which must not be confused. One has to do with secondary laws, which change with the more or less changeable will of the legislature. Such instability can exist in an orderly and well-established society. Often it is a necessary consequence of a people's political constitution. The other has to do with the very basis of society, the principles which engender the laws. Such instability cannot exist without disorder and revolution. America offers an example of the first kind of instability. For forty years, we have been tormented by the second. By confusing the two, many people conceive exaggerated hopes and fears and make incorrect comparisons."[61] This key idea is presented to the reader of *Democracy in America* in almost the same terms,[62] except that the explicit reference to France is omitted, which I think is quite significant. In America, Tocqueville observes, the Republic exists "without conflict, without opposition, without trial, by tacit agreement, through a kind of *consensus universalis*."[63] In France, however, there has been no real consensus since the Revolution. Tocqueville is well aware that it would be both futile and dangerous to insist on the point, so that he never fully expresses in his work the thought he had in mind while writing it.

More precisely, Tocqueville argues that in France there has been sufficient consensus on postrevolutionary society, that is, on civil equality, but not on the government of that society, on the political form of the regime. His own political preferences are not so obvious from his published work as from his preparatory notes. Nevertheless, it must have been fairly clear to French readers in 1835 that Tocqueville was not a member of what was then called the American School, which Guizot had denounced in 1833: "There are the republicans of the past . . . and then there are the republicans of the future, the pupils of the American School. Among them there are young people, sincere men whose minds are preoccupied by the doctrines of the United States . . . I shall simply say that those who regard the United States government as the normal state of society, as the ultimate goal toward which every society must evolve, seem to me quite childishly ignorant of human nature and social conditions."[64]

Perhaps Tocqueville's views concerning the distant future were not very far from those of the American School (which is just another name for moderate republicans),[65] but for the present and the immediate future he expressed a different political ideal in a note written in preparation for *Democracy* in which he examines ways of moderating majority rule: "If I lived among a democratic people, I would prefer a monarchical to a republican constitution; I would rather see two legislative chambers than one, a judiciary appointed for life rather than elected magistrates, and provincial governments rather than a centralized administration. All these institutions can be combined with democracy without diluting its substance."[66] The inspiration for this ideal was as much the English monarchy as the American Republic, but it is closer to American practices than was the program of the American School, which rejected bicameralism, federalism, decentralization, and life terms for judges—all the principal checks and balances.[67] In Tocqueville's view, the French republicans, even the moderates, did not clearly distinguish between those American institutions that were essentially American and those that were typically democratic, because they confused, more than they were aware, their image of democracy with an idealized image of the First Republic.

Montesquieu distinguished between regimes whose object is not liberty (republics, whether aristocratic or democratic, absolute monarchy, and despotism) and limited monarchies on the English model, whose object was liberty and which embodied the separation of powers—what would soon be called "constitutional monarchies."[68] Tocqueville wished to adapt the general principles of those regimes to the democratic social state by means of a true decentralization, a gradual curtailment of the king's powers, and parliamentary government.

JOHN STUART MILL thought that Tocqueville was confounding aristocratic government with an idealized image of English-style constitutional monarchy. But he does not dwell on this minor cavil and in his first commentary does not deal with the defects of democratic government.[69] On the whole, he felt that the book was valuable for its remarkable impartiality and for being the first instance of the application of a truly scientific method to the study of politics. As for the practical conclusions to be drawn from it, Mill felt that, apart from a few ideas still tainted by an overly aristocratic view, these tended toward what he called "Radicalism."[70] Tocqueville never repudiated this interpretation, and he might well have been a Radical himself had he lived in England, where liberal and revolutionary passions did not mingle as in France.[71]

As to the real benefits of democracy, Mill and Tocqueville were in total agreement: the general tenor of the law promotes the good of the greatest number, and rulers cannot champion interests contrary to those of the majority of the governed.[72] But the majority can be mistaken as to its own true interests; hence the value of democratic government depends on its capacity to educate its citizens, and particularly on its capacity to educate them politically. By granting rights to all citizens, democracy teaches man to respect himself and the law and instills a spirit of enterprise. Democratic freedom gives strength to society, which manifests itself in a prodigious diversity of actions and exchanges, mobilizing the energies of all and not allowing men to remain isolated from one another.[73] These are tremendous, crucial advantages, and Tocqueville analyzes them from a social, moral, and pedagogical standpoint; but he never treats them on the same terms as such specifically political problems as security, power, authority, and national prestige. *Democracy in America* treats politics as a realm of means; it focuses on the example of the United States in 1832 and thus manages to say almost nothing about political ends of this sort.[74] The final criteria of judgment are individual and social rather than political. In reality, what guides Tocqueville's reflection is the quest for liberty, a goal that he believes to be important not only for the individual and society but also for political organization as such.

The Federal Constitution

Ever since Montesquieu,[75] the idea of constitution had been intimately associated in the minds of all liberals with the idea of political organization for the purpose of securing liberty. Of all Montesquieu's disciples, the Americans proved most successful. If nations are remembered by history for their most extraordinary achievements, France will be remembered for the Revolution and America for its Constitution. Tocqueville did not believe that the American Revolution could be compared with the efforts of revolutionary France, "the victim of attack by all of Europe." For him, America was most original not for its Declaration of Independence or its war against Great Britain but for its Constitution. "What is new," he wrote, "in the history of societies is the sight of a great people, alerted by its legislators that the wheels of government had ground to a halt, without haste or fear turning its eyes upon itself, plumbing the depths of the evil, biding its time for two full years while searching at leisure for a remedy, and, once that remedy was found, submitting to it voluntarily without obliging mankind to shed a tear or a drop of blood."[76] Hannah Arendt seems not to have paid sufficient attention to this passage, for in her book *On Revolution*[77] she expresses her astonishment at Tocqueville's indifference to the American Revolution[78] and the theories of its artisans. Yet she presents an argument similar to Tocqueville's when she shows that the greatness of the American Revolution lay in its having founded a new political order by embodying the principle of liberty in its Constitution.[79] She contrasts the American Revolution, which succeeded where the French failed but did not create a revolutionary tradition, with the French Revolution, which gave rise to a myth that has survived despite the revolutionaries' inability to provide France with a constitution. On this point Tocqueville and Arendt differ not as to the substance of their case but rather in the subtle, often implicit, way in which Tocqueville proceeds with his comparison.

This is not the place to examine Tocqueville's commentary on the Constitution, which has been ably investigated by the authors of the Yale School. I shall therefore simply pay tribute to the work of George

Wilson Pierson and James T. Schleifer, especially their accounts of the origins and significance of Tocqueville's ideas about American federalism.[80] I shall limit myself to a few remarks directly pertinent to the argument of this chapter.

In essence, of course, the Constitution is an embodiment of the idea of limitation of powers (of both the states and the federal government); it is noteworthy for the checks and balances among the various branches of the federal government and for the attribution of powers to the states.[81] I shall comment first on Tocqueville's reflections upon the overall significance of American federalism and second on the lessons that he believed could be drawn from the United States Constitution.[82]

INITIALLY, FAITH IN the future of the Union was weak. No one believed that the Constitution, the fruit of difficult negotiations, would last. Franklin found it too monarchical, Washington too democratic. But this compromise agreement ultimately proved solid, and people were forced to admit that their fears had been excessive. Although Tocqueville was not the only one to have harbored unwarranted doubts about America's future, he was among the first to have recognized the originality of the federal system and the new theory on which it was based, a theory "that should count as a great discovery in the political science of our time."[83] He saw clearly that, within the federal government's limited domain, its orders were addressed directly to its citizens: "The American states which gathered in 1789 agreed not only to allow the federal government to dictate laws to them but also to enforce its laws itself."[84] Thus he grasped the crucial feature that distinguished a federal state from a mere confederation, which must rely on its member states to carry out its decisions.[85] He agreed with Hamilton (*The Federalist*, nos. 15, 16, and 23) on the principle that the subjects of the Union are its citizens and not the states, but he did not follow Hamilton's thinking all the way down the line, for he failed to grasp the precise reason why Americans were subjects of the Union: namely, that it was established by exercise of their sovereignty and not, as Tocqueville believed, by means of a pact among preestablished political entities.

Nor did Tocqueville see that ratification of the Constitution made the people the source of sovereignty and creator of an entirely new political system—as Madison put it, "the fountain of all power." If political authority is based on the consent of the governed, it is clear that local, state, and federal authorities are not natural objects but human conventions; hence it makes no sense to argue, as Tocqueville does, that the towns or the states are somehow natural political bodies and that the federal government depends on "legal fictions," or to draw the conclusion that "the sovereignty of the Union is a work of art; the sovereignty of the states is natural. It exists by itself without effort, like the father's authority over his family."[86] In this and many other passages we find the reflections of a historian and politician more concerned with mores than with laws, and not the logical analysis of a jurist.

This fact accounts for certain of Tocqueville's errors of judgment, particularly as to the future of the Union, as well as for certain contradictions in his work.[87] Although the chapter on the federal Constitution follows shortly after the commentary on *The Federalist* and approvingly cites the leading Federalist lawyers, Story and Kent, on the crucial question of the nature of the Union and the powers of Congress, Tocqueville seems to have been impressed by the views of Jefferson, who argued that the Union was the result of a pact among existing political entities and who, at the end of his life, developed a theory of "elementary republics," which he saw as nothing less than basic cells of political society.

For the first time in the history of the world, a great nation, the United States, was lastingly constituted as a republic. Thanks to federalism, moreover, it combined the advantages of a large country with those of a small one—the strength and progressiveness of a large state with the prosperity and freedom of a small republic, and above all with the qualities of patriotism and public spirit for which the ancient democracies had always been envied. All this is perfectly compatible with Montesquieu's theory that there is a natural affinity between democracy and small states; indeed, Tocqueville makes shrewd use of an exception formulated by Montesquieu himself concerning the federal republic, a "constitution which has all the internal advantages of republican government and the external strength of the monarchic." Hamilton had used this argument before Tocqueville.[88] Note, moreover, that it is valid only where federalism is accompanied by increased centralization of government, which was the case in America in 1789 but not in France under the Girondins. At the end of his remarks on American federalism, Tocqueville is quite clear about the reasons why France cannot, without grave risk, adopt a form of decentralization that would fracture its sovereignty.[89] In the preceding pages he had several times pointed out that successful establishment of a federal system requires that certain specific conditions be met and that very few nations find themselves in such a position.[90] Again, the question arises whether the American success was a unique exception.

NEVERTHELESS, IT IS possible to draw conclusions of general import from the American experience, and it is remarkable that as regards the various branches of government and the principle of separation of powers these conclusions are diametrically opposed to the practices of the French revolutionaries. I touched on this point in the preceding chapter in regard to the judiciary, and I now want to consider the legislative and executive branches.

For my purposes it is of little concern that the federalists based their view of executive power on George III, the state governors, and Cromwell's *Instrument of Government*,[91] for I am primarily interested not in the origins of the federal Constitution but rather in the fundamental contrast between a constitution that vests executive power in one man and the widely held view of the French Conventionals that executive power in a republic must be collegial. Both the Constitution of 1793 and the Constitution of the Year III (adopted two years later) provided for a collegial executive: twenty-four members in the first case (article 62), reduced to five in the second (article 132). A single executive was so powerfully linked in people's minds with the monarchy that as late as Year VIII it was deemed prudent to provide the First Consul with two adjuncts; but no one was fooled, and when people were asked what was in the Constitution, they answered, "Bonaparte!" By Tocqueville's day the question was moot; the republicans themselves accepted the views of the American School in this regard, and Tocqueville was free to undertake a cool and detailed comparison of the powers of the French constitutional monarch with those of the American President. Nevertheless, he could not help concluding with the remark that, beyond constitutional differences, both heads of state were subject to the true ruling power, that of public opinion: "In America this proceeds by elections and laws, in France by revolutions."[92]

The French republicans of Tocqueville's day were bitterly opposed to a bicameral legislature, reflecting both their attachment to the Constitution of 1793 and their suspicion that a second chamber would become a refuge for aristocracy.[93] By contrast, Tocqueville set out to show that the Americans were able to create a second legislative chamber without making it an aristocratic institution.[94] He concluded that a bicameral legislature was an advance over a unicameral one, an advance from which every representative regime, including democratic ones, could benefit: "This theory, all but unknown to the ancient republics, introduced into the world, like most great truths, almost by chance and neglected by many modern nations, has finally been accepted as an axiom by today's political science."[95] Unfortunately, the French revolutionaries, guided by misunderstood Cartesian logic, rejected the lessons of experience, and Tocqueville was unable to persuade his colleagues on the Constitutional Commission of 1848 to reject the revolutionary tradition of a unicameral legislature.

Even in America, democracy took various forms; the contrast between constitutional order and instability cut across the differences between peaceful America and revolutionary France. In New England, for instance, republican government was orderly and calm, whereas in the West it was quite wild and unruly; even the central government, federalist in the past, had been subjected to intense democratization under Jackson. That Tocqueville applied the comparative method to his study of American political realities is a fact all too often neglected. He concluded that the various state constitutions were inferior to the federal: "The federal government is more just and more moderate than the governments of the states," as well as better protected against the principal dangers to democracy: domination of the legislature by the will of the electorate and concentration of all powers in the legislative branch.[96]

CONCENTRATION OF POWER in the legislature, which posed a threat to the states of the Jacksonian Republic, had forty years earlier been one of the most striking characteristics of the French Constitution of 1793. Early in the French Revolution, however, the leaders had shown themselves more favorable to the idea of separation of powers and a system of checks and balances. The Monarchians, disciples of Montesquieu and admirers of the English monarchy, including Mounier, Malouet, Lally-Tollendal, Mallet du Pan, and Clermont-Tonnerre, defended the principles of the absolute veto and the second hereditary chamber but very quickly lost all influence over the course of political events. Badly beaten in the voting of 10 and 11 September 1789, they were relegated to the opposition after the "October Days."[97] They cannot be held responsible for the idea of an absolute separation of powers or for the failure of the institutions established by the Constitution of 1791 to function smoothly. Indeed, Mounier had pointed out that in England the powers were not completely separated and concluded: "In order that the powers remain forever divided, they must not be entirely separated."[98]

This moderate interpretation of the separation of powers is similar to the one Madison published in *The Federalist*,[99] as well as to that of other American writers. In France, one nineteenth-century liberal tradition interpreted Montesquieu in this way; Destutt de Tracy and Benjamin Constant belonged to it, as did Tocqueville and his late disciple Edouard Laboulaye. Tocqueville's commitment to the princiaration of powers is known to us not from his theoretical writings but from his description of it in *Democracy in America* and his speeches to the Constitutional Commission in 1848.

All of Montesquieu's liberal disciples interpreted the British constitution in the same moderate way, reconciling the principle of separation of the powers of government with the need for them to work together.[100] Listen to Madison: "On the slightest view of the British constitution we must perceive that the legislative, executive, and judiciary departments are by no means totally separate and distinct from each other."[101] A simplistic treatment of this question inevitably distorts Montesquieu's description of the English constitution as well as his conclusions. The absolute separation of powers under the Constitution of 1791 led to absolute war among them, as Laboulaye observed.[102]

Montesquieu's American interpreters distorted his thought far less than most members of the Constituent Assembly, for, as Tocqueville observed, lack of political experience tends to encourage faith in abstract political theories that put distance between the thinker and reality.[103] To those who objected that the proposed federal Constitution failed to respect the "political axiom" of separation of powers, Madison, by examining the constitutions of England and of various American states, showed that the principle ought to be interpreted with moderation in order to remain faithful to the illustrious Montesquieu, "the oracle who is always consulted and cited on this subject."[104] Montesquieu, he wrote, "did not mean that these departments ought to have no partial agency in, or no control over, the acts of each other."[105] He simply meant that there was no liberty where all power of both types (and, a fortiori, of all three types) was concentrated in the same hands: "When, in the same person or corps of magistrates, the legislative power is combined with the executive power, there is no liberty, because it is to be feared that the monarch or senate may make tyrannical laws in order to execute them tyrannically. There is also no liberty if the power to judge is not separated from the legislative and executive power."[106] When the three powers, the three state organs, are separate, the law is guaranteed respect, resulting in security for all citizens.

That is as far as Madison goes in his comments, although Montesquieu, after examining the most favorable conditions for the execution of the law, goes on to seek assurances of moderate legislation and guarantees that the sovereign will exercise his power in a moderate manner. For this, the supreme organ of sovereign power must be politically composite; it must embody different political principles and forces. So much is clear from what Montesquieu says about the two chambers of the legislature: although their composition is heterogeneous, both are equally necessary. Tocqueville accepted all of this but argued that the difficulty of providing the necessary counterweights and of constituting politically and socially differentiated forces was always greater in democratic societies, whose very logic drove them toward uniformity and concentration of powers.

Democracy and the Tyranny of the Majority

In reality, Tocqueville was rather skeptical about so-called constitutional guarantees; the phrase never appears in his work. He was aware that constitutions cannot survive in the face of strong revolutionary impulses, and in America he observed a powerful democratic movement which in many ways posed a threat to the federalist legacy. The people to whom he spoke were frank about their worries: "We are currently experimenting with unlimited democracy," he heard, for instance, from a lawyer named Walker, "but will we be able to tolerate it? No one can yet say that he knows."[107] Tocqueville shared these fears and at times wondered whether the mores of the Americans—their civic-mindedness and tradition of liberty—would be enough to hold the defects of democracy in check. In his notebook, for example, he wrote: "A wholly democratic government is a machine so dangerous that even in America they have been obliged to take a host of precautions against the errors and passions of democracy: the establishment of two chambers, the governors' veto, and above all the institution of judges."[108] Would these precautions prove sufficient in a country where the democratic government reinforced certain defects of the democratic social state?

Taken together, these fears suggested the horror of a possible tyranny of the majority, which Tocqueville first heard about from his friend Jared Sparks.[109] In the course of his research in the United States, Tocqueville met mainly the political adversaries of General Jackson, and in the end he was greatly—perhaps too greatly—impressed by the prospect of a tyranny of the majority, to which he devoted an important chapter of volume one of *Democracy*.[110] This chapter, among the best known and surely the most widely discussed in the book, is a composite of disparate elements, and Tocqueville does not tie them together in any rigorous way. The argument takes up both questions of law and questions of fact; it is sometimes political, sometimes sociological in nature. An effort is required on the reader's part to decide when Tocqueville is discussing the defects of democracy in general and when he is talking only about excesses observable in certain states.

The question of law is treated in the middle of the chapter, where Tocqueville, denouncing what he calls the "tyranny of the majority," is in fact attacking the theory of unlimited popular sovereignty.[111] He distinguishes between lawful tyranny and arbitrary rule,[112] and he shows how the tyranny of the majority can be exercised in the name of the law and yet be contrary to justice, as when the government defends only the rights and interests of the majority, refusing to recognize those of the minority. Thus, from a legal standpoint, tyranny of the majority is a form of injustice which consists in the failure to recognize the rights of the minority. The political right of the majority to govern cannot be challenged; tyranny begins only when no limits to that right are recognized. Injustice occurs when what Tocqueville calls the omnipotence of the majority is embodied in the institutions of government. Unfortunately, distinctions that are clearly stated at the beginning of the chapter become blurred toward the end, when the effects of this new form of tyranny are analyzed.[113]

In concluding the chapter, Tocqueville cites Jefferson and Madison in support of his thesis: that if America ever loses its freedom, it will be because it never learned how to limit popular sovereignty. As Madison wrote in *The Federalist* (no. 51): "It is of great importance in a republic, not only to guard the society against the oppression of its rulers; but to guard one part of the society against the injustice of the other part." It is a pity, however, that Tocqueville did not cite the nearby passage in which Madison shows that the United States as a whole is safe because the nation is "broken into so many parts, interests, and classes of citizens, that the rights of individuals or of the minority will be in little danger from the interested combinations of the majority."[114] Tocqueville probably preferred not to discuss this notion of changing, flexible majorities or to consider the diversity of interests and opinions in a Republic so vast; in two brief notes he restricted the criticisms set forth in the chapter to the governments of particular states, leaving the federal government beyond reproach.[115] At this time (1834–35), when French attitudes toward the United States were changing rapidly, it was customary to draw a contrast between the good America and the bad. Although Tocqueville does not repeat the commonplace contrast between Washington and Jackson, he does contrast two forms of American democracy: at the federal level he sees a stable, limited democracy respectful of justice and minority rights, while in certain states he finds extreme forms of democracy characterized by unstable laws and "omnipotence of the majority." Here, all power tends to become concentrated in the legislature, which is itself subject to the changing will of the majority; this undermines the rule of law and saps the power of the representatives, infringing individual rights when these come into conflict with the wishes of the majority. The French Revolution had taught Tocqueville the danger of a process whereby extreme democracy undercuts democracy itself.[116]

Perhaps Tocqueville underestimated the value of constitutional guarantees. When he examines how the Americans temper the tyranny of the majority, the only remedies he mentions are judicial guarantees and the absence of administrative centralization.[117] Many critics have accused him of overestimating the danger of a tyranny of the majority while remaining silent about the dangers that may come of tyrannies exercised by certain minorities.[118] They are right as far as they go, but they fail to distinguish between Tocqueville's political argument and his far more original sociological argument. When he examines the power of the majority over thought,[119] he opens an original avenue of research, which he will pursue later (in volume two): "I do not know any country where there is, broadly speaking, less independence of spirit and genuine freedom of discussion than there is in America."[120] He shows that the majority's power to censor, greater than that of the Inquisition,[121] serves to stem the expression of any thought alien to itself. Without relying on the authority of the law or on any visible form of violence, this type of social control depends on internalized norms to eradicate even the desire for opposition.

With this profound idea Tocqueville went beyond the liberals of his day to explore the social roots of liberty. Of all extra-institutional factors affecting liberty, freedom of thought is the most indispensable, and Tocqueville shows that, contrary to what many of his countrymen believed, democracy and freedom of thought are not necessarily synonymous. Unfortunately, his most novel ideas on this score are mingled with common French and American opinions of the day. Furthermore, he failed to point out that the greatest threat to liberty in France came from the government, whereas in America it came from society. Thanks partly to Mill's criticisms, but above all to the progress of his own thought, he freed himself in volume two from the shackles of convention that had imprisoned his most original ideas. In the margin of a draft of a chapter on the new despotism,[122] he noted: "In this painting lies all the originality and profundity of my idea. What I wrote at the end of my first work was trite and superficial."[123]

5 ✖ *Political Interlude: From America to Parliament*

Democracy in America met with prodigious success from the moment of its publication. Within weeks newspapers and journals of every stripe were filled with praise. The number of reviews and the warmth of admiration reflect not only the book's exceptional quality but also its impact on public opinion. The book-seller Charles Gosselin, located in Paris on the rue Saint-Germain des Prés, had advertised in the newspapers that *De la démocratie en Amérique* by Alexis de Tocqueville would appear, complete with a map of the United States, on 27 January 1835; Tocqueville was described as an attorney in the Royal Court at Paris and one of the authors of a book entitled *The Penitentiary System in the United States.*[1] By April, Gosselin told Tocqueville that "it appears you have written a masterpiece,"[2] and there was talk of a second edition.

On 14 June 1835 the *Revue des Deux Mondes* published a very favorable article by François de Corcelle. Most extraordinary, and a cause of some misunderstanding, was the fact that the press was nearly unanimous in hailing the book as a masterpiece, from the highly legitimist *Gazette de France*[3] to Armand Carrel's republican paper *Le National,*[4] not to mention such moderate papers as *Le Constitutionnel*, close to Thiers; *Le Globe*, liberal and Saint-Simonian; the *Journal des Débats,*[5] organ of the Party of Resistance; and above all *Le Temps,*[6] where

Sainte-Beuve was unstinting in his praise: "The excellent work of M. de Tocqueville . . . M. de T.'s excellent manner, at once empirical and philosophical . . . The approbation of Chateaubriand, Royer-Collard, and Lamartine has been expressed sufficiently publicly that one can subscribe to it without fear of being taken in by appearances. It is a long time since a book of political science and observation has so stimulated and satisfied the interest of thoughtful people."

To this day the work has inspired the admiration of thoughtful liberals, whose names are too numerous to list. I shall mention only a few: George Grote, Charles Sumner, James Bryce, Lord Acton, Harold Laski, and George W. Pierson, Edouard Laboulaye, Lucien Prévost-Paradol, Emile Faguet, Bertrand de Jouvenel, and Raymond Aron. All rank *Democracy in America* among the masterworks of political philosophy, and many would agree with Royer-Collard, who wrote his friend Becquey in 1835 that "to find a work to compare it with, you have to go back to Aristotle's *Politics* and [Montesquieu's] *Esprit des lois*."

Divergences of opinion did not begin to appear until volume two, a more philosophical, abstract, and difficult work than its predecessor, was published in 1840. Sainte-Beuve, changing his tone, deplored the fact that "the moralizing and meditative part here outweighs the observation."

Tocqueville was disappointed by the comparative failure of volume two,[7] but he quickly grasped the reason for it, as is shown by a letter to Mill dated 18 October 1840: "When I was talking solely about democratic society in the United States, people understood immediately. If I had spoken of our democratic society in France as it is today, they also would have understood well enough. But using notions derived from American and French society, I wanted to portray the general features of democratic societies for which no full model yet exists. That is where I lose the ordinary reader."[8] This explanation is so clear that it obscures other equally important reasons for the public's reticence. Volume two does indeed present what we would now call a model of democratic society, and sociological speculation of this kind was far in advance of its time. But it is equally certain that the French public in 1840 was simply less interested in the United States and its institutions than it had been in the 1830s. Its republican illusions had been dashed, soon followed by its liberal illusions. By 1835 French public opinion had turned critical of the United States, depriving volume two of the curiosity of republicans, the sympathy of pro-

Americans, and the favor of aspiring liberals, all of which had contributed to the success of volume one.[9]

In July 1834 Tocqueville answered a question from his publisher about the title of his work by saying that he wished it to be *De l'Empire de la démocratie aux Etats-Unis*.[10] In November 1839 he wrote Mill: "I arrived in Paris two days ago to oversee the printing of the book on which I have been working for the past four years and which is the sequel to the other one; it is called *L'influence de l'égalité sur les idées et les sentiments des hommes*."[11] No doubt Gosselin persuaded him to stay with a title that had enjoyed such great success in 1835: *De la démocratie en Amérique*. Nevertheless, Tocqueville's uncertainty about what to call his work shows that the relation between volumes one and two is neither simple nor clear. In a brilliant paper Seymour Drescher has even argued that they are really two different works.[12]

What holds this masterpiece together? Does its unity extend beyond its title? Did the author clarify and extend his thinking between 1835 and 1840, or did he write volume two merely to correct the errors of volume one? Why did he feel the need to write a sequel? True, he had more or less promised one to his readers,[13] but there were also other reasons, having to do with Tocqueville's desire to fortify his ideas by actively engaging in political life. To understand the genesis and significance of volume two, we must delve into Tocqueville's manuscripts and correspondence, and we must ask how Tocqueville's plans for a political career affected his theoretical work. G. W. Pierson has called attention to the importance of the thinking and reading that Tocqueville did after his return from America, which he drolly calls Tocqueville's "second journey" to the United States.[14] I want now to examine the final stage of that second journey: from America to parliament.

After the First Success: Tocqueville's Political Plans

Tocqueville's first political act was the publication of *Democracy in America* in 1835. At that time it was quite natural to think that a major literary success would open the door to a brilliant political career. Received with honor in the best salons, Tocqueville did not forget the plan conceived in his youth: "We must forge the political man in us," he had written to Beaumont as early as 1829.[15] Gustave de Beaumont had enjoyed considerable success with his *Marie, ou l'esclavage aux*

Etats-Unis. Less profound than his friend but also less somber, always affable and gay, more like the other liberals of his day than Tocqueville was able to be, and sometimes imprudent,[16] Beaumont would be his friend's irreplaceable ally in many a political battle, just as he had been his traveling companion in youth. A passionate, unselfish concern for the public good and for liberty was the cement that held their friendship together. They traveled in 1835 to England and Ireland, which they had visited before in 1833; there Tocqueville discovered the industrial revolution and clarified his economic, social, and political ideas, while Beaumont gathered material for a book that he published in 1839: *Ireland: Society, Politics, and Religion.* The years 1835–1840 were a happy time for the two young men, full of ideas and plans. In 1835 Tocqueville married an Englishwoman, Marie Motley, a cultivated woman without money or title. In his parents' eyes she was not at all a good match, but Tocqueville saw it as a marriage for love. In June 1836 Beaumont married a granddaughter of General Lafayette. By 1837 both men were working to complete their books and to get themselves elected deputies.

What were Tocqueville's political ideals at this point? To an old school friend, frightened by his democratic notions, Tocqueville offered reassurance: "You think that I am going to put forward radical, almost revolutionary theories. You are wrong. I have shown, and I shall continue to show, a strong and reasonable affection for liberty . . . but at the same time I shall profess so great a respect for justice, so true a love of law and order, and so deep and reasoned an attachment to morality and religion that I cannot believe that people will fail to see me as a new kind of liberal or that they will confound me with today's party of democrats. That is my whole plan."[17] Was this really a political plan? The goals are clearly stated, but there is no timetable; nothing is said about means or about obstacles to overcome. The letter is more a statement of political ideals than a "plan." Tocqueville's aim was to reunite "the two or three great things that we see separated," namely, religion, morality, and liberty.[18] A rather naive, idealistic interpretation could be given to Tocqueville's phrase "a new kind of liberal." And why was this unbeliever so determined to join the "spirit of religion" to the "spirit of liberty"? In any case, the end of the letter suggests that Tocqueville believed his goal to be unattainable: "To persuade men that respect for divine and human laws is the best way to remain free and that freedom is the best way to remain honest and religious—that cannot be, you may say. I, too, am tempted to believe it. Yet it is true, and whatever the risk, I shall attempt to live accordingly."[19]

It is a great pity that this letter is cited so often, as though it expressed Tocqueville's political ideals in their entirety. The letter actually expresses a moral ideal, and it is only in the following letter, written in response to Stoffels' probing, that Tocqueville touches on the political aspect:

You tell me, with much reason, that revolutions are great evils and rarely serve to educate a people; that prolonged agitation is already most unfortunate, and that respect for law comes only from stability of laws . . . all things that I believe profoundly. I do not think that there is a man in France less revolutionary than I am, or who more thoroughly detests what is called the revolutionary spirit . . . What am I, then, and what do I want? For clarity's sake, let us distinguish between ends and means. What is the end? What I want is not a republic but a hereditary monarchy. I would even prefer a legitimate to an elected one such as we have, because it would be stronger, particularly outside our borders. What I want is a central government dynamic within its own sphere of action . . . a clearly delineated sphere . . . I think that a government of this kind can exist, and that at the same time a majority of the nation can take care of its own affairs; that political life can spread almost everywhere; and that there can be both direct and indirect exercise of very extensive political rights. I want the general principles of government to be liberal, with as much freedom as possible left to individual action, to personal initiative. I believe that all these things are compatible. More than that, I am profoundly convinced that there will never be order and tranquillity unless we do succeed in combining them.

As for means, with all those who agree that this is the goal toward which we must proceed, I am immediately conciliatory. I am the first to admit that we must proceed slowly, with all due precautions and respect for the law. I am convinced that our present institutions suffice to achieve the result I have in view. Far from wishing that the laws be violated, I preach an almost superstitious respect for law. But I want the laws to tend little by little and gradually toward the goal I have just indicated, rather than make futile and dangerous efforts to reverse the course of history. I want the government itself to shape mores and customs in such a way that people can do without its intervention in many cases where such intervention is still either necessary or needlessly invoked. I want citizens to be involved in public life to the extent that they are deemed capable of making a useful contribution, rather than kept out at all costs . . . In sum, I have a clear concept of an ideal government which is by no means revolutionary or unreasonably agitated and which I think it is possible to establish in our country. Yet I also understand, better than anyone else, that such a government (which is nothing but an extension of the one we have) cannot be established without mores, habits, and laws which do not yet exist and which can be introduced only slowly and with the utmost precaution.[20]

Such was Tocqueville's political creed as he embarked upon his career in politics. His liberalism was new, with respect to both means and ends, as compared with the "revolutionary spirit" which animated "today's party of democrats"—clearly he meant in France, for we know that, had he lived in England, he would not have hesitated to join Mill and the "radicals." The clearest indication of Tocqueville's prudent and patient liberal reformism is to be found, in the letter to Stoffels, in his designation of the enemy: the revolutionary spirit. Tocqueville set a new goal for liberalism: to extricate the liberal passions from the revolutionary ones with which they had long been intertwined. This, I think, was the political significance of his plan to become a new kind of liberal; but his ambitions were in fact broader, for he aimed to reconcile liberalism with elements that had been accidentally severed from it by the Revolution, namely, justice and religion.

In Tocqueville's view, liberalism's attempt to make a comeback under the Restoration had ended in failure. Liberalism had become implicated in anticlericalism and Bonapartism, parts of the revolutionary legacy, and its own ranks were filled with yesterday's liberals, men incapable of shedding the intellectual habits of aristocratic society. After 1830 Tocqueville had every reason to believe that French liberalism not only could but must be given a fresh start. The revival of religious sentiment and the death of Napoleon II[21] offered a favorable opportunity. But the main task remained: to separate liberal passions from revolutionary ones.

IN 1836 THE regime seemed to have achieved stability; the riots and uncertainty of the early years had been overcome. Open rebellion and covert legitimist plots against the new monarchy gave way to years of peace, security, and prosperity. The end of rioting had aroused hopes in Tocqueville, as evidenced by a letter he wrote to John Stuart Mill on 24 June 1837: "Since the riots have ended and the fear of a violent, anarchic revolution has receded, the nation is gradually returning to its liberal and democratic instincts. But this development is still not much in evidence; it is clearer in the elector than in the elected ... I am nevertheless convinced that if peace abroad and at home continues, we shall every day, and despite the government, be drawn closer to a more liberal state of affairs. But may God preserve us from riots! They seem to threaten the government and thereby injure only liberty." Indeed, the Laws of September 1835, passed in the wake of Giuseppe Fieschi's attempt on the life of Louis-Philippe, already signified a retreat from the liberties recognized by the Charter. Tocqueville remained steadfastly opposed to these laws, which marked the culmination of the "policy of resistance." Royer-Collard, long his model, had broken relations with Guizot on account of them. While Tocqueville looked for signs of a liberal revival, Guizot maintained that it was necessary to continue the policy of resistance. He concluded his speech of 24 March 1836[22] with the following cry:

> Make no mistake: however necessary and legitimate, revolutions always suffer from the grave disadvantage of undermining and toppling governments. And when the government has been undermined and toppled, the most important thing for society, for its freedom as well as its tranquillity, for its future as well as its present, is to lift up and strengthen that fallen government, to restore its stability and dignity, its respect and consideration. That is what the Chamber has done since 1830, or at least, that is what it has begun, for God knows, not everything has been done! No, with us all is begun, nothing is finished, everything is to be carried on.

Tocqueville agreed with Guizot's goals but was vehemently opposed to his methods, calling instead for an extension of political liberty.

But his expectations were disappointed. The regime's victory over the republican rioters led not to a rebirth of liberalism but to a revival of the king's personal power, to a crisis of the parliamentary regime,[23] and to a degradation of the public spirit. The political climate in 1836, following passage of the Laws of September 1835,[24] was already quite different from what it had been in early 1835 when *Democracy in America* was published. On 19 November 1836 Royer-Collard pointed this out to Tocqueville, who was already at work on volume two: "Since you wrote, many things have changed. I do not believe that the democratic spirit has been affected or that mores have been altered. But that is the only area in which this singular spirit is making progress and bearing its full fruit."[25] Tocqueville's intuition was confirmed by his old friend: liberal and democratic tendencies were still making progress in French mores, whereas the government had turned toward personal rule by the king, backed by his administration. These two opposite tendencies made the regime fragile, as neither Tocqueville nor Royer-Collard failed to observe.[26]

Nor did the precariousness of the regime escape the attention of its principal leaders, who were quite capable of seeing what was happening outside the confines of the narrow electorate. Guizot, not content merely to govern, felt a clear need to consolidate the regime and establish the new dynasty on a firm footing. On 25 March 1836 he declared: "Society needs to organize itself, to rediscover long-lost principles of order." On 15 February 1842 at the Palais Bourbon he said: "We have to found a new society, new institutions, a new dynasty."[27] Yet he sensed, even in conservative ranks, a lack of understanding of the true need for social order and the insidious influence of revolutionary maxims.[28] To impose his views he could think of nothing better than to raise the specter of revolution.[29] As for the king himself, he had grown up with the Revolution and was well aware of its underground force, always at work; at times he doubted his ability to end the great Revolution and one day he said to Guizot: "To defeat it would take a prophet."[30]

ACCORDING TO THE official theory preached by the Party of Resistance, the Revolution of 1830 was a mere change of dynasty that led to the establishment of a true parliamentary monarchy; comparison with the English revolution of 1688 was much in vogue. In reality, everyone sensed, and Guizot knew perfectly well, that the Revolution of 1830, while apparently destroying nothing, had in fact diminished society's traditional resilience. The king could leaf through the newspapers and judge from the popular caricatures of himself just how far disrespect for the monarchy had gone. On 16 August 1830, Tocqueville, judge-auditor at Versailles, had taken the oath of allegiance to the new regime in order to prevent an even worse government from coming to power and to allow the country one last chance at constitutional monarchy. In public he never failed to pay the head of the July Monarchy the respect he was due, but his *Souvenirs* and *Conversations with Nassau Senior* leave no doubt as to his sentiments, and his unpublished manuscripts mention his "hatred of the king."[31]

He could not accept a regime in which the king governed through a willing prime minister, manipulating parliament by means of corrupt practices which were clearly facilitated by the large number of deputies who were also government employees.[32] Thus in 1837,[33] when for the first time Tocqueville presented himself to the electors of Valognes, he refused the assistance that his cousin, Count Molé, was only too happy to offer.[34] Had he accepted, his career would have been assured. But he declined the offer and was therefore forced to run against a "ministerial" candidate; the cry "No nobles!" rang out, and Tocqueville lost the election.

IN 1838 A coalition of the most important parliamentary leaders— Guizot, Thiers, and Odilon Barrot—was formed against Molé and the king's personal government. Duvergier de Hauranne was the first to demand "replacement of personal power by a parliamentary regime in which the Chamber has the right to the final say."[35] Somewhat later Thiers coined the famous phrase that caught the popular fancy: "The king reigns and does not govern." An all-out attack on the "ministry of the court" was launched in December 1838. Molé defended himself magnificently, but the Address he proposed carried by a bare majority (221-208). After dissolution of parliament, those enfranchised to vote, the *pays légal*, were called upon to resolve the debate. The coalition returned with 240 deputies compared with 200 on the government side, but its electoral success precipitated a crisis that lasted for more than two months, as the majority found itself in opposition rather than in power. On 12 May 1839 Armand Barbès and Louis Blanqui, leaders of the Four Seasons Society, attempted an insurrection in the Saint-Denis and Saint-Martin quarters; it was quickly put down, but that very night the Chamber bestowed its confidence upon the ministry of Nicolas Soult, whom the king had appointed along with others of the second rank. The coalition's plans had gone awry. It had succeeded only in diminishing respect for both the crown and parliament. Rémusat notes in his *Memoirs* that 1839 marked the beginning of a period of indifference to and even contempt for the system inaugurated in 1815,[36] and many analysts, Lamartine and Charles Montalembert foremost among them, saw this as one of the causes of the Revolution of 1848.[37]

Tocqueville had clearly foreseen the dangers of the coalition, and in his letters to Royer-Collard he pointed out that he had been a candidate of the opposition, not of the coalition.[38]

Elected in March 1839, Tocqueville sat between Thiers's center-left party and Odilon Barrot's dynastic left.[39] His friend Gustave de Beaumont soon joined him.[40] No doubt Tocqueville dreamed of founding a new party, as is suggested by his letter to Beaumont of 7 May 1838.[41] Once elected, he sought to attract some of the sixty new deputies, but all melted into the existing factions. Incapable of winning adherents with his oratory—cold and all too visibly superior in his meticulously prepared delivery—and indifferent to the ordinary exchanges and rituals of parliamentary life, he quickly became an isolated figure, caught between the center-left and the dynastic left. Unable to rally support, he strove above all to preserve his independence. This is not the place to delve into his reasons for supporting Thiers's second ministry despite his suspicion of Thiers.[42] He opposed the Soult-Guizot ministry,[43] at first for reasons of foreign policy, and then, after 1842, for almost all aspects of its program; I shall have more to say later about the reasons for this opposition. In 1846 Tocqueville joined a group of center-left dissidents led by Dufaure, who later served as president of the council under the Third Republic, along with his closest political allies, Corcelle, Rivet, and Lanjuinais. This was the seed of a new party and the end of Tocqueville's isolation, but the revolution of February 1848 upset the group's plans. On the whole, Tocqueville's career in parliament under the July Monarchy leaves the impression that his great political intelligence never found the employment to which it was suited. In a letter to Royer-Collard dated 27 September 1841, Tocqueville himself put his finger on the principal, that is to say, the political, reason for his failure: "The liberal but not revolutionary party which alone would suit me does not exist, and, to be sure, it has not been given to me to create it."[44]

Royer-Collard and Tocqueville

During the years when he was writing volume two of *Democracy in America*, which were also the years when he was trying to get elected to parliament, no one exerted more influence on Tocqueville than Royer-Collard. In philosophy as in politics, Royer served as a model and adviser, a master and confidant. He was also a friend and, as Tocqueville said, "almost a father."[45] Royer-Collard was seventy-two in 1835 when Tocqueville, then thirty, was introduced to him.

From his Jansenist childhood in the village of Sompuis in Champagne, Royer-Collard retained a very strict sense of duty, along with a strong desire for justice and a proud stiffness in conversation, a trait that accorded well with his imperious character. "The somewhat Roman grandeur of character of the Great Arnauld [Antoine Arnauld,

1612–1694, the great Jansenist theologian] was softened without turning corrupt in Royer-Collard, through contact with reality and his determination not to compromise with it but to bend it to his will."[46] In fact, Royer-Collard no longer turned for salvation to Jansenism, which he saw as an amalgam of philosophy and religion, a source of moral precepts. He read and constantly meditated upon Montesquieu's *Esprit des lois*, a few Greek and Latin classics, the English economists, and the Jansenist writers of Port-Royal. Except for Montesquieu he hated the writers of the eighteenth century, but he had read and reread the great Cartesians and had discovered Thomas Reid long before Joseph Joubert, President of the Council of Public Instruction, appointed him in 1811 to the chair of History of Philosophy, with the support of Louis de Fontanes, head of the imperial university.

Through his influence, the legacy of eighteenth-century philosophy, transmitted to the nineteenth century by the Idéologues, was given a "spiritualist" inflection.[47] Victor Cousin succeeded him at the Sorbonne, and the young Guizot was his protégé. During the Restoration he was the leader of the Doctrinaires, a small group which then included Camille Jordan, the Count de Serre, Quatremère de Quincy, and Barante, as well as Guizot[48] and Rémusat in their youth.

As a young lawyer imbued with the spirit of 1789, Royer-Collard was horrified by the excesses of the Revolution. When a member of the Council of the Five Hundred, after the coup d'état of the Directors against the Councils on 18 Fructidor, Year V, he subscribed to a "monarchism of reason, not sentiment" and became a secret adviser to the future Louis XVIII. In his view the Empire was "one of the greatest corruptions perpetrated upon human reason."[49] After plotting for the Restoration, he fought against its most dangerous divagations, and his reputation as a political orator reached its apogee in his great debates with La Bourdonnaye and Louis de Bonald. He supported freedom of the press, and the work in which he expressed his liberal views on this issue was particularly well known.[50]

THERE ARE MANY similarities between Tocqueville's ideas and Royer-Collard's, and many of their political views were identical. As a deputy from Vitry-le-François, Royer-Collard was an unenthusiastic supporter of the July Monarchy, which he deemed France's last chance at constitutional monarchy. His thought was not so narrowly legalistic as it is sometimes portrayed,[51] for he held that institutions ought to be based on mores and argued as early as 1822 that attention had to be paid to their evolution. He must have read *Democracy in America* as a confirmation of his views in this regard, while its young author found in Royer-Collard a judgment of the July Monarchy similar to his own and a political Jansenism perfectly suited to his taste. The correspondence between the two men in the years 1835–1840 reveals the development of a bond between master and disciple as well as the great influence that Royer-Collard had on the writing of volume two. Tocqueville consulted him on all matters of importance in those years: on his reading, his philosophical musings, the individualism of the French, the future of the regime, and his entry into the French Academy and into parliament. He read, pen in hand, a volume of speeches that Royer-Collard had delivered during the Restoration, a gift from the author.[52]

Many of the Doctrinaires' fundamental ideas were taken up by Tocqueville,[53] in particular the view that absolute sovereignty belongs not to the people but to reason and justice and that duration bestows legitimacy upon existing powers. Yet one senses a certain nostalgia in Tocqueville's notes on Royer's speech in praise of legitimacy, delivered on 17 May 1820: "Conjunction of liberty with legitimacy raised to the level of providential necessity, absolute condition of government: separate liberty from legitimacy and you go to barbarism."[54] Like Royer-Collard, Tocqueville knew the need for "legitimate war against privilege,"[55] but he was not so attached as the Doctrinaires to the *régime censitaire* [voting based on property qualifications], whose weaknesses he saw better than anyone else.[56] Above all, he borrowed from the Doctrinaires their conception of individual rights, less abstract and legalistic than that of Benjamin Constant, and at the same time, owing to the Doctrinaires' concern for harmony between mores and laws, more ethical and concrete.

Tocqueville was impressed by Royer-Collard's ideas and by his introduction of morality into politics, his "application of morality to great things,"[57] but he also admired him for having achieved a position of unchallenged intellectual authority while retaining his own independence; under the July Monarchy this was reduced to mere moral authority, but in the halcyon years of the Restoration Royer-Collard had wielded real political influence. As a young elected representative, Tocqueville made the mistake of following Royer's example of independence, failing to realize the importance of patience and of circumstances in making such an apparently independent role possible.

Tocqueville's notes on Royer-Collard also contain some criticisms which shed light on how Tocqueville intended to correct his teacher's ideas in order to extend their influence: "Profound but exaggerated contempt of M. Royer for the present time. Great side that escapes him: transitional era that he does not see." Indeed, Royer's great inferiority to Tocqueville comes from the fact that he was unable to conceive of the possibility of a democratic order,[58] but at least he was able to appreciate the true worth of his disciple's contribution.[59]

For the most part, Tocqueville retained Royer-Collard's ideas, which he believed would prove even more applicable under the July Monarchy than they had been under the Restoration. His notes on Royer end thus: "The Restoration was possible only after the July Revolution, after the initial effervescence had died down. True and original idea to be given prominence."[60] After the July Revolution, that is, after the destruction of aristocracy but not of royalty—in other words, once the Revolution begun in 1789 had ended—it became possible to reconcile monarchy with the principles of 1789 in a true parliamentary monarchy.

CONCENTRATING ON THE need to combine monarchy with a liberal but nonrevolutionary spirit, Tocqueville summarized Royer-Collard's ideas in a letter to his friend Freslon (8 July 1858). Because of its importance to my argument, and despite its length, I will reproduce this letter virtually in its entirety:

All of M. Royer-Collard's principal actions are in fact linked by just two ideas; one of these is greater and more his mistress than the other, but both are guiding influences on his mind:

1. M. Royer-Collard believed strongly throughout his life that one could and should distinguish between the liberal spirit and the revolutionary spirit. He passionately desired the destruction of the Old Regime and was horrified by any thought of its return. With extreme ardor he wished for the abolition of privileges, equality of political rights, and human freedom and dignity. He always detested the spirit of adventure, violence, tyranny, and demagoguery that has remained typical of the revolutionary mind throughout the world. He firmly believed that the Old Regime could be overthrown without giving in to the revolutionary spirit. He aspired to draw something other than that spirit out of revolution itself! He never believed that all aspects of the old French society had to be destroyed, but only the obstacles to the modern spirit, to a well-balanced liberty, to equality of rights, and to the opening of all careers and all destinies to every man's hope. The Revolution accomplished, he always sought to bring institutions into conformity with this ideal and, insofar as it was possible or desirable to do so, to join the past together with the present. Is there

a single detail of his life that does not accord perfectly with this ideal? I do not know. But study his whole life, and you will see that this was the ideal that guided and explained it.

2. M. Royer-Collard's second leading idea, which was quite similar to the first though not in the least derivative of it, was this: M. Royer-Collard always held that the institution of royalty was, in France, a necessary institution. It was pleasant to observe the singular effect that this doctrine sometimes produced, mingled as it was with the most indocile sentiments and the most republican nature I have ever encountered. Horror of the court, yet immutable adherence to the idea of a king. Of all royalties, the one that seemed to him most apt to maintain the great liberal and modern institutions which he desired above all else and spent his entire life defending, at times against revolutionaries, at times against the ultras and the émigrés, was the royalty of the eldest branch. I have never seen a man more exempt from what might be called legitimist passions or less passionately attached to a dynasty or a family, yet at the same time more convinced that the best possible outcome of the Revolution was the royalty of the eldest branch, controlled and held in check by all the institutions that could ensure the triumph of the new ideas. His lifelong dream was to enable the new spirit to coexist with the old family, each upholding the other. All in all, however, liberalism was always his aim, and the monarchy of the princes of the eldest branch the means . . .

I have always considered the passionate sincerity and incomparable eloquence that he exhibited in defending two theses which, in the minds of many people, embody contraries, to be one of the most extraordinary sights I have ever witnessed. You had to hear him talk about the Revolution. No one could better evoke the grandeur of that time and its superiority over our own, notwithstanding its failings and its violence. The finest words that have ever been spoken about what may be called the great conquests of '89 came from his mouth. The bitterest words I have ever heard about the vices of the Old Regime and about the foolish and ridiculous behavior of the émigrés and ultras were spoken by him. But when it became necessary to describe the tyrannical violence, unruly passions, bloody madness, and intolerance of what he called the revolutionary spirit, he was Tacitus.[61]

In this letter Tocqueville is talking as much about himself as about Royer-Collard. If there was a difference between the two men, it was that Tocqueville, the aristocrat, was less devoted than the commoner Royer-Collard to the "royalty of the eldest branch." In essential respects, however, the similarity in their two standpoints is striking, especially in view of the fact that they lived their political lives in very different times and circumstances.

While writing volume two of *Democracy in America*, however, Tocqueville had another prime confidant: John Stuart Mill, intellectually and politically a very different man from Royer-Collard. It was to Mill that Tocqueville wrote in late 1835: "Of all those who have kindly attempted to interest the public in me, you are the only one who has fully understood me."[62] Mill understood better than Royer-Collard the part of Tocqueville's thought that looked toward the future, toward democracy. But at the heart of the political thinking of both Royer-Collard and Tocqueville was a vision of the French Revolution and a concern that Mill scarcely divined: namely, how to defend the values of 1789 while combating the revolutionary spirit. If Tocqueville shared Royer-Collard's goal of freeing the liberal spirit from the revolutionary one, he nevertheless dealt with a more complex question— and a different future—in volume two of *Democracy*: how to distinguish the democratic spirit from the revolutionary one. This approach unified the two sides of his thinking, which his two most important nineteenth-century readers had understood separately, the one reflecting upon the French past, the other upon the democratic future.

The Genesis of Volume Two

In overall conception as well as in each of its four parts, volume two of *Democracy in America* attempts to answer a fundamental question: how to distinguish between what is democratic and what is revolutionary in egalitarian ideas, feelings, and mores. But Tocqueville's approach to this question changes from section to section of the work, as does the nature of his answer. Study of his manuscripts and correspondence reveals the evolution of his thought from 1836 to the end of 1839, as I shall show in the next four chapters, which closely follow the four major parts of volume two.

Let me first, however, discuss the origins and structure of volume two as a whole. Throughout the period of planning and writing this volume, Tocqueville was influenced by Royer-Collard, whose intellectual authority was at its peak in 1836 and the first half of 1837. From the correspondence between the two men, it is clear that a slight shadow fell over their relations from late June 1837 until the end of that year as a result of Tocqueville's political ambitions. Nevertheless, from June

1836 to the end of 1837 relations between the two men attained a peak of intimacy and trust. Tocqueville had already written a first draft of the chapters devoted to the influence of equality on ideas, and from October 1836 to March 1838 he worked on the sections concerning the role of sentiments and mores in democratic societies. In this phase of his work he consulted Royer-Collard about his philosophical reading and all sorts of deep issues, especially the subordination of politics to ethics.[63] Royer-Collard strongly encouraged Tocqueville to pursue his philosophical vocation but sought to discourage his political ambitions.

During 1838 and up to the time of Tocqueville's election in March 1839, relations between the two men remained quite close. Tocqueville did not hesitate to confer with Royer about his concerns and doubts as an author.[64] But when he consulted with him on the question of individualism in June 1838, he did so in a very roundabout manner, and the reader cannot help thinking that he did not want to raise this crucial issue directly for fear of touching on an area of serious disagreement. On 30 August 1838 he announced to Royer-Collard that he had just finished what he called his "final chapter"—actually the entire final section of the work, entitled "On the Influence of Democratic Ideas and Feelings on Political Society." In March 1838 he had begun revising the early parts of the text, especially the first section, in which he made substantial changes. Finally, in March 1839, Tocqueville's election led to a marked deterioration in relations between the two men.

Royer-Collard had never approved of Tocqueville's political plans, but in 1839 his disapproval was sharper than it had been in 1837. He did not answer the letter in which Tocqueville announced his success, responding only to the next one, dated August; this interruption of five months in their correspondence reveals the cooling of relations that had taken place between them. From March 1839 until August 1840 this coolness is apparent, at first in Royer-Collard's silences,[65] followed by his "very strong" criticism of the young deputy's naive errors,[66] and finally, four months after the publication of volume two, in Royer-Collard's judgment of the work, which combined praise with some serious reservations.[67] Tocqueville allowed eleven months to pass before writing again, and from July 1841 until Royer-Collard's death in 1845 he wrote only five letters; one of them hardly veils his pleasure at not having to encounter Royer-Collard's censorious gaze in the Chamber,[68] while another offers fundamental criticism of Royer-Collard's pessimistic vision of history and reveals how glad Tocqueville was to free himself from an influence which had weighed on him so heavily in 1836–37.[69]

All in all, the relationship between Tocqueville and Royer-Collard conformed to a simple pattern: Tocqueville found a master, almost a father, and then slowly freed himself from his master's influence. When we take a closer look, however, we find that changes in the relationship correspond quite closely to different periods in the writing of volume two of *Democracy in America*, as subsequent chapters will make clear. For now I want simply to give an overall assessment of Royer-Collard's influence on the writing of volume two.

In his letter of 29 June 1837 Tocqueville expressed, with some embarrassment, his desire to be elected deputy.[70] Royer-Collard answered: "To act would be imprudent in all respects . . . In a period of instability it is not good to enter public life when very young . . . A great reputation, which you hold to be the most precious good in this world, is more likely to be achieved today through books like yours than by mounting the rostrum."[71] Despite this advice, repeated by Royer in his letter of 28 September, Tocqueville decided to stand for election at Valogne; he declined the assistance offered by his cousin, Count Molé, then President of the Council, and felt the need to explain this refusal to Royer-Collard, who was a friend of Molé's.[72] "I would have preferred that things not go this far; I hope that they will go no farther," Royer-Collard answered.[73] A short while later, when the young candidate wrote of his failure, his mentor responded: "I certainly did not want to see you fail; nevertheless, I prefer it this way . . . It is not wise to have committed yourself so early, with the danger of being thrown violently off the track, so violently that you will never get back on."[74]

In 1837, Royer-Collard wanted mainly to convince Tocqueville that he would not find in politics the greatness he yearned for.[75] By 1839 the nature of their disagreement had changed. As early as April 1838, Royer-Collard had indicated to his young friend that he supported Molé: "My patriotism consists in defending the present Ministry in the person of its leader. Not that I admire him, but I think him wiser and more honest . . ."[76] Thus in the 1839 elections, Royer-Collard intended to support Molé against the coalition of oppositions.[77] When Tocqueville announced his election to Royer and sent him copies of his campaign speeches, he was careful to explain that he was opposed to Molé but not a member of the coalition: "I said that the opposition and the coalition were two distinct things, and this is in fact what I think." He also reminded Royer of his desire to enter the Chamber "in a state of perfect independence."[78] But that distinction has little force, and the notion that a young deputy would be "independent" makes no sense; at most it might apply to the brief interval after the elections during which places were assigned in a new Assembly.

TOCQUEVILLE WAS WELL aware of the importance of his debut in parliament. On 11 March 1839 he wrote to Beaumont: "Over the next six months I am going to play the game of my life."[79] He played very badly. Priding himself on his independence, he hoped to gather around him newly elected deputies who supported the idea of electoral and parliamentary reform. But the hope of electoral reform was consigned to oblivion immediately after the election, as Rémusat recounts in his *Memoirs*: "The idea of a reform of this kind had figured importantly in the most recent elections. Some new deputies, among whom the foremost was Tocqueville, the last superior man to be elected to the Chambers of the Monarchy, along with Beaumont, Lanjuinais, Corcelle, and even Louis de Carné, had entered parliament with exaggerated prejudices as to the gravity of the malady and with the noble purpose of putting an end to it."[80] The commission set up at the time to study the question included Odilon Barrot and Tocqueville and was chaired by Rémusat, who summarized its conclusions thus: "We would have proposed our views at once and would have done it well had we not been held back by the fear of calling into question the composition of a newly elected Chamber after two successive dissolutions in a short space of time. My mandate was to make an appeal on behalf of reform without establishing the basis for it or indicating the urgency. This frequently cited report, which is praised far more than it deserves because it was merely a commonplace of constitutional theory,[81] launched a long series of memorable debates."[82] In these debates and in preparatory meetings, Tocqueville showed a lack of capacity for effective action and at times a want of the requisite prudence and clear vision.[83] He admitted as much in a letter to Royer-Collard dated 8 August 1839, in which he confessed to having been manipulated by Barrot, for which he received a severe rebuke from his teacher.[84]

While the two men both sought to distinguish between liberal and revolutionary ideas, it is clear that by 1839 they no longer drew the same practical conclusions from their theoretical reflections. They entertained different relations with the left, and in March 1839 they were diametrically opposed in their identifications of the "revolutionary spirit." In a campaign speech Royer-Collard denounced the revolutionary attitudes of the antigovernment coalition,[85] while Tocqueville opposed Molé. In 1836–37 it was possible for Tocqueville to understand the distinction between liberal ideas and passions and their revolutionary deformation in the same way as Royer-Collard did; after March 1839 this ceased to be the case. And we shall see in subsequent chapters how this important issue influenced Tocqueville in the writing of volume two.

Royer-Collard declined to consult with Tocqueville about the final form of the work. On 8 August, Tocqueville informed him that he wished to make one last revision, important enough that it would take a considerable period of time. "What I have seen of the inside of politics over the past few months has made me feel the need to revise certain parts of my work which I had thought finished. That will take time, and I do not know if I will find it between now and the next session."[86] But Royer-Collard did not want to hear about any revision that would take account of current political events: "Do not make haste to rewrite your book if the spectacle that you have had before your eyes for the past few months has led you to make major changes. When you have made those changes, further experience will suggest others, and so on year after year. Thus you will never lift your book above the age in which you live or assume the standpoint of general truth, without consideration of time or place . . . You were truly independent; you must regain that independence or break your pen."[87] Royer-Collard urged Tocqueville to devote all his strength to completing a work of political philosophy, but Tocqueville wanted his book to be a political act as well. Royer's influence on the final section of the work was certainly very small, for this was the most political section; it was written last and was no doubt the main focus of the final revisions made by Tocqueville in 1839.

BY CONTRAST, ROYER'S influence on the first two sections of volume two, which deal with the distinction between democratic and revolutionary ideas and feelings, is quite apparent. If this distinction, inspired by Royer-Collard, is the central idea of the work, it is surprising that it is not stated in the introduction. Study of the Yale manuscripts shows that Tocqueville devoted considerable time to writing a major introduction to volume two but in the end decided not to publish it, contenting himself with a brief preface.

James T. Schleifer, in his excellent book on the origins of *Democracy in America*, reports that Tocqueville had planned to acknowledge and correct, in the introduction to volume two, certain errors that had been made in volume one; in particular, he planned to indicate that he no longer believed in the weakening of the federal bond in America. He also wanted to explain that the purposes of his two volumes were different: "The first book is more American than democratic. This one is more democratic than American."[88] Nevertheless, sometime between the beginning of 1838 and the end of 1839, Tocqueville threw out this introduction—inexplicably, according to Schleifer.[89] But I believe that this decision can be explained with the aid of the Yale manuscripts and knowledge of Tocqueville's increasingly personal reworking of the theme of "democracy and revolution."

Initially, he thought only to extend Royer-Collard's distinction between the liberal and the revolutionary spirit by applying it to the study of democracy. But in so doing he encountered difficulties, as is apparent from this draft introduction in the Yale archives: "The great difficulty in the study of Democracy is to distinguish what is democratic from what is revolutionary"; and in the margin he has added: "This is very difficult because examples are lacking. There is no European nation in which democracy has become established, and America is in an exceptional situation."[90] America's situation was exceptional precisely because democracy had been able to establish itself there without a major revolutionary crisis. By contrast, in France, even assuming that the political regime and civil society had achieved a durable equilibrium, ideas and feelings—"mores," as Tocqueville would say—were still subject to the influence of the Revolution. If the American situation with respect to the relation between democracy and revolution was unique, then a work centered on the study of that relation should not focus primarily on American evidence.[91] That is why volume two of *Democracy* had to be more abstract and "less American" than volume one. And beyond the transparent veils of abstraction, volume two would obviously be a work with many more chapters that could be characterized as "French." The great differences that strike the reader who turns from volume one to volume two are accounted for by the author's determination to resolve a problem which he had taken from Royer-Collard.

Tocqueville's solution hinges on distinguishing the effects of democracy from those of revolution on the basis of intensity: the "effects of democracy, and particularly the harmful effects which are exaggerated in the time of revolution during which the democratic social state, mores, and laws are established."[92] This is an idea we encountered earlier, in our analysis of volume one, albeit in a less explicit form, more derivative of Montesquieu's reflections on the corruption of democracy by the extreme spirit of equality. The formula used there had the advantage of being more in keeping with traditional political philosophy, but it also had two drawbacks: for one thing, it offered no objective criterion for determining at what point democracy became excessive or how it was linked to revolutionary excess; more important, it failed to explain why the revolutionary spirit survived long after the Revolution was over and had apparently achieved its ends. For Tocqueville the main question was why the revolutionary spirit remained so active in France long after the Revolution of 1830.

The manuscripts reveal Tocqueville's many doubts about the best way to present these ideas. A subtitle of sorts indicates: "Idea of Preface or Final Chapter."[93] But a few lines later, in the margin of the passage just cited on the exaggeration of the effects of democracy by revolution, Tocqueville wrote: "Idea to be shown head on at the beginning or end of the work and in profile throughout." This note gives the key to the structure of the work, which can be unraveled through study of the manuscripts, political analysis of the period 1836–1839, and knowledge of Tocqueville's relations with Royer-Collard.

The reader can actually verify that the theme of democracy and revolution structures the four major parts of volume two—"in profile," as Tocqueville puts it. It dominates part four, in which the author shows that revolution and war are the most powerful "accidental" causes of centralization[94] and describes, in a famous chapter, "What Sort of Despotism Democratic Nations Have to Fear."[95] The originality of this chapter lies in the fact that the democratic despotism it describes no longer owes any of its features to revolutionary despotism. Part three contains a brilliant chapter that demonstrates, contrary to a widely held opinion of the time, that "great revolutions will become rare" in democratic societies.[96] Part two, which revolves around the notion of democratic individualism, devotes a chapter to showing how individualism is greater after a democratic revolution than at other times.[97] And the first few chapters of part one seek to distinguish democratic philosophy from its prerevolutionary and revolutionary deformations.[98]

After studying the drafts of the preface in notebook CV, k, 1, of the Yale archives, I have come to the following hypothesis. In 1836 and 1837, Tocqueville, as the manuscripts from this period show, was trying to extend Royer-Collard's ideas, especially those pertaining to the first two parts of volume two. His goal was to distinguish between what is democratic and what is revolutionary. After the elections of November 1837, Tocqueville's relations with Royer-Collard became somewhat less confidential than before, and he began to see that Guizot and even Royer were too conservative in their use of the contrast between orderly liberalism and unruly revolution. He therefore sought to distinguish the liberal spirit from the revolutionary spirit in order to lay the groundwork for a broader liberalism, which by 1836 or 1837 should have been possible since the danger of revolutionary riots had passed. By contrast, Guizot continued to raise the specter of revolution in his fight against the liberal and democratic opposition. We know that in February 1838 Tocqueville was still mulling over his preface, and that in March he completed his chapter on revolution,[99] whose main thesis is the opposite of Guizot's. In this period he saw that it might be difficult and inopportune to treat the theme of democracy and revolution in the preface. His experience with volume one had taught him that most readers remembered the political theme of the introduction rather than the content of the analyses that formed the heart of the book. Thus we can understand his hesitation in February 1838 ("Idea of the Preface or the Final Chapter")[100] and his reasons for wanting to broach the subject gradually.[101] Little by little, what Tocqueville called variously his "final chapter," "last chapter," or "concluding chapter" grew in size between June and October 1838 until it became part four of the published work.[102] In all probability, the choice was made not to treat the central theme, democracy and revolution, in the preface when Tocqueville felt that his views on the subject were no longer those expressed in the drafts written in 1836 and 1837.

Tocqueville's correspondence bears witness to the magnitude of the revisions made in October and November 1838, especially on the first few chapters, which constitute the work's real philosophical introduction.[103] In the next chapter we shall see how and why the author decided to follow this course rather than stay with his original plan to begin the book with the chapters on individualism. On this notion, fundamental to Tocqueville's thought and to the conception of volume two, Royer-Collard was still consulted, although in a most roundabout fashion. But Royer declined to exert any influence over the book's final form, and there is reason to believe that Tocqueville's revisions concerned mainly, though not exclusively, the final and most political part of the work.

Begun under the influence of Royer-Collard, the work gradually evolved as its author gained increasing independence. Once he reached his more personal conclusions, he retraced his steps and eliminated from the initial chapters early ideas that testified to his outgrown dependence on Royer-Collard. As we follow the elaboration of the book's major themes in the next four chapters, we shall on occasion come across residues of the various stages of Tocqueville's thinking. And we shall also see how political circumstances, so different in 1839 from what they had been in 1836, changed the meaning of the central distinction between the liberal and the revolutionary spirit.

Two Democracies

After such scrutiny, the unity of the work can be seen in a new light, with its lines of continuity and internal cleavages. In one of the most brilliant articles ever written on *Democracy in America*, Seymour Drescher argued that volume two was a different work from volume one.[104] Reflecting on French politics in two very different periods, 1833–34 and 1836–1839, Tocqueville in 1840 reached very different conclusions, according to Drescher, from those he had held in 1835: fear of the tyranny of the majority gave way to concern about political apathy and the waning of the public spirit. Affirmation of the irresistible progress of democracy gave way to fears of a new industrial aristocracy. Most important, the final part of volume two asserted an essential correlation between democracy and centralization, whereas the descriptions of America in 1835 suggested the contrary. As so often happens in the world of scholarship, Drescher's original and penetrating article so clearly pointed up the hitherto unnoticed differences between the two *Democracies* that a unity which had once seemed obvious was now discredited. Drescher himself no doubt saw the truth clearly, and he would probably admit that there do exist elements of continuity between the two works, as James T. Schleifer has rightly pointed out.[105]

PART THREE

Democracy and Revolution

6 ⚭ *Enlightenment or Barbarism*

The Revision of 1838

In the letter in which Tocqueville announces to Royer-Collard (30 August 1838) that he has just finished writing volume two of *Democracy in America*, he notes how different it is from volume one: "Now that I can see almost the whole of the book, I notice that there is much more discussion of the general effects of equality on mores than of the particular effects that it produces in America. Is that a flaw?"[1] In 1840 the French public was much less curious about America and its institutions than it had been immediately after the Revolution of 1830; around 1834 or 1835 French attitudes toward the United States had abruptly turned from sympathetic to critical.[2] Then, too, the more abstract analysis of volume two was likely to repel many readers, as Tocqueville was only too well aware.[3] Nevertheless, he chose, in revising his text, to rewrite the beginning in keeping with the philosophy of the whole as he understood it after having completed the draft of the final sections.

Tocqueville's correspondence with Beaumont reveals the magnitude of the revisions carried out between October and December 1838, when Tocqueville said that after throwing a hundred pages into the fire, he had rewritten the destroyed chapters.[4] Comparison of the working manuscript with the printed text indicates that a hundred pages of manuscript correspond to roughly forty-five or fifty pages of the book; hence we can assume that the first ten chapters of volume two were rewritten entirely or at least modified extensively between October and

December 1838. Study of both the manuscript[5] and the final text[6] seems to confirm this hypothesis.[7]

The surviving notes for these chapters reveal Tocqueville's concern that he would repeat ideas developed in the early chapters in later ones, particularly in the chapter on revolutions.[8] He therefore gave up the idea of a "major preface," on which he was still working as late as February 1838. Since the initial chapters would adequately treat the distinction between what is democratic and what is revolutionary, it would have been superfluous to dwell on this subject in an introduction. It is true that for a period of time Tocqueville planned to begin the work with the chapters on individualistic sentiments,[9] but on the advice of Louis de Kergorlay he decided to place the methodological chapter first,[10] and therefore he had no further reason to include a "major preface."[11]

From the outset, the chapters devoted to "the influence of democracy on the intellectual movement in the United States" raised the central question that Tocqueville had inherited from Royer-Collard, namely, how to distinguish between the liberal spirit and the revolutionary spirit. But Tocqueville's reflections on this subject led him to confront two distinct problems. One was historical: Was the development of democracy identical with the progress of civilization? The other was more fundamental, concerning the relations between religion and philosophy. After examining Tocqueville's response to these two questions, we will be better equipped to understand the nature of the "new political science" he wished to construct.

American Society and Democratic Society: A Difficult Distinction

First, however, I want to consider a question that must be answered if volume two of *Democracy in America* is to be properly understood. Many commentators have found it difficult to decide how much of Tocqueville's thought concerns America alone and how much is valid for democratic society in general. Raymond Aron pointed out the ambiguity of volume two in this respect.[12] Nevertheless, I think that analysis of the text is useful in reducing uncertainty to a minimum.

Upon opening volume two, the reader is struck by the fact that the chapter titles often refer to America or Americans (in nearly thirty out of seventy-five cases), whereas the actual text distinguishes much less frequently between the American and the general case. It might seem that some titles, not justified by the contents of the chapter to which they apply, were chosen solely for rhetorical effect or perhaps to attract "that class of readers that wants mainly to know America." It may even appear, at first sight, that the distinctions are less clearly established than in volume one, which stressed the singularity of the American "point of departure" and the exceptional quality of American popular education and mores.[13] There, in his search for the "principal causes that tend to maintain the democratic republic in the United States,"[14] the author had separated out the accidental, or purely American, causes, such as the absence of neighbors and of a major capital, religion, dynamism, the frontier, and the country's general prosperity.

Volume two of *Democracy in America* demands a more attentive reading, for the distinctions it makes are less sharply delineated. Tocqueville quite often hints at more than he actually says, and, in constructing his ideal type of democracy, he sometimes borrows—very discreetly—traits from French society.[15] Furthermore, the final chapters of the book, from chapter twenty of part three on, are exclusively devoted to the tendencies of democratic societies, and America is no longer mentioned.[16]

By contrast, part one describes the differences between the intellectual attitudes of Americans and those characteristic of democratic society as such. For instance, the reason why Cartesian philosophy, despite its essentially democratic nature, is less widely accepted by Americans than by the French has to do with two specific features of American history: the fundamental role of Puritanism in the inception of Anglo-American society; and the fact that "the Americans have a democratic social state and a democratic constitution, but they have not had a democratic revolution."[17] Intellectual as well as emotional individualism is thus democratic in both origin and essence, but it is exacerbated by revolution.[18]

At the end of the chapter on Catholicism in the United States is a passage of great importance. In future democratic societies, Tocqueville says, men will exhibit just two attitudes toward religion: either they will be Catholics or they will not be Christians.[19] In other words, the Protestant churches have no future; they represent a passing phase in the religious history of mankind. In opposition to a widely held theory, Tocqueville denied the existence of an essential link between Puritanism and democracy. A few pages later, he notes that Americans are less drawn to the theater than other democratic peoples because of Puritan prohibitions.[20] But any affinities between the peculiar features of Protestant sects and American democracy is purely a matter of historical accident. The deepest justification of democratic society lies in a kind of moral universalism which more logically accords with the universalism of the Roman Catholic Church.

As for science, letters, and the arts in the United States, the situation is "entirely exceptional,"[21] because America has reaped the benefits of English culture without having had to produce it. The American evidence by no means proves that democratic peoples are unfit for culture, although Tocqueville does say that they have no literature,[22] and that utilitarian ends take precedence over truth and beauty.[23] Utilitarianism is of necessity a pronounced characteristic of democratic societies, but Tocqueville remarks that "the Americans in this respect exhibit to an excessive degree a tendency that will, I believe, be found, although to a lesser degree, in all democratic peoples."[24] The author also noted that the military burdens of the Americans were exceptionally light[25] and that almost all farmers owned the land they farmed. "America is therefore unique in this as in other respects, and it would be a mistake to take it as an example."[26]

It is possible to distinguish between the characteristics of American society and those of democratic societies in general, particularly in the first part of volume two. But difficulties mount in parts two and three, where Tocqueville deals with sentiments and mores, relying on the United States as virtually his sole example of a democratic society.

His contemporaries did the same thing. The chapters which seemed most descriptive to the readers of 1840 were those devoted to the American family and national character.[27] But even in the chapters dealing with women and the family,[28] Tocqueville combined philosophical reflection with factual reportage. "Democracy," he wrote, "loosens social bonds but tightens natural bonds."[29] When he says that democracy softens the mores of a society, we may wonder whether he is describing American mores or elaborating the ideas of Roussseau.[30] After chapter eighteen of part three, however, no further doubt is possible: the remaining chapters concern democratic societies in general, for war, revolution, and centralization are subjects of little relevance to the United States of the 1830s.

With the foregoing remarks I do not claim to have eliminated all the ambiguities, but only to have circumscribed the problem. The difficulties are greatest in part two, for in parts one and three Tocqueville is careful to emphasize the bonds between America and England— boldly at the beginning of the book, where he notes the unique position of intellectual life in the United States, and more discreetly but still clearly in the middle. To be sure, the final chapters of part three are very general,[31] but they are obviously concerned with democratic societies in the distant future, which leaves no room for ambiguity. But a French reader under the July Monarchy would have had no trouble interpreting part two as a liberal political program advocating return to the principles of the Charter, rejection of the laws of 1834 and 1835, freedom of the press and of association, and, more generally, broader political freedoms. The most "American" chapters of part two have a strong French orientation and hint at policies to be adopted in the immediate future. To understand them properly, we must answer the following question: To what extent were the political practices that had made America successful valid as a model for other democratic societies? Could they be transferred to France? I shall return to this question in the next chapter.

Democracy and Civilization

During his travels in America Tocqueville made the following notation in his diary: "Why, when civilization spreads, do prominent men diminish? Why, when knowledge becomes the common possession of all, do great minds become rarer? Why, when there is no longer a lower class, is there no longer an upper class either? Why, when the masses obtain knowledge of government, does society lack great geniuses to guide it? America places these questions squarely on the agenda. But who can answer them?"[32] Tocqueville was far from being the only person who was convinced that America had seen its finest hour in the Revolutionary War. Indeed, it was a commonplace among Frenchmen under the July Monarchy that American civilization had been on the decline since the end of the eighteenth century.[33] Did Tocqueville at least provide an original interpretation of the theme of democracy and civilization?

The manuscripts contain pessimistic reflections which in the end their author did not wish to make public. At moments he feared a return of barbarism: "Save ourselves from a new invasion of barbarians. The barbarians are already at our gates, and we amuse ourselves with talk."[34] He also wrote: "This time the barbarians will not come from the frozen North; they will rise in the bosom of our countryside and in the midst of our cities."[35] Was this no more than a banal rhetorical exercise, soon abandoned? Or was it a consequence of identifying, symbolically and historically, the barbarian invasions with revolution, as Gaetano Mosca has so ably done?[36] Tocqueville went so far as to relate the theme to a general theory of development: "Influence of democracy on mores and ideas. Influence of the progress of equality on the human intelligence. Disappearance of the intellectual classes, of theoretical talents; possible return to barbarism in this way, everyone being absorbed by practical concerns."[37]

Nothing like such an extreme fear of a return to barbarism appears in volume one of *Democracy in America*. Schleifer, who was the first to point this out in a particularly original chapter of his book, gives no explanation for it.[38] Why did Tocqueville censor or correct himself? Probably because in 1835 he no longer feared revolution so intensely as his correspondence shows he did in 1831 and 1832.[39] Tocqueville worried seriously about a return to barbarism only when the democratic movement in France seemed likely to assume a violent and uncontrolled form, with the outbreak of revolution and civil war. The final text, published in 1835, after the riots of 1832 and 1834 had faded in memory, uses the term "barbarism" only in a manner worthy of Condorcet: Tocqueville speaks of the barbarism of the Middle Ages, of feudal barbarism.[40] And in the preparatory notes for volume two, Schleifer has found the following observation, which contrasts sharply with the diary notes: "Equality of conditions seems to me very apt to hasten the progress of the human spirit."[41] On the whole, Tocqueville's fear of a return to barbarism in the period 1831–1835 reflects his fear of new revolutions far more than his doubts about civilization in America or in other democratic societies yet to come.

NEVERTHELESS, VOLUME TWO was not free of doubts about the future of civilization, doubts that were expressed in the most solemn terms in the final lines of the book: "The nations of our day cannot prevent conditions of equality from spreading in their midst. But it depends upon themselves whether equality is to lead to servitude or freedom, knowledge or barbarism, prosperity or wretchedness." In this final flight of rhetoric Tocqueville was probably more emphatic than he needed to be in order to convey an accurate impression of his thinking. Other passages show, however, that his fears, if they had not altogether disappeared, had changed considerably; fear of a violent return of barbarism, of a kind of invasion that would destroy civilization, diminished as the threat of revolution in France abated. Only then did the enduring risks of democracy emerge: stagnation and even, if certain initiatives were not taken, decadence.[42]

By breaking down stable, traditional bonds, democracy isolates individuals and weakens the resistance not only of the social fabric but of individuals themselves; this, Tocqueville says, is because "feelings and ideas are renewed, the heart expands, and the human mind advances only through reciprocal action of man upon man."[43] In democratic countries, therefore, all progress depends on knowledge of association, and if the importance of this veritable *science-mère*[44] is neglected, regression may result: "In order for men to remain civilized or to become so, they must develop or perfect the art of association in proportion as the equality of conditions increases."[45] Otherwise the transition from aristocracy to democracy may lead to barbarism: "A people among whom private individuals lost the power to do great things on their own without acquiring the faculty to do them together would quickly return to barbarism."[46] Thus the art of association is not, as is sometimes said, merely a way of creating new intermediary bodies, a substitute for the political function of the aristocracy of old—namely, to resist the central authorities—but, more fundamentally, a prerequisite for progress and, indeed, for the maintenance of civilization. Struggle against the errors of individualism is necessary for safeguarding political freedom. In the intellectual and moral sphere as well, associations have an equally important role to play in the preservation of civilization. Should they fail in this role, civilized society would begin to regress, making democratic government impossible: liberal democracy would degenerate into despotism. "Democratic government, which is based on such a simple and natural idea, nevertheless presupposes the existence of a highly civilized and highly educated society. At first one might think that democratic government existed from the beginning of the world, but upon taking a closer look it is easy to see that it could only come toward the end."[47]

From Guizot's lectures Tocqueville had borrowed an idea of the advance of civilization along with the notion that the reign of the middle classes in France was the culmination of the most recent stage of progress. But the first few chapters of volume two make it clear that he no longer shared the confident optimism of the doctrinaire historian. Even a democratic society which had developed the capacity to associate could stagnate, Tocqueville believed, because democracy and intellectual freedom are not necessarily linked. Having denounced the tyranny of the majority in volume one,[48] he showed early in volume two "how the operation of certain laws of democracy would extinguish the intellectual freedom that the democratic social state encourages, in such a way that the human mind, having thrown off the shackles formerly imposed upon it by classes or individuals, would firmly chain itself to the general will of the greatest number."[49] In democratic societies, intellectual conformity, coupled with the paramount influence of practical affairs on intellectual life to the detriment of basic research, threatens to stifle intellectual progress, much as it was stifled in China.[50] Guizot had linked the progress of civilization to the growth and eventual dominance of the middle classes. By contrast, Tocqueville believed that the attitudes and passions of the middle classes, invested mainly in business, would distract democratic societies from the need for major intellectual and moral innovations and even social progress.[51] This might lead to stagnation, camouflaged by the constant bustle and the taste for innovation of a secondary order,[52] "such that mankind will arrest its progress and limit its aims, bend its spirit and turn ever inward upon itself without producing new ideas; man will wear himself out in small, isolated, and sterile actions; and though constantly in motion, humanity will cease to advance."[53]

The democratic social state makes great intellectual and moral revolutions unlikely. As for culture, Tocqueville, in his great chapter on revolution, links the democratic spirit to sterile conformism and utilitarianism and expresses the fear that great innovations leading to major progress for mankind are becoming as rare as great intellectual and moral revolutions.

But this is a risk that can be avoided, not a certainty. What is more, intelligence and culture are highly appreciated by democratic societies, so that the number of people who cultivate the arts, letters, and sciences will increase, as will intellectual activities of all kinds. Natural inequalities will tend to create not a fixed intellectual aristocracy,[54] but a "multitude of opulent or well-to-do individuals" with sufficient leisure to pursue activities of the mind.[55] These views, expressed quite early in volume two, reveal a Tocqueville markedly more optimistic in 1840 than he had been between 1831 and 1835. He refuses to believe that evolution toward democratic society inevitably means decadence, yet he seems to think that the most likely outcome is some sort of stagnation. Perhaps he also wanted to repudiate overly conservative interpretations of his work. In any case, he is determined to distance himself from those who condemn the future of culture in democracy on the basis of the American example. American culture is unique because of its Puritan and English origins,[56] and it would be idle to attempt to draw any general conclusions from a study of cultural life in the United

States.[57] In the final analysis, the effects of equality on culture are ambivalent; they can lead to either decadence or progress,[58] or, more likely, to an equilibrium in which a multitude of disorganized actions will cancel one another out.

Mill criticized Tocqueville for having confused, at least in appearance, the effects of democracy with those of civilization.[59] But the passages just examined make it clear, I think, that Tocqueville carefully distinguished progress toward a democratic society from the progress of civilization. Unlike equality, whose effects Tocqueville believed to be ambivalent, he held that liberty was a necessary condition for progress, whose effects were always positive.[60]

Philosophy and Religion

Tocqueville's idea of progress is difficult to pin down. His chapter on the "idea of the infinite perfectibility of man"[61] does not give an adequate idea of his thinking on the subject. Tocqueville's view of this fundamental Enlightenment doctrine is best approached by way of his thoughts on the relation between philosophy and religion and on the nature of political science.

But before examining the sections of *Democracy in America* that deal with philosophy and religion, I want to pause a moment to consider Tocqueville's ideas about metaphysics. These are better expressed in letters than in his published works. In particular, two of his letters— one written at the beginning and the other at the end of his intellectual life—give an idea of the atmosphere in which he wrote his major works.

From Philadelphia on 22 October 1831, Tocqueville wrote to one of his friends:

> Life is neither a pleasure nor a pain but a serious business which is thrust upon us and which it is our duty to discharge as well as we possibly can . . . I have derived great inner strength from this idea . . . When I began to reflect, I thought that the world was full of proven truths and that one had only to look in order to discover what they were, but when I set myself to studying particular objects, I saw nothing but insuperable doubts. I cannot tell you . . . what a horrible state this discovery left me in.[62] This was the unhappiest time of my life. I can only compare myself to a man who, seized by dizziness, believes that the floor is giving way beneath his feet and that the walls are shaking all around him. Even today I look back upon that time

with horror. I can say that I then fought hand-to-hand with doubt, and that few have done so in greater despair.[63] Ah! Ultimately I convinced myself that the quest for absolute, demonstrable truth, like the search for perfect happiness, was an effort to achieve the impossible. Not that there are no truths worthy of man's entire conviction; but be assured that they are few in number. As for the immense majority of things about which we need to know, we have only probabilities, approximations. To despair that things are so is to despair of being a man, for that is one of the most inflexible laws of our nature. Does it follow that man must never act because he is never sure of anything? That is not my view. When I have a decision to make, I carefully weigh the pros and cons, and rather than despair of my inability to convince myself fully, I proceed straight toward the goal that seems to me the most probable, and I proceed as though I had no doubt at all. I act in this way because experience has taught me that on the whole it is better to set out with a quick and vigorous step on the wrong path than to waver in uncertainty or act feebly.[64]

One must therefore accept the fact that proof can rarely be achieved. But, you will object, whatever one does, it is a painful thing to take risks when in doubt. I certainly view doubt as one of the great afflictions of our nature, second only to disease and death.[65] But it is because I have that opinion of it that I do not understand why so many people impose it upon themselves gratuitously and for no purpose. That is why I have always considered metaphysics and all the purely theoretical sciences, which are useless for the realities of life, as voluntary torments that man deliberately inflicts upon himself.[66]

What, then, were those few proven truths of which Tocqueville was entirely convinced and which he deemed indispensable? Another letter, to his friend the philosopher Louis-Firmin Bouchitté,[67] dated 8 January 1858, answers this question specifically:

I would have taken a passionate interest in the philosophical studies that have occupied all your life had I been able to derive more profit from them.[68] But whether from deficiency of mind, lack of courage in pursuing my plans, or the peculiar nature of the subject matter, I always reached a point where I found that all the notions that the sciences provided me took me no farther, and frequently took me less far, than I had reached at once with the aid of a small number of very simple ideas, which indeed all men have more or less grasped. These ideas lead easily to belief in a first cause, which remains utterly evident and utterly inconceivable; to the fixed laws which the physical world allows us to see and which we must assume to exist in the moral world; to the Providence of God, hence to His justice; and to the responsibility of man, who has been allowed to know that there is good and evil, hence another life. I confess to you that, beyond this revelation, I have never found that the subtlest metaphysics provided me with clearer notions on these matters than the crudest common sense, and this made me rather ill disposed toward it. What I have called the bottom that I cannot touch is the why of the world, the plan of this creation, of which we know nothing, not even our bodies, let alone our minds; the reason for the destiny of that singular being that we call man, who has been granted just enough enlightenment to see the wretchedness of his condition but not enough to change it . . . That is the bottom, or rather, those are the bottoms which my mind would like to touch but which will always remain infinitely beyond my means of knowing the truth.[69]

That is Tocqueville's philosophy, Cartesian in its origin and principal conclusions but even more Pascalian in its anguish over the limits of reason. Like Pascal, whom Victor Cousin, the leading philosopher of the July Monarchy, presented as a skeptic, Tocqueville, encouraged by his friend and cousin Louis de Kergorlay, had learned to reason in terms of probabilities.[70] The letters just cited speak for themselves, although they fail to make clear Tocqueville's belief that the knowledge necessary for practical choice among probabilities can come only from subtlety, experience (above all, practical experience), and history. The letter to Bouchitté uses the word "philosophy" in a very narrow sense, in keeping with the following definition from a draft of *Democracy in America*: "Self-contained exercise of thought, distinct from practice and action."[71] This was no doubt the meaning that Bouchitté attached to the term, but Tocqueville's philosophical vision was infinitely broader; in addition to the Cartesian foundations just mentioned and the elements of praxeology borrowed from Pascal and Kergorlay, which had more to do with the art of politics than with practical philosophy as such, it also embraced history, which for Tocqueville meant the history of ideas more than the history of events.

Tocqueville constantly questioned himself, his age, and history concerning the moral and political consequences of Christianity and the revolution it had produced in man's ideas of freedom and equality. In ethical matters Tocqueville's positions are quite clear, but in religion he is uncertain. His doubts were not assuaged, as Descartes's had been, by the God of philosophers and scientists, and if his anxieties were alleviated, like Pascal's, by divine revelation, this happened only in his final moments.[72]

Always professing a kind of spiritualism,[73] he seems not to have accepted all of Catholic theology, but he did subscribe to the essential tenets of Christian ethics. His passion for the good as well as his scruples, doubts, and inability to settle for what he called unbelief give his spiritual struggles a Pascalian cast. Nevertheless, in his published work he does not deal with theology or even religion, but only with the political and moral functions of religion. All that he wrote on the subject might have been prefaced with this warning, which Montesquieu placed at the head of book twenty-four of *Esprit des lois*: "I shall therefore examine the various religions of the world only with respect to the good that is derived from them in the civil state, whether speaking of what is rooted in heaven or what springs from the earth. Since in this work I am not a theologian but a political writer, it may contain things that are not entirely true except according to a human way of thinking, not having been considered in relation to more sublime truths."

From the beginning of *Democracy in America*, Tocqueville praises the Americans for their marvelous ability to combine "the spirit of religion" with "the spirit of freedom": "Far from harming each other, these two apparently opposed tendencies work in harmony and seem to lend mutual support. Religion regards civil liberty as a noble exercise of men's faculties, the world of politics being a sphere intended by the Creator for the free play of intelligence. Religion, being free and powerful within its own sphere and content with the position reserved for it, realizes that its sway is all the better established because it relies only on its own powers and rules men's hearts without external support. Freedom sees religion as the companion of its struggles and triumphs, the cradle of its infancy, and the divine source of its rights. Religion is considered the guardian of mores, and mores are regarded as the guarantee of the laws and a pledge for the maintenance of freedom itself."[74]

Tocqueville admired this alliance of the spirit of religion with the spirit of freedom, but like all liberals he also believed in the need for separation of Church and State. The Christian religion contains the "divine source" of the rights of man.[75] Unfortunately, at the time Tocqueville was discovering America, many French liberals, still under the influence of the early Idéologues, were either hostile to or ignorant of Christianity. Tocqueville, who despaired over this state of affairs, gave a historical explanation of the divorce in France between the religious and the liberal spirit: "Through a conspiracy of peculiar events, religion temporarily became enmeshed with the authority that democracy overthrew, often repudiating the equality that it loves and condemning liberty as an adversary, whereas by joining hands it might have sanctified its strivings."[76] In the final years of the Restoration antireligious sentiment had peaked, and by the time Tocqueville wrote volume one the pendulum had begun to swing the other way.[77] Tocqueville's great project at this time was to reconcile religion with the values of 1789, as he confessed to his friend Stoffels in a letter written on 24 July 1836:[78] "What has always struck me in my country, but even more so in the past few years, was the sight of the men who prized morality, religion, and order lined up on one side and those who loved freedom and equality before the law lined up on the other. I found this spectacle one of the most extraordinary and deplorable ever to have been witnessed by the eyes of man, for all the things that we thus separate are, I am certain, indissolubly linked in the eyes of God. They are all holy things, if I may express myself in such terms, because man cannot achieve greatness and happiness in the world unless all are combined. From that time on I have believed that one of the noblest enterprises of our time would be to show that these things are not incompatible; that, on the contrary, they are joined together by a necessary bond, such that each one is weakened by being severed from the others."[79]

By 1843, however, in a letter to his brother Edouard,[80] Tocqueville was forced to concede that such a reconciliation would have to be put off for years through the fault of the clergy, who, not content with freedom of education, wanted the Church to control the schools. After Louis Napoleon's coup d'état, Tocqueville was disgusted by the fawning of the French clergy, whom he accused of having encouraged the Pharisees while avoiding true political commitment, using religion and personal salvation as a pretext. Tocqueville's letters to Madame Swetchine, his confidante in these years,[81] show that he expected the clergy to set the example for more liberal, more meaningful civic education. He feared that misguided and exclusive religious passions would destroy public virtues.[82]

Nevertheless, in his book on the Old Regime, Tocqueville admitted that he had overcome some of his old prejudices against the French clergy when he discovered that they possessed what he prized above all else: great public virtues.[83] He continued, however, to believe that Christianity's greatest weakness was the ease with which it was able to neglect the civic virtues: "The duties of men to one another as citizens, the citizen's obligations to the fatherland, seem to me poorly defined and relatively neglected in Christian ethics. That, it seems to me, is the weak point of that admirable moral system, just as it was the only really strong point of ancient morality."[84] So Tocqueville wrote to Joseph-Arthur de Gobineau; in letters exchanged by the two men in 1843 and 1844, Tocqueville confronts his correspondent's attacks, ready to cast himself in the role of defender of Christian morality as long as its principal defect is recognized.

> I am not a believer (which I scarcely say to praise myself); yet unbeliever that I am, I have never been able to prevent myself from feeling a profound emotion upon reading the Gospel. Several of its teachings, which are among the most important, have always struck me as absolutely new, and, even more, the whole constitutes something quite different from the corpus of philosophical and moral ideas that previously governed human societies. I cannot conceive that in reading this admirable book, your soul did not, like mine, rejoice in drawing its breath from a vaster, purer atmosphere.[85]

What is more, the moral value of the Gospel has by no means been exhausted in the modern era:

> The most notable moral innovation of the moderns consists, I think, in the prodigious development and novel reformulation of two ideas that Christianity had already brought to the fore: namely, the equal right of all men to the goods of this world, and the duty of those who have more to come to the aid of those who have less . . . Christianity made benevolence—or, as Christians call it, charity—a private virtue. We make it increasingly a social duty, a political obligation, a public virtue . . . In this way, a social and political morality has been established which the ancients understood imperfectly at best and which is a combination of the political ideas of antiquity and the moral notions of Christianity.[86]

Here we encounter, in a new form, what I earlier called the principle of continuity, by which Tocqueville set great store. It was this principle that guided him in his search for an equilibrium;[87] "Christianity is the great source of modern morality," and conversely, modern morality "is Christianity applied in a more enlightened world, through different political forms, to a different social state. In short, these are new consequences derived from an ancient principle."[88]

In his September 1843 letter to Gobineau, Tocqueville described the threefold moral transformation accomplished by Christianity:

It altered the relative positions of the virtues. Rude and savage virtues had headed the list; Christianity placed them at the end. Gentle virtues, such as humanity, pity, indulgence, and even forgiveness of injuries were last; it placed them ahead of all the others. That was the first change. The realm of duties had been limited. Christianity extended it. Scarcely did it embrace the citizens of one city. Christianity made it embrace all mankind. It had encompassed primarily the masters; Christianity included the slaves. It placed in a blinding light equality, unity, and human fraternity: that was the second change. The sanction of moral laws had been more in this world than in the other. Christianity placed the purpose of *life* after life and thus gave morality a purer, more immaterial, more disinterested, higher nature: that was the last change.[89]

After this veritable moral revolution, the changes introduced by modern morality appear not as genuine innovations but rather as signs of the weakening of religious faith.[90] In the final analysis, Tocqueville was willing to accept the moral content of the French Revolution because he saw it as a consequence of the Christian revolution.[91]

ALTHOUGH TOCQUEVILLE STATES clearly and frequently that Christianity lent an immense impetus to the sentiment of equality, he does not state as directly that it gave men freedom.[92] He can readily conceive of the idea of moral equality, whose relations with Christian morality he was able to elucidate. The idea of liberty, moral and political, was always at the center of his thought; but rarely do we find him reflecting on spiritual liberty as it relates to Christianity. Indeed, it is striking that his most philosophical reflections on democracy and religion, in the first two sections of volume two, are based not on the teachings of the Christian revelation but on the idea of God and that of a responsible and immortal soul.[93] A man like Jefferson would have found nothing repugnant in these pages, and one cannot help thinking that despite his Pascalian outlook, Tocqueville, at the time he wrote *Democracy in America,* had encountered only "the God of the philosophers and scientists."

Nor is he definite about the fate of religion in the democracies of the future. He confines himself to a remark that can only increase the uncertainty of his readers as to his true feelings: "Our nephews will increasingly divide into just two camps, some abandoning Christianity entirely, the rest joining the Roman Church."[94] Since democracies need religion, and establishing new religions is out of the question,[95] he believed that, in the absence of faith, external adherence to Christianity was, for political reasons, the least unsatisfactory solution. Two interpretations of *Democracy in America* are therefore supported by the text: one philosophical, advocating respect for established religions inspired by Christian morality, and the other Catholic, with the stipulation that Church and State remain separate.[96] Tocqueville was unwilling and perhaps unable to resolve this question, which touched on his personal doubts. It seems likely (although on such a question one cannot be certain) that his own interpretation was closer to the first; the second amounted to a hope rather than a prognosis for mankind as well as for himself. His philosophical reflections cannot conceal his fundamental doubts, which were ultimately responsible for his vacillation between, on the one hand, justifying democratic Christianity on grounds of historical continuity and morality and, on the other hand, suggesting that religion in the future would be merely another name for the values upon which social consensus was based. For his own time and the immediate future, he championed the first view.

As for the second view, a dangerous germ, possibly fatal to freedom of thought, lurks within it: the tyranny of public opinion. Indeed, in democratic societies, "faith in public opinion will become a sort of religion, of which the majority will be the prophet."[97] The power of this collective consciousness is evoked in terms that anticipate Durkheim: "An immense pressure of the spirit of all on the mind of each."[98] Unlike Durkheim, however, Tocqueville did not believe that society worships itself; given the current state of mankind, he believed that the Christian religion was the best guarantee of freedom of thought, provided that Church and State were kept strictly separate. For not only did Christianity unite men around their highest shared values, it also protected each individual from the pressure of the group by recognizing that each person has a unique spiritual destiny. Tocqueville was the first to show that unless democracy was supported by some higher ideal, it would run a constant risk of degenerating into ideology. Like the prophets before him, he called upon religion to smash the idols of the day and to combat the tendency of the majority to ascribe to itself unlimited authority.

IN THE FIRST few chapters of volume two, Tocqueville not only extends the analysis of the tyranny of the majority begun in volume one but also broaches the new theme of individualism, which he acknowledges to be both valuable and dangerous. The first chapter, "On the Philosophical Method of the Americans," is a splendid opening that sheds new light on the ideological problems of modern democracies and provides a sociological interpretation of Western culture since the Reformation.[99] This is the true introduction to the work and, in particular, to part one, which is entirely devoted to studies in the sociology of democratic cultures. According to Tocqueville, the chief characteristic of democratic thought is individualism: "Each man withdraws deep into himself and from there pretends to judge the world."[100]

Spontaneously, and without necessarily having heard of Descartes, the Americans had adopted his philosophical method. Tocqueville traces the history of the method of individual self-scrutiny from Luther to Descartes and beyond, to the philosophers of the eighteenth century, who, unlike Descartes, were no longer content to apply it only to philosophical questions but fashioned from it a weapon for use in political combat. Tocqueville then offers a sociological explanation: this method "was discovered in an era when men were becoming increasingly equal and similar. It could be brought into wide use only in centuries when conditions had at last become approximately similar and men almost identical. The philosophical method of the eighteenth century is therefore not only French but democratic, which explains why it was so readily accepted throughout Europe, whose face it did so much to change."[101] Even if people in America do not study Descartes, the United States is the country where his precepts are most closely followed.[102] In France, Descartes's heirs had moved a long way from their master's teachings.

Why did philosophical individualism remain democratic in America, whereas in France it was transformed into revolutionary philosophy? To this fundamental question Tocqueville provides several answers, some more fully developed than others. At the end of the first chapter he makes a crucial point, which shows why he thought that the United States was an exception among democracies: "The Americans have a democratic social state and constitution, but they have not had a democratic revolution."[103] Now, a revolution necessarily increases the effects of democratic individualism.[104] What remains to be explained, however, is why eighteenth-century philosophy took a revolutionary turn in France (even before the Revolution) but not in America. Two answers are given: first, religion was a stronger counterweight in America than in France;[105] and second, the French liked to treat political problems in terms of general ideas, whereas the Americans did not.[106] The second point is quite far-reaching in its implications, as Raymond Aron has pointed out,[107] and Tocqueville believed in it strongly enough to include and amplify it in his *Old Regime*:[108] "The Americans form a democratic people which has always taken charge of public affairs itself,"[109] whereas the French had long been handicapped because "our political constitution still prevented us [in the eighteenth century] from rectifying these ideas through experience."[110] But volume one, especially in its concluding chapter, had shown that in politics, above all "true enlightenment is born of experience."[111]

In a democratic society, intellectual individualism may take different forms; it may exhibit either a liberal or a revolutionary cast. The problem (which Tocqueville took from Royer-Collard) was to distinguish between them. Tocqueville gives his answer in the first five chapters of volume two—especially in chapter two, where he shows that the proper use of liberty requires recognition of its limits, and in chapter five, where he attempts to define those limits.[112] "For my part," he wrote, "I doubt that man can ever tolerate both complete religious independence and full political freedom at the same time; and I am inclined to believe that he who has no faith must serve and he who is free must believe."[113] Democracies, just as much as other regimes, must be able to call upon intellectual and moral authority; the only questions are, how much authority, and where should it be located: in public opinion, philosophy, or religion?[114] For the sake of intellectual freedom it is essential that public opinion, with all its fluctuations and enthusiasms, not be the sole arbiter; it is equally essential that the liberal spirit not suddenly[115] cast doubt upon the historic fund of basic values upon which the social and political order rests. By contrast, the revolutionary spirit ignores the significance of duration and does not hesitate to destroy authority, for it nourishes the illusion that authority can easily be recreated through the instantaneous fusion of individual wills. In America, philosophical individualism remained liberal in spirit. In France, political inexperience and the philosophers' opposition to the legacy of the past, especially religion, transformed the Cartesian method into a revolutionary implement.

Might the Americans be better Cartesians than the French? In conduct, yes, says Tocqueville;[116] and the first few chapters of volume two clearly show that, for him, eighteenth-century philosophy represented a distortion of Descartes's thought. Yet the Yale manuscripts[117] show a good deal of indecisiveness in the writing of these chapters, which Tocqueville began in 1836 and revised in 1838. Much of the rewriting concerned the question of relations between philosophy and religion.[118] Tocqueville's most serious doubts, I think, concerned eighteenth-century French philosophy, about which he says that, "leaving aside its anti-Christian passions, which were only an accident . . . it was not French but democratic."[119] But a few pages later on he says: "The eighteenth century exalted the individual . . . It was revolution, not democracy . . . The philosophy of the eighteenth century was more revolutionary than democratic. Scrutinize it for what was revolutionary and what was democratic."[120] Inspired by Royer-Collard, this scrutiny led to the recasting, in 1838, of the early chapters of volume two. Individualism, which in 1836 Tocqueville had seen as revolutionary, now assumed a dual significance: ordinarily it was democratic, but in excessive amounts it became revolutionary. Ultimately, Tocqueville in volume two took the position that eighteenth-century French philosophy was democratic,[121] and he delineated the precise circumstances that prevented it from taking a revolutionary turn in America.[122] In France, however, these restraints were absent, and the lack of political freedom transformed the philosophical method into an impassioned but abstract revolutionary ideology.[123] Subsequently, the Revolution itself aggravated the instability of ideas and beliefs.[124]

"A New Political Science"

In a speech that Tocqueville delivered in 1853, near the end of his life, to the annual public meeting of the Academy of Moral and Political Sciences, he defined political science in terms of its subject, the behavior of societies; its foundations, political philosophy and history; and its hierarchical structure, ranging "from the general to the particular, and from pure theory toward written laws and facts."[125] The first section of volume two contains chapters of very different levels of generality, which are not ordered in the best possible way; nevertheless, it is easy to identify their philosophical framework and, from chapters one, eight, and twenty, to reconstruct the theoretical foundations of Tocqueville's political science.

First, it is clear to Tocqueville that the faults of the historians of the democratic age are the opposite of those encouraged by individualist philosophizing. Whereas the latter encourages excessive intellectual and moral freedom, the historians underestimate the role of individuals in history and overemphasize general causes in their explanations. What is more, "they deprive . . . nations themselves of the ability to alter their own fate and subject them either to an inflexible Providence or to a kind of blind fate."[126] To democratic man the great democratic revolution and the forward march of progress seem irresistible. But for Tocqueville neither of these is necessary as such. To be sure, society will inevitably become increasingly egalitarian. This can lead either to the reign of freedom or to a new form of servitude. Looking back to the past, moreover, there was no reason why the French Revolution had to follow the course that it did, despite the claims of some historians. Furthermore, increasing equality and enlightenment could result in either progress or stagnation, perhaps even in a new form of barbarism.

The chapter on progress is therefore central; here Tocqueville treats individualism in philosophy and history,[127] the twin pillars (in his view) on which political science must rest. At the beginning of the chapter, moreover, he points out that "the idea of human perfectibility . . . is in itself a great philosophical theory,"[128] one of those great ideas that political science can grasp at more than one level of generality— not only in philosophical and historical terms but also in relation to everyday life, for its "consequences can be seen constantly in practical affairs."[129] He then gives a political critique of the theory of progress, which in many respects anticipates modern methods in the sociology of knowledge: "Aristocratic nations are naturally inclined to restrict the limits of human perfectibility unnecessarily, while democratic nations sometimes extend them unreasonably."[130] Because man's confidence in himself attains its maximum in great revolutions,[131] it is easy to see how Tocqueville read Condorcet.[132] He accepted Condorcet's ideas about the future of equality, but he did not believe in certain progress and would never have written, as Condorcet did, that "all signs suggest that the human race will not relapse into its barbarism of old."[133] He distinguished, in fact, between moral and political progress, on the one hand, and the progress of science, on the other, and thus would have opposed the Condorcet who wrote: "All errors in politics and morals stem from philosophical errors, which are themselves linked to physical errors."[134] Unfortunately, Tocqueville did not pay sufficient attention to progress in science and technology, a failure which contributed to his excessively static view of democracies, but he was quite right to see accident where Condorcet saw only necessity. His purpose was not to combat all the theses of Condorcet and his disciples, the Idéologues, but rather to correct the course of the Idéologue movement, with which in many respects he himself was associated.[135] Condorcet and

Tocqueville both belonged to the enlightened, liberal aristocracy, imbued with the spirit of 1789; but the former gave voice to the revolutionary spirit, whereas the latter hoped to define the true spirit of democracy. Like Royer-Collard, Tocqueville believed that the essential thing was to distinguish between the liberal and the revolutionary spirit and to show that, in politics, knowledge does not come from abstract reasoning based on the model of the natural sciences. He never tired of pointing out that "true enlightenment is born of experience."[136]

Auguste Comte, in his *Plan for Scientific Works Necessary for the Reorganization of Society,* attempted to build on the work of Montesquieu and Condorcet in order to make politics a science.[137] Unlike Tocqueville, he accepted Condorcet's idea of continuous progress stemming from advances in knowledge, but he reproached Condorcet for not having repudiated the critical philosophy of the eighteenth century, a point on which he was rather close to Tocqueville. The founder of positivism shared with the author of *Democracy in America* the project of establishing a new political science to guide society out of the transitional period, to which the former referred as the "age of criticism" and the latter as the age of the "great democratic revolution." But one was the prophet of the scientific age and the other of the democratic age. Tocqueville refused to link moral progress to scientific progress, and in this respect he diverged from positivism. To the end of his life he pondered the failure of the Enlightenment to establish or even to conceptualize political liberty.[138] His judgment was not nearly so negative as that of Burke, however. He carried on in the critical tradition of eighteenth-century philosophy: the first part of volume two examines the conditions under which the intelligence can function properly in a democratic society, as well as the danger that it will fall under the sway of some ideology. At the heart of his new political science[139] he placed freedom; his conception of history, unlike that of the positivists, had room for risk. And the first object of the new political science was to distinguish between democracy and revolution, between the liberal spirit and the revolutionary spirit.

7 ✣ Prosperity or Misery

The Birth of Individualism

By studying Tocqueville's working manuscript in the Yale archives, Schleifer could pinpoint his first use of the term "individualism" in volume two.[1] It occurs in a note dated 24 April 1837 in the margins of the chapter on the "philosophical method of the Americans." In this note the author raises the question of a necessary equilibrium between intellectual authority and independent individual thought. As we saw in the preceding chapter, what Tocqueville feared most was intellectual conformism. In this regard, the first chapter of volume two is a continuation of Tocqueville's anxious thoughts about the "tyranny of the majority" at the end of volume one. Not only in his first work but also in his letters, Tocqueville frequently alludes to the importance of "egoism" as a characteristic of human relations in democratic societies. It is worth noting[2] that he began using the concept of individualism in place of egoism when he wanted to cast intellectual independence in a relatively favorable light.

From 1838 on, the word "individualism" becomes quite common in the manuscripts, whereas "egoism" becomes increasingly rare. By this time Tocqueville was involved in revising volume two: the first few chapters of part one and several chapters of part two. These parts focus on the intellectual and moral aspects of individualism, which is the key concept in all the analyses: as Tocqueville noted in his drafts, "Individualism has effects of two kinds, which must be distinguished and treated separately: 1) moral effects—hearts are isolated; 2) intellectual effects—minds are isolated."[3]

In the final text the order is reversed: first ideas, then feelings. In June 1838, however, Tocqueville planned to begin the work with two chapters on the influence of democracy on feelings, as this note, found among the drafts, makes clear: "Perhaps begin the whole book with chapters on individualism and the taste for material pleasures; almost everything stems from that, both in ideas and in feelings."[4] But between October and December 1838, Kergorlay came to help him with the revisions[5] and persuaded him to take a different course, as this note, dated December, shows:

> Of all the chapters which precede chapter nine, where I am now,[6] there is not one in which I have not felt the need to assume that the reader knew either what impelled democratic peoples toward individualism or what impelled them to a taste for material pleasures. The experience of these eight chapters therefore tends to prove that the two chapters on individualism and material pleasures ought to precede the rest. L. [Louis de Kergorlay] thinks that, whatever the logical reasons for beginning with those two chapters, the chapter on method must be kept at the beginning. He says it offers a splendid introduction and immediately forces the reader to take a lofty view of the subject.[7]

Note, however, that the plan finally adopted was not the one that most clearly highlights the originality of volume two as compared with volume one, whose reflections on the tyranny of the majority it seems instead to continue. But volume one dealt only with American social groups and types; the analysis of the role of the individual in volume two is entirely new. A full and clear explanation of this is not given until the beginning of part two, which somewhat diminishes the force of the innovation. Note, too, that the distinction between democratic society and revolutionary society (which exacerbates individualism), a distinction of crucial importance in both parts one and two, is less fully emphasized in the introduction than it would have been had the other plan been adopted.

What is more, when it came to the drafting of part two, Royer-Collard's influence was rivaled by that of Mill, Nassau Senior, and other economists. The structure of this part of the book is therefore more complex and perhaps less clear than it might have been.[8] Since the notion of individualism had just been discovered, this was perhaps unavoidable; the term was new and lent itself to a variety of uses.[9]

In its three most common meanings, individualism referred to (1) the doctrine of the rights of man and political liberalism; (2) economic liberalism and, more specifically, the doctrine of laissez-faire; (3) the romantic cult of personality. Joseph de Maistre and Louis de Bonald attacked this revolutionary doctrine, which, they argued, led to the atomization of society; Balzac, for his part, accused the Revolution of having altered the laws of inheritance in such a way as to destroy the family spirit. Tocqueville may also have been familiar with the Saint-Simonian use of the term.[10] Unlike the counterrevolutionaries, Tocqueville says that individualism is democratic in origin, not revolutionary.[11] To him, the ideas of the liberal economists and, at times, the more extreme ideas of the Saint-Simonians seemed to reveal a hidden danger: that public spirit would decline and politics be devalued in favor of private pursuits. In America he found not only a less pejorative use of the word "individualism" than in Europe but also a different quality in the phenomenon itself, a quality he attempted to define.[12]

According to Tocqueville, individualism can lead either to prosperity or misery, servitude or freedom. In order to understand his recommendations, his ideas about individualism must be studied in relation to democratic society, to the democratic revolution, and to economic life.[13]

Individualism and Democracy

"Individualism," Tocqueville wrote, "is a calm and considered feeling which disposes each citizen to isolate himself from the mass of his fellows and withdraw into the circle of family and friends; with this little society formed to his taste, he gladly leaves the greater society to look after itself."[14] This statement is as neutral and objective as possible. One finds no hint of revolutionary clamor or struggle or desire to put the rights of the individual above those of the society; the term seems to imply nothing more than civic indifference.

Tocqueville refuses to identify individualism as a social fact with individualism in the moral sense, which some people equate with egoism: "Egoism is a passionate and exaggerated love of self which leads a man to think of all things in terms of himself and to prefer himself to all."[15] For Tocqueville's contemporaries it was easy to accept the idea that egoism is exaggerated self-love and that self-love is a primitive passion, prior to reflective thought. Hence Tocqueville was able to distinguish between egoism and individualism in these terms:

"Egoism springs from a blind instinct; individualism is based on misguided judgment rather than depraved feeling. It is due more to inadequate understanding than to perversity of heart."[16] If individualism is based on misguided judgment, it can be dispelled by truth, whereas egoism cannot be eliminated by substituting adequate for inadequate ideas.[17] Hence it would seem that individualism is not an inevitable evil: eliminate the misguided judgment upon which it is based and it will disappear. What is this misguided judgment? Tocqueville chose to defer his answer until the end of the chapter that we are now examining, and we would do well to follow his lead, because the error of individualism does not become apparent until we know its origins and effects.

Egoism differs from individualism not only by nature but also by its effects: "Egoism sterilizes the seeds of every virtue; individualism at first only dams the spring of public virtues, but in the long run it attacks and destroys all the others too and finally merges with egoism."[18] Individualism appears first in the form of a disease of the public spirit; between egoism and individualism there is a gap created by what Rousseau called the "social contract." Egoism is a defect in the nature of the individual, individualism a defect in the nature of the citizen. Is the fundamental political problem the same for Tocqueville as it was for Rousseau, namely, to "denature man," that is, to transform the individual into the citizen? If so, the principal obstacle is none other than individualism, which "dams the spring of public virtues." But to say that individualism "finally merges with egoism" does not mean that it becomes a matter of blind instinct, but only that it takes the form of a social philosophy that justifies and masks man's natural egoism.[19] It is in this sense, and this sense only, that individualism merges with egoism. Once the public virtues are weakened, the civic spirit is abdicated altogether, and the city is no longer able to impose its moral order on man. Tocqueville's idea is that the public virtues not only contribute to the common good but also help foster and cultivate the private virtues, however distinct the two may be in theory. This thought, worthy of Rousseau and the philosophers of antiquity, stands at the heart of his work.

"Egoism," Tocqueville continues, "is a vice as old as the world. It is not peculiar to one form of society more than another. Individualism is of democratic origin and threatens to grow as conditions proceed toward equality."[20]

The authorities disagree as to the origins of modern individualism. Some trace the source to the English Revolution of 1688, others to the theories of Locke. Still others lay the blame at the door of contractualist theories and doctrines of natural law. They often see the Declaration of the Rights of Man and of the Citizen as the culmination of those doctrines. Still others look to the individualism of the Reformation or even to Christianity itself. Confusion reigns, possibly because the notion of individualism is hard to pin down. As André Lalande observed in his *Vocabulaire de la philosophie*, individualism is a "bad term, highly equivocal, whose use gives rise to continual sophisms."

Tocqueville was confronted with two dominant theories of individualism: one traced its origins to the French Revolution; the other, to England, the Reformation, the theories of Locke, and above all to liberal economics. He preferred a third theory of his own devising, based upon his experiences in the United States: that individualism originated in democracy. Once again, the distinction he makes between democracy and revolution sets him apart from other thinkers with whom his name is commonly associated.

"In aristocratically and hierarchically constituted countries, the government never directly addresses all the governed. Men being dependent upon one another, it is enough to command the first and the rest will follow."[21] Individualism has no reason to exist unless the individual as such enjoys a political existence; he acquires that existence only through belonging to a hierarchy, within which personal bonds are political bonds. Eliminate that hierarchy, destroy the intermediary bodies, and the individual is left to stand alone against the state. Gone are the concrete, vital bonds of common interest, which had held together the social and political fabric of the state. Once personal relations[22] lose the quality of being political relations in an immediate sense, political problems as such cease to be of immediate concern to individuals.

As each class of society draws closer to and mingles with other classes, its members become indifferent to one another, almost strangers. Under aristocracy, the subjects of the monarch form a long chain, which stretches from the peasant to the king; "democracy," writes Tocqueville, "breaks the chain and separates the links."[23] He sounds almost like Royer-Collard, who wrote: "We have seen the old society perish and, with it, the domestic institutions and independent magistracies that flourished within it. The Revolution left only individuals; the dictatorship that ended it consummated its work in this respect: it dissolved even the, as it were, physical association of the commune; it dispelled every trace of the magistracies, which defended the rights of which they formed the repository . . . An unprecedented spectacle: from society reduced to dust arose centralization."[24]

There can be no doubt that Tocqueville pondered deeply this idea of his primary teacher. But his thinking was original in two ways as compared with that of the illustrious Doctrinaire. What Royer-Collard sees as effects of the Revolution, Tocqueville attributes to the equalization of conditions. He does not believe that the impact of 1789 by itself "reduced society to dust." For him, individualism stems not from democratic government but from democratic society, that is, a society whose chief characteristic is equality of condition. Tocqueville believed that the French aristocracy had been losing political power since the fourteenth century and that French society was becoming increasingly democratic. In *The Old Regime* he substantiated this belief and showed how centralization, far from being born, as Royer maintains, in the Revolution, had developed through six centuries of monarchy. In treating individualism, therefore, Tocqueville was obliged to correct his teacher's ideas. Where Royer had distinguished only between the liberal spirit and the revolutionary spirit, Tocqueville introduced a further distinction between democracy and revolution; the two men differ, moreover, as to the origins of individualism. In the final analysis, Tocqueville's theory is much farther from the theories of the counter-revolutionaries than Royer's.

TOCQUEVILLE NOT ONLY parted company with Royer-Collard but also diverged from the teachings of Guizot, who preached a doctrine favorable to the middle classes: "As social equality spreads, there are more and more people who, though neither rich nor powerful enough to have much hold over others, have gained or kept enough wealth and enough understanding to look after their own needs. Such people owe no man anything and expect little from anybody. They form the habit of thinking of themselves in isolation and imagine that their whole destiny is in their own hands."[25] Far from agreeing with Guizot that the rise of the middle classes established reason in government, Tocqueville argued precisely the opposite: that the triumph of the middle classes is the triumph of individualism, which is the exact opposite of political reason—a "mistaken judgment," as Tocqueville calls it. Because the middle classes "form the habit of thinking of themselves in isolation and imagine that their whole destiny is in their own hands," they take refuge in their private affairs and enjoy the benefits of an era in which their dominance is assured. The supremacy of private affairs is the supreme good that they expect from modern liberty. Tired of political life after the tribulations of Revolution and Empire, they aspire only to repose. Louis Girard, in his course on liberalism, called attention to the prominence of the theme of repose in the work of Destutt de Tracy, Madame de Staël, and Benjamin Constant.[26] One of its most striking expressions can be found at the beginning of Constant's *Esprit de conquête*, where he considers the attitudes of modern nations toward war: "The unique goal of modern nations is repose, and with repose, wealth, and as the source of wealth, industry."[27]

This, in Tocqueville's eyes, is a sign of moral collapse. It is the result of the "damming up of the public virtues" by individualism, whose effects are exacerbated by revolution. When this occurs, political judgment is so distorted that political liberty ceases to be seen as anything other than a guarantee of private liberties. In the final analysis, individualism rests on an error; when Constant extols "the salutary and fecund isolation of man in a broadened, leveled world," when he praises "the proud and jealous isolation of the individual in the fortress of his rights,"[28] he commits an error of judgment by placing too wide a gulf between civil society and political society. Guizot makes the same mistake in encouraging the French to cultivate their material interests rather than seek broader participation in political life.

The individualist is wrong to isolate the man from the citizen; he is mistaken in thinking that individual ties are essentially and totally distinct from political ties. He is deluded in believing that liberty is a "natural" condition. It is a product of a certain type of society, namely, democratic society, and of a certain relation between that society and the governing power. As a result of increasing social equality and the French Revolution, it is true that personal relations were no longer immediately political. In a mediated form, however, these personal relations did retain their political quality, although this was no longer apparent to the casual observer, since all concrete and individualized images of political society had been eliminated from civil society. The images were gone but the idea remained, unchanged but more difficult to perceive.

In these circumstances, the philosopher's task became one of giving advice about the proper means of civic education. In Tocqueville's view, the role of towns and associations was to teach individuals anew that they were indeed citizens, as well as to understand that private interests and public interests are inextricably intertwined. Individualism could then be seen as the great threat to the future of the democratic age. The malady was curable, however. But before it could be cured, it had to be recognized and not glossed over by apologetic doctrine. Unfortunately, contemporary liberals were not exempt from this vice, and Tocqueville's diagnosis implied the need for somehow transcending liberal individualism.

The fate of the individual, far from being entirely in his own hands, depends on the preservation of common values, most notably security, prosperity, liberty, and national grandeur.[29] As a political philosopher and sociologist, Tocqueville points out that the individual does not take precedence over the "city." Nevertheless, he holds that the individual is of infinite value, and he feels a very powerful and sincere attachment to individualism in its nobler forms, along with an acute sense of the degradation of individualist ideals.

"IT IS TO 1789," Tocqueville writes, "a time of inexperience, to be sure, but also a time of generosity, enthusiasm, virility, and grandeur, a time of immortal memory, to which men will turn with admiration and respect long after those who saw it for themselves have disappeared. The French were then proud enough of their cause and of themselves to believe that they could be equals in freedom."[30] Unlike Maistre and Bonald, Tocqueville denounces individualism as the corrupter of democracy only in the name of individual pride and love of liberty. Never, not even in the dark days of the Second Empire, did he lose his confidence in the individual and his freedom: as he wrote to Gobineau on 24 January 1857,

> In my view, human societies, like individuals, amount to something only through the use they make of their freedom. That liberty is more difficult to establish in democratic societies like our own than in certain of the aristocratic societies that preceded it, is something I have always said. But I should never be so bold as to say it is impossible. I pray God never to make me think that I must despair of success. No, I will not believe that the human race, which stands at the summit of visible creation, has become, as you say, a degenerate herd and that nothing remains to be done but to surrender it defenseless and without hope to a small number of shepherds, who, after all, are no better animals than we are, and often worse.[31]

IN THIS ADMIRABLE text Tocqueville summed up his moral and political credo, which Jean-Jacques Chevallier has characterized as a "credo of confidence in man treated as man; in better education; and in liberty, the only leaven of perfectibility in both societies and individuals."[32] Because of his great faith in liberty, Tocqueville argued that the purpose of any political association must be to perfect the individual.

His program for defense of the individual is clearly outlined at the end of *Democracy in America*: "We should lay down extensive but clear and fixed limits to the field of social power. Private people should be given certain rights and the undisputed enjoyment of such rights. The individual should be allowed to keep the little freedom, strength, and originality left to him. His position in the face of society should be raised and supported. Such, I think, should be the chief aim of any legislator in the age opening before us."[33] Tocqueville is thus an individualist, in the sense that for him the end of society is the good of individuals.

Individualism and Economics

Tocqueville's name is also connected with the question of individualism in another way: his examination of what he called the "theory of self-interest properly understood."[34] Several chapters of volume two are devoted to questions of economics. In this Tocqueville differed not only from Constant, who refused to consider utilitarian matters in connection with his reflections upon justice, but also from the Doctrinaires. Yet it would be a mistake to suppose that he completely accepted utilitarian thinking or liberal economic theory. For him, utility was a value of a secondary order, and he treats it only because he has no choice. In the drafts of volume one he expressed the reasons for his interest in utilitarian doctrines: "If morality were strong enough by itself, I would not think it so important to relate it to utility. If ideas of what is just were more powerful, I would not speak so much about the idea of utility."[35] Tocqueville believed that utilitarian arguments and economic theories held some measure of pedagogical and practical value provided they remained subordinate to a clear vision of the moral and political necessities.[36] Tocqueville shared with Sismondi the rather unusual distinction of being politically liberal yet at some distance from economic liberalism. He was willing to accept any measure that encouraged individual initiative, yet he never became a dogmatic liberal. He was afraid that the extreme forms of liberal economic theory would encourage individualistic illusions and vices and lead to neglect of the common good.

In order to discover the general outline of his economic philosophy, it is convenient to examine his theoretical principles before considering his views on commerce and industry as they relate to liberty and democracy. Then we can turn to the question of what conditions are conducive to prosperity or poverty in democratic societies.

ABOARD THE SHIP that was carrying them to America, Tocqueville and Beaumont studied Jean-Baptiste Say's *Cours complet d'économie politique*, which was published in 1828 and 1829. Among their interlocutors in America were numerous partisans of the theory of self-interest; in particular, Albert Gallatin, John Quincy Adams, and Edward Livingston had all been influenced by Bentham.[37] But Tocqueville and his friend were interested in many subjects other than economics, and when they were received by Nicholas Biddle, president of the National Bank, Tocqueville questioned him almost exclusively about the American party system.[38] On their trip to England in 1835, Tocqueville and Beaumont discovered the industrial revolution and again made an effort to study economics, in which they relied on the advice of their friend Nassau Senior, who gave them his *Outline of the Science of Political Economy* (London, 1836). The two young travelers might also have learned a great deal from their conversations with John Stuart Mill, but to judge by his correspondence with Tocqueville they talked mainly about political philosophy, perhaps also about the philosophy of economics, but not about economics per se.[39]

All things considered, these early readings and conversations could not have done much more than incline Tocqueville and Beaumont in the direction of economic liberalism.[40] The work of Alban de Villeneuve-Bargemont was something else again, and in my view not enough attention has been paid to his influence on Tocqueville.[41] Born into an old and authentically noble family, Alban de Villeneuve-Bargemont had a career in some ways reminiscent of that of Tocqueville's father. He served as a prefect under the Restoration until 1830. In the Nord in 1828, his contacts with impoverished workers set him to thinking, and upon his retirement he began a study of French and foreign writers on economics.[42] In particular, he read Smith, Say, Sismondi, Jacques Droz, and especially Malthus prior to publishing his *Treatise* in 1834.[43]

Villeneuve-Bargemont believed that Adam Smith and his followers had treated only production, and he approved of Sismondi and Droz for establishing the welfare of the majority as the proper subject of political economy. Nevertheless, he was critical of the Saint-Simonians for wanting to reorganize society, social inequality being in his view inevitable. For him, the only indisputable basis for a society in harmony with man's nature was the Christian religion, and he sought to effect a synthesis between Christian charity and political economy: "Charity exercised in the name of society becomes a veritable science, whose theory and principles can be rigorously proved."[44] Artificial increase of needs through industry struck him as dangerous, and his most technical writing concerns the establishment of agricultural colonies. He favored legislative intervention in the economy, but for him social economy had to be based primarily on education and religion.

Although Tocqueville was not, strictly speaking, a disciple of Villeneuve-Bargemont and did not share all of his principal conclusions, the two men did have similar attitudes toward economics and economists. Both were suspicious of industry and its excesses, hardly surprising in men whose families were politically legitimist and highly traditionalistic. Both rejected the narrow individualism that was being preached at the time by such liberal economists as Charles Dunoyer or, somewhat later, Frédéric Bastiat; even more significant, perhaps, both men rejected the liberals' optimistic vision of man and society. Last but not least, both were inclined to see social phenomena as effects of moral causes, so that logically both looked at economics in moral terms. In 1845 Tocqueville was one of the founding members of the Annals of Charity, and in 1847 he was also among the founders of the Society of Charitable Economy, two organizations inspired by Armand de Melun, the leader of the "social legitimists" and a disciple of Villeneuve-Bargemont.[45]

AT THE TIME he wrote volume two, Tocqueville's economic knowledge was limited,[46] and he was afraid of allowing himself to be influenced by Michel Chevalier's *Letters on North America*, published in 1836.[47] He may even have feared being drawn into competition with Chevalier on topics of which he was not a master and which were of only secondary interest to him. In any case, the chapters of volume two concerned with economics are scattered through the book with no semblance of logical design; the second half of part two treats not economics as such but the moral and political effects of the pursuit of prosperity in democratic societies. In the moral sphere, Tocqueville argued, individualism produces consequences of two kinds: it isolates individuals by weakening their civic spirit (chapters one through nine of part two), while it exacerbates the desire for material well-being, which in turn aggravates the problem of individualism.

Americans, however, had been able to combat the pernicious effects of individualism through their knack for association and by linking religion with liberty. They were also able to combine moral strength with self-interest. Hence they managed to avoid the worst, yet remained anxious in the midst of their prosperity. From the moment of his arrival Tocqueville noted that self-interest was the bond that held American society together.[48] The country, he said, was ruled by a "refined and intelligent egoism," quite different from the crude and unenlightened egoism characteristic of France in a period of transition.[49] With the aid of the travel diaries, we can follow Tocqueville's thoughts on this subject to the point where he first uses the phrase "self-interest properly understood."[50] Tocqueville was thus led to rediscover one of the key ideas of the Idéologues, inherited from Condorcet himself: "Is not self-interest, improperly understood, the cause of the most common actions contrary to the general good? Are not violent passions frequently an effect of habits to which people surrender only as the result of a mistaken calculation or out of ignorance of the means to resist their first impulses, to temper them, divert them, and control their consequences?"[51] The Americans seemed to have inherited the optimism of the Enlightenment, as Tocqueville notes in the draft of volume one: "Most Americans believe that a correct understanding of self-interest is enough to induce men to be honest."[52]

Volume two is markedly less optimistic. The theory of self-interest properly understood is favorably described as "the best suited to the needs of men in our time." It is "not a very noble doctrine, but a clear and certain one."[53] Better to perfect than to combat it, for it has its value. Still, it is not sufficient: "One must therefore expect that private interest will more than ever become the chief if not the only driving force behind all behavior. But we have yet to see how each man will interpret his private interest. If citizens, attaining equality, were to remain ignorant and coarse, it would be difficult to foresee any limit to the stupid excesses into which their selfishness might lead them."[54] Man's twofold nature, spiritual as well as material, requires physical pleasures but cannot be satisfied by them alone.[55] As an example, Tocqueville cites the ability of the Americans to combat the corrupting tendencies of individualism not only through "enlightenment" and the theory of self-interest properly understood but also through religion and, above all, with the aid of associations and political freedom.[56] He clearly did not believe that harmony between private interests and the general interest was a self-evident truth. Not trusting the "invisible hand" invoked by Adam Smith, he recommended political remedies on the grounds that "liberty brings together those whom equality divides."[57]

It is easy to measure the ground covered since Montesquieu, who had made virtue the principle of democracy, a role that Tocqueville reserved for self-interest properly understood.[58] Nevertheless, Tocqueville attached less importance to the logic of self-interest than Montesquieu did. Montesquieu shows how the economic nature of things produces moral effects that serve as a corrective to human passions: "And it is fortunate that men are in a situation in which, when their passions inspire in them the thought of being wicked, it is in their own self-interest not to be."[59] The commercial spirit, he believed, would temper the arbitrary violence of political passions; his friend Jean-François Melon, a Bordeaux merchant, had published in 1734 a *Political Essay on Commerce*, a copy of which was in Tocqueville's library. The central point of the work was that the spirit of commerce and the spirit of conquest are mutually exclusive. Montesquieu himself, when he discussed commercial democracies, argued that the commercial spirit brought with it frugality, moderation, order, and tranquillity.[60] Along with his friend Melon he helped to establish the doctrine of "gentle commerce."[61] Following them, Benjamin Constant also drew a contrast between the spirit of conquest and that of commerce. For Tocqueville, however, it was democracy that tempered manners, not commerce.

Tocqueville did not share Montesquieu's optimism, as is clear from chapter fourteen of part two of volume two. Like Montesquieu, he did believe that there is a close and necessary relation between economic, commercial, and industrial activity and liberty.[62] But he was also capable of describing a situation which, though unnamed, closely resembled that of Guizot's France: "When the appetite for material pleasures develops more rapidly than enlightenment and habits of freedom in a [democratic] people, there comes a time when men lose control of themselves at the sight of new goods there for the taking. Preoccupied with the single thought of making a fortune, they no longer see the close connection that exists between the private wealth of individuals and the prosperity of all."[63] In an extreme form, this is the "mistaken judgment" upon which individualism is based, and it is hardly surprising that under such conditions civic values are neglected. "There is no need," Tocqueville continues, "to deprive such citizens of what rights they possess; they voluntarily give them up. The exercise of their political duties seems to them a waste of time, which distracts from their business . . . These people believe that they are following the doctrine of self-interest, of which they have but a crude idea, and in order to attend more fully to what they call their affairs, they neglect the chief affair, which is to remain their own masters."[64] In other words, by following Guizot's advice ("Enrich yourselves through work and saving"), the French were preparing not for the exercise of political freedom but for its opposite.

This chapter ends with a prophecy of crisis, the most remarkable forecast in all of Tocqueville's work,[65] in which he states, as early as 1840, the underlying reasons for Napoleon III's success: "If, at this critical juncture, a shrewd and ambitious man manages to seize power, he will find that all the avenues of usurpation are open . . . I willingly concede that public peace is a great good; nevertheless, I do not want to forget that many nations have arrived at tyranny in good order . . . A nation that asks nothing of its government but the preservation of order is already enslaved in its heart. It is a slave of its prosperity, and a man may come to cast it in chains."[66]

The relation between economy and liberty in Tocqueville is thus almost the opposite of what it was in Montesquieu and in many liberals. Montesquieu had asserted that commerce brings liberty;[67] for Tocqueville, who prefers to emphasize the danger to liberty in excessive love of material goods, this is only a partial truth. According to him, liberty engenders commerce and prosperity, rather than the other way around.[68] Furthermore, "an excessive love of prosperity can impair prosperity" itself;[69] and emphasis on utility, if not made subject to higher goals, can destroy prosperity as well as liberty. If Tocqueville is willing to accept, with some reservations, the "political consequences of Descartes," he is much more doubtful about what I shall call, following Bertrand de Jouvenel,[70] the "political consequences of Hobbes," for he knows that absolute individualism and materialism lead to despotism.

DURING HIS TRAVELS in America, Tocqueville did not show the same interest in the nascent industry of the country as he did in commerce and agriculture. While in Boston he neglected to visit the factories in nearby Lowell, about which Michel Chevalier wrote an interesting letter.[71] He stayed in Pittsburgh without visiting a single mill. There is nothing surprising about his attitude, which was shared by nearly all travelers of the time, accustomed to thinking of America as an essentially agrarian and commercial nation. It required Chevalier's keen powers of divination to see in the first American factories the seeds of a potent industrial power. Tocqueville's discovery of industry and, with it, of a potential for new forms of dependency and even slavery came during his trip to England in 1835.[72] He was horrified by Manchester[73] but much less frightened by Birmingham, where there were few large factories and many small industries.[74] The lot of workers was less harsh and less unhealthy and the gulf between the classes narrower in the latter city than in the former, where "civilization" and "barbarism" lived side by side.[75]

These travel notes, written ten years before Engels published his *Condition of the English Working Class*, contain the seed of what eventually became the final chapter of volume two, part two: "How an Aristocracy May Be Created by Industry." Tocqueville's criticism, which questions the wisdom of an excessive division of labor, is quite radical.[76] He has more to say, however, about the emergence of a new master class, a new aristocracy, "one of the harshest that has ever existed on earth," and he shows how the gulf between master and worker has increased: "The one more and more resembles the administrator of a vast empire, the other, a brute."[77] Yet in the conclusion to this chapter, he notes that the phenomenon is atypical:[78] it is, he says, "a monster within the social state . . . in the midst of today's broad democracy." Several chapters later,[79] he asserts that the workers' interests will ultimately prevail and that wages will rise: an extraordinary prediction, which came true only long after it was made and which flew in the face of the trend toward lower wages in France in the period 1815–1850.[80]

For Tocqueville, democracy is rooted in ideas, feelings, and mores that can change only slowly. He was also aware of what we would nowadays call systemic effects: a new element might be added to an existing system, but in the end it would be integrated, at least in part, into that system. Nevertheless, he did not believe that the harmony of interests would come about of its own accord, and at the end of the chapter on wages he suggests the need for legislative intervention. In this he may have been borrowing from Villeneuve-Bargemont, who advocated a form of minimum wage.[81]

In the final chapters of *Democracy in America*, however, the industrial class is no longer viewed as an exception. Tocqueville refers to a "great revolution"—the industrial revolution—and says that "after having been the exceptional class" the industrial class "threatens to become the principal and in a sense the only class."[82] Yet Tocqueville's chief fear in these final chapters is not so much the specter of a new industrial aristocracy as the threat of bureaucratic domination. Is this a contradiction? I think not, for in Tocqueville's view the new industrial aristocracy was a passing phenomenon, as this note, made in June 1838, suggests: "All newly born societies begin by organizing themselves as aristocracies. Industry is now subject to this law."[83] Ultimately, democracy will always win out, but the question is, what kind of democracy—liberal or despotic?[84]

THE EFFECTS OF economic progress are ambiguous, as Tocqueville was careful to note. Mill criticized him, quite wrongly, for having confused the trend toward greater equality with other tendencies of modern commercial society, the suggestion being that Tocqueville ascribed to equality some phenomena that ought to be seen instead as effects of growing prosperity.[85] I think I have shown that this was not the case; in any event, Tocqueville's chapter on the risks of a new industrial aristocracy would suffice to prove the point, that economic progress and the progress of democracy are not the same thing.[86] Tocqueville's analysis of the relations between economics and politics shows that economic individualism can lead either to prosperity or to misery or to new forms of servitude.

Individualism and Revolution

Individualism waxes as political liberty wanes. It also receives a strong impetus from democratic revolution, as is suggested by the very title of chapter three, part two: "How Individualism Is More Pronounced at the End of a Democratic Revolution Than at Any Other Time." Individualism is democratic in origin, but revolution intensifies its effects: "Democracy inclines men not to seek closer ties with their neighbors, but democratic revolutions make them flee one another and perpetuate, in the midst of equality, hatreds born of inequality."[87] Revolutionary passions outlive revolution itself and foster individualism, not only by perpetuating hatreds born of battle but also by making the newly independent feel "intoxicated with their newfound power," so that they exhibit "a presumptuous confidence in their strength" and "think only of themselves."[88] The hope is that with the passage of time things will return to normal.

*   *   *

184 Democracy and Revolution

AT FIRST SIGHT, this distinction, based on the intensity of the phenomenon, between democratic individualism and revolutionary individualism would seem to meet the requirements laid down by Royer-Collard. It is hard not to notice, however, that the criterion of intensity lacks precision and rigor. Furthermore, the correspondence between Tocqueville and Royer-Collard shows that when Tocqueville was obliged to consult Royer on the subject, he approached it in a very roundabout way, without even using the word "individualism." Consider Tocqueville's letter of 23 June 1838 (written at a time when the chapters on individualism were already complete and Tocqueville was considering placing them at the beginning of the book); in describing his Norman neighbors he wrote: "These people are honest, intelligent, fairly religious, tolerably moral, very steady. But disinterest is a quality they possess in very small degree. The selfishness of this area is admittedly very unlike that of Paris, which is so violent and often so cruel. It is a mild, tranquil, but tenacious love of one's private interests, which gradually absorbs all the other feelings of the heart and stanches almost all the sources of enthusiasm. With this selfishness they combine a number of private virtues and domestic qualities which together make them honest men and poor citizens."[89] These same lines might not seem out of place in the travel diaries that Tocqueville kept while in America. They describe a "democratic" individualism from which "revolutionary" features are wholly lacking. If this were the only kind of individualism in France, the distinction would lose much of its political interest and would no longer coincide with the distinction between America and France.

To this letter Royer-Collard responded thus: "You have feelings against the region in which you live. But your Normans are France, they are the world. Prudent, intelligent selfishness: the phrase describes the respectable men and women of our age quite accurately. They are worth neither more nor less on that account."[90] Tocqueville never brought up the subject again. Perhaps he wondered whether the national character had changed since the time of Montesquieu, for what he saw around him no longer resembled the portrait of the French in *Esprit des lois*: "If ever there were a nation sociable in humor, openhearted, joyful, tasteful, and able readily to communicate its thoughts, lively, agreeable, bright, sometimes imprudent, often indiscreet, yet full of courage, generosity, frankness, and scrupulously honorable, it would be a mistake to attempt to hobble its manners with laws for fear of hindering its virtues."[91]

In his American travel diaries and in volume one of *Democracy*, Tocqueville explained the superiority of democracy in America as a result of political education[92] and intelligent use of the theory of self-interest.[93] At the behest of Royer-Collard, Tocqueville undertook in volume two to distinguish between democratic characteristics and revolutionary ones. He never succeeded more fully, perhaps, than in the famous chapter on postrevolutionary individualism, which ends with a sentence that I have already cited several times because I think it is the key to the entire work: "The Americans have this great advantage, that they attained democracy without the sufferings of a democratic revolution and that they were born equal instead of becoming so."[94] A certain ambiguity remains, however, when this sentence is read in the light of the remainder of the chapter. Individualism has two aspects: in a negative sense it tends to weaken the civic spirit and isolate individuals, but in a positive sense it focuses attention on economic well-being. Yet Tocqueville is not clear about the role of the industrial revolution, about which he says nothing in part two of volume two. It would, I think, be compatible with his view to say that the industrial revolution, like other revolutions, also exacerbated individualism. The final chapter of part two denounces the hard and selfish ways of the great industrialists. Nevertheless, the idea of the industrial revolution is not mentioned before part four.[95]

Tocqueville was extremely preoccupied with the political apathy of the French in the years 1835–1840. To be sure, his theory of individualism predicted it, but to have conformed strictly to that theory, apathy should have diminished as the Revolution of 1830 receded into the past. Instead, Tocqueville believed it was on the rise, encouraged by the lure of business. The intellectual framework inherited from Royer-Collard was becoming daily less appropriate to the current state of the country. It had stimulated Tocqueville's thinking when he first sat down to work on volume two, but by 1838 it had become an obstacle to further progress. This, I think, is all that is necessary to explain the obvious lack of intellectual confidence in Tocqueville's letter to Royer-Collard of 23 June 1838, just quoted.

IT WAS PRECISELY this question of the origins of individualism that caused Tocqueville to diverge intellectually from Royer-Collard and to break radically with his counterrevolutionary theory. Tocqueville's notion of individualism was at odds with the widespread belief that the Declaration of Rights was the cause as well as the ultimate expression of individualism. While Tocqueville acknowledged that the postrevolutionary period was one of heightened individualism, he admired (as did Royer-Collard, for that matter) the spirit of '89, which he took to be the exact opposite of individualism. But whereas Royer-Collard had done little to resolve this apparent contradiction, Tocqueville dwelt on it at length in *The Old Regime and the French Revolution*.

Concerning, in particular, the feelings and passions of the men of '89, he says that these "had become like a new religion, which, by producing some of the great effects that religion has produced in the past, rescued them from selfish individualism and drove them to heights of heroism and devotion, often making them careless of all the petty things that we possess."[96] Individualism was not born in 1789 but had developed under the Old Regime, and Tocqueville devotes a chapter of his book to showing how, at the end of the Old Regime, the French had become both more alike and more isolated from one another than at any other time in their history.[97] Nothing distinguished the educated classes from one another except the disparities in their respective rights, which created a wide gulf between them. Political liberty, which had vanished, could no longer hold men together, and society broke apart into a multitude of small groups, each jealous of its privileges. "Each of the thousand small groups of which French society was composed thought only of itself," Tocqueville wrote. "It was, if I may put it this way, a sort of collective individualism, which prepared people for the veritable individualism that we are experiencing now."[98] On the following page he states that this collective individualism was "the most mortal . . . of all the maladies that afflicted the constitution of the Old Regime and condemned it to perish." Furthermore, it was "the crime of the old royalty" to have consolidated this division of classes in the hope of exploiting it.

Far from being an effect of the French Revolution, individualism was one of its primary causes: "When the various classes of old France reestablished communication sixty years ago, they at first touched one another's sore points exclusively; they came together only to tear one another apart. Even today their jealousies and hatreds still survive."[99] Tocqueville's second great work was written some twenty years after the first, which it complements and illuminates. It shows, just as

Democracy does, that the origin of individualism is "democratic," for in Tocqueville's lexicon "democracy" refers more commonly to a state of society than to a political regime. The Old Regime in its final centuries had already begun the trend toward greater equality. In any case, the "genealogical" analysis in Tocqueville's later masterpiece clearly demonstrates that individualism began to develop in France long before the Revolution.

During the transitional period between pure aristocracy and pure democracy, individualism first takes the form of a corruption of aristocracy and later that of a "childhood disorder" of democracy. The signs and causes of the malady are always the same: decline of local institutions and virtual disappearance of political freedom. It is striking that the only passage in *The Old Regime* in which Tocqueville compares French with American institutions deals with local freedoms. As he sadly concludes in his comparison of rural towns in America with eighteenth-century French communes: "They resemble each other, as much as a living thing may resemble a dead one."[100] He devoted a chapter, moreover, to showing "how the destruction of political freedom and the separation of classes caused almost all the maladies of which the Old Regime died."[101] *Democracy in America* may have left doubts as to the relative importance of the various causes of individualism, but it left none about the best remedies for its ills and, more generally, for disorders born of equality: "I say, moreover, that to combat such ills as equality may produce, there is but one effective remedy: political freedom."[102]

Indeed, if individualism is a childhood disorder of democracy, it also represents, even in the oldest and most firmly established democracy, a threat to the democratic social state. Furthermore, the allure of wealth, heightened by the progress of industry, always threatens to dissuade individuals from devoting their time and energy to their responsibilities as citizens.

Civic Spirit and Political Freedom

All of Tocqueville's work is a meditation on the civic spirit. In reading him it is easy to feel at times that one is reading an author of antiquity, so powerful is his insistence that man cannot fulfill himself unless he is fully a citizen.[103] Yet he also shows the utmost respect for the value of the individual, which prevents the comparison from being pushed too far. His work was the last great theoretical embodiment of civic humanism, whose influence can be seen in the Renaissance and in both the American and French revolutions. Rousseau had also been a civic humanist but with his eye fixed on the past; he sacrificed the individual to the citizen. Better than anyone else, Tocqueville posed the central problem of modern political philosophy: how to respect the individual while preserving the citizen.

His proposed remedies for the disease of individualism included political education,[104] association, and broader political rights. Of all the ways of democratically combating the evils of democracy, he considered political freedom the most important. The attachment of such importance to political freedom points up one of the differences between Tocqueville's sociology and that of Mill, who suggests that one way to avoid the decline that would result from the domination of the industrial and commercial class is to maintain a vigorous agriculture along with a leisure class and an educated class.[105]

It is wrong to see Tocqueville's critique of the dangers of individualism as a moral condemnation. It is based on a sociological analysis, which reveals the "error in judgment" involved in the belief that individuals can be self-sufficient. A political Jansenist, Tocqueville, unlike Bonald and de Maistre, is not critical of all aspects of individualism. On the contrary, his analysis of democratic societies had convinced him of the need to defend the rights of individuals and to protect their intellectual independence and moral freedom. Nevertheless, he believed that individualism had reached excessive heights in postrevolutionary France, leading to undue neglect of civic duties; Constant's writings were a symptom of this. The remedies he finally proposes are political: encourage associations and protect political freedoms. These, he says, will not only cure the ills born of individualism but will, for that very reason, protect the future of civilization.[106] "Feelings and ideas are renewed, the heart enlarged, and the understanding developed only by the reciprocal action of men one upon another."[107]

Nevertheless, even if political freedom can be established or developed in one nation by imitation of the political institutions of another, there is no guarantee that the civic spirit of the former will be of the same quality as that of the latter. What good are the best laws if the citizens of a country do not have an adequate conception of their political obligations? The American system requires not only free institutions but also a certain level of education and a tradition of liberty. In other words, its success depends on the Americans' civic spirit, what Montesquieu would have called their "virtue," which Tocqueville preferred to define as an equilibrium between private interests and the public good.[108]

Could the political remedies that the Americans had used successfully against the characteristic ills of democracy be carried over to France? We encountered another form of this question earlier: To what extent had the Americans been successful?[109] Which of the analyses in part two of volume two were valid only for America, and which applied to democratic societies in general? To answer these questions we must answer the classic question of political philosophy: Do good laws make good citizens?

Tocqueville was well aware that the civic spirit of the French would never be the same as that of the Americans, because a people's civic spirit is an expression of what Montesquieu called its *esprit général*.[110] But he believed that the introduction of political liberty in France would gradually create "habits of freedom" that would ultimately foster a civic spirit capable of overcoming postrevolutionary individualism. Like Montesquieu, but looking at America as much as at England, he wondered "how the laws might contribute to shaping the mores, manners, and character of a nation."[111] His fullest answer to this question is set forth in part two of volume two: political liberty is the universal remedy, useful and necessary in all democratic societies, in France just as much as in the United States. In the case of France, moreover, it was a prerequisite for any improvement in public mores. Despite the persistence of political apathy and a revolutionary spirit, Tocqueville remained hopeful and patient: if political freedom could be reestablished, the public spirit would be reborn in an unpredictable and peculiarly French form.

Underlying all of *Democracy in America*, particularly volume two, is a dialectic of the universal and the particular, the democratic and the American. The peculiarities of the United States are explained in terms of the English and Puritan origins of American society coupled with the prosperity of the American economy. Above all, as already stated, "the Americans have this great advantage, that they attained democracy without the sufferings of a democratic revolution and that they were born equal instead of becoming so."[112] In part two of volume two Tocqueville shows, better than anywhere else, the extent to which America can serve as a model for other democratic societies. In America it was possible to distinguish between what was American and what was democratic, whereas it would have been much more difficult to distinguish between what was democratic and what was revolutionary in France.

The conclusions that Tocqueville drew from his study of America may be seen as a development of an observation recorded in his travel diary on 1 October 1831: "In America free mores make free political institutions; in France it is up to free political institutions to make free mores. That is the aim to be striven for, but without forgetting the point of departure."[113] In the French case, the "point of departure" was the French Revolution, which did not make matters any easier.

8 ❧ Democracy or Revolution

Sentiments and Mores

Part two of volume two is entitled "The Influence of Democracy on the Sentiments of the Americans," while part three is called "The Influence of Democracy on Mores Properly So Called." Why did Tocqueville distinguish between sentiments and mores? The answer is not immediately apparent, and some critics have found the organization of volume two defective on that account. In my view, however, this criticism is based on a misunderstanding, for the distinction is real, and the organization of the volume, judged by its content, is quite rigorous. Unfortunately, Tocqueville's formulation of the distinction is not as solid as his construction of the book. His definition of the word "mores" derives from the Latin, meaning habits of both heart and mind, that is, "the whole moral and intellectual condition of a people."[1] Yet in part two of volume two, presumably devoted to sentiments rather than mores, he deals, in a key passage,[2] with "habits of freedom," and many of the chapters on America's appetite for prosperity might logically have been included under the heading "mores."

The real criterion on which the distinction between parts two and three is based is not to be found in the titles that Tocqueville has given them. One must notice (as commentators, as far as I know, have hitherto failed to do) that in all twenty chapters of part two there is not a word about England.[3] Such silence in anything by Tocqueville is unusual.[4] Yet this same part of volume two contains numerous and clear allusions to France.[5] Now, the comparison of France with America makes sense only in the context of a discussion of the democratic type. By contrast, from the beginning of part three, Tocqueville is careful to point out that "the Americans are close to the English in origin, religion, language, and partly also mores. Their social condition is the only difference."[6]

Part two presents the Americans as an example of a democratic people, whereas part three considers those aspects of their mores and national character that stem from their English origins. Tocqueville, moreover, is somewhat coy about pointing out the effects of equality. Many travelers before him, both French and English, had tried their hand at describing the ways of the Americans, but Tocqueville promises to avoid the beaten path and what he calls "the eternal comparisons."[7] As a latecomer, he resolves to describe American mores in terms of their "engendering idea," with the result that the references to England have become too discreet for some readers to see.

In Tocqueville's sketch of the American character, the leading traits of the democratic type have been superimposed upon enduring features of the English character. As equality receded, there was less to distinguish the Englishman from the American, and what was most original in this early sketch was forgotten or dismissed. Around the turn of the century, for example, Bryce criticized Tocqueville for having mistaken the true identity of both the English and the Americans.[8] The author of *The American Republic* was a subject of Queen Victoria, and his point of view is readily understood: he visited the United States at a time when the cause of social equality was at a low ebb—a far cry from the Age of Jackson. Hatred of the English had disappeared, and as Anglo-American friendship grew, the deep resemblances between the two peoples became increasingly apparent.

In France, early twentieth-century commentators (such as Antoine Rédier, Roland Pierre-Marcel, and Emile Boutmy) have generally echoed Bryce's critique. Listen, for instance, to Rédier: "Tocqueville failed to see that the American was neither a free man nor a democrat but essentially an Englishman."[9] Indeed, both liberals and conservatives drew on criticism that predated Bryce by a good many years, harking back all the way to the "party of resistance" and its distaste for Tocqueville's vision of a democratic future.[10]

Even in Tocqueville's day, moreover, the European liberals most favorably disposed toward American political institutions had tastes at odds with the American way of life. Republicans by principle, many of them remained aristocrats by sensibility and education and skeptical or critical of American practices.[11] Would it not have been imprudent of Tocqueville to offer a public so dubious about American mores a book that devoted so many pages to their study? The organization of volume two shows how artfully he accommodated trends in French public opinion by scattering the most American chapters throughout the book. He clearly attempted to restore some balance of judgment.[12] He may, however, have gone too far, and in my view he paints a somewhat too rosy picture of democratic societies.[13] This is not the place for a detailed commentary on these chapters, which would require systematic comparison of travelers' accounts from this period. I shall deal only with the final two chapters of the section, the most general and most political. Devoted to war and revolution, they present not Tocqueville's observations on his travels but his reflections on the future of democratic societies.

What Is a Great Revolution?

Tocqueville uses the word "revolution" in two very different senses. Sometimes he intends the common meaning: a political crisis that leads to an important change. But at other times he has in mind the "great democratic revolution" that began at the end of the eleventh century and gradually led to the replacement of an aristocratic type of society by a democratic one.

The first meaning of the word is strictly political, and it was in this sense that Tocqueville used it at the end of his 1836 article on the French Revolution: "Everything that the Revolution did would have been done, I have no doubt, without it. It was nothing but a violent and rapid means of adapting the political state to the social state, facts to ideas, and laws to mores."[14] Earlier, Benjamin Constant had written: "When the harmony between ideas and institutions is destroyed, revolutions are inevitable."[15] Tocqueville, extensively embellishing the old liberal theme of subordinating laws to mores, went much further than Constant. His originality is most apparent, even in the very early article cited above, when he looks before 1789 to show that even prior to the Revolution, French society was in its essential features already democratic. In other words, the democratic governing principle had already won out over the aristocratic principle.

Raymond Aron has written that "the Tocquevillean concept of revolutions is essentially political. The resistance of political institutions of the past to the modern democratic movement may on occasion cause an explosion."[16] This judgment applies readily to revolutionary crises and somewhat less simply to the idea of a revolution as the substitution of one governing principle for another. For Tocqueville, however, the contrast between ideal types, between aristocracy and democracy, has both a social and a political significance. True, Tocqueville's typology is essentially political, but it is also more than that, and Tocqueville himself characterized the French Revolution as a "social and political revolution."[17] Of course, "social revolution" does not mean here what it does, for instance, when one says that the Revolution of 1848 was a social revolution. Here it is not a question of socioeconomic relations but of substituting a democratic society for an aristocratic one.

The French Revolution repeatedly provoked violent crises, but its course might easily have been different. Before visiting England for the first time in 1833, Tocqueville had been afraid that that country might be in for a period of revolutionary crisis, but at the end of his stay he noted in his diary: "If by revolution one means any major change in the laws, any social transformation, any substitution of one governing principle for another, then England is surely in a state of revolution, for the aristocratic principle, which was once the vital principle of its constitution, is daily losing strength, and it is likely that the democratic principle will take its place reasonably soon. But if by revolution one means a violent and sudden change, then England does not seem ripe for such an event, and I even see many reasons to think that it never will be."[18]

HANNAH ARENDT HAS expressed her astonishment that Tocqueville showed so little interest in the American Revolution and the theories of its artisans.[19] In actuality, he was wary of historical comparisons, and his primary purpose was to compare American democracy with the confused mixture of democracy and revolution prevalent in the ideas and mores of the French. It was not that he was uninterested in the American Revolution, but only that he refused to treat it as in some way equivalent to the French Revolution. Nothing in the American case could compare, he felt, with the grandeur of the French Revolution and of France's war against all Europe, whereas nothing in France could compare with the Constitution of the United States for wisdom of design, longevity, or power to command its citizens' respect.[20]

John Quincy Adams wrote to Tocqueville on 12 June 1837 to report that his father, John Adams, had persuaded the abbé de Mably not to write a history of the American Revolution.[21] The necessary documents were not yet available, Adams argued, and, what is more, in order to succeed the writer would need a good knowledge of the history of the colonies from their inception.[22] This, John Adams felt, would require a lifetime of work. The argument would certainly have convinced Tocqueville, had that been necessary, much as it persuaded Mably to give up his project. In fact, however, Tocqueville knew enough about the American Revolution to know that it did not exhibit the characteristics that most interested him; in particular, it did not fit his conception of the democratic revolution. From the inception of the colonies, he believed, the American social condition had been democratic.[23] An early draft also contains this note: "In America the democratic revolution is long since over, or, rather, there never was such a revolution. The Americans never had class privileges to abolish or exclusive rights to overthrow."[24]

Thus in Tocqueville's work there is not, and cannot be, any systematic comparison of the American Revolution with the French Revolution. *Democracy in America* does, however, contain scattered observations on the subject, generally in the form of a contrast between the two events. For example, Tocqueville notes that the Americans had always governed themselves and had never experienced either centralized government or revolution in the French manner.[25] In a preliminary draft of volume one, he writes: "Revolution in America. Difficulty of inducing the people to make one. Religious character of this revolution."[26] Thus he was aware of these two specific differences between the French and American revolutions, but he yet preferred not to mention them in the published work. He saw clearly the conservative characteristics[27] of the American Revolution,[28] and no doubt he agreed with Burke that, despite its use of the language of natural rights, the American rebellion was actually rooted in love of English liberties. In the end, however, he limited himself to stating that the American Revolution, unlike the French, "was produced by a mature and deliberate desire for freedom and not by a vague and undefined instinct for independence."[29] Finally, he saw no sign in America of the revolutionary ideas and passions prevalent in France.[30] He therefore had every reason to believe that, according to the French sense of the word "revolution," there had been no revolution in America. For him, moreover, this was the Americans' great good fortune.[31]

Jackson's America presented Tocqueville with a spectacle that interested him far more than the American Revolution. The whole country was in an uproar as the result of a powerful surge of democracy; yet there was no revolution and not even a risk of revolution. The fundamental laws were not threatened by changes in secondary laws; the Constitution remained immutable and respected in the midst of constant legislative turmoil.[32] Hamilton, Madison, and Jefferson had deplored the instability of the laws of the United States,[33] but perhaps, Tocqueville acknowledged, such instability was inevitable in a democratic society, and in any case it was far preferable to the French form of constitutional instability—a revolutionary rather than a democratic phenomenon. In noting these bitter comparisons in his travel diary shortly before leaving America,[34] Tocqueville adumbrated a theory he would develop later, in volume two of *Democracy in America*: that democracies are agitated and unstable but not revolutionary.[35]

AMERICA, THEN, WAS the model of democracy, France the model of revolution. The French Revolution was the world's only truly great revolution for a number of reasons—not only because of its unprecedented violence and the major wars that followed in its wake, but also because it was both "a social and a political revolution,"[36] and, with its religious overtones, set an example for the entire world.[37] The year 1789 was "a moment of moral grandeur unequaled in history,"[38] because the revolutionary spirit was one of unselfish ardor for the public good, driven by the ambition "to introduce into the world new principles of government applicable to all peoples and destined to change utterly the face of human affairs."[39]

Tocqueville convinced himself of the Revolution's grandeur by his customary comparative method. For example, when he compares the English Revolution of 1640 with the French Revolution,[40] he notes that the former did not affect the majority of the population so deeply as the latter, nor did it mobilize religious passions in the same spontaneous and profound way; even though it overturned the political constitution, it caused only superficial changes in social practices, customs, and secondary laws. The American Revolution had even less of an impact on American society; it was a strictly political revolution, whereas the English Revolution of 1640 was both religious and political. The French Revolution, in Tocqueville's view, was the greatest revolution because it embodied both aspects of what he meant by the word "revolution": a violent political crisis together with substitution of one social principle for another. The French national character,[41] combined with the antireligious passions and philosophies prevalent in the country[42] and with the political circumstances of the moment,[43] further amplified the consequences of this conjunction to the point where, in a moment of enthusiasm, the people were gripped by the desire to create a new world.[44]

Throughout his life Tocqueville remained both fascinated and horrified by the Revolution.[45] On either of his two definitions of revolution, he came to the logical conclusion that the French Revolution was the greatest of all. But long before he had begun to reason about political events, his thinking was shaped by his parents' tales of the Revolution, to which he listened as a child. His final judgment of that extraordinary time combined revulsion and criticism with admiration. What he admired above all was the spirit of '89 and the Constituent Assembly,[46] in which he found liberalism in harmony with democracy. His criticisms were directed mainly at the illusion that the political world could be created anew, even as the centralizing tendencies of the Old Regime were being perpetuated and perhaps aggravated.[47] In calling the French Revolution the greatest of all revolutions, Tocqueville intends no judgment of value. He is merely observing that no previous revolution had resulted in total upheaval. Only the Revolution of 1789 posed a simultaneous challenge to civil, political, and religious laws. At first it sought liberty and equality together, but the pursuit of equality quickly became its principal goal. By way of contrast, Tocqueville points out that the principal goal of both the American Revolution[48] and the English Revolution[49] was liberty.

Tocqueville's concept of a great revolution is consistent, but on the part of a liberal writer it may seem rather paradoxical.[50] Historically, the liberal revolutions were not the greatest revolutions, and the greatest revolution was unable to remain entirely liberal over its full course. Perhaps Tocqueville would have agreed with Hegel that the French Revolution was a "superb sunrise." But surely he would not have gone so far as to see it as "a veritable reconciliation of divinity with the world," precisely because the greatest of democratic revolutions was unable to establish the tranquil reign of freedom in France. In Tocqueville's eyes, the liberal idea had yet to be reconciled with historical grandeur.

"On Revolutionary Passions in Democratic Peoples"

In the future, Tocqueville held, it would be both possible and desirable for the French to gain gradual familiarity with freedom. He thought it unlikely, however, that France or any other democratic society would produce another great revolution. In opposition to prevailing public opinion, and in particular to Guizot, he argued that democracies do not foster revolutionary attitudes. He was well aware of the originality of the idea expressed in his chapter entitled "Why Great Revolutions Will Become Rare,"[51] and a few weeks before the publication of volume two he selected this chapter to be published in the *Revue des Deux Mondes*.[52] The working manuscript in the Yale archives reveals that it was among those chapters most thoroughly revised by the author. The first page contains the notation "Baugy, end of March, 1838."[53] At the top of the page we find three titles, all different from the one that appears in the published work: the first is "On Revolutionary Passions in Democratic Peoples";[54] the other two, crossed out with a vertical stroke, are "Why the Americans Seem So Agitated Yet Are So Unchanging" and "Why the Americans Make So Many Innovations and So Few Revolutions." The latter two titles reveal Tocqueville's original idea: to comment on the contrast between the instability of secondary laws and the stability of fundamental laws in America.[55] The starting point for these reflections is observation of the United States; the goal, as indicated by the first title, is in keeping with the program inherited from Royer-Collard: to distinguish between democratic passions and revolutionary ones. But the argument, as we shall see, changes course in midstream on account of the political situation in France at the time of writing. As a result, Tocqueville failed to heed the wise counsel recorded on the title page: "Take care in revising this chapter to make it clearer that I am talking about a remote end state and not about the period of transition through which we are still passing. This is necessary in order not to appear paradoxical."[56]

The general conclusion of this chapter is well known and has been the subject of many admiring commentaries, which generally praise Tocqueville for his originality and foresight in predicting the conservative nature of democracy at a time when his contemporaries were still confusing democracy with revolution. At the turn of the century, for instance, Emile Faguet wrote: "To say democracy is peaceful, democracy is conservative, democracy is mild-mannered to men whom the word 'democracy' inevitably reminded of the French Revolution [was] to arouse interest by insisting on a contradiction. It took some courage." Furthermore, Faguet notes, Tocqueville proved to be a very good prophet: "It is now a half century since democracy became established in France, whether in its Caesarean or republican form.

During these forty-six years it has been conservative; it has not made a revolution . . . There is no conservative instrument more robust or formidable than universal suffrage."[57]

ALTHOUGH TOCQUEVILLE'S CONCLUSIONS have been applauded and presumably confirmed by history, his argument seems rather weak. It rests on two distinct analyses, one of interests, the other of ideas, in democratic countries.

The first line of argument is quite simple: the "conservative interests" and "homely tastes" of the middle classes are inimical to revolutionary instincts,[58] and, further, in a democratic society love of property and commercial habits and practices will dissuade most men from participating in revolutionary activities.[59] Tocqueville does not dwell on the point, feeling that he has already shown adequately that democracy tends to civilize manners,[60] and that democratic societies encourage individualism and focus attention on the quest for well-being rather than on collective action.[61]

This argument founders on history and logic. The Scottish economists had pointed out as early as the late eighteenth century that progress in manufacturing and commerce had encouraged certain forms of collective action and that the mercantile classes in England had made use of "discord" and even riot to attain their ends. The work of John Millar of Glasgow (1735–1801), as well as that of Andrew Ure, shows the weakness of Tocqueville's assumptions.[62] Furthermore, Tocqueville is quick to generalize from the mores of the commercial classes to the mores of the nation, or, at any rate, of the majority. Barnave was more cautious when he wrote in his *Introduction to the French Revolution* that "the mores of a commercial nation are not in all respects the mores of the commercial classes; the merchant is thrifty, most people are spendthrift; the merchant is abstemious, the public dissolute."[63] Finally, Tocqueville used the phrase "middle classes" without making clear what he meant by it (even though he felt the need to do so).[64] In fact, it meant something quite different in America from what it did in France. To say that American society is a middle-class society means that the distribution of property and the level of social mobility are such that the vast majority of Americans can reasonably consider themselves part of the middle class. In France in 1840, however, the phrase "middle classes" referred to a minority, a mock aristocracy that dared not speak its name. Tocqueville's argument is valid for a classless society or for a middle-class society like the American; but in his book he was addressing French readers, and the notion of middle-class society as applied to France was not very convincing. Tocqueville was well aware of this, but he allowed the equivocation to remain. He could have made his argument clearer had he adhered to his resolution in the manuscript to distinguish clearly between the remote democratic future and the current transitional phase.

After presenting this first argument, Tocqueville states his conclusion in measured terms: violent action by a minority is always possible, but only a violent minority can wish for a revolution in a democracy.[65] Furthermore, social equality does not, as was commonly believed in Tocqueville's day, encourage revolution; in fact, it greatly diminishes the likelihood of a major, violent revolution. Subsequently he carries this thought one step further, imagining a "political condition which, combined with equality, might create a society more stationary than any we have ever known in our Western world."[66] Furthermore, the second half of the chapter is devoted to demonstrating the unlikelihood of great intellectual revolutions. Here, the argument should be viewed in relation to the remarks in part one concerning the strength of communal beliefs and intellectual conformism in democratic societies.[67] The author's intentions are clearly stated in a note attached to the working manuscript:

> I must be careful to avoid the improbable and paradoxical and the appearance of indulging in fantasy. As social equality makes individual minds completely independent, it should lead to intellectual anarchy and constant revolutions in accepted opinion. That is the first idea that comes to mind, the vulgar idea, the most likely at first glance. After examining things more closely, however, I find that there are limits to this individual independence in the democratic countries which I did not see at first and which make me think that beliefs should be more *common* and more *stable* than it seemed initially.[68] To convince the reader of this is already a great deal.[69] But I want to carry the argument even further and suggest that the end result of democracy will be to make the human mind too immobile and human opinions too stable. This idea is so extraordinary and so novel to the reader that it can only be limned in the background, presented as a kind of hypothesis.

The reasoning, however, is disappointing, even though in this instance Tocqueville is careful to distinguish between democracy in its final state and the transitional period of intellectual anarchy.[70] Essentially, his argument rests on two fundamental propositions. But

Tocqueville himself was doubtful about the first, and he failed to pursue the second to its logical conclusion. He begins with this assertion: "Men's main opinions become alike as the conditions of their life become alike."[71] From this premise he attempts to prove that democracies are intellectually conformist and that great intellectual revolutions are therefore impossible. Yet opposite the quoted passage on the working manuscript he made this judicious observation: "That men's opinions are naturally alike—is that the reason why they do not succumb to revolution?" Tocqueville's second premise is this antirationalist assertion: "It is less the force of an argument than the authority of a name which has brought about great and rapid changes in accepted ideas."[72] If rationality is not the decisive criterion, however, then the role of mass ideologies cannot be excluded.[73] Comparison of the remainder of the text[74] with certain notes made in writing volume one suggests that Tocqueville believed that what we now call ideologies might serve as a replacement for religion on the wane. As he put it, "When the power of a religion diminishes and no other religion is born to take its place, a prodigious revolution takes place in the human spirit without man's taking part in it or even suspecting it."[75]

WHAT IS THE ultimate theoretical value of this chapter? It lies not in the details of the argument but rather in the originality and power of the main thesis, as well as in the connections that are brought out with the preceding analyses.[76] Nowhere does Tocqueville distinguish more clearly than in this chapter between democracy and revolution, since here they are presented as opposites. But the argument seems strained and artificial and adds little to the factual observation on which the chapter really rests: "In America they have democratic ideas and passions; in Europe we still have revolutionary passions and ideas."[77]

The comparative method provided a solid starting point. In order to have proceeded from there to the elaboration of a theory, however, Tocqueville would have had to clarify the notions of final state and transitional state, the latter being one in which revolutionary passions and ideas still survive. He also would have needed to treat the dynamics of revolutionary passions rather than confine himself simply to interests and ideas. It would have been useful to show how collective action involves a danger of revolution when the different classes of society have very different ideas and attitudes about the reasons for which the action is undertaken.[78] It is surprising, perhaps, that in *Democracy in America* Tocqueville underestimated the likelihood of revolutionary idealism, whereas in *The Old Regime* he stressed the enthusiasm and disinterest of 1789.[79] It is hard not to wonder why this subtle and profound writer so oversimplified matters in this chapter, even though it is one of the longest and most thoroughly revised in the book.

But keep in mind that this philosopher was also a politician. The chapter in question is in fact a pamphlet directed against Guizot, who since 1836 had justified his "policy of resistance" by invoking the need to combat the danger of revolution, "which still weighs upon every head and which clouds and distorts man's reason."[80] Guizot saw no need to reconsider the repressive laws of 1835, whose main tenets he defended in the memorable debates of 5 and 6 May 1837, in which he figured as leader of the Party of Resistance. Tocqueville preferred reinstatement of the freedoms granted in 1830, and he decided to challenge Guizot by proving how small the risk of revolution was. In the end he chose, contrary to his original intentions, to write a dazzling if paradoxical essay. Had he aimed for rigor, had he clarified the differences between the middle classes of France and the United States, had he distinguished between the transitional and the final state of democracy, he would have diminished the polemical force of his essay, for clearly he offers no grounds for ruling out the possibility of the most violent sort of revolution during the transitional phase. Unfortunately for the value of the chapter as theory, Tocqueville chose to include in his book the speech that he would have liked to make in parliament in response to Guizot.

Throughout his parliamentary career, Tocqueville was an enemy of Guizot, even though the two men's ultimate ends were the same. In his *Memoirs* Guizot described the aims of his political allies in the cabinet of 29 October 1840: "They aspired to end the era of revolution in France by establishing the free government that France had promised itself in 1789, as the consequence and political guarantee of the social revolution that it accomplished."[81] Tocqueville pursued the same ends but differed as to the means: Guizot, and for that matter Louis-Philippe,[82] wanted to turn the interest of the French away from politics and toward their own well-being, whereas Tocqueville believed that the only way to promote stability and progress in France was to extend political freedoms in keeping with the spirit of 1789. In Tocqueville's assessment of his own "instinct and opinions,"[83] he described himself politically in these terms: "I belong to neither the revolutionary party nor the conservative party. In the end, however, I am closer to the latter than to the former, for I differ from the latter more on the question of means than of ends, whereas I differ from the former on both. Liberty is the first of my passions."[84]

Democratic Society and Political Passions

Although Tocqueville's opposition to Guizot[85] accounts for many aspects of the chapter on revolutions, it does not explain all of them. In the background lurks a very definite psychology of political passions. There were two reasons why Tocqueville did not dwell at length on revolutionary passions in a chapter which at one point he considered entitling "On Revolutionary Passions." First, he would have weakened his own position in his campaign against Guizot if he had insisted on the survival of revolutionary passions in France. Second, he sincerely believed that, despite some contrary signs, the characteristic feature of France's moral and political situation in the late 1830s was apathy.[86] Beyond the residue of revolutionary ideas and passions, the country's indifference and political demoralization were increasingly apparent.

Apathy is the most frightening consequence of democratic individualism, and Tocqueville attached such importance to the notion of individualism that he had for a time considered beginning volume two with his chapters on that subject.[87] In the final note of the work he says that apathy is the source of both anarchy and despotism.[88] The most striking difference between volumes one and two of *Democracy in America* has to do with this notion. In volume one, Tocqueville described the activity and energy of American society while expressing some fears about the force of democratic passions, which might lead to the tyranny of opinion. In volume two, however, he devoted one part to the dangers of individualism, and his gravest worry appears to have been the absence rather than the overabundance of political passion.[89] Although he treats democracies in general in volume two, he is usually thinking of France, and in writing he kept constantly in mind a concern that he had expressed a little earlier to his friend Nassau Senior: "The almost feverish activity that has always been characteristic of this country is now turning away from politics and toward material well-being."[90] Like Montesquieu, Tocqueville believed that a republic without a sufficiently intense political life was doomed to corruption. As Montesquieu put it, "Misfortune befalls a republic when there are no more intrigues, and this occurs when the people have been corrupted by money. They become cold-blooded, develop a liking for lucre but not for affairs, care nothing for government and what government proposes, and tranquilly await their wages."[91] Tocqueville added the Revolution to the list of causes of apathy.[92] He did not fully develop the theme until April 1842, however, when he accepted his seat in the French Academy.[93] From then on he clung steadfastly to this idea, which occurs again in a central place in his analysis of the Directory and yet again in his working notes for the second half of *The Old Regime*.[94]

Some years after the publication of volume two, Tocqueville made an important addition to his doctrine. In a speech delivered to the National Assembly on 17 January 1844, he worried about the slumbering public spirit: "You say that the nation is quiet; I say that it is asleep. And take it from me, it is to no one's advantage when a great nation sleeps. Everyone must fear its reawakening, for from this reawakening can come only new revolutions."[95] Thus, four years before his prophetic speech of 27 January 1848,[96] he understood that a danger of revolution still existed in France and, further, that the danger lay precisely in that attenuation of political passions which, in the polemical chapter of 1840, he had invoked in order to deny that great revolutions still posed a threat.

Was Tocqueville in contradiction with himself? Strictly speaking, the answer is no. The 1840 polemic was couched in terms of probabilities, and he never denied the likelihood of all great revolutions but only of those conducted by impassioned majorities. Nevertheless, Tocqueville not only simplified his ideas for polemical purposes, but from 1835 until 1844[97] he believed that no new revolution would occur in France. For a decade he shared the illusion of the liberals that the Revolution was over.[98] In his *Souvenirs* Tocqueville frankly admitted his mistake: "The universal appeasement and truckling that followed the July Revolution made me think for a long time that I was destined to spend my life in an exhausted and tranquil society."[99] In 1830, he added, he had "mistaken the end of an act for the end of the play."[100]

This error of political judgment certainly affected the content of volume two, in which Tocqueville exaggerated the apathy of democracy. His thinking at that time seemed to take a turn away from reality, and in part three he mused in similar fashion on the mildness of democratic mores. In view of the errors that Tocqueville himself acknowledged and the very different views expressed in his various texts, two fundamental questions have to be asked. First, does political apathy stem from democracy or from revolution? The answer is simple: from democracy, like the individualism of which it is but one consequence; nevertheless, a great revolution increases apathy to the utmost. Once again, Tocqueville is arguing that the effects of revolution are similar to the defects of democracy, but more powerful. Second, does the attenuation of political passion, or, in extreme cases, political apathy, diminish the risk of revolution? The answer to this question is more difficult, for Tocqueville's views on the matter are not so clear. They are not inconsistent, however, provided we agree that the attenuation of political passions diminishes the likelihood of a great revolution, but only up to a point; beyond a certain level of depoliticization, a reversal takes place: the regime becomes more fragile and therefore more vulnerable to revolution because it lacks public support. Tocqueville's theory gives no way of assessing where this critical threshold lies, however; it is up to the statesman to decide. In this crucial respect, the "art of governing" must make up for the failure of "political science."[101]

THE CHAPTER ON revolution is central to a group of chapters dealing with the political passions in peace and war.[102] Here we find a Tocqueville not unlike Saint-Simon, heralding the decline of the bellicose and political passions. Yet he seems melancholy about some aspects of an evolution to which Saint-Simon looked forward with glee.

Men in democratic societies, exhausted by the pursuit of power and, above all, wealth, renounce all higher ambitions. The primacy of economic values, accepted by nearly everyone, discourages most people from taking an interest in politics, and even those who seek power do so using the prudent methods of economic calculation.[103] Thus democratic societies tend to become "meritocracies,"[104] burdened with rites of passage worthy of ancient China. Wherever public employment is more attractive than independent careers, the number of those seeking such employment can grow to the point of constituting a danger to the state.[105] Democracy makes men too humble; it unduly diminishes their dignity and pride. Tocqueville recommended that an effort be made "to give them a broader idea of themselves and their species."[106]

In democratic societies, political ambition is not confined within proper bounds, is not limited to the moderation characteristic, according to Montesquieu, of the aristocratic polity: "a proportionate, moderate, and vast ambition is hardly ever found there."[107] A person who does not resign himself to mediocrity, who conceives a truly great political ambition, has little chance of fulfilling his aims and having his ambition recognized for what it is, little chance of discovering that noble emulation that flourishes where glory is loved. Ambition therefore assumes "a violent and revolutionary character" and, unable to act otherwise, seeks "success more than glory." Abandoning grandeur, it seeks domination. Nowhere does Tocqueville more fully express his psychology of the political passions than in the two final pages of the chapter on ambition.[108] His anticipation of the violent political passions of twentieth-century minorities is at least as astonishing as his more famous prediction of an "immense and protective" state.

At the beginning of the chapter, Tocqueville argues that revolutions, and especially democratic revolutions, enlarge men's ambitions. Since he shows later that democracy tends to restrict those same ambitions, this chapter clearly adds a good deal to the distinction between what is democratic and what is revolutionary. At the top of the chapter outline, which has been preserved in the Yale archives, he wrote: "It is essential to distinguish carefully between democratic revolution and democracy."[109]

The final chapters of part three, on war, show that "the military spirit and the revolutionary spirit diminish at the same time and for the same reasons."[110] Tocqueville maintains that war will become rare in the democratic era but will also change character.[111] He does not, however, describe "the profound revolution in the manner of making war" that he planned to study in the book which was to have followed *The Old Regime*.[112] Leaving aside the Saint-Simonian theme of the end of martial civilizations, these final chapters contain Tocqueville's reflections on the close connection which he believed existed between the idea of a great revolution and that of a great war. Apparently he was unable to free his mind of examples from recent French history. He was also afraid that military revolutions would threaten the future of democratic societies.[113] The drafts at Yale reveal his fear of an "aristocracy of men of war,"[114] or a "military despotism following revolution and democratic anarchy."[115] If a military government were ever established in a democratic society, "it would create a sort of fusion of the habits of the clerk with those of the soldier."[116]

In most men, democratic society tends to diminish political passions and heighten economic passions.[117] Although Tocqueville seems to be following Saint-Simon, he actually differs with him on the essential point: he does not believe that "the administration of things" can replace "the government of men," and he shows that violent elites, either political or military, may capitalize on democratic apathy in order to seize power. The analysis of political passions brings out the fundamental distinction between elites and masses. Tocqueville was the first to pose the problem of ruling elites in a democracy. He did not, however, belong to the family of disciples of Machiavelli, for among those men with strong political passions he distinguished between the violent, whether civilian or military, and those whose passions are not corrupt, "the legists" and liberal democrats who remain respectful of the law and capable of exhibiting a true civic spirit.[118] Furthermore, he did not believe that social mobility was enough to make tolerable the division between rulers and ruled; he insisted on the need for diverse forms of participation in public life. Rather than accept, as do today's "Machiavellians," the political apathy of the masses as a given, he held that to combat it was the only way to avoid the despotism of violent minorities.

The First Conclusion of Volume Two

The chapters on political passions form a powerful unit.[119] They constitute the first conclusion of the work, and the chapter on revolution forms its centerpiece. Recall that Tocqueville contemplated writing a lengthy preface to volume two, in which he would have stated his intention to distinguish between democratic traits and revolutionary traits still present in the era of transition between aristocracy and democracy.[120] From the beginning, however, he had doubts about the best place to put these arguments: "Idea for the preface or the final chapter," "Idea to be shown head on at the beginning or end and in profile throughout the various parts."[121] Indeed, we have already encountered the theme of democracy and revolution "in profile" in parts one and two. In the final chapters of part three, the original conclusion,[122] the contrast between democracy and revolution, based on the conception of Royer-Collard, is most clearly in evidence. Once Tocqueville made the decision to include in this chapter his ideas on centralization,[123] however, he was compelled to expand it far beyond what he had planned, until ultimately this single chapter grew into a whole new part of the book, part four, whose conclusion is rather different from what I am calling the first conclusion.

Tocqueville was prescient enough to appreciate, in opposition to much of French opinion at the time, the conservative capacity of democracy. Nevertheless, the central point of the first conclusion is the contrast between democracy and revolution, which is sometimes carried beyond the limits of reason. Tocqueville paints too mild a picture of democracy in part three; in later work he reverted to a more realistic view.[124] He failed to distinguish clearly enough between the long term and the period of transition. I have shown how his political ambitions prevented him from setting forth his theory in full detail and how by not fully specifying the role of the middle classes in democracy he left a good deal of vagueness in his analyses.[125] He shared the liberal illusion that the "revolution is over." He was the first to think that revolutionary messianism would disappear once the democratic process was complete. Great revolutions, he believed, are essentially transitional phenomena between the old hierarchical structures and the democracies of the future. His opposition to the counterrevolutionary tradition was twofold: first, he believed that a model for counterrevolution should not be sought in the past, and second, he held that democracy itself provided this model. Apart from its obviously sound qualities, this theory has a no less obvious defect: that it does not explain how one can be certain that the transitional phase has come to an end. Since total equality is only a dream, there is a danger that the definition of a mature democracy will remain a matter of dispute.

Finally, Tocqueville was the first thinker with insight into the role of ruling elites and ideologies in democratic societies, but he was unable to combine these insights into a persuasive theory. The Revolution of 1848 demonstrated that popular revolutions were still possible during the transitional period. Yet none could surpass the model of the great revolution that was ever present in Tocqueville's mind: the Revolution of 1789.

9 ❧ Servitude or Freedom

Distinguishing the Spirit of Equality
from the Spirit of Revolution

In a note made prior to writing part four of volume two, Tocqueville makes a statement that seems to contradict the central argument of the chapter on revolution: "Distinguish between the spirit of equality and the revolutionary spirit. Why the revolutionary spirit is more natural in democratic peoples."[1] We saw earlier that, in Tocqueville's view, the democratic spirit was opposed to the passions and ideas that make great revolutions; yet now he tells us that it is linked to the revolutionary spirit. As we read part four of volume two, however, our surprise diminishes and the contradiction gradually comes to seem justified. After 1840 Tocqueville frequently distinguished between the "revolutionary spirit" and "great revolutions," and ultimately this distinction became a basic tenet of liberal thought.[2] Indeed, it can almost be used to define the fundamental attitude of the nineteenth-century liberal: a liberal is a person who accepts the spirit of 1789 but rejects the revolutionary spirit. The peculiar difficulty faced by French liberalism is reflected in the paradoxical form of this statement, which has the virtue of concisely summarizing the central political problem faced by France in the nineteenth century. The Revolution of 1789 was the source both of freedom and of a revolutionary tradition that threatened freedom.

The revolutionary spirit is presented in a new light in the political chapters that conclude volume two, which bring out the essential connection between centralization and revolution.[3] These are admirable chapters, and they have received all kinds of praise. I shall attempt to give yet another reason for admiring them by showing that they in fact constitute the beginning of Tocqueville's second work: the true introduction to *The Old Regime and the French Revolution*.

Centralization

In his first writings on centralization,[4] Tocqueville sought primarily to distinguish between administrative centralization and governmental centralization in order to show how the United States derived the benefit of administrative decentralization without impugning the principle of political centralization. A "brilliant distinction," said Sainte-Beuve in his article in *Le Temps*; but Faguet, somewhat later, called it "illusory."[5] Suffice it to say that "government" and "administration" are too closely intertwined to permit establishing a conceptual boundary between them, and that the observable differences between the powers and responsibilities of the government and those of the administration in countries with comparable regimes are explicable essentially in terms of history and the traditions of public life. Tocqueville's distinction has little theoretical value, but it does show how he used the comparative method: he starts with a comparison of France with England and the United States, observing not so much their principles as the effects of their different institutions.[6] If we focus our attention on France, however, we find another significance to the distinction: governmental centralization is a legacy of the Old Regime, while the Revolution is described, if not as the source of administrative centralization, then at least as the cause of a considerable aggravation of that evil.[7]

Benjamin Constant denounced the dangers of excessive centralization in *On the Spirit of Conquest and Usurpation* (1814). It is likely that Tocqueville was aware of Constant's critique of centralization and even more likely that he knew the work of Henrion de Pansey, *Municipal Power*, which enjoyed a high reputation during the Restoration.[8] For Pansey, municipal government was a veritable fourth power, older than the three others and by nature both public and private, combining "the authority of the magistrate with that of the father."[9] His writings justify the concentration of political power and the diffusion of social power, which must have given Tocqueville food for thought. "In every state," Pansey writes, "there are two distinct powers: one, more moral than material but endowed with great strength by its concentration, constitutes the political authority; the other, composed of material forces disseminated throughout the society, constitutes the social power, or, what amounts to the same thing, democracy."[10] Tocqueville was also influenced by the American writers Josiah Quincy, Gray, and especially Jared Sparks, as Pierson has shown,[11] as well as by the Doctrinaires and by Guizot's courses. I do not believe, however, that the information Tocqueville requested of his friends Chabrol and Blosseville, and especially of his father, could have had much impact on his thinking, except to compel him to undertake the unpleasant task of comparing the Anglo-Saxon countries, which enjoyed administrative decentralization, with France, which had been overly centralized for far too long.[12] The reforms of 1833–1838, which maintained much of the legislation of Pluviôse Year VIII, were obviously too timid to satisfy him.[13]

England and America offered examples of strong and prosperous societies without administrative centralization; and Tocqueville, at the time of his first trip to England in 1833 as well as during his earlier travels in the United States, believed that the social vitality and economic prosperity of the two countries were related to their scanty administrative superstructures.[14] But he did not see a connection between the tendency toward centralization and the development of the democratic principle until after his second trip to England in 1835. The administrative bureaucracy established in connection with the Poor Law Amendment Act of 15 February 1834 struck him as revealing an inherent tendency of democracy, as he noted at the time in his travel diary: "Centralization, democratic instinct, instinct of a society which has finally freed itself from the medieval system of individualism. Preparation for despotism."[15] John Stuart Mill also noticed this centralizing tendency but believed that the English national character would prove a sufficient impediment; unlike Tocqueville, he did not explain it as the result of a "democratic instinct."[16] Later, he expressed his gratitude to Tocqueville for having revealed to him the drawbacks of centralization.[17] Despite "the centralizing mania which has taken hold of the English democratic party," Tocqueville believed that England was still a long way from the gravest dangers because centralization there was governmental rather than administrative.[18]

Drescher has shown that Tocqueville's second journey to England had a decisive influence on his identification of democratic and centralizing tendencies. Thereafter, Tocqueville based his prognoses on developments in Europe rather than America.[19] When he began work on the final section of *Democracy in America*, he wrote his brother Edouard that centralization in America had been delayed by circumstances that did not exist in Europe.[20]

The first chapters of part four of volume two show how the uniformity,[21] individualism, and dislike of intermediate powers characteristic of democracy contribute to centralization. Tocqueville, of course, emphasizes the need to develop as many forms of participation as possible in order to prevent public life from deteriorating into an unequal encounter between the individual and the state. I cannot, however, agree with Eugène d'Eichtal that for Tocqueville "servitude is nothing other than subjugation to a central power."[22] If it seems that Tocqueville's fears of the administration were excessive, especially during the pessimistic period in which he was completing volume two,[23] we should nevertheless be careful not to neglect the subtlety of his comparative analyses. He never falls to the level of the dogmatic liberals, who were content to oppose the idea of liberty to the alleged omnipotence of the administration. In its summary form, Tocqueville's analysis involves centralization, liberty, equality, and revolution. The following fragment contains an echo of his thoughts about England: "(1) When liberty exists before equality, it establishes habits that impede excessive development of the central government . . . (2) When equality has developed rapidly with the help of a revolution, the desire for intermediary powers disappears more quickly. Centralization becomes in some sense necessary [in the margin: two ideas relative to revolutions which have not been treated] . . . (3) The Revolution heightens hatred and jealousy between neighbors and leads sometimes the upper, sometimes the lower, classes to desire centralization."[24]

IT IS VERY DIFFICULT, moreover, to separate the idea of centralization from that of revolution in Tocqueville's work; the former always partakes of at least one of the two meanings of the latter. During the transitional period between aristocracy and democracy, or, in other words, during the course of that centuries-long process to which Tocqueville refers as the "great democratic revolution," centralization, he argues, is destined to increase.[25] During Tocqueville's most politically optimistic period, in 1836 when he wrote his article for the *London and Westminster Review*, he apparently still hoped that centralization would diminish as France moved further into the democratic era and as the revolutionary period (1789–1814) receded into the past. "The natural tendency that impels democratic peoples to centralize power is most apparent and obviously on the rise in periods of struggle and change, when there is a war over which of two principles will govern affairs."[26] By 1838, however, largely inconsequential steps toward decentralization and the increasingly obvious disposition of the king and his principal ministers had put an end to Tocqueville's hopes, and he was content to number centralization among the effects of democracy that are exacerbated by revolutionary crisis; no longer does he suggest that a decrease in the tendency is imminent. In a note written on 6 September 1839, after reading the chapter devoted to the various factors that contribute to centralization in democracies,[27] he says: "Most of the reasons I give, and surely the most important ones, have to do with a particular accident, revolution. I should therefore deal with this separately and announce in advance that I am going to concern myself with this type of special case. It is worth the effort."[28]

The reflections in the 1836 article and in the final part of *Democracy* anticipate the analyses in *The Old Regime*, of which the first half of book two is devoted to demonstrating that by 1789 administrative centralization had replaced all other powers under the old regime while still preserving their facades.[29] In this way the "great democratic revolution" influenced the political institutions and mores of the French, substituting the democratic for the aristocratic principle. Under certain specific political circumstances,[30] a liberal order could be transformed into a despotism and class conflict created.[31] Unfortunately, this was the case in France, and when the French finally wished to make reforms, centralization had left them so ill prepared for joint action that they destroyed the old order.[32] Thus Tocqueville, who in his first works had considered centralization an effect of revolution (in both senses of the word), showed at the end of his life how it could be a factor in encouraging revolutionary crises, as he believed happened in 1848 as well as 1789.[33] The revolutionary spirit was a product of the Old Regime's public mores.

Emile Faguet wittily summed up the central argument of *The Old Regime* thus: of the three existing governments—the feudal, the provincial, and the central—only one was oppressive, and the Revolution struck down the other two.[34] But the very idea of the free commune was presented to the National Assembly for the first time by Jacques Thouret as a consequence of the new principles, and it was later developed by Condorcet. Georges Lefebvre has criticized Tocqueville for not explaining why centralization reemerged, after the nation had enthusiastically done away with it in 1789.[35] Tocqueville's answer can be found, I believe, in his preliminary notes for the work that was to have followed *The Old Regime*: "Centralization was reestablished through mores, not through ideas."[36] Tocqueville's analysis does not end with ideas but strives to penetrate to the deeper level of intellectual and political habits, the true foundation of French democratic culture. Similarly, in the conclusion to volume one of *Democracy*, he had showed that American mores did more than laws to maintain the republic.[37]

PART FOUR OF volume two introduces a new and very important thought: that revolutionary ideas and tendencies, instead of gradually disappearing, might well be perpetuated by administrative centralization and the absence of sufficient political freedom. In democratic countries, "it is always to be feared that revolutionary instincts, calmed and regularized but not extinguished, may gradually be transformed into governmental practices and administrative habits."[38] In the preparatory notes to volume two is a page of reflections on the revolutionary spirit which I think is worth reproducing almost in its entirety. It begins with a search for a definition: "Appetite for rapid changes. Use of violence to bring them about. Tyrannical spirit. Contempt for forms. Contempt for established rights. Indifference to means in view of the end, doctrine of the useful. Satisfaction of the brutal appetites." The passage that follows further clarifies the difference between the liberal and the revolutionary spirit, and if there is any page in Tocqueville's work that establishes, with all the rigor of which he is capable, the nature of a distinction that was so important to his master, Royer-Collard, this is it: "The revolutionary spirit, which is everywhere the greatest enemy of freedom, is especially so among democratic peoples because there is a natural and secret connection between it and democracy . . . A revolution can sometimes be just and necessary; it can establish liberty; but the revolutionary spirit is always detestable and can never lead to anything but tyranny."[39] The only difference between Tocqueville's idea and Royer's—a considerable one—is that Royer could not have imagined that the revolutionary spirit so defined could be perpetuated through administrative and governmental practices. The spirit of 1789 was the liberal ideal, but it was soon overwhelmed by the revolutionary spirit, owing to the weight of tyrannical practices engendered by the administration of the Old Regime.

Anarchy and Despotism

In the political life of his time, Tocqueville continually confronted the risk that liberalism would degenerate into revolution. On 16 September 1842 he wrote Odilon Barrot: "What has always deeply offended me about the left is how little real liberalism one finds there. As long as the opposition does not change its instincts, it will be good for nothing but bringing on further revolutions or paving the way for despotism."[40] For Tocqueville, the swing of the pendulum from revolution (or anarchy) to despotism was an ever-present danger, an enduring feature of French history after 1789.[41] Of the two risks, despotism was the more worrisome.[42] In his working notes for volume two, Tocqueville wrote: "Those who pay attention only to the great *Revolution* fear that the world will fall into anarchy, and those who think only of the consequences of that *Revolution* worry that it will turn to despotism. One must therefore distinguish carefully between the democratic Revolution and its effects. The greatest errors of our time stem from the fact that the two things are not adequately distinguished."[43]

Sometimes, however, it is wiser not to state the truth, and Tocqueville hesitated before committing to paper the thought that the primary risk in the centralizing tendency of democracy was despotism: "In order to combat despotism, I am obliged to prove that it leads to anarchy. If it led only to itself, many of our contemporaries would willingly follow it." In the margin he adds: "If people could believe in a tranquil and stable despotism—perhaps the worst of all forms of despotism—my cause would be lost." To return to the main thread of the argument: "Anarchy is not an enduring condition; despotism is. True, our present apathy will lead either to anarchy or despotism. Yet I can still say that it will lead to despotism, because despotism is a final state."[44] For a long time Tocqueville remained unsure whether the alternation between anarchy and despotism would ever come to an end, but ultimately he concluded that in the end despotism would take root.[45] He planned to develop these ideas "with greater depth and color."[46] But in the final draft he toned down the colors somewhat, and I will therefore cite the rest of his note:

> One might think that equality arouses too great an appetite for independence to allow despotism to last and too few of the habits of independence and the means to defend it to permit liberty to endure. In the end, I think that the movement of my [illegible word: chapter?]

book?], which follows the tendency of democratic society to move toward despotism, is correct and should remain, but somewhere I must add that this movement toward despotism [is] gradual but not continuous. Equality, without established free institutions, leads to anarchy almost as energetically as to despotism. Explain why the combination of the appetite for power with the appetite for freedom, both natural in the democratic era, will give rise to successive periods of anarchy and despotism and at times to both at once.[47]

THESE PRELIMINARY NOTES[48] indicate the difficulties that Tocqueville encountered as well as his conception of the political dynamic. He was well aware that most of his compatriots did not number liberty among the primary political values and that many of them were prepared to accommodate certain forms of despotism.[49] He was convinced that the appetite and passion for liberty are likely to prove too weak in most men in democratic societies to allow freedom to be maintained permanently and without strain. He was afraid that his work would lose its immediate political utility if he contented himself with showing how tendencies inherent in democratic society lead to a tranquil form of despotism. Yet after much hesitation, he chose in the end to tell the truth: "Is it not possible to believe that in a country with social equality but without established free institutions, one could go perpetually from anarchy to despotism and from despotism to anarchy without ever achieving stability? If that were true, it would have to be said." In the margin he adds: "No, despotism would ultimately take root, increase, and finally cast its maleficent shadow over the entire country."[50] At the end of *Democracy* Tocqueville has resigned himself to the need for stating this dangerous truth, and the reader may wonder why the final text places so little emphasis on the intermediate phases of anarchy, which might have frightened some proponents of centralization sufficiently to discourage them. I have no sure answer to this question but offer the following hypothesis: at the time of the final revision, after Tocqueville's election,[51] he understood that no one in politics seriously believed in the danger of riot or a return of anarchy in the foreseeable future.[52] He also saw that the crisis precipitated by the coalition had left the country profoundly demoralized.

In chapter five of part four, Tocqueville gives a somewhat different picture of the political dynamic of his time. There, unfortunately, he no longer treats the question of an alternation between anarchy and despotism.[53] Had Tocqueville pursued his thought to the end, he would have explained in advance the repetition of revolutionary cycles in France; the cycle of 1848 resembles that of 1789, moving from anarchy to despotism.[54] In chapter five the two contrary tendencies are analyzed in new terms: "Hence two revolutions seem to be moving today in contrary directions: one steadily weakens the power of government, while the other constantly reinforces it. In no other era of our history has government seemed either so weak or so strong."[55] Raymond Aron has criticized Tocqueville for not having properly formulated the antithesis: it was the traditional powers that had grown weaker, while the power of the administration had increased. "What Tocqueville means," Aron writes, "is that government was curtailed while its sphere of action was enlarged. In reality, he is attacking the expansion of administrative and governmental functions and the curtailment of the political power of decision."[56] The comment is correct as far as the long-term tendencies are concerned.[57] But an analysis of the literal and historical context is also called for. On the same page Tocqueville shows that the two contrary tendencies generally succeed each other in the course of a revolution, following the dialectic of liberty and equality:[58] "They wanted to be free in order to become equal, and to the extent that equality established itself more firmly with the aid of liberty, it made liberty more difficult for them."[59] This analysis is concerned essentially with the medium-term political dynamic, even though the conclusion of the chapter looks forward to the distant future: "I see that nations today are restless. But I do not see clearly that they are liberal, and I fear that, when these disturbances which cause thrones to totter are over, the sovereigns will be more powerful than ever before."[60]

The political dynamic just analyzed covers the period from the Revolution (or just before) to the end of the transitional period between aristocracy and democracy. More precisely, the transitional period can be defined in terms of the conjunction of what Tocqueville calls the great democratic revolution with political oscillations which, in the final analysis, express the conflict between egalitarian and liberal passions. These political oscillations are a survival of the political "cycles" of classical thought. By linking them to the progress of equality, Tocqueville brings into play both the ancient and modern concepts of revolution. Although he imagined (in volume one and the first three parts of volume two) a rapid extinction of the revolutionary passions once the period of crisis was over, part four contains a more complex analysis which shows how centralized institutions can in fact sustain revolutionary passions.

Volume two shows that certain dispositions of democracy may become distorted during the transitional period. These include the harmful effects of individualism and the political apathy that follows a period of revolution. In his projected preface for volume two, Tocqueville had planned to stress this aspect of the subject and to analyze the "effects of democracy, particularly [the] unfortunate effects exaggerated in time of revolution." This does not mean, however, that revolution is a necessary characteristic of the transitional period, or even that the egalitarian passions must dominate the liberal passions. As the example of England shows, the centralizing tendencies may themselves encounter very serious obstacles during the transition.[61] The anarchy-despotism dialectic can be avoided,[62] and so can violent revolutionary crisis, provided that free institutions have been established in a country long enough before egalitarian demands manifest themselves.

This dynamic is valid for all democratic countries. Cycles of anarchy and despotism can appear whenever political apathy is coupled with excessive centralization. Thus America, which did not experience a transitional period in the European sense since the Americans were "born equal instead of becoming so,"[63] could prove vulnerable to the phenomenon if its civic spirit should disappear and if the administrative control of the central government were to increase.[64] In 1838, when he was writing the preface to volume two, Tocqueville was prepared to recognize the error he had made in 1835 in stating that the federal bond had weakened.[65] The final chapters of volume two are applicable to the United States; but centralization, which was accelerated in Europe and especially in France by special circumstances,[66] was restrained in America by powerful forces. The dynamic of alternation accurately describes only the postrevolutionary period in France, but it is defined in such a way that it can occur, in attenuated form, in any situation of imperfect democracy whenever apathy and centralization reach a certain critical level.

By the time he wrote volume two, Tocqueville had become aware of the industrial revolution, and he argued that industrialization was a powerful factor in centralization and one that would inevitably affect the United States. In 1835 America had seemed to represent the future of Europe. By 1840 the European present served as a backdrop against which Tocqueville painted the future of the democratic nations, America included. Europe had become the future of America.[67]

The analyses at the end of volume two leave a rather pessimistic impression because Tocqueville admits that it is impossible to herald the end of the transitional phase and the advent of the new society: "The great Revolution which created it still endures, and in what is happening today it is almost impossible to determine what must pass with the Revolution itself and what will remain after it has gone."[68] Tocqueville's immense effort to follow the trail blazed by Royer-Collard ended in failure, and it is not difficult to understand why he decided not to publish the lengthy preface in which he had planned to outline his goals.

The New Democratic Despotism

Tocqueville was more successful in distinguishing between the revolutionary and democratic forms of despotism.[69] But did he fully achieve his goal? We shall see. For now, note simply that it is much easier, and politically more effective, to contrast the two kinds of despotism than to draw a precise boundary between democratic liberty and revolutionary liberty. Montesquieu showed the way: rather than indicate what form of liberal monarchy he desired for France, he described the horrors of despotism. Similarly, at a time when Tocqueville believed that few Frenchmen would care to hear his praise of democratic liberty, he hoped to enlist them more firmly in the liberal cause by involving them in the struggle against its opposite: democratic despotism. This was obviously a shrewd political maneuver, particularly the argument that a danger of violent crisis will remain until the new despotic regime has been stabilized.[70] The theoretical value of the ploy remains to be seen, however.

Fear of despotism was Tocqueville's own earliest and most powerful political passion, but initially it was mingled with his horror of revolution; only through a slow and patient effort of mind was he able to free himself from these early images of revolutionary despotism. In working notes for volume one, he formulated what he considered the fundamental political issue (assuming that society is inevitably headed in the direction of greater equality): "Henceforth one can have only a despotism or a republic."[71] The remainder of the passage shows that by despotism he meant an absolute power similar to that of the Roman emperor, coupled with a return to barbarism.[72] Similarly, in the margin of a draft of the introduction he wrote: "We are headed toward either a republic or a despotism, and perhaps to an alternation between the two."[73] These early drafts bear the trace of memories of the Revolution; on the basis of these, as contrasted with the example of America, Tocqueville would construct his first model of democratic despotism. In fact, the notion of a "tyranny of the majority" is nothing other than an attempt to synthesize such diverse elements as the omnipotence of the majority in assemblies[74] and the tyranny of public opinion. The clearest model of the former was provided by the revolutionary assemblies of France, while the idea of the latter came from the intellectual conformism of Jacksonian America. Tocqueville suggests, moreover, that democratic society leads almost ineluctably to such a condition. As many commentators have noted, the danger of "tyranny" by one or more minorities is at least as great in modern democracies as the tyranny of the majority denounced by Tocqueville. Mill's comments no doubt helped Tocqueville see the weakness of this idea, which was subject to unduly conservative interpretation.[75] In another draft Tocqueville says: "This is the true and original picture; the one in the first volume was distorted, common [hackneyed], and false."[76]

It took him longer to free himself from the image of the tyranny of one man, especially a military hero.[77] To his American informants, most of whom belonged to the landed aristocracy, General Jackson was virtually a new Caesar, a manifestation of democratic tyranny. Tocqueville himself was both fascinated and horrified throughout his life by the genius of Napoleon,[78] "that almost divine intelligence, crudely employed to curtail man's freedom."[79] Furthermore, the profound unity of the "first conclusion"[80] shows that Tocqueville was unable to separate great revolutions from great wars and great ambitions: over these chapters "the Eagle" silently hovers.

Tocqueville's working notes show that for a long time his idea of modern despotism was bound up with that of military despotism.[81] At this point he was still afraid of an "aristocracy of men of war."[82] He wondered, in particular, if the despotism of the future might involve a "fusion of the clerk and the soldier," with society being "treated like a barracks."[83] As he wrote, however, he realized that there was no necessary connection between military and democratic despotism but that it was only an accident of recent French history. For a time he considered a compromise between martial tyranny and what he called despotism in its "mild" form.[84] But ultimately he decided to eliminate the military features from his sketch of the new despotism. He thus created a new model, unencumbered by images inherited from the revolutionary and imperial despotisms of the past.

Where does the theory of democratic despotism fit into part four of volume two? The first three chapters contrast, in general terms, free and centralized institutions, depicting their antagonism as a consequence of tendencies stemming from equality. Chapter four analyzes in detail the factors that hasten or slow the process of centralization. It is clear that the two most powerful causes, war and revolution, have amplified centralizing tendencies in Europe and especially in France, whereas in America centralization is proceeding more slowly than anywhere else. The following chapter describes the combination, in Europe, of political instability with increasing centralization, which Tocqueville associates with violent swings from anarchy to despotism. Finally, in chapter six, we come to the theory of democratic despotism itself.

Tocqueville makes three points. First, he shows the long-term institutional consequences of the conflict, inherent in democratic ideas and mores, between liberal (chapter 1) and centralizing (chapters 2 and 3) tendencies; in chapter four, he abstracts from all the special circumstances analyzed previously. Second, he seeks to show that "compromise between administrative despotism and popular sovereignty"[85] is unstable. And third, he seeks to justify his own liberal political program as a remedy for these ills (chapter 7).

TOCQUEVILLE'S POLITICAL AND philosophical intentions were not correctly perceived by his contemporaries, and to a large extent they are still misunderstood today. The reason for this is partly that his thinking ran counter to the dominant tendencies of his time and partly that some aspects of his thought are, through his own fault, fairly obscure.

To make the simplest point first, note that the political program in chapter seven is quite vague. Its title,[86] as the author notes in the margin, "means nothing at all," to which he added, rather curiously: "Anything I might want to put in its place would imply too much." Nevertheless, while noting that "such a title would suggest more than the chapter can deliver," he mentions that an ideal title would be "What must be done in order to avoid the evils that are indicated in the preceding chapters." After his parliamentary debut, marked by several disappointments, we know that he revised his text,[87] and there is reason to believe that the revision, which he himself describes as a consequence of his recent experience in parliament, involved the political chapters at the end of the work, especially chapter seven.[88] By eliminating certain aspects of his liberal program, he gave his text a timeless appearance, and by deciding not to raise the question of how to define "middle classes" and "government of the middle classes," he concealed much of his thinking about the political problems that France faced during the transitional period.[89]

The distinction between very-long-range political predictions and shorter-term prognoses is not always clear. How, for example, should the conclusion of the chapter on the new despotism be interpreted?[90]

The manuscript throws new light on the text and shows what kind of revolution Tocqueville had in mind, and why. A page of notes is attached at the end of the chapter, and among other things it contains this: "Idea that revolutions and anarchy can combine with this kind of administrative despotism—days of anarchy in years of despotism. Palace revolutions which I can easily distinguish from general revolutions, the impossibility of which I indicated earlier." In the margin he adds: "Idea to introduce somewhere in this chapter, because our contemporaries are more afraid of disorder than of servitude, and that is where the attack should be directed." Tocqueville was very discreet, however, in carrying out this resolution, so that it is quite difficult for the reader to distinguish the risk of alternation between anarchy and despotism in the relatively near term from the long-term risk of despotism in the form of a "protective state." Furthermore, the argument is rather convoluted; in the end Tocqueville abandoned the idea in the manuscripts that despotism would finally put an end to anarchy.[91] He also decided not to present his "theory of alternation" in its entirety; had he done so, this would have complemented the argument of the preceding chapter and contained in embryo an explanation for the cycle of 1848–1851.

In the end, the published text is but a pale and confused version of Tocqueville's thinking. It is difficult for the reader to make out his true intention, which is to distinguish between the new democratic despotism on the one hand and revolutionary despotism on the other (whether that of the Roman Empire, the Reign of Terror, or one of the attenuated forms of revolutionary despotism characteristic of the late transitional period). Finally, in the chapter that follows the theory of the new despotism, Tocqueville introduces an important new idea, but he fails to give it sufficient prominence: "It is always to be feared that revolutionary instincts will become more mild and regular without being extinguished and that they will gradually be transformed into governmental practices and administrative habits."[92] He should have placed greater emphasis on this idea, which helps to explain the transition from a period of alternating anarchy and despotism to the mature, final form of despotism; it marks a radical break with the psychology of revolution set forth in the first conclusion.

Hence it is not very surprising that contemporaries did not understand the final portion of the work, even though many of them favored centralization. Guizot, for example, had concluded his course on the history of French civilization thus: "All things considered, the centralization characteristic of our history has brought France more prosperity and grandeur, and a happier, more glorious fate, than it would have obtained had local institutions, local independence, and local ideas remained sovereign or even merely preponderant."[93] Broadly speaking, French opinion was closer to the views of Guizot and Carné than to those of Tocqueville; people regarded centralization not as a characteristic of the transitional period but as a signal conquest and an enduring necessity.

Today's critics, like Tocqueville's contemporaries, have provided no analysis of democratic despotism that clarifies the differences between it and revolutionary despotism and demonstrates that it is one of the possible stable outcomes of the alternation between anarchy and despotism. No one has shown that, according to Tocqueville's conception of the political dynamic, short-term oscillations ultimately lose their revolutionary character and that, as democratic mores take hold, political passions subside and give way to increasing administrative centralization. In the most stable countries, moreover, the two tendencies do not alternate but develop simultaneously: extension of the activities of the state goes hand in hand with weakening of its authority as well as waning of the political sentiments and passions. That is why the despots of the future will be more like guardians than tyrants.[94]

Before Tocqueville's day, Edmund Burke, Madame de Staël, and Benjamin Constant were critical of the links between democracy and despotism. Yet all cast their aspersions essentially on revolutionary despotism, and their works ceased to provide effective support to the liberal cause and became increasingly outmoded as the risk of a great revolution seemed to diminish.[95] It was left to Tocqueville to develop the theory of democratic despotism by drawing a careful distinction between it and the ancient and revolutionary forms of despotism.

He would have been better understood had he couched his theory entirely in the conditional; but for artistic reasons, no doubt, he did not adopt the style that Montesquieu had employed, for reasons of prudence, in the second of the great "English" chapters of his *Esprit des lois*.[96] Tocqueville contented himself with what seemed to him a clear statement: "I want to imagine the features under which a new despotism might come into the world."[97] After this use of "might", he reverts to the present indicative. But nothing in the text warrants the interpretation that he was actually making a prediction. He was simply describing what would happen if the liberal spirit was not aroused by the exercise of freedom in associations, in the press, and in the courts. Fortunately, many of the remedies recommended by Tocqueville are today in use in the great liberal democracies. Nevertheless, many readers mistake a provisional hypothesis for a prediction; furthermore, they take it for granted that we are now living in the age of democracy and that Tocqueville is painting the misfortunes of the present time or the imminent future. Yet the characteristic signs of the age of transition— great wars, great revolutions, great political passions—abound in the twentieth century, and Tocqueville never made it clear precisely when the period of transition would end and the age of democracy begin. Perhaps the transitional period will never end, and the vision of the future will be only a myth:

> I see an innumerable multitude of men, alike and equal, constantly circling around in pursuit of the petty and banal pleasures with which they glut their souls. Each one of them, withdrawn into himself, is almost unaware of the fate of the rest. Mankind, for him, consists of his children and his personal friends. As for the rest of his fellow citizens, they are near enough, but he does not notice them. He touches them but feels nothing. He exists in and for himself, and though he still may have a family, one can at least say that he has not got a fatherland.
>
> Over this kind of men stands an immense, protective (*tutélaire*) power which is alone responsible for securing their enjoyment and watching over their fate. That power is absolute, thoughtful of detail, orderly, provident, and gentle. It would resemble parental authority if, fatherlike, it tried to prepare its charges for a man's life; but, on the contrary, it only tries to keep them in perpetual childhood. It likes to see the citizens enjoy themselves, provided that they think of nothing but enjoyment. It gladly works for their happiness but wants to be sole agent and judge of it. It provides for their security, foresees and supplies their necessities, facilitates their pleasures, manages their principal concerns, directs their industry, makes rules for their testaments, and divides their inheritances. Why should it not entirely relieve them from the trouble of thinking and from all the cares of living?[98]

As is only fitting in a disciple of Montesquieu, Tocqueville's model of democratic despotism simply inverts the essential moral and political characteristics of liberal democracy while preserving its formal features, in particular its central representative institutions. In appearance, the state serves the society and individuals; in reality, it no longer acts in accordance with its fundamental law. It diverges from its purpose when, rather than encouraging individual liberties, it curtails them. It perverts social regulation, substituting itself for the spontaneous action of society. By stimulating the various forms of individualism, it discourages the public spirit, thereby destroying what Montesquieu considered the "principle" of the regime and resulting in its corruption. All the centers of collective action lose their vitality: local institutions, associations, and social movements wither or disappear.[99] Montesquieu showed that despotism, with its passion for uniformity, destroys the intermediary bodies required by a moderate monarchy.[100] Similarly, Tocqueville shows that democracy deteriorates into a new form of despotism when it destroys all the centers of collective action between the individual and the state. Democracy naturally tends in that direction, but this tendency can be corrected: "Individual independence and local freedoms will always be products of art. Centralized government will be the natural thing."[101]

Montesquieu described the despotism of one man; Tocqueville painted a more complex picture of despotism growing out of the feelings and ideas of the men whom it would oppress,[102] for democracy degenerates of its own inner tendencies whenever liberal sentiments subside.[103] The point of the model is to show that democracy, left to its own devices, lacks the necessary strength to avoid corruption. Democracy initially derives its sole force from revolutionary passion; once the regime becomes established, democracy survives only as long as the liberal sentiments remain vital. Without the seasoning of liberalism, it becomes insipid and eventually decays.

In a master stroke Tocqueville portrayed this new form of corruption by contrasting it with revolutionary despotism. This procedure was no doubt also the source of some exaggerations: his portrait of democracy is too mild. Raymond Aron, in a temperate critique of this passage, in which he finds "lucid forebodings, excessive fears, and unmistakable errors," observed that "mild regimes have not established protective (*tutélaire*) despotisms," and further, that "when regimes have established despotisms, they have been protective only secondarily but primarily violent and ideocratic."[104] The errors that Aron criticizes are not so much Tocqueville's, however, as those of certain of his interpreters, most notably the extreme liberals of the Friedrich von Hayek school. Note that if "mild" regimes[105] have not established protective despotisms, it is because they have put Tocqueville's recommendations into practice. They are pluralist democracies that not only tolerate a diversity of world views but also organize public life on several levels by means of associations, political parties, trade unions, and professional organizations, as well as local institutions and a variety of information media. As for the despotism of our time, which we call totalitarianism, Aron is correct in saying that it is violent and ideocratic first and protective only second. But this is because totalitarianism combines revolutionary despotism with protective despotism, which is not surprising if we are still in the transitional stage.[106] Aron might have agreed, for his main point seems to be that for the time being the prophecy of a mild despotism has not been fulfilled, which is quite correct.[107]

Tocqueville is a political theorist whom some want desperately to turn into a prophet. Prophecy was indeed one of the maladies of the Restoration and the July Monarchy,[108] and Tocqueville spoke the language of his day. Yet he was careful only to indicate major trends, always making it clear that men could, by their own actions, promote either servitude or freedom; actual situations in the past or present are always mixtures of the pure democratic forms and must be analyzed in terms of their history and politics. In Montesquieu's case it is possible to wonder whether he was describing despotism or constructing a theoretical model. (I am inclined to think that he was constructing a theoretical model.) In the case of Tocqueville's "democratic despotism," no doubt is possible: it is clearly a theoretical construction.

Tocqueville was also a politician, whose circumstantial judgments, whether right or wrong, must be distinguished, insofar as it is possible to do so, from his theoretical conclusions. Did he ascribe too much importance in his political career to the fight against administrative centralization? This is where I would agree with Aron that his fears were "excessive" even if some of his "forebodings" were lucid.[109] Tocqueville did not ascribe such crucial theoretical importance to administrative centralization because he held that the liberal state was the minimal state; unlike many of his contemporaries, he was not guilty of this error. But he was the first to understand that undue administrative intervention would spell the end of a government of law, which for him was the same thing as liberal government.[110] His idea was quite different from that of the liberals of his own day as well as from that of Hayek and some other modern liberals who, like Hayek, apply economic forms of argument to these questions. Liberal democracy is a regime that derives its strength and legitimacy from public opinion. If administrative centralization and increasing state intervention sap initiative and weaken liberal sentiments, public opinion will suffer, and so will a regime that derives its power from that opinion. If voters care about nothing but their own interests and cannot choose representatives in an intelligent way, the regime will become corrupt.[111] And it is not, I think, alien to Tocqueville's thought to add that if government intervention and regulation increase unduly, the very idea of the law and of representative institutions is thereby diminished.[112]

Tocqueville described in advance the reasons for the constitutional instability from which France suffered throughout the nineteenth century, until the Third Republic finally became established on a secure footing: "A constitution that is republican at the top and ultramonarchic in all its other parts has always seemed to me an ephemeral monster."[113] Looking beyond his own century, he foresaw that the legislature might be reduced to a mere symbolic repository of sovereignty and that economic and social problems would for most men take the place of political problems. Finally, he made a decisive contribution to the theory of modern democracy by showing that, since a government of the people was impossible to achieve in a large-scale modern society, the idea of democracy cannot be adequately embodied in a system that simply allows the nation to choose its own representatives; several levels of choice and delegation of authority are also essential.[114]

THE MANUSCRIPTS ENABLE us to reconstruct a theory that is rather obscurely presented in part four of the second volume of *Democracy in America*. I have already said enough about Tocqueville's reasons for not expressing his ideas in full. The most important impediment to frank communication between him and his public was that Tocqueville, in 1840, did not believe that his readers shared his view that liberty should be ranked foremost among political values. He also knew that "liberty is always a little disturbing,"[115] and he did not want his fellow citizens' pusillanimous love of tranquillity to stand in the way of what he believed to be necessary reforms. Consequently his calculations: "To make use of democracy in order to moderate democracy is the only avenue of salvation open to us . . . It is primarily a question of proving that it is with the aid of liberty that we can hope to prevent license. Everything is there. In order to succeed, fear must be put to work on behalf of liberty."[116] The strength of the egalitarian passions dominates volume one; volume two is imbued with a melancholy sentiment of the weakness of liberal passions,[117] while egalitarian mores are depicted as quite mild. Clearly, Tocqueville wished to offer a very benign portrait of democracy in order to make his liberal program as unfrightening as possible. He therefore eliminated much of his theory of the alternation between anarchy and despotism. What is more, his extraordinary portrait of democratic despotism tends to eclipse all the rest. In the end, it is difficult for the reader to distinguish between medium-range political analyses and long-term reflections on the future and on the final choice between servitude and freedom.[118]

Thus, the second conclusion of the work is not clearly differentiated from the first. The final chapters of part three describe the waning of political passions and the low probability of great revolutions and great wars in the distant future of democratic society. Part four, which is concerned primarily with the transitional period, shows in a veiled way that some danger of "anarchy" still exists and that the political process will ultimately lead to one of two possible forms of democracy at the end of the transitional phase. The second conclusion contains two important new ideas. The first is the theory of democratic despotism, which Tocqueville composed during a lengthy period of isolation, eliminating all the residue of ancient and revolutionary despotism whose images still figured prominently in the first conclusion. The other major innovation is the idea that revolutionary instincts may gradually be transformed into "governmental practices and administrative habits."[119] First presented here, this connection between revolution and centralization is one of the major themes of *The Old Regime*,[120] where Tocqueville fleshes it out by showing how centralization helps not only to perpetuate the revolutionary spirit but also to engender and nourish it.

Tocqueville's work can therefore be divided into two groups of texts: one consisting of *Democracy in America* minus the political chapters at the end of volume two, and the other consisting of everything else. Until the middle of 1838 Tocqueville believed that he had a simple way of distinguishing between democracy and revolution, but later that year, as he wrote the final chapters of *Democracy*, he discovered that the revolutionary spirit can long outlive the revolution and that its fate is bound up with that of centralization. Previously, he had thought of institutions as a reflection of ideas and mores, but now he maintained that they have a life of their own and that they create, or at least encourage, forms of the public spirit that are not a mere reflection of the social state and may even be in conflict with the ideas and mores that express this state. He was forced to recognize that his strenuous effort, inspired by Royer-Collard,[121] to distinguish between democracy and revolution had ended in failure: "The great revolution . . . is still going on, and in what happens in our time it is almost impossible to ascertain what must pass away with the Revolution itself and what will remain after it."[122] One thing was clear, however: that the revolutionary spirit could endure, and could transform itself, thanks to administrative centralization.[123] The final part of volume two might have been entitled "Democracy and Revolution," whereas the first three parts had led to a conclusion in which the two terms were still contrasted in an optimistic way: "Democracy or Revolution." Tocqueville's reflection on the transitional phase led to a discovery that creates a sharp division in his work, more significant than the break that Drescher saw between the two *Democracies*.[124]

This division is crucial; because of it, there can be no certainty that the transitional period will ever end. The prospect of a pure democracy, untainted by revolutionary and aristocratic residues, becomes a point on a distant horizon. Even if Tocqueville still believed in 1840 that there was no danger of revolution in France, he had already embraced a system of thought which contains in embryo the notion of a revolutionary tradition. He wrote the *Souvenirs* and *The Old Regime* to explain the continuity of that tradition beyond the apparent alternation of anarchy with despotism. Most readers do not read *The Old Regime* beyond the volume published in 1856, and many see the kinship between the theory of the continuity of the French administration and the final reflections in *Democracy in America*. To go beyond this, to grasp the fact that Tocqueville also wanted to describe the formation of the French revolutionary tradition, one must read the preparatory notes for the unfinished second volume, which Tocqueville wanted to entitle simply "The Revolution."[125]

At the origin of *The Old Regime* lies this thought from the *Souvenirs*, written in 1850:

And now the French Revolution begins again, for it is always the same. The farther we proceed, the more remote and obscure its goal becomes. Are we coming—as new prophets, possibly as foolish as their predecessors, assure us we are—to a social transformation more thorough and profound than our fathers ever wished for and than we ourselves can yet conceive; or must we simply end up in that intermittent state of anarchy which is the well-known, chronic, and incurable malady of old peoples? As for myself, I cannot say; I know not when this long voyage will end. I am tired of mistaking deceptive mists for the shore, and I often wonder whether that terra firma for which we have been searching so long actually exists or whether our destiny is not rather to ply the seas forever![126]

Conclusion: The Ambivalence of Democracy

To HASTY READERS, the architecture of Tocqueville's work in general, and of each of his two great books in particular, seems simple. Everyone is pleased to recognize the elegance and reliability of his eyewitness accounts and the wisdom contained in the sometimes penetrating insights to which they think his thought can be reduced—or, rather, his "thoughts," since it is taken for granted that his work consists, on the one hand, of a philosophy of democracy and, on the other hand, of a historical explanation of the origins of the French Revolution. Disciplinary differences between historians and sociologists only reinforce the natural predilections of American and French writers to encourage this dual approach, the main drawback of which is to destroy the unity of the work and to hide its complexity and richness.

Admittedly, Tocqueville's vocabulary is not as precise as his ideas; in particular, he used the words "democracy" and "revolution" in very different ways without always explaining what he was up to. In his defense, however, it can be said that he showed better than anyone else how the meanings of these old words had changed almost before his eyes. For it was the French Revolution that altered the meaning of the word "revolution," and it was American democracy that set the example of the first modern democracy, so different from what the ancients or Rousseau had meant by the term. It is absurd, moreover, to expect Tocqueville to meet the standards of rigor required of a contemporary sociologist, when he was dealing with new and still changing realities. In any case, his political vocabulary was more reliable than that of his contemporaries, and more than any of them he has taught us to understand these novel historical phenomena.

He did so, moreover, with no trace of dogmatism, and he is quite safe from the reproach that his friend John Stuart Mill leveled at Comte: namely, that in his late speculations he succumbed to an uncontrolled desire for unity and systematization.[1] For Tocqueville, diversity was a part of man's nature, and he was too keenly aware of the existence of conflicts of value to have any interest in majestic syntheses. Between individuals and groups tensions due to opposing values were inevitable, and there was no guarantee that society would ever achieve equilibrium or even that any science of action could infallibly demonstrate how its members ought to behave. Nevertheless, throughout his life Tocqueville guided himself by referring to one fixed point: for him, political liberty was the preeminent value. But since he knew that the majority of his contemporaries did not share his view, he was sometimes forced to resort to subterfuge in setting forth his ideas. His political ambitions led him to make certain omissions, as we have seen, and these impaired the presentation of his ideas. He was quite frank about his disappointment with the "wretched world of parliament" which he inhabited for ten years.[2] From all his political experience he derived only one personal reward, when he served briefly in Odilon Barrot's second cabinet as minister of foreign affairs, which restored his confidence in himself.[3] Death prevented him from completing his great work on the Revolution, moreover; so there are many reasons to argue that his work has no apparent unity.

It is my contention, however, that Tocqueville's mind was always occupied by one thought, whose development we can follow through his constant need to contrast democracy with revolution, democratic culture with revolutionary culture. These are the unifying themes in Tocqueville's thought, whose enduring interest and importance I have sought to demonstrate through study of the working manuscript of *Democracy in America*, unpublished notes in the Yale archives, and fragments intended for the unfinished work on revolution. To conclude, I want to show the unity that exists among the three interim conclusions identified in the preceding chapters, in the hope that this will help to show how Tocqueville based his liberalism on a "new political science" as well as to clarify the relation between democracy and liberalism.

The Three Conclusions of the Work

The first conclusion comes at the end of part three, volume two, of *Democracy in America*.[4] It shows that the political passions of democratic societies are at odds with such vast ambitions as war and revolution. This comes as no surprise to the reader who remembers the beginning of volume one, where Tocqueville points out that America presents an accurate image of democracy precisely because its origins can be traced to Puritanism rather than to a revolution.

The portrait of American institutions, which is often considered Tocqueville's masterpiece, has rightly attracted the attention of readers, but it is a mistake to view it as nothing more than a commentary on the Constitution and laws of the United States. Had it been only that, Tocqueville would hardly have surpassed the authors of *The Federalist*, to whom, incidentally, he owed a great deal. In reality, *Democracy in America* offers the first philosophical theory of modern democracy, a far cry from the dogma of the First Republic and the *Social Contract*. Tocqueville's is a philosophical theory, but at the same time, as Mill observed, it is inductive and analytic, unlike the theories of Bentham and his disciples or those of the eighteenth-century philosophes.[5] For the first time the object of study is representative, pluralistic democracy. Tocqueville examines not only its federal and local structures but also the diversity of opinions and interests represented. He shows how reverence for the Constitution and common moral convictions shared by various religious sects gave America the unity it needed to balance its diversity. Yet it is impossible to fail to see that even in analyzing the machinery of the American Constitution, Tocqueville is thinking of France: executive power vested in one man and a legislature divided into two chambers were aspects of the American system that contrasted sharply with the dogmas of the Convention; and the separation of powers in America was based on an interpretation of Montesquieu more faithful than the one current in France and, in particular, at odds with the rigid ideas of Sieyès. And Tocqueville tirelessly contrasts the power of the American judiciary with the bankruptcy of French justice under the Revolution. American democracy provided him with a model of a government of law, whereas the Revolution symbolized the reign of violence.

All in all, the stability and longevity of the American Republic resulted from its laws far more than from any favorable circumstances, and even more from the mores of the Americans than from their laws: this is the basic conclusion of volume one;[6] and volume two would develop that point further by contrasting democratic ideas, sentiments, and passions with those bearing the stamp of revolution. Encouraged in this project by Royer-Collard, Tocqueville wrote the bulk of volume two with the purpose of establishing this distinction, to which he attached the greatest importance; this effort culminated in the first conclusion of the work, the chapter in which he asks why great revolutions will become increasingly rare in democratic societies.[7] In America the tendencies of democracy could be observed in their pure state, and the first conclusion can be seen as the result of comparative analysis based on a notion so fundamental to an understanding of Tocqueville's thought that I have already quoted it several times: "The Americans have this great advantage, that they attained democracy without the sufferings of a democratic revolution and that they were born equal instead of becoming so."[8] In France, however, where the republican ideal was still largely confused with the constitution of 1793, the First Republic embodied the opposite of the American model: a regime whose democratic features were effaced by the pressure of the Revolution. The two faces of the democratic Janus are thus easily identified.

The final part of volume two gives the work a very different conclusion, apparently the opposite of the first one. Instead of being based on a supposed antithesis between democratic and revolutionary characteristics, it asserts that, thanks to centralization, the two can coexist for a long time, perhaps even permanently. In democratic countries, "it is always to be feared that revolutionary instincts, calmed and regularized but not extinguished, may gradually be transformed into governmental practices and administrative habits. Hence I know of no country in which revolutions are more dangerous than in a democracy, because apart from the accidental and ephemeral ills which they are ever bound to entail, there is always a danger of their becoming permanent and, one may almost say, eternal."[9] Previously, Tocqueville had thought that with the passage of time the consequences of the Revolution would disappear and the European countries would, after a period of transition, experience a situation comparable to that of the United States. America was held up as the future of Europe; but in this second conclusion of his work Tocqueville argued that centralization was inevitable in democratic societies and that, although the United States had been more successful in slowing it than the European countries, it would nevertheless eventually follow Europe's lead.[10] The notion of a transitional period, so often invoked by Tocqueville, became obsolete, or, rather, it changed its form: no longer was it conceived of as a temporary mixture of aristocratic, democratic, and revolutionary elements, but as a permanent fusion of revolutionary with democratic characteristics. And there was one further change. Tocqueville always believed that free mores were the most reliable means of sustaining free institutions and that, in return, free institutions helped free mores to take firm root. But previously he had argued that discord between a society's characteristic mores and its laws could only be temporary or trivial: either such discord was soon corrected by spontaneous evolution or appropriate reforms, or there would likely develop a prerevolutionary situation of turbulence. Now, however, he admitted that a gap between mores and laws could survive long after revolution had ended, keeping forms of the revolutionary spirit alive within democratic society itself.

Tocqueville at this time abandoned the idea of imagining the distant future of democracy on the model of *The Federalist*, but, unlike Comte before him and Marx after him, he did not on that account give up on the ideal of liberal democracy. His political science acquired a new sophistication as he abandoned his initial conception, which had been based on a tripartite philosophy of history, according to which historical time falls neatly into three epochs—an oversimplification, like all philosophies of this sort. Thus, the transformation of the notion of the transitional period was among the more significant ways in which Tocqueville deepened his thought. At first he had imagined a period intermediate between the remote past and the distant future, the past corresponding to the ideal type of pure aristocracy, the future to pure democracy. Eventually he came to understand that it was a mistake to confuse purity of type with remoteness in time and that every concrete historical situation is a mixture of elements taken from different ideal types. The United States presented an apparent exception to this rule, but here, too, Tocqueville's thinking evolved: at first he saw America as a pure expression of the democratic principle, and in volume two he showed why America was exceptional. It was not so much the absence of aristocratic elements (for there was no dearth of these in the English legacy, and the Americans had assimilated the best of them as a means of safeguarding their liberties), as it was the absence of great revolutions, great wars, and centralization. By 1840 Tocqueville no longer based his vision of the future on the happiest years in the history of the American Republic. For both the United States and the nations of Europe, dangers lay ahead: the dangers that centralization carries with it.

These new ideas foreshadow themes that Tocqueville would develop in *Souvenirs* and *The Old Regime*; the final section of *Democracy in America* is closer to those two works than it is to the rest of the book of which it is a part. The idea of a revolutionary tradition, contained in embryonic form in the final passages of *Democracy in America*, is the real subject of *The Old Regime*, while *Souvenirs* recounts the resurgence of the spirit of 1793 among the revolutionaries of 1848. But *The Old Regime* adds a new analysis of how centralization in a society of orders (or, as Tocqueville preferred to say, a society of classes, rigidly separated from one another) contributes to the formation of the revolutionary spirit. In all democratic societies and societies in the process of becoming democratic, centralization leads to a sort of political corruption. In societies with a high degree of social mobility, however, the ultimate danger, in its most extreme form, is democratic despotism.[11] By contrast, in societies where the classes are rigidly separated, centralization first helps foster the revolutionary spirit[12] and later becomes the primary instrument of revolutionary despotism. The unfinished second volume of the work, on the subject of revolution, would have examined the nature of this revolutionary tradition and would probably have developed certain ideas from the *Souvenirs* concerning its regressive aspects. This unfinished third conclusion to the work is obviously in perfect harmony with what I have been calling the second conclusion of *Democracy in America*, while the second conclusion is at odds not only with the first but with most of the rest of the book.

The Unity of the Work

Now that we have isolated the two halves of Tocqueville's work, can we find the principle of unity that holds it together? As we have seen, the two halves do not coincide with his two great books; the boundary line passes between parts three and four of volume two of *Democracy in America*. I propose calling the first half of that volume "Democracy or Revolution" and the second half "Democracy and Revolution."

Must we conclude that Tocqueville changed his mind sometime between the end of 1838 and the end of 1839? Having previously stressed the importance of his omissions and corrections after his election in

1839, I shall say nothing more about that subject here. There is no denying that, while Tocqueville remained firmly wedded to certain principles, his work was influenced by his doubts and by the changing political situation. The major change has to do with centralization, which he first conceived as a typical institutional feature of the age of transition but later came to see as an institution typical of democracy itself. In England he saw that, although democratization led to centralization, it did not, in a country where aristocracy was overt, lead to the formation of a revolutionary spirit.[13] In a country like France, however, which had experienced a great revolution and which possessed a very ancient centralizing tradition, centralization perpetuated certain forms of the revolutionary spirit. Tocqueville's principal deliberate omission was his failure to discuss the "middle classes" and the critique of government based on them at the end of *Democracy*; this is the cause of considerable confusion, for it prevented him from distinguishing as clearly as he should have done between the imminent future of French society and the prospects for democracy over the long term.

For these reasons, the two conclusions of *Democracy in America* seem to contradict each other, whereas in reality they do not deal with the same question. The first treats perfect democracy, a classless society on the American model, which could only be relevant to the distant future of the European countries, while the second treats imperfect democracies, born of revolution, in which democratic and revolutionary features may be combined for some time, possibly forever. It is not necessarily contradictory to assert, on the one hand, that in certain situations these features may occur in combination over a considerable period of time and, on the other hand, that pure democracy and revolution have nothing in common. In 1840 Tocqueville understood that progress toward equality would be neither so rapid nor so widespread as he had believed in 1835, and that the industrial revolution would, for some unforeseeable period, create new kinds of inequality, perhaps even harsher than that of the Old Regime but destined to diminish as democracy progressed. The situation had become more complex, but the main idea, that of a dynamic of democracy, was maintained. Once Tocqueville's undeniable fluctuations and imprecisions are recognized, it is easy to see that they affect the presentation of his ideas rather than their content; though they may cloud his meaning, they do not seriously damage his coherence.

The unity of Tocqueville's thought, as well as of his conclusions, is clear once one realizes that, for him, the first and most crucial of political realities is the public spirit as fashioned by political institutions and the exercise of political choices and, even more, by ideas and mores, or, to use a more contemporary vocabulary, by a political culture. All of Tocqueville's reflections, from his first travel diaries to the final fragments of *Revolution* (the projected second volume of *The Old Regime*), are concerned with democratic culture and its relation to revolutionary culture. His relatively unsuccessful career as a politician, and in particular as a member of the Constitutional Commission of 1848, tended to reinforce this natural inclination, and when he was working on *The Old Regime* he wrote to his friend Corcelle: "I am thoroughly convinced that political societies are not what laws make them but what, in advance, they are prepared to be by the sentiments, beliefs, ideas, and habits of heart and mind of the men who compose them, as nature and education have made them."[14] In its totality, Tocqueville's work can indeed be seen as a reflection on the civic culture of democratic societies. He analyzed, as a sociologist would do, the conditions under which democratic societies form their political ideas and ideals. For him, experience of political freedom, together with the political science that can be derived from such experience, constitutes the best guarantee against the distortions of ideology. A reader always has the right to ask in the name of what authority a writer claims to be able to denounce an ideology; Tocqueville, like Marx and Pareto, responds by invoking the science of history and the experience of a special kind of political practice. For him, that special practice is the experience of a free people, and he constantly shows that in politics a sense of reality and political liberty are one and the same.

Democratic culture risks two forms of corruption, which, to borrow the language of Aristotle, we may call excess and deficiency. Of the two, corruption through excess of freedom is the less likely, and Tocqueville prefers, especially in volume one of *Democracy*, to describe corruption resulting from the "extreme spirit of equality." Taking his inspiration from Montesquieu, he shows the connection between this form of corruption and revolutionary disturbances. The "tyranny of number" is the most striking example of corruption of this kind. Subsequently, Tocqueville came to think that this danger was increasingly unlikely, and in volume two and later works he worries mainly about corruption through deficiency. He explicitly considers the possibility of an industrial aristocracy, although he argues that this new form of inequality cannot last. His most serious concern was a deficiency of liberal sentiment, which he thought might lead to a new kind of democratic despotism. The revolutionary tradition, which he describes in his last works, can be characterized as the result of a mutual exacerbation of the spirit of extreme equality and the waning of liberal sentiment (which began in the French Revolution and continued steadily thereafter).

Using the comparative method, Tocqueville sought to discover why liberalism had been unable to establish itself in France as it had done in the Anglo-Saxon countries, even though the spirit of independence was fiercer in France than anywhere else.[15] The usual answer to this question, as banal as it is wrong, is that in France conservatism usurped the place of liberalism; this does not explain why the French should have become more conservative than their neighbors. Tocqueville's reflections on the precarious state of democratic culture in France and its tendency to become corrupted into revolutionary culture suggests another explanation: that it was the violence of the first revolutionary shock, followed by a series of other revolutions, that made it hard for liberalism to take root in a soil which had long been rendered inhospitable to it.

A "New Kind of Liberal"

Very early, Tocqueville wanted to define himself as a "new kind of liberal," and his work can be seen as an effort to establish liberalism on a new foundation, avoiding both its obsolete aristocratic forms and the distortions that lie in wait in democracies. He translated Montesquieu's views into the democratic context while returning to Montesquieu's methods and political principles, eschewing the distortions of liberalism that had preceded and accompanied the Revolution. To do this, moreover, he contributed greatly to the development of a sociology of political knowledge.

This led him, first of all, to redress certain misguided tendencies of eighteenth-century philosophy, particularly its excessive optimism. He showed that democratic societies have a tendency to overestimate the possibility of progress, particularly in revolutionary periods; knowing this, we can understand how he wished to correct Condorcet. He also rejected the fatalism of the historians of the democratic era, preferring to see the future in terms of probabilities. His critique of eighteenth-century political philosophy went to the very root, to the idea of natural equality, which he interpreted as the product of a centralized

society moving toward equality, whose institutions no longer corresponded to the social condition. He was highly suspicious of the idea
of a natural order, especially in the form in which it was presented by
the Physiocrats, for he was convinced that human societies are based
not on nature but on history and that political and cultural factors
become inextricably intertwined. Eighteenth-century French philosophy was for him the model of a revolutionary distortion of Cartesian
thought, which he took to be the characteristic philosophy of the
democratic era. In the chapters on individualism in *Democracy in America* he shows why democratic societies tend to see themselves primarily
in economic terms. Tocqueville's sociology of knowledge is most strik-
ingly revealed in his discussion of individualism: he shows how the
illusion of individual independence is created by the disappearance of
the most obvious traditional social ties, while at the same time inter-
dependence (what Durkheim would call "forms of organic solidarity")
actually increases and diversifies. Tocqueville adds that this individualism is particularly exaggerated immediately after a revolution, an
observation that is the key to his attitude toward Benjamin Constant,
as well as the reason for his remaining aloof from the form of liberal
individualism that was concerned mainly with private values and saw
political liberty not as valuable in itself but only as a guarantee of civil
liberties.

The principal threat to democratic societies comes from the fact that
freedom is granted to men who do not understand its value and treat
it as a second-class political good, less important than tranquillity and
prosperity. For that reason Tocqueville is careful not to limit his
reflection to the political sphere; his researches and his plea on behalf
of freedom are threefold.[16] He shows how the absence of liberty poses
a threat, first, to progress[17] and, eventually, to material prosperity;[18]
finally, he describes the danger of democratic despotism. Those commentators who have, up to now, stressed only the political dimension
of Tocqueville's work have mutilated his thought and rendered it
incoherent and almost absurd. Had he pitched his argument solely on
the political level, he would have been quite wrong to paint the portrait
that he did of a "mild and protective" despotism, which he knew better
than anyone else was in itself insufficient to inspire horror in the
bourgeoisie.

Democratic despotism, first described in theory by Tocqueville,
grows out of tendencies inherent in democratic society itself, out of the
difficulties that society faces in living with freedom. Liberals before

Tocqueville had dealt only with monarchic, revolutionary, and imperial forms of despotism: in all of these an overweening state forcibly imposes its will on society. Democratic despotism is something very different, for it is a response to the demands of a society in which liberal sentiments are no longer strong enough. Here again, Tocqueville moved from historical observation to the essence of the phenomenon as he began to explore his own ideas more deeply. Initially he identified democratic despotism with the Revolution and Empire, but later, as he sought to separate out the historical, revolutionary elements from the enduring tendencies of democratic society, he discovered the true nature of democratic despotism, which should be seen as a theoretical countermodel to liberal democracy. This transition from comparative history to the "new political science" reveals the symmetry of the two theoretical models of despotism. Both are disturbances of the equilibrium between state and society. The despotism that stems from society itself is no less a danger than the abuse of political power that is visited upon society. Although the two phenomena are easy to distinguish in theory, in concrete, historical situations they actually occur in combination; it was Tocqueville's genius to show how each reinforces the other. The two faces of democracy reveal an indelible ambivalence.

Tocqueville did not confuse the liberal state with the minimal state, because he understood that the liberal state was, by definition, a government of law, whereas the minimal state was but one historical form assumed by the liberal opposition to monarchical and revolutionary despotism. Unlike ordinary liberals, however, he sought not to combat but to compensate for the growth of the central government, which he knew to be inevitable. He was thus the originator of the pluralist theory of democracy. Nevertheless, although his quest for an equilibrium between state and society is based on sound principles, it results in recommendations, on the institutional level, which are rather too general. Tocqueville was no legal scholar, and, like Rousseau's great legislator,[19] he was more concerned with mores than with laws. For in mores, or what we would nowadays call *mentalités* or cultures, lies the secret of the political future. Like Montesquieu, moreover, Tocqueville believed that the way to reform mores was not with laws but with other mores.[20] He is without peer when it comes to demonstrating that the justice of political and social relations ultimately depends on a proper relation between liberty and equality in civic culture.

Tocqueville never cited Condorcet or Constant or even Madame de Staël and Chateaubriand, to whom he owed so much, and he did not refer to either Guizot or Royer-Collard, to whom he owed even more. The most extraordinary thing is that he hardly mentions Montesquieu, of whom he was the greatest disciple and whose example he frequently follows quite closely. No doubt he had a good deal of author's pride and perhaps an excessive desire to be original, and to seem so. This psychological explanation, however, though not false, has the disadvantage of not pointing out the true and very powerful originality of his work as distinct from the calculated effort to give the impression of originality: he established liberalism on a new foundation by identifying those dangers within democratic culture that most threatened to erode its liberal component. He believed that, without liberalism, democracy could not survive, and he painted a portrait of the new democratic despotism to make this clear to others. He knew that French political culture was a most dangerous amalgam of the psychology of the "middle classes" and the revolutionary tradition, and he spared no effort to give the French people the means to identify these two distortions of true democracy. This was one of the principal purposes of the "new political science" that he created.

To combat ideological distortion and, more generally, the evils produced by democratic society, Tocqueville recommended freedom as the best of remedies. Was this a liberal ideology or a philosophy of liberty? Each reader will answer this question in his or her own way. I have given reasons for my own answer throughout this study: Tocqueville was a philosopher of liberty and a sociologist of political culture. His philosophy is based on the enduring features of man's nature as a free and responsible being, who can fulfill his destiny only through the exercise of freedom in both public and private life. As for equality, Tocqueville treats it as a cultural object, associated with liberty to a greater or lesser degree depending on the particular political culture. Tocqueville's political science compares the various civic cultures of democratic societies and diagnoses them as healthy or corrupt; it offers liberals instruments of discrimination and vigilance, necessary tools of civic education.

Selected Bibliography
Notes
Index

Selected Bibliography

Works on Tocqueville

Aron, Raymond. *Auguste Comte et Alexis de Tocqueville, juges de l'Angle-terre*. Zaharoff Lecture for 1965. Oxford: Clarendon Press, 1965.
———*Dix-huit leçons sur les sociétés industrielles*. Paris: Gallimard, 1962.
———*Essai sur les libertés*. Paris: Calmann-Lévy, 1965.
Barth, Niklas Peter. *Die Idee der Freiheit und der Demokratie bei Alexis de Tocqueville*. Zurich: Engen Koller, 1953.
Battista, Anna Maria. *Lo spirito liberale e lo spirito religioso: Tocqueville nel dibattito sulla scuola*. Milan: Jaco Book, 1976.
Birnbaum, Pierre. *Sociologie de Tocqueville*. Paris: Presses Universitaires de France, 1970. With bibliography.
Brogan, Hugh. *Tocqueville*. London: Fontana, 1973.
Brunius, Teddy. *Alexis de Tocqueville: The Sociological Aesthetician*. Upsala, 1960.
Burckhardt, Carl. *Alexis de Tocqueville*. Frankfurt: Bilnisse, 1959.
Chevallier, Jean-Jacques. *Les grandes oeuvres politiques de Machivael à nos jours*. Paris: Armand Colin, 1949.
Diez del Corral y Pedruzo, Luis. *La demistification de la antiguedad clasica por los pensadores liberales, con especial referencia a Tocqueville*. Cuadernos de la "Fundacion Pastor," no. 16. Madrid: Taurus Edicions, 1969.
———*El liberalismo doctrinal*. Madrid, 1945.
———*La mendalidad politica de Tocqueville con especial referencia a Pascal*. Madrid: Ediciones Castilla, 1965.
Drescher, Seymour. *Dilemmas of Democracy: Tocqueville and Modernization*. Pittsburgh: University of Pittsburgh Press, 1968.

————*Tocqueville and England.* Cambridge, Mass.: Harvard University Press, 1964.

Eichtal, Eugène d'. *Alexis de Tocqueville et la démocratie libérale.* Paris: Calmann-Lévy, 1897.

Fabian, Bernhard. *Alexis de Tocqueville Amerikabild.* Heidelberg: Carl Winter, 1957.

Faguet, Emile. *Politiques et moralistes du XIXe siècle.* Paris: Société Française d'Impression et d'Edition, 1903.

Fournière, Xavier de la. *Alexis de Tocqueville.* Paris: Librairie Académique Perrin, 1981.

Freund, Dorrit. *Alexis de Tocqueville und die politische Kultur der Demokratie.* Bern and Stuttgart: Verlag Paul Haupt, 1974.

Furet, François. *Penser la Révolution française.* Paris: Gallimard, 1978.

Gargan, Edward. *Alexis de Tocqueville: The Critical Years, 1848–1851.* Washington: Catholic University of America Press, 1955.

Geiss, Immanuel. *Tocqueville und das Zeitalter der Revolution.* Munich, 1972.

Gibert, Pierre. *Tocqueville: Égalité sociale et liberté politique.* Paris, Aubier Montaigne, 1977.

Girard, Louis. *Le libéralisme en France de 1814 à 1848. Doctrine et mouvement.* Paris: CDU-SEDES, 1967.

Goldstein, Doris S. *Trial of Faith: Religion and Politics in Tocqueville's Thought.* New York: Elsevier, 1975.

Göring, Helmut. *Tocqueville und die Demokratie.* Munich and Berlin: Verlag von R. Oldenburg, 1928.

Gorla, Gino. *Commento a Tocqueville "l'idea dei diritti."* Milan: Giuffré, 1948.

Hartz, Louis. *The Liberal Tradition in America.* New York and London: Harcourt Brace Jovanovich, 1955.

Hereth, Michael. *Alexis de Tocqueville: Die Gefährdung der Freiheit in der Demokratie.* Stuttgart: Verlag W. Kohlammler, 1979.

Herr, Richard. *Tocqueville and the Old Regime.* Princeton: Princeton University Press, 1962.

Janet, Paul. *Histoire de la science politique dans ses rapports avec la morale.* 4th ed. Paris: Felix Alcan, 1913.

————*Philosophie de la Révolution française.* Paris: Libraire Germer-Baillière, 1975.

Kellenberger, Peter. *Mensch und Staat bei Alexis de Tocqueville.* Gallen, 1954.

Kiesinger, Kurt Georg. *Di Prognosen des Grafen Alexis de Tocqueville am Beginn des industrialen Zeitalters.* Karlsruhe, 1961.

Laboulaye, Edouard. *L'Etat et ses limites.* 2nd ed. Paris: Charpentier, 1863.

Lamberti, Jean-Claude. *La notion d'individualisme chez Tocqueville*. Paris: Presses Universitaires de France, 1970.

Laski, Harold J. *The Rise of European Liberalism*. London: Allen & Unwin, 1936.

Lawlor, Mary. *Alexis de Tocqueville in the Chamber of Deputies: His Views on Foreign and Colonial Policy*. Washington: Catholic University of America Press, 1959.

Lerner, Max. *Tocqueville and American Civilization*. New York: Harper and Row, 1969.

Leroy, Maxime. *Histoire des idées sociales en France*, vol. II, *De Babeuf à Tocqueville*. Paris: Gallimard, 1962.

Lively, Jack. *The Social and Political Thought of Alexis de Tocqueville*. Oxford: Clarendon Press, 1965.

Lucchini, Laurent. *De la Démocratie en Amérique: Ce que ce texte a d'essentiel pour la politique aujourd'hui*. Paris: Seghers, 1972.

Mahieu, R. G. *Les enquêteurs français aux Etats-Unis de 1830 à 1837*. Paris: Honoré Champion, 1934.

Mantaz, H. *French Criticism of American Literature before 1850*. New York, 1917.

Mayer, J.-P. *Alexis de Tocqueville*, 2nd ed. Paris: Gallimard, 1948.

——*Political Thought in France from the Revolution to the Fourth Republic*, rev. ed. London: Routledge and Paul, 1949.

Meyer, Martin. *Der Begriff der Freiheit im Denken Alexis de Tocqueville*. Zurich: Hörgen, 1955.

Meyers, Marvin. *The Jacksonian Persuasion*. Stanford: Stanford University Press, 1957.

Michel, Henry. *L'idée de l'Etat*. Paris: Hachette, 1896.

Mill, John Stuart. *Dissertations and Discussions*. London: Parker, 1869. Vol. II, pp. 1–83, contains two review essays on *Democracy in America* first published in the *London and Westminster Review* in 1835 and in the *Edinburgh Review* in 1840. These essays, or commentary, have also been reproduced as an introduction to the 1961 Schocken edition of *Democracy in America*, trans. Henry Reeve.

Mueller, I.-W. *John Stuart Mill and French Thought*. Urbana: University of Illinois Press, 1956.

Nantet, Jacques. *Tocqueville*. Paris: Seghers, 1971.

Pierre-Marcel, Roland. *Essai politique sur Alexis de Tocqueville*. Paris: Alcan, 1910.

Pierson, George Wilson. *Tocqueville and Beaumont in America*. New York: Oxford University Press, 1938.

——*Tocqueville in America*. Gloucester, Mass.: Peter Smith, 1969. An abridged version of the preceding work.

Poggi, Gianfranco. *Images of Society. Essays on Sociological Theories of*

Tocqueville, Marx, and Durkheim. Stanford: Stanford University Press, 1972.

Polin, Claude. *De la Démocratie en Amérique: Profil d'un oeuvre.* Paris: Hatier, 1973.

Poussin, Guillaume-Tell. *Considérations sur le principe démocratique qui régit l'Union américaine et la possibilité de son application à d'autres états.* Paris: Librairie Charles de Gosselin, 1841.

Prévost-Paradol. *Essais de politique et de littérature.* Paris: Michel Lévy, 1859–1863.

Probst, George E. *The Happy Republic: A Reader in Tocqueville's America.* New York: Harper and Row, 1962.

Rau, Hans-Arnold. *Tocquevilles Theorie des politischen Handels Demokratie zwischen Verwaltungsdespotismus und Republik.* Cologne: Handen, 1975.

Redier, Antoine. *Comme disait M. de Tocqueville.* Paris: Perrin, 1925.

Rémond, René. *Les Etats-Unis dans l'opinion française, 1815–1852.* 2 vols. Paris: Armand Colin, 1962.

Richter, Melvin. *Essays in Theory and History: An Approach to the Social Sciences.* Cambridge, Mass.: Harvard University Press, 1970.

———"Tocqueville's Contribution to the Theory of Revolution," in Carl Friedrich, ed., *Revolution.* New York: Atherton Press, 1966.

Sainte-Beuve, Charles. *Causeries de lundi,* vol. V. Paris: Garnier, n.d.

Salomon, Albert. *In Praise of Enlightenment.* New York: World, 1963.

Schieferdecher, Adelheid. *Ein Vergleich der Anschauungen Edmund Burkes und Alexis de Tocquevilles über die französische Revolution.* Berlin, 1971.

Schleifer, James T. *The Making of Tocqueville's Democracy in America.* Chapel Hill: University of North Carolina Press, 1980. With bibliography.

Senior, Nassau William. *Des fragments des entretiens de Tocqueville avec Nassau Senior, 1848–1858,* published as an appendix to Eugène d'Eichtal, *Alexis de Tocqueville et la démocratie libérale.* The complete conversations will soon be published in the *Oeuvres complètes,* thanks to the work of Miss Kerr and Mr. Hugh Brogan.

Simon, Canon G. A. *Histoire généalogique des Clerel, seigneurs de Rampan-Tocqueville, 1066–1954.* Caen, 1954.

Simpson, M. C. M., ed. *The Correspondence and Conversations of Alexis de Tocqueville with Nassau Senior.* 2 vols. London, 1872.

Songy, Gaston. "Alexis de Tocqueville and Slavery Judgments and Predictions." Ph.D. dissertation, Saint Louis University, 1969.

Spitz, David. *Democracy and the Challenge of Power.* New York: Columbia University Press, 1958.

Taupier, Michel. *La décentralisation dans l'oeuvre d'Alexis de Tocqueville.* Travaux juridiques et économiques de l'Université de Rennes, vol. 28. Rennes, 1967.

Vossler, Otto. *Alexis de Tocqueville: Freiheit und Gleichheit.* Frankfurt: Klostermann, 1973.

Zeitlin, Irving M. *Liberty, Equality, and Revolution in Alexis de Tocqueville.* Boston: Little, Brown, 1971.

Zetterbaum, Marvin. *Tocqueville and the Problem of Democracy.* Stanford: Stanford University Press, 1967.

Articles Cited

Adams, Herbert. "Jared Sparks and Alexis de Tocqueville." *Studies in Historical and Political Science,* 16, no. 12 (1898). Johns Hopkins University, Baltimore.

Aron, Raymond. "La définition libérale de la liberté: Alexis de Tocqueville et Karl Marx." *Archives Européennes de Sociologie,* 5 (1964).

———"Idées politiques et vision historique de Tocqueville." *Revue Française de Science Politique,* 10, no. 3 (1960), 509–526.

Bastid, Paul. "Tocqueville et la doctrine constitutionnelle." In *Alexis de Toqueville: Livre du Centenaire, 1859–1959,* Paris: pp. 45–57. Paris: Editions du CNRS, 1960.

Blanc, Louis. "De la Démocratie en Amérique." *Revue Républicaine,* 5 (1836), 129–163.

Bourricaud, François. "Cotradition et traditions chez Tocqueville." *Revue Tocqueville,* 2, no. 1 (1980), 25–40.

Bryce, James. "The Predictions of Hamilton and de Tocqueville." In *Studies in Historical and Political Science.* Baltimore: Johns Hopkins Press, 1887.

Burrage, Michael. "On Tocqueville's Notion of the 'Irresistibility' of Democracy." *Archives Européennes de Sociologie,* 13, no. 1 (1972), 151–175.

Carné, Louis de. "De la démocratie aux Etats-Unis et de la bourgeoisie en France." *Revue des Deux Mondes,* 15 March 1837, pp. 653–682.

Cestre, Charles. "Alexis de Tocqueville, témoin et juge de la civilisation américaine." *Revue des Cours et Conférences,* 1 and 2 (1934).

Chevallier, Jean-Jacques. "De la distinction des sociétés aristocratiques et des sociétés démocratiques, en tant que fondement de la pensée d'Alexis de Tocqueville." Mimeographed, 26 pages. Listed as Mel. 4 55(10) in catalogue of Bibliothèque de l'Institut d'Etudes Politiques de Paris.

Corcelle, François de. "De la démocratie américaine." *Revue des Deux Mondes,* 14 June 1835, pp. 739–761.

Diez del Corral y Pedruzo, Luis. "Chateaubriand und der soziologische Ästhetizismus Tocquevilles." In *Festgabe für Carl Schmitt.* Berlin: Duncker und Humblot, 1968.

————"Tocqueville et Pascal." In *Revue des Travaux de l'Académie des Sciences Morales et Politiques*. Paris: Librairie Sirey, 1965.

————"Tocqueville et la pensée des doctrinaires." In *Alexis de Tocqueville: Livre du Centenaire, 1859–1959*, pp. 57–70. Paris: Editions du CNRS, 1960.

Drescher, Seymour. "Tocqueville's Two Democracies." *Journal of the History of Ideas*, 25, no. 2 (1964), 201–216.

Furet, François. "Tocqueville est-il un historien de la Révolution française?" *Annales*, 25, no. 2 (1970), 434–451.

Goldstein, Doris S. "A. de Tocqueville's Concept of Citizenship." In *Proceedings of the American Philosophical Society*, February 1964.

————"The Religious Beliefs of Alexis de Tocqueville." *French Historical Studies*, I, no. 4 (1960), 379–393.

Hartnett, Robert C. "Tocqueville on American Federalism." In *Burke Society Series*, I, 22–31. New York: Fordham University Press, 1945.

Jardin, André. "Tocqueville député sous la Monarchie de Juillet." *Contre-point*, 22-23 (1976), 167–185.

Lacordaire, Jean Baptiste. "Eloge d'Alexis de Tocqueville." Acceptance speech to the French Academy, 24 January 1861. Published in *Revue Politique*, 16 (October–December 1961).

Lamberti, Jean-Claude. "De Benjamin Constant à Tocqueville," *Revue France–Forum*, 203–204 (1983), 19–26.

Lukacs, John. "The Last Days of Alexis de Tocqueville." *Catholic Historical Review*, 50, no. 2 (July 1964), 155–170.

Mayer, J.-P. "Tocqueville, prophète de l'Etat moderne." *Critique*, 100–101 (1955), 884–892.

————"Les voyages de Tocqueville et la genèse de la sociologie politique." *Nouvelle Revue Française*, 1 (February 1957), 1–13.

Pappe, H. O. "Mill and Tocqueville." *Journal of the History of Ideas*, April–June 1964.

Pierson, George Wilson. "The Manuscript of Tocqueville's *De la démocratie en Amérique*." *Yale University Library Gazette*, 29, no. 3 (1955), 115–125.

————"Le 'second voyage' de Tocqueville en Amérique." In *Alexis de Tocqueville: Livre du Centenaire, 1859–1959*, pp. 71–86. Paris: Editions du CNRS, 1960.

Rémond, René. "Tocqueville et la 'Démocratie en Amérique.' " In *Alexis de Tocqueville: Livre du Centenaire, 1859–1959*, pp. 181–190. Paris: Editions du CNRS, 1960.

Rémusat, Charles de. "De l'esprit de réaction: Royer-Collard et Tocqueville." *Revue des Deux Mondes*, 35 (15 October 1861), 777–814.

Richter, Melvin. "Comparative Political Analysis in Montesquieu and Tocqueville." *Comparative Politics*, 1, no. 2 (1969), 129–159.

Rossi, R. "De la Démocratie en Amérique." *Revue des Deux Mondes,* 23 (15 September 1840), 884–904.

Sainte-Beuve, Charles. "De la Démocratie en Amérique." *Le Temps,* 7 (April 1835).

Walter, T. H. "John Stuart Mill, Disciple of Tocqueville." *Western Political Quarterly,* 13, no. 4 (1960), 880–889.

Notes

As far as possible, references to Tocqueville's works are to the definitive edition of the complete works: J.-P. Mayer, ed., *Oeuvres complètes* (Paris: Gallimard, 1959–). The publication of this edition is overseen by the National Commission for the Publication of Tocqueville's Works, which was chaired until his death by Raymond Aron. (Where it has not been possible to cite this definitive edition, references are given to the seriously flawed nine-volume *Oeuvres complètes* published in 1866 by Michel Lévy and edited by Madame de Tocqueville. The texts of this 1866 edition, compiled for the most part by Gustave de Beaumont, are often defective, and the work is incomplete.)

In the notes, the Gallimard edition is abbreviated OC, followed by a roman numeral indicating the volume number. Some volumes are further subdivided into parts or sections. In citations from these the volume number is followed by an arabic numeral indicating the part or section number, followed by a second arabic numeral indicating the page. Volumes that have no internal parts or sections are followed by a single arabic numeral indicating the page.

Thirteen volumes of the *Oeuvres complètes* have appeared so far. The two parts of *Democracy in America,* one published originally in 1835, the other in 1840, constitute volume I, which is published in two parts. The *Old Regime and the French Revolution* is OC, II, which contains both the volume published by Tocqueville in 1856, intended to be the first half of a projected larger work, and a collection of fragments and notes left by Tocqueville when he died in 1859 before completing the book. The *Souvenirs,* written in 1850 and 1851 and published posthumously, correspond to OC, XII. To make the notes clearer, I denote these three works as DA, AR, and S, respectively. These abbreviations are followed by a roman numeral indicating the volume of the work as originally published. In the case of DA, I have also indicated the part and chapter numbers, the former with capital letters, the latter with arabic numerals: thus, DA, I, A, 2 refers to volume one, part one, chapter two of *Democracy in America.* Specific page references are given in arabic after the chapter number.

Translator's note: For the most part I have translated Tocqueville's words myself. I found it helpful to consult George Lawrence's excellent translation of *Democracy in America* (New York: Doubleday, 1969); and in some instances, for the reader's convenience, I have indicated in parentheses a page reference to that work, even when my translation does not coincide exactly with Lawrence's.

Introduction

1. The most notable recent studies, those to which I am most heavily indebted, are Marvin Zetterbaum, *Tocqueville and the Problem of Democracy* (Stanford: Stanford University Press, 1967); Seymour Drescher, *Tocqueville and England* (Cambridge, Mass.: Harvard University Press, 1964), and *Dilemmas of Democracy: Tocqueville and Modernization* (Pittsburgh: University of Pittsburgh Press, 1968); and James T. Schleifer, *The Making of Tocqueville's Democracy in America* (Chapel Hill: University of North Carolina Press, 1980).

2. Paul Lambert White, professor of history at Yale, visited the châteaus of Tocqueville and Beaumont after World War I and was able to copy their travel diaries. He was preparing to publish a book when he died suddenly. His friends and disciples set up a fund to continue his work and pay for the copying of the manuscripts. G. W. Pierson, a former student of White's, did much to augment and classify the documentary materials collected subsequently and wrote a book based on the Yale collection (cited in n. 3). In addition to the travel diaries, which have now been published, and the bulk of Tocqueville's and Beaumont's American correspondence, the collection includes all of Beaumont's manuscripts and the working manuscript of *Democracy in America*, as well as rough drafts at all stages in the preparation of the text; also included are the "critical observations of my father, my brothers, and Beaumont on my work."

The Tocqueville family archives are richer still; they comprise 110 cartons classified in three categories: work, life, and correspondence (23 cartons). Some of this material has been used for the publication of the definitive edition of Tocqueville's complete works by Gallimard, under the control of a national commission chaired until his death by Raymond Aron.

3. George Wilson Pierson, *Tocqueville and Beaumont in America* (New York: Oxford University Press, 1938).

4. By contrast, there are no American works devoted exclusively to *The Old Regime*, except for Richard Herr, *Tocqueville and the Old Regime* (Princeton: Princeton University Press, 1962).

5. Worth mentioning, however, is the work of Pierre Birnbaum, *Sociologie de Tocqueville* (Paris: Presses Universitaires de France, 1970). For Aron's work on Tocqueville, see the bibliography.

6. See volume I, book 2, of the Gallimard edition of Tocqueville's Complete Works.

7. The phrase in quotes figures as the subtitle of book 2 of the *L'Ancien Régime et la Révolution* in the Gallimard edition of the Complete Works.

8. "L'Etat social et politique de la France avant et depuis 1789." This article is reproduced at the beginning of the first volume of *L'Ancien Régime* in the Gallimard edition.

9. One notable exception to this rule is Jack Lively, *The Social and Political*

Thought of Alexis de Tocqueville (Oxford: Clarendon Press, 1965), a British work which treats Tocqueville's thought as a whole.

10. This is the thesis put forward by Louis Hartz in his fine book, *The Liberal Tradition in America* (New York and London: Harcourt Brace Jovanovich, 1955).

11. For information about the abbreviations used in citing Tocqueville's work, see the headnote to these notes.

12. A. Redier, *Comme disait M. de Tocqueville*, 2nd ed. (Paris: Librairie Perrin, 1935), pp. 16–17.

13. Thibaudet was far from the truth when he characterized Tocqueville as a "minor noble." This view, which can easily be challenged on psychological and political grounds, has been refuted by the genealogical studies of Canon G. A. Simon and the history of the Tocqueville family. See Redier, *Comme disait M. de Tocqueville*, chaps. 1 and 2, as well as the forthcoming biography of Tocqueville by André Jardin.

14. Louise's sister married Louis Jean-Baptiste de Chateaubriand, the elder brother of the celebrated writer. See Chateaubriand, *Mémoires d'outre-tombe*, ed. Biré (Paris: Garnier, n.d.), II, 467.

15. Letter of 8 September 1824, cited by Pierson, *Tocqueville and Beaumont,* pp. 17–18.

16. OC, 1866 ed., VI, 307–308. Speech delivered 2 April 1853.

17. We shall see subsequently that an article that Tocqueville wrote in 1836 for the *London and Westminster Review* at the behest of John Stuart Mill contains some of the major arguments of *The Old Regime and the French Revolution*.

18. OC, XIII, 1, 373–375, and VIII, 3, 272.

19. *Democracy in America* is based on abundant documentation; on this subject see Pierson, *Tocqueville and Beaumont,* pp. 718, 739, and esp. p. 729; and René Rémond, *Tocqueville et la Démocratie en Amérique* (Paris: Editions du Centre National de Recherche Scientifique, 1960), pp. 181–190. In writing *The Old Regime and the French Revolution* Tocqueville became a veritable historian. See Georges Lefebvre's introduction to AR, I.

20. See especially the correspondence with Royer-Collard, in particular OC, XI, 19–21 and 28–30 (concerning Machiavelli, Bossuet, Plato, and Thiers's *Histoire de la Révolution*).

21. OC, XIII, 1, 148. Letter of 10 November 1836.

22. DA, I, end of introduction, p. 14: "This book follows absolutely no one else's."

23. The Doctrinaires were a group of political thinkers prominent during the Restoration. Chief among them was Pierre-Paul Royer-Collard, who was joined by Camille Jordan, the comte de Serre, Quatremere de Quincy, and Barante, as well as Guizot and Rémusat, who would part company with Royer-Collard under the July Monarchy. See Amable Barante, *La vie politique de Royer-Collard* (Paris: Didier, 1863).

24. Pierson, *Tocqueville and Beaumont,* p. 23.

25. François Guizot, *Cours d'histoire moderne* (Paris: Pichon et Didier), included the following volumes: *Histoire générale de la civilisation en Europe* (1828); *Histoire générale de la civilisation en France*, vols. I and II (1829), vol. III (1828–1830), vol. IV (1830), vol. V (1830–1832). Bibliothèque Nationale G 12658.

26. Lucien Febvre, *Civilisation, le mot et l'idée* (Paris: Publications du Centre

International de Synthèse, 1930); and Emile Benveniste, *Civilisation, contribution à l'histoire du mot*. The first use of the word occurs in Mirabeau's *Ami des hommes, ou Traité de la population*. In 1814 Benjamin Constant published *De l'esprit de conquête et de l'usurpation dans leurs rapports avec la civilisation européenne*. The word implies a historical view of society and an optimistic, positive interpretation of history, quite different from the theological view inherited from the past.

27. See François Furet, *Penser la Révolution française* (Paris: Gallimard, 1978), pp. 177–182.

28. OC, XI, 29. Letter to Royer-Collard dated 6 December 1836.

29. Louis Blanc, *L'organisation du travail* (1839), *Histoire de dix ans* (1841), and *Histoire de la Révolution* (1847–1862).

30. Paul Janet, *Philosophie de la Révolution française* (Paris: Libraire Germer-Ballière, 1975), book 1, chap. 4, and book 2, chap. 3.

31. Yale archives, CV h, notebook 3. "Outline of Introduction: A state which is neither as good as the old was nor as good as the state which could come to be . . . We share our fathers' ignorance without sharing their virtue . . . We have abandoned the virtues of the old order without accepting the ideas of the new order . . . The material Revolution is complete, the intellectual and moral part of the Revolution remain to be completed."

32. OC, XIII, 1, 375, is Tocqueville's response to Kergorlay's questions about the introduction. The letter is undated (but was probably written in late January or February 1835, as is shown by the context—that is, shortly after the publication of *Democracy in America* in January 1835). The copyist has indicated that the end of the letter was missing. Kergorlay had read the book in proof; he had been consulted about the manuscript and made numerous observations. (See Yale archives, CIII, h, *Observations critiques de mon père, mes frères, B* [= Beaumont], *Louis* [= Louis de Kergorlay].) Hence it would seem that the introduction was written after the rest of the book.

33. DA, I, B, 9, 289–330 (277–315); compare DA, II, D, 8, 336–340 (702–708). DA, I, B, 10, is a late addition, comprising texts of a rather different nature, all of which deal with questions that were currently agitating public opinion. This chapter is the rhetorical conclusion of the work, but the previous chapter is the dialectical conclusion.

34. DA, I, B, 9, 319–329.

35. DA, I, B, 9, 323 (305); see also DA, I, A, 53, last paragraph. This argument was made earlier in DA, I, A, 2.

36. OC, V, 1; see especially notebooks A and B and portable notebook no. 3.

37. Tocqueville studied for a degree in law (*licence*) between 1823 and 1826 and attended Guizot's lectures in 1829 and 1830. In 1825 Villèle, under pressure from the "ultras," was obliged to press for passage of the law concerning the émigré's *milliard*, which offered returned émigrés compensation of up to one billion francs for property seized during the Revolution.

38. As early as 1820 the duc de Broglie wrote: "In politics, I regarded the government of the United States as the future of civilized nations and the English Monarchy as the government of the present day. I hated despotism and saw bureaucratic monarchy only as a state of transition." *Souvenirs*, (Paris, 1886), I, 262.

39. This was shown, for example, by reactions to the law of primogeniture

and the law on the press proposed by Villèle but ultimately voted down (1826–1827). In *Fragments inédits sur la Démocratie en Amérique* (published in the *Nouvelle Revue Française* of 1 April 1959) we read: "Give me for thirty years a law of equal division of inheritances and freedom of the press, and I shall give you the Republic" (p. 10). When Tocqueville wrote to Kergorlay in 1835 that almost ten years had passed since he first conceived his ideas, he had in mind, I think, these most revealing debates of 1826–1827.

40. Pascal, *Oeuvres complètes*, ed. Léon Brunschvicg (Paris: Boutroux, Gazier, n.d.), III, 123.

41. J.-P. Mayer, *Alexis de Tocqueville*, 2nd ed. (Paris: Gallimard, 1948), p. 55. "Tocqueville applied Pascal's method to the political life of mankind." On this subject, see also the interesting work of Luis Diez del Corral listed in the bibliography.

42. The political intentions of the work are expressed most clearly in a letter from Tocqueville to his friend Stoffels dated 21 February 1835. OC, 1866 ed., V, 429ff.

43. He clung to this youthful conviction throughout his life. See AR, II, 114–115: "It is man's ideas and passions, and not the mechanics of the laws, that drive human affairs. It is always in the depths of men's minds that one finds the impression left by whatever may occur in the world."

44. This point has been elucidated by Lively, *Social and Political Thought*, p. 33, and by Michael Burrage, "On Tocqueville's Notion of the 'Irresistibility' of Democracy," *Archives Européennes de Sociologie* 13, no. 1 (1972), 151–175, esp. 158–159.

1. Aristocracy and Democracy

1. DA, I, B, 9, 323 (305).

2. Yale archives, CV, k, notebook 1, 7–40.

3. OC, V, 1, 203. René Rémond has shown that the features of the American national character still looked quite confused to the eyes of Frenchmen under the Restoration and really began to take shape only after 1830, with almost all the American traits originally borrowed from those of the English as the French then imagined the English to be. See René Rémond, *Les Etats-Unis dans l'opinion française, 1815–1852* (Paris: Armand Colin, 1962) I, 477–480. See also Pierre Reboul, *Le mythe anglais dans la littérature française sous la Restauration* (Lille: Université de Lille, 1962).

4. OC, V, 1, 203.

5. Mayer, *Alexis de Tocqueville*, p. 13.

6. Montesquieu, *Esprit des lois*, book 19, chap. 1.

7. OC, IX.

8. OC, V, 1, 189 (25 Nov. 1831); on French Canada see also OC, V, 1, 215.

9. OC, V, 1, 190 (25 Nov. 1831).

10. OC, V, 1, 191.

11. DA, I, B, 2, 178.

12. Most notably Pierson, *Tocqueville and Beaumont*, pp. 6–7 with note, 158–159 and note, 165–166, and 757–758; Lively, *Social and Political Thought*, pp. 49–50; Schleifer, *Making*, pp. 263–274 with notes, 345–347; and Zetterbaum, *Tocqueville*.

13. Schleifer, *Making*.

14. In sum, Schleifer holds that Tocqueville uses "democracy" to mean: (1) a fact; (2) an irresistible tendency; (3) a social revolution; (4) a social state; (5) the sovereignty of the people; (6) the practical realization of the idea of popular sovereignty; (7) the people (sometimes all the people, sometimes the "lower classes"); (8) mobility; (9) the middle classes; (10) equality of conditions; and (11) the feeling of equality. Though not unaware of the difficulties involved, I propose to collect these various meanings into two groups: (A) the democratic social state (i.e., 4, together with 1, 2, 3, 8, 10, and 11), and (B) government of the people, consisting of 5 and 6. Uses 7 and 9 can have either a political or a sociological interpretation, depending on the context. For example, DA, I, B, 5, 217: "The government of the middle classes," and DA, II, B, 10, 135: "The passion for material well-being is essentially a middle-class passion."

15. DA, I, A, 3.

16. OC, XIII, 1, 233–234.

17. DA, I, introduction, 4.

18. DA, I, introduction, 1; see also Yale archives, CV, h, Packet 3, notebook 3, 27–28. "Democracy! Don't you see that these are the waters of the Flood? Don't you see how they move ceaselessly forward by dint of slow and irresistible effort? Already they cover fields and cities, they roll over the destroyed towers of the castles and lick at the feet of thrones . . . Rather than build useless dikes, let us try to build a holy ark capable of carrying mankind across this shoreless ocean."

19. DA, I, introduction, 11; see also Yale archives, CV, h, Packet 3, notebook 3, 28: "this immense social revolution."

20. DA, I, introduction, 1.

21. Working manuscript, CVI a, vol. I, chap. 1.

22. Yale archives, CV, h, Packet 3, 5 notebooks.

23. Yale archives, CV, h, notebook 5, 7–8.

24. DA, I, A, 3: "The Social State of the Anglo-Americans;" and DA, I, A, 4: "On the Principle of the Sovereignty of the People in America."

25. Yale archives, CV, h, notebook 1, 22.

26. Unless the context indicates otherwise, "democracy" usually refers to the democratic social state in texts contemporary with *Democracy in America*. In the years during which Tocqueville was writing *The Old Regime and the French Revolution*, the term more frequently connotes political liberty. See especially AR, II, 198–199.

27. Schleifer makes the same point; see *Making*, pp. 273–274.

28. *Esprit des lois*, book 3, chap. 1.

29. Ibid., book 8, chaps. 16, 17, and 19.

30. DA, I, A, 8, 165.

31. *The Federalist*, no. 9.

32. *Esprit des lois*, book 9, chap. 1.

33. Melvin Richter, "The Uses of Theory: Tocqueville's Adaptation of Montesquieu," in his *Essays in Theory and History: An Approach to the Social Sciences* (Cambridge, Mass.: Harvard University Press, 1970), pp. 74–102.

34. OC, V, 1, 7, 235.

35. This opinion was widely held in France under the Restoration. The traits

of the American national character did not impress themselves on French opinion until after 1830. See Rémond, *Les Etats-Unis,* p. 478.

36. OC, V, 1, 208–210.

37. DA, II, B, 13, 142–145 (535–538).

38. DA, II, B, 13, 145 (538).

39. *Esprit des lois*, book 14, chap. 13.

40. Working manuscript, Yale archives, CVI a, 1, marginal annotation of the chapter on the social state (DA, I, A, 3).

41. DA, I, A, 3, 45 (50).

42. OC, V, 1, 207.

43. Pierson, *Tocqueville and Beaumont,* pp. 450–457.

44. OC, V, 1, 207.

45. DA, I, A, 2, 26–44 (31–49).

46. DA, I, A, 1, 31.

47. Seymour Drescher, *Tocqueville and England* (Cambridge, Mass.: Harvard University Press, 1964), esp. chap. 2 and, more specifically, pp. 31–32.

48. OC, V, 1, 191.

49. A notable exception is Melvin Richter, "Comparative Political Analysis in Montesquieu and Tocqueville," and "The Uses of Theory," both in his *Essays in Theory and History.*

50. OC, V, 1, 203.

51. OC, V, 1, 207.

52. DA, I, A, 2, 43 (48).

53. OC, V, 1, 207.

54. DA, I, A, 2, 27–28 (32).

55. DA, I, A, 2, 42 (46).

56. OC, V, 1, 207.

57. Schleifer, *Making,* sect. 1, chap. 1, notes that vol. I, chap. 10 of *Democracy in America* does not figure in the original outline.

58. DA, I, B, 9, 289 (277).

59. OC, V, 1, 207.

60. DA, I, B, 9, 319–323 (305–308).

61. DA, I, B, 9, 290–299 (277–285).

62. DA, I, B, 9, 292 (279).

63. DA, I, A, 1, 25 (31).

64. DA, I, A, 2, 32 (37).

65. DA, I, A, 3, 45 (50).

66. DA, I, A, 2, 27 (32).

67. OC, V, 1, 203.

68. DA, I, A, 2, 43–44 (48–49).

69. OC, V, 1, 203 and 205.

70. DA, I, A, 39.

71. DA, I, A, 3, 46 (51), and OC, V, 1, 121.

72. DA, I, A, 3, 52 (57).

73. DA, I, A, 3, 46 (51).

74. DA, I, A, 3, 50 (55).

75. DA, I, A, 3, 50 (55).

76. OC, V, 1, 282–383.

77. Arthur M. Schlesinger, *The Age of Jackson* (Boston: Little, Brown, 1953), p. 312.

78. See esp. chap. 1, sect. 3, chap. 2, sects 1 and 4; and chap. 4, sect. 1.

79. To be precise, 115 times, distributed as follows: DA, I: introduction, 3 times; A, 8 times; B, 24 times; DA II, A, 18 times; B, 20 times; C, 28 times; D, 14 times.

80. Yale archives, CV, k, notebook 1, 51.

81. DA, I, B, 5, 202 (196).

82. AR, I, Social state and politics of France before and after 1789, p. 45.

83. DA, I, B, 2, 183: "In the United States, the wealthy classes of society are almost entirely outside of political affairs." The separation of elites and exclusion of certain of them from power are phenomena exacerbated by democratic revolutions.

84. It diverges sharply from medieval thinking. See Jakob Burckhardt, *The Civilization of the Renaissance in Italy* (New York: Harper & Row, 1958), part 5, chap. 1: "Dante is following Aristotle exclusively when he says the 'nobility rests on natural excellence supported by great inherited wealth' (*Politics, V*). But in his *Ethics*, in which he says what he thinks, he calls noble that which aspires to the true good. The more humanism extended its influence over the Italian mind, the more firmly established was the conviction that man's value is independent of his birth . . . that there is no nobility other than that resulting from personal merit." Tocqueville's conception is less idealistic, but it belongs to this humanist tradition, which tends to devalue birth.

85. Robert Dahl, *Who Governs?* (New Haven: Yale University Press, 1961), esp. chap. 7. See also Dahl's *Modern Political Analysis* (Englewood Cliffs, N.J.: Prentice-Hall, 1971).

86. Raymond Aron, *La lutte des classes* (Paris: Gallimard, 1964), chap. 9, and *Démocratie et totalitarisme* (Paris: Gallimard, 1968), chap. 7.

87. DA, II, A, 13, 63.

88. AR, I, 37.

89. J.-J. Chevallier, "De la distinction des sociétés aristocratiques et des sociétés démocratiques, en tant que fondement de la pensée d'Alexis de Tocqueville" (Mimeograph).

90. DA, II, B, 2, 106.

91. DA, II, B, 2.

92. DA, II, B, 2, 105.

93. Louis Dumont, *Homo hierarchicus* (Paris: Gallimard, 1966), p. 33.

94. Tocqueville's notes on Plato will be published in the Gallimard edition of the Complete Works.

95. Tocqueville to Kergorlay, 8 August 1838, OC, XIII, 1, 41: "On the whole, I consider him a poor political theorist, but the philosopher has always seemed to me the greatest of all and his desire to introduce as much morality as possible into politics is admirable."

96. DA, I, A, 2, 29.

97. DA, I, B, 5, 240.

98. DA, II, A, 8, 39.

99. DA, II, A, 8, 40.

100. DA, I, B, 6, 255.

101. DA, I, B, 7, 271.

102. DA, II, C, 2.

103. DA, II, C, 5.

104. DA, II, C, 6, 194.

105. *Esprit des lois*, book 8, chap. 3.

106. DA, II, C, 5, 189.

107. Ibid.

108. J. L. de Lolme, *La constitution de l'Angleterre* (Geneva, 1771).

109. AR, I, 147–149; the idea occurred to Tocqueville quite early and is mentioned in his travel diaries for 1833; see OC, V, 2, 37. Montesquieu had already pointed out that an aristocracy becomes corrupt when it ceases to be anything more than a hereditary nobility. See *Esprit des lois*, book 8, chap. 5.

110. AR, I, 56.

111. Yale archives, CV, h, notebook 4, p. 37.

112. Yale archives, CV, d, p. 41.

113. Tocqueville developed this idea during his first trip to England (1833), even though that trip had been undertaken in fear of imminent revolution in France. See OC, V, 2, 36, 41 and 42.

114. OC, V, 2.

115. François Guizot, *Mémoires* (Paris, 1858–1867), VIII, p. 522.

116. François Guizot, *De la démocratie en France* (Paris 1849), p. 94.

117. S, part 1, chap. 1, esp. pp. 30–32.

118. Unpublished letter, cited from Roland Pierre-Marcel, *Essai politique sur Alexis de Tocqueville* (Paris: Alcan, 1910), p. 368.

119. OC (1866), VII, 232.

120. Yale archives, CV, g, notebook 3, p. 9.

121. Ibid.

122. Yale archives, CV, g, notebook 2, p. 18.

123. Yale archives, CV, k, notebook 2, sleeve 19.

124. Yale archives, CV, k, notebook 1, p. 21.

125. I use the phrase "political formula" here in the strong sense given it by Gaetano Mosca: namely, a formula that rationalizes and justifies the domination of a ruling class.

126. See especially S, I, 1, 30.

127. DA, II, B, 3, 108.

128. Hartz, *Liberal Tradition*, pp. 51–53.

129. OC, V, 2, 59.

130. AR, II, 108.

131. OC, V, 2, 177.

132. These articles (or "commentary") by Mill were reprinted in his *Dissertations and Discussions* (London: Parker, 1869), vol. II; the quotations used here are taken from Tocqueville's *Democracy in America*, 4th ed. (New York: Schocken, 1970), henceforth referred to as the Schocken edition."

133. This was Tocqueville's report to Mill of Royer-Collard's judgment: OC, VI, 1, 334.

134. OC, VI, 1, 302; his reaction after receipt of the second article was similar: OC, VI, 1, 329.

135. Schocken ed., II, xlvii.

136. OC, V, 1, 278. Note of 30 November 1831. This is the first expression of this idea.

137. This is true as far as one can judge from the written texts. But it is logical to assume that Tocqueville already had an idea of the remote causes when he wrote his 1836 article "L'Etat social et politique de la France avant et depuis 1789."

138. DA, II, D, 8, 338.

139. See Raymond Boudon, *Les méthodes en sociologie*, 4th ed. (Paris: Presses Universitaires de France, 1976), where the work of Montesquieu and Tocqueville is discussed in terms of social systems analysis.

140. DA, II, D, 8, 338.

141. Yale archives, CV, k, notebook 2, sleeve 18.

142. Tocqueville is primarily concerned not with the balance of social forces or social classes but with an equilibrium of values.

143. *Esprit des lois*, book 2, chap. 4.

144. DA, II, D, 8, 339.

145. OC, IX; see particularly the correspondence for 1853, and esp. p. 203.

146. DA, II, A, 20, 91. The criticism is aimed at Joseph de Maistre as well as Thiers.

147. OC, VI, 1, 27 August 1843, 345.

148. DA, I, introduction, 5, and DA, I, B, 9, 316.

149. See, for example, Zetterbaum, *Tocqueville,* chap. 1, and esp. pp. 15–16 and 19ff, where it is argued that Tocqueville did not believe in the irresistible progress of equality and aimed to construct a "salutary myth."

150. DA, I, introduction, 5; and DA, I, B, IX, 325.

151. DA, I, A, 3, 52–53.

152. This idea is supported by Albert Salomon, *Tocqueville's Philosophy of Freedom*; for a contrary view, see Pierre-Marcel, *Essai politique,* p. 87.

153. OC, IX, 24 January 1857, 281; see also DA, II, D, 8, 338, and OC, XIII, 1, 373: "I cannot believe that God has for centuries now impelled two or three million men toward greater equality of condition only to end in a despotism like that of Tiberius or Claudius."

154. DA, II, D, 8, 338.

2. Liberty and Equality

1. Philippe Buchez and Prosper-Charles Roux, *Histoire parlementaire de la Révolution (Paris 1834–1840)*.

2. Yale archives, CV, g, notebook 3, 9.

3. AR, I, 72.

4. DA, I, introduction, 9.

5. OC, 1866 ed., VI, 439.

6. Redier, *Comme disait M. de Tocqueville,* chap. 4; and Jack Lively, *Social and Political Thought,* chap. 1.

7. OC, V, 1, notebook E, De l'égalité en Amérique, 279.

8. Ibid., 280.

9. James Bryce, *The American Commonwealth* (London: Macmillan, 1888).

10. Civil equality is not to be confused with political equality or equality before the civil laws, which is only its first precondition. See DA, II, B, 1, 101: "Equality can be established in civil society yet not prevail in politics. One can enjoy the right to partake of the same pleasures, to work in the same professions, to frequent the same places, and in short to live in the same way and pursue wealth by the same means as others without all taking the same part in government." Equality of rights in civil society means equality before the law and the courts, as well as in taxation and in eligibility for public office. Such equality of rights constituted, for Royer-Collard, "the true name of democracy."

11. This complex but precise concept, expressed in an ambiguous vocabulary, has been misinterpreted by various French writers, who either considered the only legitimate equality to be equality of rights—Eugène d'Eichtal, *Alexis de Tocqueville et la démocratie libérale* (Paris: Calmann-Lévy, 1897), p. 110—or who confounded equality of conditions with equality in fact—e.g., R. Rossi, review of *Démocratie en Amérique* published in the *Revue des Deux Mondes*, 15 September 1840, p. 903.

12. OC, 1866 ed., VII, 135; here, as in the introduction, the influence of Montesquieu is obvious. Compare the next-to-last paragraph of the preface to *Esprit des lois:* "I have many times begun and many times abandoned this work . . . But when I discovered my principles, everything that I was looking for came to me."

13. DA, I, introduction, 1.

14. I shall consider the question of religious equality elsewhere. Recall, moreover, that Tocqueville attached great importance to the laws of inheritance, and hence to the elimination of primogeniture.

15. "Men are born and remain free and equal in right" (Article 1).

16. Cited in Hannah Arendt, *On Revolution* (New York: Viking, 1963), p. 65.

17. This idea has been asserted by, for example, Irving M. Zeitlin, *Liberty, Equality, and Revolution in Alexis de Tocqueville* (Boston: Little, Brown, 1971), p. 57.

18. Rousseau, *Social Contract,* book 2, chap. 7.

19. DA, II, C, 5, 188.

20. Yale archives, CV, g, notebook 1, p. 3: "What I say about the servant is always more or less applicable to the worker." See p. 4 for a similar statement.

21. DA, II, C, 5, 189. This statement is not literally true, and Tocqueville himself noted that domestics were not electors (see DA, I, B, 6, 251). In fact, the chapter concerns relations of subordination between equal citizens.

22. DA, II, C, 5, 187.

23. DA, II, C, 5, 191.

24. DA, II, C, 5, 189.

25. DA, II, C, 13, 223; see also C, 12, 219. In contemporary terms, equality based on similarity is "egalitarianism."

26. On this topic see the correspondence with Bogineau: OC, IX, 45–69 and 199–212.

27. Rousseau, *Social Contract*, book 1, chap. 9.

28. DA, II, C, 5, 191 (578).

29. Ibid., 192 (579) for the two preceding quotations.

30. Ibid., 93 (580).

31. Plato, *Republic*, VIII, 558–562.

32. *Esprit des lois*, book 8, chap. 3.

33. DA, I, A, 3, 52.

34. Ibid.

35. DA, I, A, 3, 52–53.

36. DA, I, B, 5, 204.

37. See, for example, his *Entretiens avec Nassau Senior*, 22 May 1850 (cited by Eichtal, *Alexis de Tocqueville* p. 247): "Equality is an evil mistaken for envy."

38. DA, II, B, 13, 144.

39. DA, II, B, 104.

40. DA, I, A, 3, 52–53.

41. DA, I, B, 9, 326–330.

42. DA, II, B, 1, 103.

43. Perhaps this is because Montesquieu's examples are not well chosen. See the note by M. Brethe de la Gressaye in vol. I, p. 313, of the edition of *Esprit des lois* published by the Société des Belles Lettres, 1972.

44. See, for example, OC, V, 2, 47, note of 8 May 1835: "The French spirit is to want no superior. The English spirit is to want inferiors . . . The pride of the English may be natural in man, that of the the French inherent in a particular cause. . . . The one [the Frenchman] in order to be something therefore had to destroy what was above him; the other had to attempt to reach this elevated level."

45. It is a paradox for which Tocqueville frequently strives deliberately, as he clearly does in DA, II, A, 9, and II, C, 21.

46. In preparing the final section of vol. II of *Democracy in America*, Tocqueville noted, in the margins of an outline, his goals in writing: "To unite the spirit of liberty with the spirit of equality. To separate the spirit of equality from the revolutionary spirit." Yale archives, CV, d, 3.

47. DA, II, D, 7, 328.

48. Earlier, Chateaubriand had written: "Democrat by nature, aristocrat by culture, I would quite willingly abandon my fortune and my life to the people, provided I had little to do with the mob." Cited in Bourlanges, p. 96.

49. Cited in Redier, *Comme disait M. de Tocqueville*, pp. 46–48.

50. See Paul Bastid, *Benjamin Constant et sa doctrine* (Paris: Armand Colin, 1966), p. 1100.

51. Cited ibid., p. 734.

52. Cited in Paul Bastid, *Sieyès et sa pensée* (Paris: Hachette, 1939), p. 3.

53. In this I disagree with Edouard Laboulaye, a distant disciple of both men. See his *L'Etat et ses limites*, 2nd ed. (Paris: Charpentier, 1863).

54. OC, VIII, 1, 93.

55. OC, VI, 1, 55.

56. OC, XIII, 2, 233, 15 December 1850.

57. OC, IX, p. 20, n. 10.

58. AR, I, 217.

59. *Esprit des lois*, book 9, chap. 6. Lefebvre, in his introduction to AR, p. 10, cites a passage which shows that Tocqueville was not altogether a stranger to feudalism: "The French nobility, born of conquest as were the other nobilities of the Middle Ages . . ." Lefebvre concludes that "in this sense, Boulainvilliers,

Montesquieu, and other exemplars of eighteenth-century aristocratic literature nourished the thought of Tocqueville."

60. OC, IX, 19.

61. AR, I, 62.

62. AR, I, 176.

63. AR, I, 62.

64. Raymond Aron, *Essai sur les libertés* (Paris: Calmann-Lévy, 1965), pp. 22–23.

65. Strictly speaking, the final ingredient also derives from the Germanic idea. The aristocratic idea is already a synthesis of the Germanic and Christian ideas.

66. AR, I, book 3, chap. 1.

67. DA, II, D, 4, 305, and similarly, DA, II, B, 1, 104.

68. *Esprit des lois*, book 11, chap. 2.

69. DA, I, A, 2, 42 (46–47).

70. AR, I, 84.

71. Ibid.

72. DA, II, B, 15, 151.

73. OC, IX, 47.

74. Here again Tocqueville differs with Chateaubriand, who drew a rather different distinction between the two species of liberty: "One belongs to a people's childhood; it is a child of mores and virtue. This was the liberty of the early Greeks and early Romans, and of the American savages. The other is born of a people's old age; it is a child of enlightenment and reason. This is the liberty of the United States, which replaces that of the Indian." *Voyage en Amérique*, 1827, in Chateaubriand's *Oeuvres complètes*, ed. Pourrat (Paris: Didier, 1964), XII, 288.

75. DA, II, "Observations sur l'ouvrage de M. Cherbuliez, *De la démocratie en Suisse*," 356.

76. DA, I, A, 2, 34, 39–40, and DA, I, A, 5, 58–67.

77. A preliminary statement of the ideas later expressed in the address to the Athenaeum in 1819 can be found in Constant's brochure *De l'esprit de conquête et de l'usurpation* (Paris, 1814), in which he described the efforts of the revolutionaries to impose the ancient form of liberty upon a modern nation (see chaps. 6–8).

78. It is essential that these two forms of liberty be clearly distinguished; in some cases they are diametrically opposed. Because of this, Tocqueville's thought is occasionally difficult to grasp. For a balanced analysis, free of dogmatic bias, see A. Passerin d'Entrèves, *La notion de l'Etat* (Paris: Sirey, 1969), pp. 249–275. See also the excellent chapter on liberty in Lively, *Social and Political Thought*. Giovanni Sartori, *Théorie de la démocratie* (Paris, n.d.), rightly points out that freedom of participation is made possible by independence, and not the reverse.

79. Yale archives, CV, g, notebook 3, 9.

80. AR, I, 62.

81. *Esprit des lois*, XI, 4.

82. OC, V, 2, 91.

83. OC, VI, 1, 293–294; on instinctive feeling and taste for liberty, see also AR, II, 344–345.

84. This was an original and fertile idea that would subsequently be elabo-

rated upon by many writers, in particular Bertrand de Jouvenel, *Du pouvoir* (Geneva: Bourquin, 1947). See esp. p. 400: "The system of civil and political liberty has proved viable as long as it has been extended to men who acquired the mores associated with it. But it has not been viable when it encompassed strata for whom liberty was nothing compared with political power, who expected nothing from the one and hoped for everything from the other."

85. DA, II, B, 11, 139.

86. DA, II, D, 4.

87. Yale archives, CV, h, notebook 4, 36–37. Preparation for DA, I, A, 3, 52–53.

88. DA, II, B, 1, 101–104. The manuscripts in the Yale archives (CV, d) show that this chapter was written at the same time as the beginning of part four. In these drafts it is difficult to distinguish this chapter from DA, II, D, 1. Up to the last minute Tocqueville hesitated about where to place the chapter in the volume, and he was not even sure about where to put it in the work. It does not appear in the Yale working manuscript or in the last of the chapters to be included in the first three parts of DA, II (Yale archives, CV, f, packet 4). In the end, it was Tocqueville's friend Kergorlay who persuaded him to publish the chapter (Yale archives, CV, k, notebook 2, 1–2).

89. Chateaubriand: "The principle of aristocracy is liberty, just as the principle of democracy is equality," preface to *Ouvrages politiques*, 1926, in *Oeuvres complètes*, XXIX, 289.

90. DA, II, D, 5, 308.

91. Yale archives, CV, d, subsection of first file: Outline of chapter.

92. Yale archives, CV, g, notebook 2, 16.

93. DA, II, D, 1, 295.

94. DA, II, D, 5, 320.

3. The Primacy of Law

1. DA, I, B, 7, 261 (250).

2. Cited in Bastid, *Benjamin Constant*, p. 739.

3. Benjamin Constant, *Oeuvres* (Paris: Gallimard, 1957), p. 1071.

4. Ibid.

5. Ibid., p. 1076.

6. DA, I, B, 7, 262 (251).

7. Constant, *Oeuvres*, p. 1070.

8. Ibid., p. 1073.

9. Ibid., p. 1075.

10. Bastid, *Benjamin Constant*, p. 727.

11. Royer-Collard: "The question is whether morally the law can do whatever it pleases. We say that it cannot, that it is itself subject to right, or, to put it another way, to justice, and that wherever justice is subverted by the law there is oppression and tyranny." Speech cited in Dominique Bagge, "Le conflit des idées politiques en France sous la Restauration" (diss., University of Paris, 1952), p. 117.

12. DA, I, B, 6, 248–250.

13. AR, I, 89–90.

14. DA, I, B, 6, 248.

15. DA, I, A, 2, 41.

16. DA, I, B, 6, 249 (239).

17. Chateaubriand, *Mémoires d'outre-tombe* (Paris: Garnier, n.d.)

18. DA, I, B, 6, 250.

19. DA, II, B, 8.

20. Hobbes, *Leviathan*, chap. 15: "The right of nature, which writers commonly call *jus naturale*, is the liberty each man hath to use his own power, as he will himself, for the preservation of his own nature . . . A law of nature, *lex naturalis*, is a precept or general rule, found out by reason, by which a man is forbidden to do that which is destructive of his life, or taketh away the means of preserving the same . . . For though they that speak of this subject, use [sic] to confound *jus* and *lex*, *right* and *law*; yet they ought to be distinguished: because *right* consisteth in liberty to do or to forbear, whereas *law* determineth and bindeth to one of them; so that law and right differ as much as obligation and liberty; which in one and the same matter are inconsistent."

21. See Leo Strauss, *Natural Law and History*.

22. AR, I, 89.

23. AR, I, 90.

24. DA, II, A, 3 and 4.

25. DA, II, A, 4, 25.

26. AR, I, 198.

27. AR, I, 194.

28. DA, II, A, 4, 25.

29. Clinton Rossiter, *The Political Thought of the American Revolution* (New York: Harcourt, 1963), pp. 81–145.

30. See François Bourricaud, *Le bricolage idéologique* (Paris: Presses Universitaires de France, 1980), chap. 2.

31. Earlier, Condorcet had shown in his *Esquisse d'un tableau historique des progrès de l'esprit humain* (9th era) that he clearly understood how the idea of inalienable rights was associated with certain specific historical conditions, and he pointed out the significance of the American Revolution in this respect. Ernst Cassirer makes the same point in his *Philosophy of the Enlightenment*. Yet Condorcet's lack of political experience, abstract cast of mind, and predilection for mathematical forms of reasoning obscured the differences between America and France as well as the political consequences of those differences.

32. Raymond Polin, *L'obligation politique* (Paris: Presses Universitaires de France, 1971), pp. 149–150.

33. Pierre-Marcel, *Essai politique,* p. 183.

34. In Chapter 6 I shall consider freedom of education and freedom of thought, which are not mentioned here, and I shall have more to say about religious freedom. Economic freedoms will be examined in Chapter 7.

35. Pierre-Marcel, *Essai politique*, esp. pp. 180, 182, 193n, 195n, 197, 103, 208, 220, 229, 239, 246, and 253.

36. Ibid., pp. 177–272. The following works are most often cited: Constant, *Principes de politiques;* Rossi, *Cours de droit constitutionnel;* Rémusat, *Politique libérale;* Laboulaye, *Le parti libéral, L'Etat et ses limites,* and *Cours de politique*

constitutionnelle; Broglie, *Vues sur le government de la France*; Jules Simon, *La liberté politique;* Vacherot, *La démocratie libérale*; and Esmein, *Eléments de droit constitutionnel.*

37. Pierre-Marcel, *Essai politique,* p. 180; it is Pierre-Marcel who has italicized the word "probably." On this point see Jean-Claude Lamberti, "De Benjamin Constant à Tocqueville," *France-Forum,* no. 203–204 (April–May 1983), 19–26.

38. Letter to Stoffels, 24 July 1836, OC, 1866 ed., V, 433.

39. DA, I, B, 4, 198.

40. DA, I, B, 4, 199–201.

41. DA, II, B, 7, 126.

42. The law of 16 February 1834 concerning associations was still more stringent than the penal code inherited from the Empire (article 291 at 195). See Rémusat, *Mémoires de ma vie* (Paris: Plon, 1958–1967), III, pp. 65–67; and Guizot, *Mémoires,* III, p. 230. On the three laws of 9 September 1835, cf. Rémusat, *Mémoires,* pp. 135–138: these laws "mark the culmination of the politics of resistance" (p. 137). The third law was criticized by Royer-Collard for infringing the freedom of the press; Royer chose this occasion to break with Guizot.

43. DA, II, B, 7, 125. Cf. Rémusat (*Mémoires,* III, 67): "Although this right subsists in countries that obtained their freedom long ago, it had never been called for in a sustained and forceful manner by the liberal opposition of the past twenty years . . . The clubs of the Revolution had left memories too fresh and too odious to permit the liberal party to number among its customary demands the right to reestablish them."

44. Pierre-Marcel (*Essai politique,* pp. 201–204) has shown with great subtlety that in regard to freedom of the press Tocqueville was the disciple of Royer-Collard more than of Constant. He quotes (p. 203) an unpublished paper of Tocqueville's: "The Restoration was little more than a long war between press and government. The years that have elapsed since the July Revolution have offered the same spectacle, with the difference that under the Restoration it was the press that ultimately vanquished the government, whereas nowadays it is the government that triumphs over the press." On the Revolution of 1830 and freedom of the press, there is a transparent allusion in DA, I, B, 3, 192–193: "The time of sudden revolutions." On freedom of the press in general, see DA, I, B, 3, 185–193, and DA, II, B, 6, 118–121.

45. DA, II, B, 7, 122.

46. DA, II, B, 105: "Individualism is the result of an erroneous judgment rather than a depraved sentiment." On this question, in order to avoid tedious repetition, I shall allow myself to refer to my own previous work, *La notion d'individualisme chez Tocqueville* (Paris: Presses Universitaires de France, 1970).

47. DA, II, B, 5, 117.

48. DA, II, B, 7, 123.

49. Pierre-Marcel, *Essai politique,* p. 197, cites Tocqueville's influence on Broglie (*Vues sur le gouvernement,* p. 190), Laboulaye (*Le parti libéral,* p. 185), Jules Simon (*La liberté politique,* p. 150), Renouvier (*Science de la morale,* beginning of vol. II), Taine (*Origines de la France contemporaine,* III, 264, and VIII, 8, 162), and Le Play and Renan.

50. DA, II, D, 7, 330.

51. DA, II, B, 5, 116.

52. See Albert Salomon, *Tocqueville, Moralist and Sociologist* (1935), p. 266; and F. Pillon, "Césarisme ou républicain," *La Critique Philosophique*, no. 24 (18 July 1872). Pillon was the managing editor of the journal, whose leading figure was Charles Renouvier.

53. DA, II, B, 2 and 3.

54. Emile Faguet, *Politiques et moralistes du XIXe siècle* (Paris, Société Française d'Impression et d'Edition, 1903), p. 218.

55. Marcel Prelot, *Histoire des idées politiques*, 3rd ed. (Paris: Dalloz, 1966), p. 445.

56. Ibid.

57. Contemporaries referred familiarly to the "additional act" to the Constitution of the Empire as the "Benjamine."

58. Cicero, *Oratio pro Cluentio*.

59. AR, II, 344.

60. DA, I, B, 6, 248–250.

61. AR, I, 134.

62. AR, I, 177.

63. DA, I, A, 5, 70.

64. Compare Montesquieu, *Esprit des lois*, XI, 3: "In a State, that is, a society in which there are laws, liberty consists solely in being able to do what one must will and in not being compelled to do what one must not will."

65. See Rousseau's letter to the marquis de Mirabeau, written five years after the *Social Contract*: "The great problem in politics, which I compare to that of squaring the circle in geometry, is to find a form of government which puts the law above man . . . If, unfortunately, such a form cannot be found, and ingenuously I admit that I believe it cannot be . . ." *Correspondance* (Paris: Colin, 1927–1934) XVII, 155.

66. Rousseau, "Huitième lettre écrite de la montagne," *Ecrits politiques* (Paris: Gallimard, 1959), p. 842.

67. Rousseau, *Social Contract*, book 2, chap. 3: "The general will is always right and always contributes to public utility, but it does not follow that the deliberations of the people are always righteous to the same degree . . . There is often a great deal of difference between the will of all and the general will."

68. See, for example, in France, Raymond Carré de Malberg, *La loi, expression de la volonté générale* (Paris: Sirey, 1931); and, in England, Edward Dicey, *Introduction to the Study of the Law of the Constitution* (London, 1889).

69. DA, II, D, 7, 333.

70. S, 87.

71. DA, I, B, 6, 249.

72. OC, IX, 57. Letter to Gobineau, 2 October 1843.

73. AR, II, 371.

74. DA, I, B, 7, 261–262 and B, 10, 413.

75. DA, I, B, 7, 261–262.

76. *Esprit des lois*, I, 3.

77. Ibid., I, 1, and XIX, 14.

78. Michel Villey, *Philosophie du droit* (Paris: Dalloz, 1978).

79. *Esprit des lois*, XIX, 4, paragraph 2. Paragraph 1 reads: "Several things govern men: climate, religion, laws, maxims of government, examples of things past, mores, and manners, from which a general spirit is formed." Tocqueville's "moral conception" of rights corresponds to what Montesquieu calls "examples of things past and mores." Tocqueville's "political conception" is the equivalent of what Montesquieu refers to as the effect of "laws and maxims of government."

80. Ibid., book 8, chap. 8.

81. DA, I, A, 2, 32.

82. The revolutionaries had erred, Tocqueville believed, in attempting to make all rights stem from a single source, that is, in having treated the law as a logical construction. See DA, I, A, 8, 121: "Over time a people develops different interests and consecrates a variety of rights . . . Hence it is only at the inception of a society that its laws can be completely logical."

83. OC, V, 1, 179. On this point Tocqueville is also indebted to Rousseau: see *Social Contract*, book 2, end of chap. 12: "I am speaking of mores, customs, and above all opinion, things unknown to our politicians but upon which the success of everything else depends; things with which the great lawgiver occupies himself in secret, while he appears to limit himself to specific regulations which form only the arch of the vault, while mores, slower to take shape, ultimately form the unshakable keystone."

84. See Bertrand de Jouvenel, *Du pouvoir*, esp. chaps. 13 and 16. The inspiration for this remarkable work is very close, I think, to that of Montesquieu and Tocqueville.

85. Locke, *Second Treatise on Civil Government*, chap. 11, especially paragraph 135.

86. OC, V, 1, 250–256. "Notes on Kent."

87. See Max Lerner, *La civilisation américaine* (Paris: Seuil, 1961), chap. 8. The fundamental work on this question remains Oliver Wendell Holmes, Jr., *The Common Law* (Boston, 1881).

88. DA, I, B, 8, 274–282.

89. On these two approaches to justice, see DA, II, C, 18, 238: "Sometimes they are at odds, but never are they entirely one and never do they destroy each other."

90. DA, I, B, 6, 251, and, in the same sense, OC, V, 1, 270–271. See also the fragments published for the first time in the *Nouvelle Revue Française*, 1 April 1959, p. 11: It is not in the nature of a democratic power to lack for material strength, but to lack for moral strength, stability, and intelligence. I will grant, if you like, that democratic governments have more strength than others, but less wisdom.

91. DA, I, A, 8, 141.

92. Yale archives, CV, h, notebook 5, 39.

93. Ibid. See also DA, I, A, 6, 100: "its passive nature."

94. DA, II, D, 7, 331; see also 358: "The idea of an independent judiciary is a modern idea."

95. The main ideas call for comparison with chap. 18 and esp. chap. 19 of Constant's *Principes de politique* (Paris, 1815).

96. DA, I, A, 6, 100 (99–100).

97. DA, II, 358 (account of Victor Cherbuliez's *De la démocratie en Suisse*).

98. DA, I, A, 5, 73 and 82.

99. DA, I, A, 6, 103.

100. For Mill's review, see *Democracy in America,* Schocken ed. (1970), p. xxiv.

101. Ancient Athens practiced a rudimentary form of oversight: anyone who proposed to the assembly a law deemed contrary to the fundamental traditions of the city could be taken before the courts and accused of unlawful activity (*graphe para nomon*). Demosthenes wrote his "discourse for the crown" in response to such a charge.

102. See also the articles by Hamilton in *The Federalist*, nos. 78–83. Tocqueville was aware that Jefferson was of the opposite opinion. He had studied Jefferson, as well as L. P. Conseil's *Mélanges politiques et philosophiques extraits des mémoires et de la correspondance de Thomas Jefferson précédés d'un essai sur les principes de l'école américaine* (Paris: Paulin, 1833), where he could have read (p. 85) that "Jefferson and the men of his school were greatly worried about the steadily growing power of the judiciary, and . . . they pointed to the establishment of this power as the principal weakness of the Federal Constitution and a permanent threat to American liberty." On this question and many others, Tocqueville was closer to Hamilton and Madison than to Jefferson.

103. DA, I, A, 8, 141. See Arendt, *On Revolution*, esp. chap. 5.

104. Yale archives, CV, h, notebook 5, 39: "Examine the doctrine that makes judges the arbiters of a law's constitutionality. Such a maxim can prevail only where the doctrine that the Constitution is superior to all the authorities that emanate from it is accepted."

105. Bryce, *American Commonwealth*. On the place of the Supreme Court in the American power structure, see DA, I, A, 8, 152–154.

106. DA, I, B, 8, 277 (266): "The lawyer belongs to the people by interest and birth and to the aristocracy by habit and taste; he is, as it were, the natural link between the two, the ring that joins them."

107. DA, I, B, 8, 274–281: "The American aristocracy is found at the bar or on the bench."

108. DA, I, B, 8, 276 (265). And he says later: "When an aristocracy closes its ranks to lawyers, it creates particularly dangerous enemies, because although they are beneath it in wealth and power, their work makes them independent of it, and their education makes them feel equal to it."

109. AR, I, 173–175; see also AR, II, 364.

110. AR, II, 363–364.

111. AR, II, 364.

112. *Esprit des lois*, XI, 6.

113. Ibid., 11.

114. Created by the constitution of the Year VIII, the Conseil d'Etat was given the responsibility of examining suits against the administration, with the final decision being vested in the head of the executive branch, that is, the First Consul.

115. Constant, *Principes de politique*, chap. 19, p. 1205.

116. Ibid., chap. 18, p. 1198.

117. DA, I, B, 8, 284–285; see also OC, V, 1, 181, 201, 243, 296–304, 304–318,

325–330. Pierson (*Tocqueville and Beaumont,* chaps. 28 and 29), pointed out that the chapter on lawyers and juries (DA, I, B, 8) is almost entirely contained in the travel notes for September 1831.

118. Pierre-Marcel, *Essai politique,* pp. 92, 181–201.

119. See OC, 1866 ed., IX, 74–75, "Report on the treatise on administrative law by M. Macarel." Tocqueville failed to understand that the development of administrative courts and administrative law could constitute a counterweight to the power of the administration.

4. Democratic Government

1. Yale archives, CV, h, notebook 2, 68–73: "On the different ways in which one can conceptualize the republic." This is the draft of DA, I, B, 10, 412–413.

2. DA, I, introduction, 9 (16); see also DA, I, B, 5, 231: "It would be an insult to republicans to call by that name the oligarchy that reigned over France in 1793."

3. DA, I, B, 10, 412–413 (395–396).

4. DA, I, A, 4, 54.

5. DA, I, A, 8, 125.

6. Yale archives, CV, h, notebook 1, 78.

7. Even Jefferson, in his inaugural address of 1801, asserted that if the will of the majority is to carry in all circumstances, that will must be legitimate and reasonable.

8. OC, V, 1, 184, 25 October 1831.

9. Yale archives, CV, j, notebook 2, 2; text partially incorporated in DA, I, B, 7, 262.

10. DA, I, A, 4, 57–58, and A, 8, 168–169.

11. DA, I, A, 5, 64. Under the influence of his friend Jared Sparks, Tocqueville seems to have placed some credence in the theory that the community is the source of sovereignty. Sparks had ably combined this theory with that of the social pact and natural liberty. For a critique, see Pierson, *Tocqueville and Beaumont* p. 410n.

12. Yale archives, CV, h, notebook 1, 24–25, 75, and notebook 2, 48, 80–81. Compare *The Federalist,* no. 39.

13. See Pierson, *Tocqueville and Beaumont,* esp. chaps 30 and 55. Pierson has compiled a list of Tocqueville's informants and indicated his sources. The three principal sources are the Collection of the Laws of Massachusetts, probably given him by Senator Gray, a volume entitled *The Town Officer,* given him by Josiah Quincy, president of Harvard, and above all Jared Sparks's essay *On the Government of Towns in Massachusetts.* Sparks was the author of a remarkable book, *The Life of Gouverneur Morris,* and Tocqueville met him in Paris in 1828. Senator Everett, the Unitarian minister Joseph Tuckerman, and Major Richard, mayor of Philadelphia, also provided Tocqueville with information; another important influence was the "distinguished lawyer" Ambrose Spencer, who had been in Congress and was serving in the New York State Legislature when Tocqueville met him. The depth of Tocqueville's investigation is evident from his travel notes for September and October 1831: OC, V, 1, 89–90 (Quincy); 94 (Gray); 95–96 (Sparks); 103–104 (Richard); 242–243 (Tuckerman).

14. DA, I, A, 5, 59 and 66 (62–63, 68–69).

15. Henrion de Pansey, *Du pouvoir municipal* (1820), quoted from 3rd ed. (Paris: Barrois et Duprat, 1833), pp. 1 and 7. De Pansey (1742–1829), a lawyer and scholar, translated from the Latin and published in 1773 the *Traité des fiefs* by Dumoulin, and then in 1789 published his own *Dissertation du droit féodal*, which Chateaubriand used as a source on the early years of monarchy. De Pansey served as president of one of the chambers of the Court in 1807 and was appointed Conseiller d'Etat while he was still serving as judge, an unusual procedure. Among his other works: *De l'autorité judiciaire en France* (1810), *Des assemblées nationales en France après l'établissement de la monarchie jusqu'en 1814* (1826). For de Pansey, the law of 14 December 1789, which restored genuine power to the communes of France, was "the wise and best pondered law of all those we owe to the Constituent Assembly."

16. Cited in Redier, *Comme disait M. de Tocqueville*, pp. 271–272.

17. Yale archives, CV, h, notebook 5, 4.

18. DA, I, A, 4, 56 (60).

19. DA, I, A, 5, 60 and note 2.

20. See Maurice Barbé, *Etude historique des idées sur la souveraineté en France de 1815 à 1848* (Paris, 1904).

21. A similar idea is expressed in DA, I, A, 4, 54.

22. On the failure of the Restoration, see OC, V, 1, 182.

23. Certain liberals of Tocqueville's day suggested that the remedy lay in extending the right to vote. Tocqueville disagreed, calling instead for "moralization" of the electoral system and greater powers for local government. See Pierre-Marcel, *Essai politique* pp. 232–245.

24. Yale archives, CV, h, notebook 1, 5.

25. Mill, *Dissertations*. This work contains Mill's two reviews of *Democracy in America*, from 1835 and 1840, originally published in the *London and Westminster Review*.

26. OC, V, 1, 205–206; see also 256–257 and 278.

27. DA, I, introduction, 5: "To educate democracy . . . gradually to substitute knowledge of affairs for its inexperience, knowledge of its true interests for its blind instincts . . . A wholly new world needs a new political science."

28. DA, I, A, 5, 59 (local government); B, 7, 123 (political associations); B, 8, 286 (jury). On the inadequacy of education, see DA, I, B, 9, 318, and OC, V, 1, 220–221.

29. *Esprit des lois*, IV, 4.

30. Ibid., 5.

31. Mill, *Dissertations*, I, xv–xvii and II, xx.

32. Ibid., I, xxi.

33. Ibid., I, xxx. Mill would later express a similar idea in *Considerations on Representative Government*: "Men as well as women need political rights not only in order to govern themselves but also in order to prevent others from misgoverning them." [Retranslated into English from the French translation—Trans.]

34. OC, 1866 ed., VII, 24. For Montesquieu, see *Esprit des lois*, I, 3: Laws "must be suited to the people for which they are made, and it is the rarest of chances if those of one nation can be made to fit another."

35. Armand Carrel, writing in the newspaper *Le National* on 29 May 1832,

stated: "Since our first Revolution, we have moved steadily closer to that Anglo-French concoction known as the American Constitution."

36. See, for example, Rémond, *Les Etats-Unis*. Around 1834 or 1835 there occurred a sudden reversal of opinion, and sympathy for the United States vanished. See *Democracy in America*, II, parts 3 and 4.

37. OC, 1866 ed., VII, 23. Letter of 3 June 1831.

38. DA, I, B, 9, esp. 292. See Chapter 3 of this book, fourth section, for my comments.

39. DA, I, prefatory note to 12th ed., p. xliv.

40. Mill, *Dissertations,* I, xxvi.

41. DA, I, B, 5, 202 (196). See also Yale archives, CV, k, notebook 1, 52, for a similar idea in a draft for the preface of vol. II.

42. OC, VIII, 1, 141. Letter to Beaumont, 14 August 1834.

43. OC, 1866 ed., V, 428–429.

44. OC, VI, 1, 302.

45. The problem of democratic representation was still so new that Madison (in *The Federalist*, no. 10) draws a contrast between a republic (representative) and a democracy (pure). The notion of "representative democracy" is a triumph of political vocabulary due in large part to Tocqueville; in any case, it did not occur until after *The Federalist*'s time.

46. OC, VI, 1, 303–304. The theory of representative democracy is not to be found in Montesquieu, who dealt primarily with ancient democracy: see *Esprit des lois*, II, 2. But he does present a clear notion of representation (XI, 9), along with a theory of representative government, in his "English" chapters (XI, 6, and XIX, 27).

47. This was also the opinion of the moderate republicans of the "American School." See L. P. Conseil, *Mélanges politiques et philosophiques extraits des mémoires et de la correspondance de Thomas Jefferson, précédés d'un essai sur les principes de l'Ecole américaine*, p. 27: "The government of the people by itself, in which the republic is based on the participation of all citizens in the election of all delegates to whom they entrust the exercise of the three powers: legislative, judicial, and executive."

48. DA, II, App., "Report on the work of M. Cherbuliez entitled *De la démocratie en Suisse*," 356–357. The cantons in which pure democracy was practiced lacked representative bodies; their democracy was "of another age." In other cantons, with representative democracy, the use of the popular veto caused representative government to degenerate into pure democracy. It was precisely this veto, this requirement of popular approbation, that Rousseau considered essential for popular sovereignty.

49. DA, I, B, 5, 208.

50. DA, I, B, 6, 241.

51. Mill, *Dissertations,* I, xxxiv–xxxvii; see also I, xi.

52. See esp. DA, I, B, 6, 242, and B, 5, 204 and 233.

53. DA, I, B, 5, 208–209, 214–216, 216–229, 229–231, 231–234, 236–240.

54. DA, I, B, 5, 203–205; cf. Montesquieu, *Esprit des lois*, II, 2.

55. DA, I, B, 5, 233.

56. DA, I, B, 5, 204–205.

57. Rémond, *Les Etats-Unis,* II, 696–714, esp. 702–708.

58. DA, I, B, 6, 243.

59. DA, I, B, 5, 209; letter from Jefferson to Madison dated 20 December 1787; *The Federalist,* no. 62 (Madison) and no. 73 (Hamilton).

60. *Esprit des lois,* XIX, 27, 576.

61. OC, V, 1, 196.

62. DA, I, B, 10, 415.

63. DA, I, B, 10, 416.

64. Cited in Robert G. Mahieu, *Les enquêteurs français aux Etats-Unis de 1830 à 1837* (Paris: Honoré Champion, 1934), p. 92.

65. It should be noted, however, that Tocqueville always regarded Lafayette as a dangerous demagogue.

66. Yale archives, CV, j, notebook 1, 41–42. It is clear that "democracy" here means "democratic social state." A muffled echo of this passage can be found in DA, II, A, 2, 19, paragraph 2, and DA, I, B, 7, 264.

67. See for example, Conseil, *Mélanges politiques,* pp. 42–58, 79–85.

68. *Esprit des lois,* XI, 4, 5, and 6.

69. Mill deals with only one defect, the omnipotence of the majority (*Dissertations,* I, xxxviii–xxxix). He realized that his commentary was somewhat more favorable to democracy than Tocqueville's book (OC, VI, 1, 299).

70. Mill, *Dissertations,* II, vi–vii.

71. On this subject see the correspondence between Mill and Tocqueville for the second half of 1835: OC, VI, 1, 291–306, esp. 294.

72. Destutt de Tracy, in his *Commentaire de l'Esprit des lois* (1806), argued that any form of government included in Montesquieu's classification could lead to despotism if it tended to satisfy not the general and permanent interests of its citizens but the particular interests of one man (under monarchy) or of a group of men (in a republic).

73. DA, I, B, 6, 241–257, and Mill, *Dissertations,* II, xix–xxi.

74. DA, I, B, 6, 233. The necessary warning was given, however.

75. *Esprit des lois,* XI, 5 and 6.

76. DA, I, A, 8, 114.

77. Arendt, *On Revolution.*

78. Ibid., p. 85.

79. Ibid., chaps. 4 and 5.

80. Pierson, *Tocqueville and Beaumont;* Schleifer, *Making,* pp. 87–120.

81. See André and Suzanne Tunc, *Le système constitutionnel des Etats-Unis d'Amérique,* 2 vols. (Paris: Domat-Montechrestien, 1954); Frederick A. Ogg and Perley O. Ray, *Essentials of American Government* (New York: Century, 1932); Alexander Hamilton, John Jay, and James Madison, *The Federalist* (New York: Bantam, 1982).

82. What follows is based primarily on DA, I, A, 8, 113–174; DA, I, B, 10, 380–412; and OC, V, 1, 266–270. DA, I, A, 8 cites from *The Federalist,* nos. 12, 15–22, 32, 30–36, 41–42, 45, 51, 52–66, 67–77, 78–83. *The Federalist* in its entirety helped to shape Tocqueville's thought, and the texts that had the greatest influence on him (such as Madison's no. 10 on "factions") are not necessarily cited. See Tocqueville's judgment in DA, I, 116: "*The Federalist* is a fine book, which, though

specific to America, ought to be familiar to the statesmen of all countries." This was also the judgment of Talleyrand and Guizot (see Esmein's preface to the French translation of *The Federalist,* published by the Librairie Générale de Droit et de Jurisprudence in 1957).

83. DA, I, A, 8, 159.

84. Ibid. See also OC, V, 1, 267.

85. Here again, however, Tocqueville's vocabulary is less precise than his analysis. In the same passage (DA, I, A, 8, bottom of p. 158) he speaks of the United States as a "confederation." It should be noted, however, that this ambiguous usage of "federation" and "confederation" was common at the time.

86. DA, I, A, 8, 168 and 171.

87. See Schleifer, *Making*, pp. 102–111, which examines the texts in detail but does not give a rigorous account of Tocqueville's legal misunderstandings. Such an account can be found in Robert C. Hartnett, *Tocqueville on American Federalism* (New York: Fordham, 1945), pp. 22–31. On the relaxation of the federal bond, see DA, I, B, 10, 403. By 1838 Tocqueville was prepared to acknowledge his mistake (Schleifer, *Making*, p. 111).

88. DA, I, A, 8, 163–167; *Esprit des lois*, IX, 1; *The Federalist*, no. 9.

89. DA, I, A, 8, 174.

90. DA, I, A, 8, 168–172; see OC, V, 1, 269. These conditions include an educated populace, a tradition of self-government, homogeneity of mores and interests, and peaceful neighbors.

91. On this subject see Esmein's excellent analysis in his preface to the French edition of *The Federalist*.

92. DA, I, A, 8, 126.

93. See, for example, Conseil, *Mélanges politiques*, pp. 52–58. Once again Conseil presents, in the name of the American School, a theory of republicanism quite remote from American experience. Under the July Monarchy the republicans' disaffection with the United States was expressed chiefly in the political sphere, through opposition to bicameralism and federalism. See Rémond, *Les Etats-Unis*, II, 667–673. Between 1795 and 1848 a majority of the French favored bicameralism. In his report on the Constitution of the Year III, Boissy d'Anglas put forward an idea that would uncontestably hold sway for the next half century: that the disorders and misfortunes of the Revolution were due to the arbitrariness of the unicameral assembly.

94. Benjamin Constant favored a hereditary peerage, and he managed to gain Napoleon's reluctant approval of the idea. See articles 3–5 of the *Acte additionnel aux Constitutions de l'Empire du 22 avril 1815*. Count Hervé de Tocqueville was named peer of France in 1828. His son Alexis never defended the principle of a hereditary chamber.

95. DA, I, A, 5, 85. When he says "introduced into the world . . . almost by chance," does he mean that there was nothing necessarily aristocratic about the second chamber? It is hard to say. Pierson, *Tocqueville and Beaumont*, p. 729, proves that Tocqueville had read J. L. de Lolme, Montesquieu's finest eighteenth-century disciple, whose *La Constitution de l'Angleterre* (Geneva, 1771), book 2, chap. 3, shows rationally that every representative regime requires a bicameral legislature.

96. DA, I, A, 8, 158; see also DA, I, B, 7, 257n and 264; and *The Federalist*, no. 51.

97. François Furet and Denis Richet, *La Révolution française* (Paris: Fayard, 1973), pp. 92 and 106; the second chamber was rejected on 10 September by a vote of 849 to 89 with more than 100 abstentions.

98. Cited in Edouard Laboulaye, *Histoire des Etats-Unis* (Paris: Charpentier, 1870), III, p. 292.

99. *The Federalist*, no. 47; see *Le Bicentenaire de l'Esprit des lois: Montesquieu, sa pensée politique et constitutionnelle* (Paris: Sirey, n.d.). On Madison and Montesquieu, see Paul Bastid, *Montesquieu et les Etats-Unis*, and Charles Eisenmann, *La pensée constitutionnelle de Montesquieu*.

100. There is also a *strict* interpretation of the separation-of-powers theory, more juridical than political, whose early twentieth-century exponents included Jellinek and Laband in Germany and Duguit and Carré de Malberg in France. For these authors, separation of powers means that the three governmental powers are exercised by three bodies composed of entirely different elements among which there are no relations and therefore no possibility of influence. See, for example, Carré de Malberg, *Contribution à la théorie générale de l'Etat*, II (Paris: Sirey, 1922). For an opposing view, favorable to the moderate interpretation, see Charles Eisenmann, *L'Esprit des lois et la séparation des pouvoirs: Mélanges Carré de Malberg* (Paris, 1933), pp. 165ff.

101. *The Federalist*, no. 47, p. 399; see also Laboulaye, *Histoire*, p. 291.

102. Laboulaye, *Histoire*, p. 293. This is also true, in my view, of the Constitution of the Year III; but Laboulaye, a great admirer of Boissy d'Anglas and Daunou (p. 303), does not say so.

103. DA, II, A, 4; and AR, I, book 3, chap. 1.

104. *The Federalist*, no. 47, p. 244.

105. Ibid., p. 245.

106. *Esprit des lois*, XI, 6, paragraphs 5 and 6.

107. OC, V, 1, 129, 3 December 1831. Walker was "a very distinguished young lawyer from Ohio."

108. OC, V, 1, 178; see also p. 61 (on the judges) and p. 68 (on the two chambers).

109. OC, V, 1, 96, 29 September 1831. Sparks had a great influence on Tocqueville, as Pierson has shown in great detail (see his *Tocqueville and Beaumont*, esp. chaps. 30 and 55).

110. DA, I, B, 7, 257–272.

111. DA, I, B, 7, 261–264.

112. DA, I, B, 7, 264.

113. DA, I, B, 7, 268–270. Tocqueville is here concerned with both the political and moral effects of the tyranny or omnipotence of the majority. In particular, he is responding to a question often raised at the time: Why was America no longer producing such remarkable politicians as in the past? On this subject see Rémond, *Les Etats-Unis*, II, 704–708.

114. *The Federalist*, no. 51, p. 264; cited in part in DA, I, B, 7, 271. In his conclusion, Madison went so far as to state that "a coalition of the entire nation will rarely occur for motives other than justice and the general interest." Guil-

laume-Tell Poussin criticized Tocqueville on these grounds in his *Considérations sur le principe démocratique qui régit l'Union américaine et la possibilité de son application à d'autres états* (Paris: Librairie Charles de Gosselin, 1841), p. 144.

115. DA, I, B, 7, 257n and 271n. Schleifer, *Making*, pp. 112–120, emphasizes the differences between Tocqueville's conception of the majority and Madison's, relying primarily on DA, I, B, 7, 262: "What, therefore, is a majority taken collectively other than an individual who has opinions and usually interests contrary to those of another individual, called the minority?" It is true that in this passage Tocqueville's notion of majority appears to be something of "a fixed, abstract entity." But elsewhere he uses the notion in a manner very similar to Madison; see DA, I, A, 8, 163: "The more numerous a people is, and the more diversified the nature of its intellects and interests, the more difficult it is to form a compact majority." On the other hand, Schleifer is quite right to observe that one of the paradoxes in Tocqueville's work is that he fears the tyranny of the majority yet praises the moral and political climate in the townships, where the worst instances of American conformism are found.

116. See also Yale archives, CV, b, 26: "How democracy leads to tyranny and may destroy freedom in America." On p. 25 Tocqueville emphasizes the confusion of powers, and on p. 26 he says that "the tyranny of one man may seem more tolerable than the tyranny of the majority." Compare this with the letter from Jefferson to Madison dated 15 March 1789 and cited at the end of DA, I, B, 7, 272. See also Rémond, *Les Etats Unis*, II, pp. 708–713, for French views of America's future: many foresaw a return to aristocratic society or military dictatorship, and after the election of Jackson "people looked forward to an American Bonaparte" (p. 708).

117. DA, I, B, 8.

118. Mill, *Dissertations,* I, xxxviii, and II, vi and xxvi; Bryce, *American Commonwealth*, chap. 84; Pierson, *Tocqueville and Beaumont*, p. 766; David Spitz, *Democracy and the Challenge of Power* (New York: Columbia University Press, 1958), chap. 5.

119. DA, I, B, 7, 265–270. I am following Tocqueville's terminology; it would have been better, perhaps, to speak of tyranny of opinion, but Tocqueville does not distinguish adequately between political and sociological concepts. Spitz, *Democracy*, notes that the pressure of public opinion can be observed in all societies.

120. DA, I, B, 7, 266.

121. DA, I, B, 7, 267; the comparison stems from a conversation with M. Stuart. See OC, V, 1, 115, 1 November 1831.

122. DA, II, D, 6.

123. Yale archives, CV, g, notebook 2, 80; see also p. 79: "This is the true and original portrait; the one in the first volume was distorted, common, and false."

5. Political Interlude

1. Official missions of inquiry to foreign countries were much in vogue in the early years of the July Monarchy. See Mahieu, *Les enquêteurs,* chap. 1. Michel Chevalier went to the United States to study the railroads and from there wrote his famous *Letters on North America*. Tocqueville and Beaumont obtained a commis-

sion to study the American penitentiary system, which was the official pretext for their travels in the United States between April 1831 and January 1832. Their investigation led to a report published in 1833 under the title *Du système péniten-tiaire aux Etats-Unis et de son application en France*, including an appendix on the penal colonies and statistical notes. The book won the French Academy's Month-yon Prize, which it shared jointly with Necker de Saussure's *L'Education progressive*.

2. OC, VIII, 1, 151.

3. *Gazette de France*, 3 February 1835. This was the least kind of all the reviews. It began: "M. de T. is an attorney, and as such he pleads the case of American Democracy." The article was harsh on America and harsher still on the "revolutionary" government of Louis-Philippe, but it ended with an homage to Tocqueville.

4. On 19 January, *Le National* published an excerpt from the work, the chapter on political judgment (DA, I, A, 7), and on 7 June and 25 June it published two highly laudatory articles signed A.S.(?), in which Tocqueville was judged to be one of "the superior men" who can "enlighten democracy" and "in a sense com-plete its governmental education in the interest of society." The second article contains this very just observation: "Thus the first fact that must strike those who study the history of the United States and its legislation is the total absence of the contradiction that results in France from the struggle between revolution and counterrevolution."

5. The *Journal des Débats* published two articles, one on 23 March and the other on 2 May 1835. "This is a beautiful book, a book unlike any other." Tocque-ville was compared to Blackstone and Montesquieu. A passage summarizing one of the articles expresses the prevailing attitude of the paper: American democracy "shares the characteristics of the conservative institutions of the ancient peoples." One cavil is given amid the praise: "He believed too much in the title of his work, in the frontispiece on American laws, he believed too much in democracy in the United States." As one might expect, the tone of the articles is very different from that of *Le National*. It is remarkable, almost astonishing, that the two papers' judgments were so similar in regard to a political work on America, given that the *Journal des Débats* considered *Le National* to be its principal adversary and re-proached the rival journal for constantly voicing its opinions about the United States.

6. *Le Temps*, 7 April 1835.

7. OC, XI, 92. Letter from Tocqueville to Royer-Collard, 15 August 1840: "As for the great public—great in number—the book is little read and poorly understood. This silence pains me. I examine my conscience and suffer. I ask myself if in fact there is anything of value in this work."

8. OC, VI, 1, 330.

9. Rémond, *Les Etats-Unis*, vol. II, chap. 1.

10. OC, VIII, 1. Letter from Tocqueville to Beaumont, 14 July 1834.

11. OC, VI, 1, 326.

12. Seymour Drescher, "Tocqueville's Two Democracies," *Journal of the His-tory of Ideas*, 25, no. 2 (1964), 201–216.

13. DA, I, introduction, 12. In 1835 he avoided treating democratic ideas and mores so as not to compete with the book written by his friend and traveling

companion, Gustave de Beaumont: *Marie, or Slavery in the United States* (Stanford: Stanford University Press, 1958).

14. G. W. Pierson, "Le 'second voyage' de Tocqueville en Amérique," in *Alexis de Tocqueville: Livre du Centenaire, 1859–1959* (Paris: Editions du CNRS, 1960).

15. OC, VIII, 1, 93.

16. Heinrich Heine, *Allemands et Français* (Paris, 1848), p. 313: "[They] complement each other as well as possible. One is the severe thinker, the other full of unctuous sentiments, like the pitcher of vinegar and the pitcher of oil."

17. Letter to Eugène Stoffels, 24 July 1836, in OC, 1866 ed., V, 433–434.

18. Ibid., 434.

19. Ibid., 435.

20. OC, 1866 ed., V, 436–438. Letter of 5 October 1836.

21. Napoleon II died on 22 July 1832.

22. Thiers had been named Prime Minister on 22 February. On 6 September he was succeeded by Count Molé, and Guizot became Minister of Public Instruction.

23. Paul Marie Pierre Thureau-Dangin entitled book 3 of his *Histoire de la Monarchie de Juillet*, (Paris: Plon, 1904–1909), which dealt with the period 1836–1839, "The Crisis of Parliamentary Government."

24. In a letter written in 1837 and cited by Thureau-Dangin, Tocqueville protests against the Laws of September 1835 and their consequences.

25. OC, XI, 27.

26. OC, XI, 43.

27. Cited in Pierre de la Gorce, "Louis-Philippe," *Revue des Deux Mondes*, April–May 1931, pp. 152, 155. This article clearly exposes Guizot's true ambition and the weaknesses of the regime.

28. Ibid. In this connection, a contribution of Guizot's to the debate on secret funds (3 March 1837) is cited.

29. Rémusat, *Mémoires*, III, 199. In the debates of 5 and 6 May 1837, Guizot figured as the leader of the party of resistance, eclipsing Molé. Whereas Thiers maintained that the repressive Laws of September 1835 were no longer so necessary, Guizot asserted the need to battle revolutionary subversion by appealing to all the conservative forces in the country. For Tocqueville's opinion of this debate, see his letter to Beaumont of 14 May 1837, OC, VIII, 1, 182–185.

30. Cited in de la Gorce, "Louis-Philippe," p. 158.

31. S, 31–35; and Eichtal, *Alexis de Tocqueville*, p. 237.

32. See Louis Girard et al., *La Chambre des Députés en 1837–1839* (Paris: Publications de la Sorbonne, 1976), p. 48: of 457 members of parliament, 206 were government functionaries. Functionaries accounted for more than 52 percent of Molé's majority (120 out of 229), but for only 39 percent of the opposition coalition (73 out of 191), and 36 percent of those of undetermined affiliation (13 out of 37).

33. In September 1836 the king, in disagreement with Thiers over foreign policy, split with him and called upon Molé, who governed with Guizot until April 1837, when Guizot and three of his colleagues resigned. Molé cooperated in establishing a more royal, less parliamentary government, and as a reward the king made him head of the cabinet. In the course of his ministry, when many good things

happened, Molé attempted to extend the "castle party," and the dissolution of parliament in November 1837 resulted in a new chamber with a docile majority, more than half of whom were functionaries.

34. Concerning Tocqueville's political career, the much anticipated book of André Jardin is still in preparation. See his article "Tocqueville député sous la Monarchie de Juillet," *Contrepoint*, no. 22–23 (1976). See also Mary Lawlor, *Alexis de Tocqueville in the Chamber of Deputies* (Washington: Catholic University of America Press, 1959). The best study currently available in French remains Pierre-Marcel, *Essai politique*.

35. Duvergier de Hauranne, *Des principes du gouvernement représentatif et de leur application* (Paris: Just-Tessier, 1838), p. 43.

36. Rémusat, *Mémoires*, III, 223–261.

37. This is also the central thesis of Thureau-Dangin, *Histoire,* III, 392–398.

38. Royer-Collard's speech to his electors in March 1839 was very hostile to the coalition and denounced its "revolutionary spirit": "We are witnessing, gentlemen, a great manifestation of our country's critical state, which leaves far behind the noise of parliamentary debate. The agitation produced by the July Revolution, driven from the streets where it was repressed, has taken refuge, found shelter in the heart of the state; there, from a secure place, it harasses the government, debases it, strikes it impotent, and makes its position all but impossible. Beneath the deceptive cloak in which it wraps itself, this is the revolutionary spirit. I recognize it by the hypocrisy of its words, the foolishness of its pride, its profound immorality . . . Tired institutions, betrayed by mores, are hard put to resist . . . We are entering, gentlemen, a new era; great evils threaten us. We must learn to deal with them . . . The throne of July is attacked; I wish it were not shaken." The complete text is in OC, VIII, 1, 362n.

39. Tocqueville took seat no. 319, according to the official plan of the Chamber of 1839. In a letter from him to François de Corcelle we find this humorous note: "In our campaigns, judgment must depend on external signs. In those folks' eyes, where you put your behind is a matter of the first importance." He expressed the wish that the word "left-wing" would "remain attached to his memory until the end of time."

40. In 1837 and 1839 Beaumont had failed to win election at Saint-Calais in the Sarthe.

41. OC, VIII, 1, 294–296. In January 1840 he again considered the idea, but had to declare it impracticable for the immediate future. On this subject see the unpublished letter to Stoffels cited by Pierre-Marcel, *Essai politique*, p. 318.

42. Thiers's second ministry lasted from 1 March to 20 October 1840.

43. The Soult-Guizot ministry came to power on 29 October 1840 with Soult as prime minister and Guizot as minister of foreign affairs; he quickly became the most powerful man in the government. Officially, however, Guizot did not become prime minister until 1847.

44. OC, XI, 108; see also Pierre-Marcel, *Essai politique*, p. 338, for an unpublished letter from Tocqueville to Odilon Barrot dated 16 September 1842: "What has always deeply wounded me about the left is the lack of real liberalism that one finds there: the left is still far more revolutionary than liberal. As long as the

opposition does not modify its instincts, it will be good only for bringing on revolutions or to make despotism's bed."

45. OC, XI, 121. Letter of condolence from Tocqueville to Madame Royer-Collard, 9 September 1845: "Royer-Collard was an admirable example for all of France, a great mind. He will survive as one of the noblest and most admirable figures in our history. But for me he was also something more. He had made me accustomed to look upon him as almost a father."

46. Sainte-Beuve, cited in Langeron, *Un conseiller secret de Louis XVIII: Royer-Collard* (Paris: Hachette, 1956), p. 20. Sainte-Beuve also voiced other judgments, rather different in tone, of Royer-Collard, whom he called "the most worldly-emancipated of the Port-Royalistes" as well as "the gravest and most authoritative man of his time."

47. See François Picavet, *Les idéologues* (Paris: Alcan, 1891) and George Gusdorf, *Les sciences humaines et la pensée occidentale* (Paris: Payot, 1978), vol. VIII. Picavet distinguishes three generations of Idéologues: in the first he places those who had died or published their principal works prior to 1800, including Condorcet, Volney, Sieyès, Roederer, Lakanal, Dupuis, Saint-Lambert, Laplace, and Pinel; in the second, those who exerted the greatest political influence on their contemporaries, including Cabanis, Destutt de Tracy, Daunou, and in some respects Benjamin Constant; the leading names of the third generation are Laromiguière, Gerando, and Maine de Biran. This last generation saw a marked return to spiritualism, whose leading philosophical exponents were Maine de Biran and Royer-Collard. On the philosophical differences between the two men see Gabriel Madinier, *Conscience et mouvement* (Paris: Nauwelaerts, 1967), p. 188: "Royer-Collard protested against those who substituted causality for substance. This error, the opposite of Spinoza's, was what the most vaunted discoveries of modern philosophy ultimately came down to; Royer-Collard was therefore a long way from Biran."

48. See Barante, *La vie politique de Royer-Collard*. Pierre-François de Serre, Keeper of the Seals in 1818, pressed for and won freedom of the press. When he again served as Keeper of the Seals in the second Richelieu ministry, he opposed the liberalism of his Doctrinaire friends and broke with them on that account.

49. OC, XI, 102.

50. His definitive break with Guizot came over the Laws of September 1835, which increased the number of press offenses. Note that the use of the term "doctrinaire" to refer to Guizot and his friends, especially after 1835, actually designates a faction within the party of resistance; these were not the same Doctrinaires who had surrounded Royer-Collard during the Restoration—a relatively more liberal group. On the debate over the Laws of September 1835, see Rémusat, *Mémoires*, III, 135–138.

51. See, for example, Prelot, *Histoire*, p. 450. In reality, Royer-Collard took no part in the elaboration of the Charter (see Langeron, *Un conseiller secret*, p. 93); Barante, in his *Souvenirs*, shows how Royer-Collard had gradually developed a theory of the Charter in opposition to the ultras, but his political philosophy was more than this.

52. OC, XI, 97–104. Tocqueville's letter to Royer-Collard of 28 July 1841 shows (p. 96) that the book of speeches had been given to Tocqueville years earlier.

He read some of them while working on volume two of *Democracy in America* and probably completed his study and note-taking in 1841.

53. Luis Diez del Corral, "Tocqueville et la pensée des Doctrinaires," pp. 57–71, esp. 68–69, in *Alexis de Tocqueville: Livre du Centenaire, 1859–1959* (Paris: Editions du CNRS, 1960).

54. OC, XI, 98–99.

55. OC, XI, 99.

56. See Diez del Corral, "Tocqueville," pp. 65–67.

57. OC, XI, 24.

58. Rémusat made this point in his article "De l'esprit de réaction: Royer-Collard et Tocqueville," in *Revue des Deux Mondes*, 35 (15 October 1861), 777–814: "The point of difference between them . . . is clear. Royer-Collard, more skeptical and more easily offended or perhaps simply older and more tormented by memories of the Revolution, could not help feeling that it was impossible for a government to exist in order, or even to exist at all, in a democratic society."

59. OC, XI, 54. Letter from Royer-Collard to Tocqueville, 21 November 1837. See also the letter from Royer-Collard to his friend Becquey, in which he declares, speaking of *Democracy in America*: "M. de Tocqueville has written a very beautiful book that is not of our time . . . to find something to compare it with you must go back to Aristotle's *Politics* and Montesquieu's *Esprit des lois*, which I have read five times. I have made fifty pages of excerpts, which I find an inexhaustible source of instruction and pleasure" (quoted from OC, XI, 5).

60. OC, XI, 104.

61. OC, 1866 ed., VI, 442ff.

62. OC, VI, 1, 302.

63. OC, XI, 19–21, 25 August 1836 (Machiavelli, Bossuet, Plato); 28–30 (Thiers and his *Histoire de la Révolution*); 18–31 (politics and ethics).

64. OC, XI, 59, 67, 71.

65. Besides from the interruption of their correspondence, another example of "silence" was Royer-Collard's highly evasive response when Tocqueville asked him to support his candidacy for the Académie Française. The subject never came up again. Tocqueville was elected to the Academy on 23 December 1841.

66. OC, XI, 82–83.

67. OC, XI, 93–94, 29 August 1840.

68. See the letters from Royer-Collard to Molé for September and November 1839, cited by André Jardin in his introduction to the volume of correspondence between Tocqueville and Royer-Collard: OC, XI, 8–9.

69. OC, XI, 114–116. Letter of 15 September 1843.

70. OC, XI, 33–36. Tocqueville's embarrassment was due in part to the fact that he had had a conversation with Royer-Collard in which the latter came to the opposite conclusion (see p. 35).

71. OC, XI, 38. Letter from Royer-Collard, 21 July 1837. Royer-Collard seems to have guessed, as the remainder of his letter shows, that Tocqueville, despite his talent as a writer, would not be a great orator.

72. OC, XI, 48. The letters from Tocqueville to Molé dated 12 and 23 September, along with Molé's reply of 14 September, were published in OC, 1866 ed.,

VI, 71–77. On this exchange of letters, see Pierre-Marcel, *Essai politique*, pp. 298–299.

73. OC, XI, 49–50, 24 October 1837.

74. OC, XI, 53–54, 21 November 1837.

75. In November 1837, in a speech of thanks to the electors of Vitry-le-François who had supported him for forty years, Royer-Collard declared: "Politics is now stripped of its grandeur, dominated by what people call material interests." The speech is reproduced in Barante, *La vie de politique*, II, 522–524. I cited earlier the beginning of the excerpts contained in OC, XI, 53n. Tocqueville knew this speech: see OC, XI, 52, postscript.

76. OC, XI, 62.

77. Three quarters of the coalition was made up of members of the Party of Movement (that is, the center-left of Thiers, the dynastic left of Odilon Barrot, and the radical left, which called itself that because it was no longer allowed to call itself the republican left); this group was reinforced by the Doctrinaires, led by Guizot, by a quarter of the legitimists, and by three quarters of the Third Party. See Girard, *La Chambre des députés*, pp. 46ff. The coalition included 9 of 11 former ministers of Louis-Philippe.

78. OC, XI, 76–77. Tocqueville to Royer-Collard, 7 March 1839.

79. OC, VIII, 1, 364.

80. Rémusat, *Mémoires*, III, pp. 262–263.

81. Guizot, in *Mémoires,* VIII, 524–530, skillfully defends himself against the charge of having caused the Revolution of 1848 by opposing reforms, and especially electoral reforms (such as broadening the base of eligible voters). He points to the vague, temporizing, and ultimately negative conclusions of the Rémusat Commission of 1839 and shows that Thiers, in 1840, had again rejected the idea of reform. Rémusat is not being falsely modest; his statement that the report was praised far more than it deserved is to be taken literally. About the dynastic left in particular, Guizot says (p. 526) that they "basically wanted the conservative policy to succeed. They reproached us for carrying that policy too far, for preaching it too loudly . . ."

82. Rémusat, *Mémoires*, p. 264.

83. At this stage Tocqueville wanted an electoral law that would be not "more radical" but "more moral." Pierre-Marcel, *Essai politique*, p. 211, cites an unpublished document whose date he sets at 1840: "As for electoral reform, my feeling is this: I absolutely reject any lowering of the *cens* [property qualification] or equivalent adjunctions. I want an election law that is not more radical but more moral, an electoral system that would render corruption through government appointments more difficult."

84. OC, XI, 81, and Royer-Collard's response, 82–83.

85. See note 38.

86. OC, XI, 79. Letter from Tocqueville, 8 August 1839.

87. OC, XI, 83. Letter from Royer-Collard, 17 August 1839.

88. Yale archives, CV, k, notebook 1, 53.

89. Schleifer, *Making*, p. 29.

90. Yale archives, CV, k, notebook 1, 52. A few pages earlier we find a similar passage: "All the existing democratic peoples are more or less in a state of revo-

lution. The state of revolution is a special state, which produces certain effects that must not be confounded and that are peculiar to it. The difficulty is to recognize in democratic peoples what is revolutionary and what is democratic."

91. Yale archives, CV, k, notebook 1, 48: "One of the principal ideas of the preface, I think, should be to show briefly all the dissimilarities that exist between American democracy and our own."

92. Yale archives, CV, k, notebook 1, 51. It is difficult to date the drafts contained in the notebooks, because Tocqueville worked on loose sheets which he shifted about and reclassified according to his idea of the moment. Sometimes, however, a note is dated. In the two notebooks designated CV, k, we find texts from different times: the earliest are from January 1837, the latest from May 1839; several carry dates from the year 1838. On the whole, the notebooks give the impression that they were considerably augmented and revised in 1838. Hence the interest of the following fragment: "Preface, 5 February 1838: Point out that I was led in the second work to reconsider subjects already touched on in the first or to modify some of the opinions expressed there. Necessary outcome of such a large work done in two parts. Allow glimpse of the idea of recasting the whole thing later on." In the Bonnel copy, this fragment comes slightly before the text cited above (which was probably written earlier) and is a sort of annotation added in February 1838. On the same page (51) of the Bonnel copy, we find the subtitle: "Idea of Preface or Final Chapter."

93. Yale archives, CV, k, notebook 1, 51. See the preceding note.

94. DA, II, D, 4.

95. DA, II, D, 6.

96. DA, II, C, 21.

97. DA, II, B, 3.

98. This subject will be treated in the next chapter.

99. DA, II, C, XXI; on the title page of the manuscript in the Yale archives he wrote "Baugy, end of March 1838."

100. Yale archives, CV, k, notebook 1, 51.

101. See text after note no. 93.

102. These dates are certain: OC, VIII, 1, 317, letter from Tocqueville to Beaumont of 30 September 1838.

103. OC, VIII, 1, 321, letter from Tocqueville to Beaumont, 19 October 1838; OC, VIII, 1, 325, letter from Tocqueville to Beaumont, 5 November 1838; OC, VIII, 1, 323, letter from Tocqueville to Beaumont, 5 December 1838.

104. Drescher, "Tocqueville's Two Democracies."

105. Schleifer, *Making*, p. 285. Diametrically opposed to Drescher's interpretation is Max Lerner's argument that volume II in its entirety is nothing but a development of those chapters in volume I that deal with the tyranny of the majority. This argument can be found in the introduction to Tocqueville, *Democracy in America* (New York: Fontana, 1968), p. 91.

6. Enlightenment or Barbarism

1. OC, XI, 71.

2. Rémond, *Les Etats-Unis,* part 4.

3. Some of these analyses are more philosophical and detailed than those in volume I; but others are vast generalizations made on the basis of insufficient data, and Tocqueville's conclusions seem arbitrary, as some of his greatest admirers have noted: for example, Royer-Collard, OC, XI, 93; and, more recently, Raymond Aron, *Les étapes de la pensée sociologique* (Paris: Gallimard, 1967), p. 254. Rossi, in his review of volume II in *Revue des Deux Mondes*, September 1840, took malicious pleasure in contradicting Tocqueville's argument in DA, II, A, 7: "What Causes Democratic Nations to Incline toward Pantheism."

4. OC, VIII, 1, 317, letter from Tocqueville, 19 October 1838; OC, VIII, 1, 325–326, letter of 5 November; OC, VIII, 1, 328–329, letter of 5 December; see also letter from Tocqueville to Royer-Collard, 20 November 1838, OC, XI, 73.

5. Yale archives, CV, a, packet 8, contains only five pages on the "influence of democracy on ideas," which are notes from 1836; CV, j, notebook 1, packet 2, contains what remains of the notes used in preparation for DA, II, A. Some of these are from 1836, others from 1838. The destroyed pages probably belonged to CV, a; and file CV, j, remains as testimony to the 1838 revision of the first section of DA, II.

6. The first ten chapters of volume II contain many passages that were obviously written after passages that appear later in the book. The most notable of these are the following: chap. 1, p. 12, paragraphs 3 and 4; chap. 5, p. 29, paragraphs 5, 6, 7, and p. 33, paragraph 1, written after section B; chap. 3, p. 24, paragraph 2, written after sects. B and C; chap. 10, p. 48, paragraph 2, written after DA, II, C, 21; chap. 2, p. 19, last paragraph ("a new physiognomy of servitude"); chap. 5, p. 29, paragraph 1, and chap. 9, p. 43, paragraphs 3, 4, 5, and 6, written after the final section. It may be possible to identify the end of the rewritten section with precision, since chap. 10 contains a specific allusion to DA, II, C, 21, while the immediately following chapters contain no allusions to the rest of the text.

7. The hypothesis and its confirmation are my own. Schleifer, *Making*, p. 30, indicates only that the first two chapters were rewritten. This is correct, but so were the eight subsequent chapters.

8. Yale archives, CV, j, notebook 1, p. 1.

9. Yale archives, CV, k, notebook 1, p. 12. Note made in June 1838: "Perhaps begin whole book with chapters on individualism and taste for material pleasures. Almost everything flows from that, both in ideas and in sentiments."

10. Yale archives, CV, k, notebook 1, p. 11.

11. On this point I disagree with Schleifer, *Making*, p. 29, who maintains that Tocqueville gave up his preface sometime between the beginning of 1838 and the end of 1839 for inexplicable reasons.

12. Aron, *Les étapes*, p. 252.

13. DA, I, A, 2, and DA, I, A, 2 and 3.

14. DA, I, B, 9.

15. For example, DA, II, B, 3 and 15, and DA, II, C, 20.

16. This actually occurs from chap. 18 on, but chaps 18 and 19 contain brief references to America.

17. DA, II, A, 1, 14.

18. See also DA, II, B, 3.

19. DA, II, A, 6, 36.

20. DA, II, A, 19.

21. DA, II, A, 9.

22. DA, II, A, 13.

23. DA, II, A, 10 and 11.

24. DA, II, A, 10, 47.

25. DA, II, C, 22, 270.

26. DA, II, C, 6, 194.

27. For the French view of the American national character, see Rémond, *Les Etats-Unis,* II, pp. 478–480. Compare DA, II, C, 3, 15 and 16, on the essential features of the American character as perceived by the French: impassiveness, gravity, and national pride.

28. DA, II, C, 8–12.

29. DA, II, C, 8, 205.

30. DA, II, C, 1; see esp. p. 174 on the sentiment of pity.

31. DA, II, C, 18–26.

32. OC, V, 1, 188, 6 November 1831, diary no. 3. See also OC, V, 1, 121, 5 November 1831.

33. Rémond, *Les Etats-Unis,*, II, pp. 704–708.

34. Yale archives, CV, b, 28–29.

35. Yale archives, CV, h, notebook 3, 31.

36. Gaetano Mosca, *The Ruling Class* (New York: McGraw Hill, 1939), chap. 8.

37. Yale archives, CV, b, 32.

38. Schleifer, *Making*, chap. 16.

39. OC, 1866 ed., letter from Tocqueville to his mother dated 21 August 1831: "I was still convinced that a crisis was imminent and civil war soon to follow" (p. 54); to his brother Edouard, 10 September 1831: "at the beginning of a period of revolution like the present" (p. 60); and to his cousin, the Countess of Grancey, 5 May 1832 (p. 114). Bear in mind the great fear of 1832, the year of the cholera and the "ragpickers' riot" in April, followed by the uprising of the republican clubs in June. As early as the end of 1831 Tocqueville had received alarming news in America, and distance lent an even darker cast to events. The first two letters cited above arrived in France only a short time before the pessimistic journal entries of November 1831.

40. DA, I, B, 10, 344: "In what we call German institutions I am therefore tempted to see nothing but barbarian habits and in what we call feudal ideas nothing but the opinions of savages." DA, I, conclusion, 429: "The constant wars and barbarism of the Middle Ages . . ." Schleifer, *Making*, does not mention these passages, which suggest the need for major changes in the picture he draws.

41. Yale archives, CV, k, notebook 1, 20. In the preceding pages (18–20), Tocqueville shows that a democratic people cannot escape barbarism by itself; his thoughts on the origins of civilization are not without similarity to Rousseau's; for example, he writes: "If peoples remain democratic, civilization can never arise in their midst, and if by chance it insinuates itself among them, they cease to be democratic." But this holds true only in the initial stages of civilization, and things change as the beginnings recede into the past; see DA, I, B, 5, 215, last paragraph.

42. DA, II, A, 10, 51: "Because Roman civilization perished in the wake of the

barbarian invasion, we are perhaps too inclined to believe that civilization can perish in no other way. If the lights that guide us ever go out, they will fade little by little, as if of their own accord." See also p. 52, and DA, II, B, 1, 104 (next-to-last paragraph).

43. DA, II, B, 5, 115–116.

44. DA, II, B, 5, 117.

45. Ibid.

46. DA, II, B, 5, 114.

47. DA, I, B, 5, 215. In the working manuscript, Yale archives, C, VI, a, vol. II, we read: "Democratic government is the masterwork of civilization and enlightenment."

48. DA, I, B, 265–268. All his life Tocqueville believed that freedom was the primary condition for all great intellectual creations; see AR, II, 345.

49. DA, II, A, 2, 19.

50. DA, II, A, 10, 52. Here Tocqueville is inverting the image of China put forward by certain eighteenth-century reformers, most notably the Physiocrats. See also AR, II, 369–371.

51. DA, II, C, 21, 266: "The ardor they place in business prevents them from burning for ideas." See also pp. 261–262 and 269.

52. DA, II, C, 21, 262, paragraph 3.

53. DA, II, C, 21, 269.

54. On this point, Tocqueville differs with Mme de Staël and her aristocracy of enlightenment: "Political equality, an inherent principle of any philosophical constitution, is viable only if you classify differences of education with even greater care than feudalism took with its arbitrary distinctions." See Mme de Staël, *De la littérature* (Geneva: Droz, 1959), Discours préliminaire. Tocqueville clung to the idea of a cultivated elite but rejected that of a fixed hierarchy of the enlightened.

55. DA, II, A, 9, 44–45.

56. DA, II, A, 9, 42.

57. For the same reason it is impossible to draw any conclusions from French progress in the exact sciences during the Revolution; the case is too special, according to Tocqueville (DA, II, A, 10, 47–48). A few lines earlier, however, he wrote: "When a violent revolution occurs among a very civilized people, it cannot fail to give a sudden impulse to feelings and ideas." This is the first remark in his work on the Revolution's powers of cultural creation, and it is quite new compared with the conclusion of his 1836 article (AR, I, 66).

58. DA, II, A, 8, 39–40.

59. See Mill's introduction to the Schocken edition of *Democracy in America*. In his memoirs Mill, too, expressed his fear of the intellectual conformism of democratic societies and, like Tocqueville, held that in a transitional era people would benefit from the intellectual impulse of democratic revolution.

60. Yale archives, CV, k, notebook 2, 55: "Necessity to introduce liberty in a democratic nation in order to impart the necessary impetus toward things of the mind . . . Democracy without enlightenment and freedom could reduce mankind to barbarism."

61. DA, II, A, 8, 39–40.

62. This crisis occurred around 1822, when Tocqueville was 16 or 17. I touched on its religious aspect earlier (at the beginning of chap. 1).

63. Apart from the crisis of 1822–23, Tocqueville's correspondence reveals other times when he suffered acute bouts of doubt and anxiety. Pierson, *Tocqueville and Beaumont*, p. 682, mentions an episode of this kind that occurred in 1832, when Tocqueville returned from America. In 1838 he suffered what seems to have been an intellectual crisis (OC, XI, 59, letter to Royer-Collard, 6 April 1838). Subsequently came a period of respite, which lasted into the 1850s. During the 1840s Tocqueville's existential anxieties seem to have abated (see OC, XIII, 2, 100, letter to Kergorlay, 21 October 1841), but they did not disappear entirely (OC, XIII, 2, 106, 25 October 1842).

64. The distinction between thought and action and the assertion that action can and must be resolute even in the absence of certitude are the most Cartesian aspects of Tocqueville's thought. Yet Tocqueville does not seem to have overcome his philosophical doubts as felicitously as Descartes did.

65. See also letter to Corcell, 1 August 1850, OC, 1866 ed., VI, 153–154.

66. OC, 1866 ed., VII, 80–84. The addressee, Mr. Charles X, is not clearly identified; perhaps it is Charles Stoffels.

67. Tocqueville met Bouchitté at Versailles in 1824 or 1825; the latter was a former professor of history at the Collège de Versailles, Inspector of the Paris Academy, and later rector of the Academies of Eure-et-Loir and Seine-et-Oise. He wrote a history of proofs of the existence of God as well as works on the fine arts in relation to morality and religion.

68. Tocqueville was interested in the relation between abstract ideas and collective behavior, not in pure philosophy. Compare OC, 1866 ed., VI, 301, letter to M. de Corcelle, 16 October 1855: "Abstract ideas which pertain to man eventually affect, I know not how, the mores of the crowd." See also AR, II, 114–115.

69. OC, 1866 ed., VII, pp. 476–477.

70. Yale archives, CV, k, notebook 1, 42: "Dare to state somewhere L's [Louis's] idea that a distinction must be made between absolute assertion, certainty, and Pyrrhonism, that the system of probabilities is the only true, the only human, system, provided that probability causes one to act as energetically as certitude." This passage is found among the drafts of the preface to volume II. Kergorlay set forth his views on probability in a long letter dated 2 March 1838 (OC, XIII, 2, 19–21). Pascal is cited in volume II as an intellectual hero (DA, II, A, 10, 49), and his famous wager is analyzed (DA, II, B, 9, 131). On probabilism in Tocqueville's day, see F. Mentré, *Cournot et la renaissance du probabilisme au XIXe siècle* (Paris: Rivière, 1908).

71. Yale archives, CV, a, 36.

72. "Doubts never left him. He died with them, I am sure," said his friend Beaumont. Redier, *Comme disait M. de Tocqueville*, pp. 290ff, is determined to refute this testimony by proving that Tocqueville died a believer at peace with God and with the sacraments of the Church, administered on 16 April 1859. On 6 April he had taken Easter communion. For a similar view, see abbé Louis Baunard, *La foi et ses victoires dans le siècle présent* (Paris, 1884), II, 327–331; and John Lukacs, "The Last Days of Alexis de Tocqueville," *Catholic Historical Review*, 50, no. 2 (1964), 155–170, which relies on detailed accounts written by the nuns who attended

Tocqueville during his final illness. On Tocqueville's religious thought, the most complete and accurate account is that of Doris S. Goldstein, *Trial of Faith, Religion, and Politics in Tocqueville's Thought* (New York: Elsevier, 1975).

73. DA, I, B, 9, 310; DA, II, A, 9, 44; DA, II, B, 12, 140; DA, II, B, 15, 151–152; and OC, XIII, 1, 388–389.

74. DA, I, A, 2, 42–43 (47). In his correspondence Tocqueville noted that American religion often came down to morality. See OC, XIII, 1, 225–238, letter to Kergorlay, 29 June 1831, esp. 227: "Faith is obviously inert. Go into one of the churches (I mean the Protestant churches) and you will hear talk of morality but not the slightest word of dogma. Nothing that can shock one's neighbor in the slightest, nothing that can arouse an idea of dissidence." See also Yale archives, CV, g, notebook 1, 173: "Tendency of democracy to view religion as a useful thing, a human institution, to extinguish the ardor of zeal, to turn men away from looking to heaven." Also, Yale archives, CV, j, notebook 1, p. 1: "The weakening of beliefs is far more general and complete during the democratic revolution than it is when democracy is established." Thus beliefs are weaker in France than in America, but only temporarily.

75. Faguet, *Le libéralisme* (Paris, 1903), p. 320: "Certainly Christianity was the foundation of the rights of man, as I have often repeated, but what makes me even surer of myself is that Taine said the same thing before me, and what makes me surer still is that Montesquieu said it before Taine." He could have added Tocqueville and Laboulaye to the list.

76. DA, I, introduction, 9; see also AR, I, book 1, chap. 2, esp. p. 83, and book 3, chap. 2.

77. See Tocqueville's letter to Lord Radnor, May 1835, OC, 1866 ed., VI, 43–51. Paul-Louis Courier and Pierre Béranger are good bellwethers; see Jean Touchard, *La gloire de Béranger* (Paris: Armand Colin, 1962). In the history of liberal thought, however, the religious spirit is not nearly so estranged from the liberal spirit as Tocqueville seems to believe. Under the Restoration, Mme de Staël professed a liberal Christianity of Protestant inspiration, also influenced by Fénelon. See Gwinne, *Madame de Staël et la Révolution française* (Paris: Nizet, 1969), pp. 156–163. In 1789 Necker himself had published *L'importance des opinions religieuses*. And Benjamin Constant wrote that "free peoples are religious peoples" and that "a free government needs religion, because it needs disinterestedness." He held that religious feeling was natural and said of himself: "I am too skeptical to be an unbeliever." His writings contain the notion of a progressive religion; see H. Gouhier, *Benjamin Constant, les écrivains devant Dieu* (Paris: Desclée de Brouwer, 1967), pp. 43, 61, 65–86, and 106–107: "Constant was opposed to two widely held opinions: first, that religion is a natural ally of despotism, and second, that the absence of religious feeling is favorable to freedom."

78. In this letter (which I quoted in part and commented on in Chapter 5) Tocqueville describes himself as "a liberal of a new species." On the political significance of this formula, see Chapter 8; as for its religious and political significance, Tocqueville was not so original as he claimed (see n. 77). Yet it was a relatively new thing to want to reconcile the Catholics of his milieu with the liberal spirit.

79. OC, 1866 ed., V, 432; also Yale archives, C, I, b, three undated documents.

80. OC, 1866 ed., VII, 212–213, 6 December 1843.

81. Letter of 20 October 1856, cited by Mayer, *Alexis de Tocqueville* pp. 148–149.

82. OC, XIII, 2, 328. Letter to Kergorlay, 4 August 1857.

83. AR, I, 173.

84. OC, IX, 46. Letter from Tocqueville to Gobineau, 5 September 1843.

85. OC, IX, 57. Letter from Tocqueville to Gobineau, 20 October 1843.

86. OC, IX, 47, letter to Gobineau, 5 September 1843; see also AR, I, 83–84.

87. Equilibrium is always to be sought in civilization as well as in the individual: equilibrium and not synthesis—neither the word nor the idea of synthesis appears in Tocqueville's work.

88. OC, IX, 59. It is interesting that in a speech delivered in France on 1 June 1980, Pope John Paul II asserted that liberty, equality, and the rights of man were Christian values.

89. OC, IX, 46–47.

90. OC, IX, 58; see also Yale archives, CV, h, notebook 4, 164: ". . . unless by a specific action of Providence religions lose a part of their power over man's soul as the world that gave birth to and nurtured them recedes into the past." Religion may still correct certain utilitarian tendencies in the United States, but it can no longer oppose them. See DA, II, 5, 34.

91. Proudhon was in many respects a disciple of Tocqueville, as has been pointed out by Mayer, *Alexis de Tocqueville*, p. 159, following G. Sorel, *Illusion du progrès* (Paris, 1927), p. 258. Both men shared a belief in the intervention of Providence in history, and both stressed the influence of mores, equality, and justice. Above all, both believed that a single great revolution is unfolding continuously through all of history, a revolution marked by certain revelatory crises: the Christian revolution, the age of Luther and Descartes, the Revolution of 1789. All of this is directly inspired by *Democracy in America*. But when Proudhon affirms that the generation of 1848 was assigned the mission of accomplishing a fourth mutation, he parts company with Tocqueville. See Daniel Guérin, *Proudhon, oui et non* (Paris: Gallimard, 1978), part I.

92. His work contains no statement so clear as the following, written by Laboulaye, who was in many respects his disciple: "Among the Ancients, the gods were attached to the walls of the city and existed only with the permission of the Senate or Caesar. To proclaim that God has rights was to destroy the unity of despotism. Therein lies the germ of the revolution which separates the ancient from the modern world . . . The sovereignty of God forever broke the tyranny of the Caesars. Indeed, from the day that sovereignty is recognized, the immortal soul has duties and therefore rights—rights and duties which are independent of the state and over which the prince has no authority. Conscience is emancipated, the individual exists." *La liberté antique et la liberté moderne* (Paris, 1863), p. 110.

93. DA, II, A, 5, 6, 7, and part of 1 and 2; DA, II, B, 9, 12, 15, and part of 16 and 17. See two much more sharply defined positions: Jacques Maritain, *Christianisme et démocratie* (Paris: Hartmann, 1945); and Henri Bergson, *Les deux sources de la morale et de la religion* (Paris: Alcan, 1932), p. 304.

94. DA, II, A, 6, 36. When Tocqueville arrived in America, Catholicism there was on the rise. The Catholic clergy and bishops were French (see Rémond, *Les Etats-Unis*, pp. 121–160). Tocqueville carried with him letters of introduction from

a family friend, Monseigneur Cheverus, formerly archbishop of Boston. Hence his judgment should not surprise us. A century later Jacques Maritain, visiting the United States during the postwar Catholic revival, drew similar conclusions in his *Réflexions sur l'Amérique* (Paris: Fayard, 1858), chaps. 4, 9, 10, 11, and 19. Tocqueville believed no more than Chateaubriand that there was an essential link between Puritanism, or even just Protestantism, and democracy or liberalism. For him these religious forms were transitory, much as the government of the "middle classes" had only a transitory value. See Yale archives, CV, h, notebook 2, 85: "Protestantism is the government of the middle classes applied to the religious realm."

95. DA, II, A, 2, 17, penultimate paragraph. On the need for a positive religion, the religious future of France, and the principle of authority in religion, see OC, V, 1, 99–101, a very interesting conversation with the celebrated Unitarian preacher William Ellery Channing. Tocqueville always rejected the idea of natural religion, which for him had no political value. But he was clearly interested in the idea of a positive religion, which would be as close as possible to natural religion. He saw clearly, however, that this was possible only in America. In France, positive religion would quickly become as revolutionary as natural religion. See also his letter to Kergorlay, 29 June 1831, OC, XIII, 225–238, esp. 226–231.

96. See, for example, the article by Father Gibert, "Incroyance nouvelle et religion à venir," *Etudes*, December 1966, pp. 611–627.

97. DA, II, A, 2, 19; Yale archives, CV, j, notebook 1: "Faith in public opinion is the religion of democratic centuries and the majority is its prophet . . . In America, the moral power of the majority. The faith that people have in it. It is a true religion" (p. 10). "The moral empire of the majority may to some extent be destined to replace religion or to perpetuate a few, if it protects them. But then religion would live as public opinion more than as religion" (p. 8). Compare DA, II, A, 2, 18, penultimate paragraph.

98. DA, II, A, 2, 18.

99. The originality of this chapter lies in its systematic character and its profundity of thought. But Tocqueville very likely knew the works of Mme de Staël, *De la littérature* (1800) and *De l'Allemagne* (1813), which contained earlier contributions to both the sociology of knowledge and political theory.

100. DA, II, A, 1, 12; for the elaboration of the early chapters of DA, II, see Yale archives, CV, j, notebook 1.

101. DA, II, A, 1, 13.

102. In America the Enlightenment did not create a "revolutionary" state of mind in the European sense of that term, not even during the American Revolution; see Rossiter, *Political Thought*, p. 145: "Never have a people engaged in revolution been so anxious to convince themselves and the world that they were not really revolutionaries at all." A measure of reaction against Enlightenment philosophy and French ideas had occurred in in the United States by 1790, however; see Merle Curti, *The Growth of American Thought* (New York: Harper & Row, 1964), chap. 8.

103. DA, II, A, 1, 14.

104. Yale archives, CV, k, notebook 1, 52; revolution exacerbates the instability of beliefs peculiar to democratic societies.

105. Ibid. See also DA, II, A, 5.

106. DA, II, A, 3, and esp. 4.

107. Aron, *Les étapes,* p. 253.

108. AR, III, 9, 193–201.

109. DA, II, A, 4, 25.

110. Ibid.

111. DA, I, B, IX, 318. Note the continuity of this chapter with the first five chapters of DA, II. DA, I, B, 9, 307–308, contains an early critique of the eighteenth-century French philosophes as well as of Spinoza and Cabanis, whereas the Americans are praised for their use of practical knowledge and experience (pp. 315–319) as well as religion, to ensure the success of democracy.

112. DA, II, A, 5, 28 (443): "General ideas respecting God and human nature are therefore the ideas above all others which ought to be withdrawn from the habitual action of private judgment . . ."

113. DA, II, A, 5, 29. Note that, despite its title, chapter 5 has little to say about the United States; its import is in fact quite general. Only the final page refers to the American situation, showing how utilitarianism is allied there with religion.

114. DA, II, A, 2, 17.

115. It is all a question of proportions; Tocqueville's thought is permeated with a relativist spirit. But no future development is ruled out. When Mosca says that it is very dangerous to make a sudden change in a regime's "political formula," he is close to Tocqueville; he was greatly indebted to Taine, hence indirectly to Tocqueville.

116. DA, II, A, 1, 11: "America is therefore the country where Descartes's precepts are least studied and best obeyed."

117. Yale archives, CV, j, notebook 1.

118. CV, J, notebook 1, pp. 1–6: philosophy and religion are natural antagonists, and both are necessary; but "it is obvious that the democratic social state must make Philosophy predominant." And on p. 59: "I am firmly convinced that if one sincerely applied the eighteenth-century philosophical method to the search for the true religion, one would easily discover the truth of the dogmas taught by Jesus Christ, and I believe that one would reach Christianity through reason as well as faith." See also OC, V, 230: "What struck me in conversation with Mr. Power [the high vicar of New York] was . . . that he looks upon the Enlightenment as favorable to the moral and religious spirit."

119. CV, j, notebook 1, 31; this occurs again in DA, II, A, 1, 13, last paragraph.

120. CV, j, notebook 1, 11; in his acceptance speech to the French Academy, Tocqueville reconsidered the question of how the philosophy of the eighteenth century had turned revolutionary. OC, 1866 ed., IX, 5; see also AR, I, book III, chaps. 1, 2, and 3.

121. DA, II, A, 1, 13, last paragraph.

122. DA, II, A, 1, 14–15.

123. DA, II, A, 4.

124. Yale archives, CV, k, notebook 1, 52.

125. OC, 1866 ed., IX, 120, and speech cited, pp. 117ff. Political philosophy was divided into four groups of disciplines: the general philosophy of government (treated most notably by Plato, Aristotle, Machiavelli, Montesquieu, and Rousseau); international law; special sciences such as penal law, political economy, and

so on, not directly dependent on philosophy; and commentaries on and interpretations of constitutions, treaties, laws, and so forth.

126. DA, II, A, 20, 91.

127. DA, II, 1 (philosophical method), 8 (progress), and 20 (history) form a coherent whole. Schleifer, *Making*, p. 21, points out that Tocqueville had originally planned to include a chapter "on the moral sciences." Schleifer maintains that this plan was abandoned, but I think that Tocqueville's ideas on the subject were incorporated into chapters 1, 8, and 20. Yet to chapter 20, the logical conclusion of the group, he added a chapter 21, on "parliamentary eloquence." In this he was following the lead of Mme de Staël, who ended the second part of her *De la littérature* with a chapter on eloquence and its role in republican government.

128. DA, II, A, 8, 39. See also AR, I, 207–208 and 224.

129. DA, II, A, 8, 39.

130. DA, II, A, 8, 40; see also AR, I, 224.

131. DA, II, A, 14; DA, II, A, 10, 47 (last three paragraphs); DA, II, C, 21, 267.

132. No citation, no proof, exists that he did read Condorcet, but there is a strong presumption in favor of the hypothesis. Of all his sources, Tocqueville is most determined to hide those influenced by the Idéologues, especially in the first part of volume II, whose content evokes both Condorcet and Mme de Staël's *De la littérature*. The latter work expressed the Idéologues' thought as fully as Destutt de Tracy's *Commentaire de l'Esprit des lois*, which Tocqueville read and worked on (see Pierre-Marcel, *Essai politique*, p. 94). He is also known to have read Volney.

133. Condorcet, *Esquissse d'un tableau historique des progrès de l'esprit humain* (Paris: Editions Sociales, 1971), p. 249. In Tocqueville's eyes, the Empire was a regression. He probably mulled over this thought of Mme de Staël's: "I constantly come back, therefore, to all the evidence for the perfectibility of the human race. This is no idle theory, but the result of observation of the facts. One must avoid metaphysics, which lacks the support of hope; but one must not forget that in corrupt centuries what is called metaphysics is anything less narrow than selfish calculation or less positive than self-interest" (*De la littérature*, conclusion of first discourse). Tocqueville owes more than is commonly believed to Mme de Staël; what she called narrow, selfish calculation he denounced as excessive individualism, which he saw as the primary cause of democracy's corruption and regression.

134. Condorcet, *Esquisse*, p. 243.

135. His attitude toward the Idéologues was much less negative than Chateaubriand's. Certainly he had nothing in common with Helvetius or Condillac, but he had some affinity with Condorcet and Tracy. Above all, he shared a common vision of man with the Idéologues of the third generation (Gerando, Biran, Laromiguière), spiritualists who were close to the Doctrinaires and to the ideas of Mme de Staël. Tocqueville's thought had many features in common with that of the Idéologues: both attached great importance to ideas, particularly new ideas, as well as to equality; both were interested in America—its revolution, its institutions, Jefferson; both were opposed to the Empire; both were passionately committed to progress, yet aware that it was neither necessary nor the same in all realms.

136. DA, I, B, 9, 318; Tocqueville was particularly critical of the Physiocrats' claim to have established a deductive social science.

137. Auguste Comte, *Plan des travaux scientifiques nécessaires pour réorganiser la société* (Paris: Aubier, 1970), pp. 131–134 (on Montesquieu), 135–137 and 141–146 (on Condorcet).

138. This was still true of the second-generation Idéologues, the Constituents of the Year III. Daunou conceived of political liberty only as a means of guaranteeing civil liberty and individual happiness. Tracy confused the search for liberty with the search for happiness. For Tocqueville, political liberty was the supreme value, and its role was far greater than that ascribed to it by the Idéologues.

139. DA, I, introduction, 5.

7. Prosperity or Misery

1. Schleifer, *Making*, p. 252. The word "individualism" does not appear in volume I of *Democracy in America*. Schleifer's remark is true only for Tocqueville's published work, however. In the travel diaries the word "individualism" occurs in a note dated 11 May 1835 (OC, V, 2, 49).

2. Here I am following Schleifer's pertinent observations: *Making*, pp. 251–253.

3. Yale archives, CV, g, notebook 3.

4. Yale archives, CV, k, notebook 1, 12.

5. OC, VIII, 1, 328–329. Letter from Tocqueville to Beaumont, 5 December 1838: "Louis . . . has been very useful to me."

6. He is referring to DA, II, A, 9.

7. Yale archives, CV, k, notebook 1, 11.

8. To add still further to the complexity, some of the chapters on economic questions were moved to part 3 (chaps. 5, 6, and 7).

9. Koenraad Swart, " 'Individualism' in the Mid-Nineteenth Century (1826–1840)," *Journal of the History of Ideas*, January–March 1962, pp. 77–90. The term was included in the dictionary of the Académie Française in 1836 (supplement to the 6th ed., 1835).

10. Swart, "Individualism," p. 79, mentions the first use in the newspaper *Le Producteur* in 1826. P. J. Rouen expressed his regret that the economist Dunoyer reduced economics "to the narrow proportions of individualism," a legacy of the eighteenth century. Michel Chevalier, in his *Lettres sur l'Amérique du Nord* (1836), called attention to the "individualistic" character of Americans, especially Yankees. Contrary to what Schleifer says (*Making*, p. 245), Reeve's 1840 English translation of *Democracy in America* does not contain the first use of "individualism" in a language other than French; this honor belongs to the translations of Chevalier's *Lettres* into German (1837) and English (1839); I take this information from Swart, "Individualism," p. 86.

11. DA, II, B, 2 and 3.

12. Rémond, *Les Etats-Unis*, II, 670, points out that between 1833 and 1835 some journalists described the American Republic as "individualistic."

13. In the next two sections of this chapter I shall summarize certain ideas

from an early book of mine: *La notion d'individualisme chez Tocqueville* (Paris: Presses Universitaires de France, 1970).

14. DA, II, B, 2, 105 (506).

15. Ibid.

16. Ibid. Recall that the term "individualism" did not appear in volume I.

17. This distinction does not appear in the first drafts; for example, Yale archives, CV, g, notebook 2, 35: "Each man in his home, each man for himself. That is the natural instinct which must be corrected." Schleifer, *Making*, chap. 17, gives a thorough analysis of Tocqueville's early thinking (1831–1837) on the relations between democracy and egoism. It is worth noting, however, that in his early writings Tocqueville contrasted two forms of egoism: narrow egoism as opposed to self-interest properly understood in terms of reason and practical experience.

18. DA, II, B, 2, 105.

19. In volume I Tocqueville distinguished between two forms of patriotism, instinctive and reflective. At the time, the term "individualism" was not available to him, and he used egoism in contexts where "individualism" would have been perfectly suitable; for example, DA, I, B, 5, 246 and 252: "In certain countries, citizens accept only with a kind of reluctance the political rights accorded them by law. They feel deprived of the time required to deal with matters of common interest, and they like to confine themselves within a narrow egoism hemmed in by four hedgerows."

20. DA, II, B, 2, 105 (507).

21. DA, II, C, 8, 201.

22. In an aristocracy, personal relations are marked by the "spirit of individuality," which is practically destroyed by the democratic social state; see DA, II, C, 26, 288n. Tocqueville distinguishes between individualism and the spirit of individuality, almost to the point of opposing them. He found the spirit of individuality at a maximum in aristocratic England; see OC, V, 2, 60, note of 30 May 1835.

23. DA, II, B, 2, 106.

24. Royer-Collard, quoted in Barante, *La vie politique*, II, pp. 130–131.

25. DA, II, B, 2, 106 (508).

26. Louis Girard, *Le libéralisme: Doctrine et mouvement* (Paris: CDE, 1973), I, 77.

27. Constant, *Oeuvres*, p. 960.

28. Cited in Prelot, *Histoire*, pp. 446–447.

29. Tocqueville also maintained that Providence intervenes in history, but his work contains no reflection on predestination and grace. He held that American individualism stemmed from democracy, not from Puritanism. He refers to Puritanism only in order to explain certain negative characteristics of American culture, such as the relatively limited development of the arts (DA, II, A, 9, 41), especially theater (DA, II, A, 19, 87–88). The beneficial effects of religion on mores are ascribed not to Puritanism but to religion in general.

30. AR, I, 247–248.

31. OC, IX, 280–281.

32. OC, IX, 35.

33. DA, II, D, 7, 334 (701).

34. DA, II, B, 8.

35. Yale archives, CV, h, notebook 4, 30.

36. Long afterward, John Stuart Mill would also attempt, in his *Utilitarianism* (1861), to go beyond individualistic utilitarianism by subordinating utility to justice (chap. 4). Like Tocqueville, Mill invoked the feeling of moral obligation, but he related it to the progress of civilization, whereas Tocqueville's doctrine derived from civic humanism. Neither was guilty of the error of which Mill accused Comte's "religion of altruism": "He committed the error which is often wrongly imputed to the entire class of utilitarian moralists: he wanted the rule of conduct also to be its exclusive motive." Retranslated from Georges Clémenceau's French translation, *Auguste Comte et le positivisme* (Paris: Germer Baillière, 1868), p. 146.

37. Curti, *Growth*.

38. OC, V, 1, 122–123.

39. Mill published his *Principles of Political Economy* in 1848, and there is no mention of it in his correspondence with Tocqueville.

40. Note, however, that Tocqueville, for political reasons, took almost no part in the French free trade movement: his district was highly protectionist. He made no major speech in the Chamber on an economic subject, and the *Journal des Economistes* noted that his reports stopped short of discussing economic issues. He voted in favor of state subsidies for the railroads. Tocqueville believed that the principles of political economy were undeniably true, but he judged the applications of those principles from the standpoint of a moralist or a politician. See his letter to Lord Radnor, 5 November 1843, OC, 1866 ed., VI, 119–120.

41. A. de Villeneuve-Bargemont, *Traité d'économie politique chrétienne, ou recherches sur la nature et les causes du paupérisme en France et en Europe*, 3 vols. (Paris, 1834). Tocqueville had read this work before presenting his "Memoir on Pauperism" to the Academy of Cherbourg in 1835. This memoir opened with the observation that in a wealthy country like England one-eighth of the population lived on public relief. (Nassau Senior had supplied Tocqueville with documents concerning the Poor Act Amendment of 1834; see also OC, V, 2, 49, 71, and 153.) Countries that seemed less developed had fewer indigent citizens. Compare this with the opening of Villeneuve-Bargemont's *Treatise*: "True pauperism, which is to say, the growing distress of the working population, originated in England" (I, 24). Economic development resulted in prosperity for the majority but in poverty for a growing minority. Tocqueville wrote: "The industrial class, which provides for the welfare and pleasure of the greatest number, is exposed to miseries which would be virtually unknown if this class did not exist."

42. Count Hervé de Tocqueville served as a prefect until 1828, when he was named peer of France. As prefect at Metz (1817–1823), he had to deal with a serious economic crisis and was successful in his efforts. His reports, like those of Villeneuve-Bargemont, were held in high esteem. Both men are excellent examples in the finest tradition of the French civil service; both came from pious families and hewed throughout their lives to firm religious convictions.

43. On Villeneuve-Bargemont and his work, see Jean-Baptiste Duroselle, *Les débuts du catholicisme social en France* (Paris: Presses Universitaires de France, 1951),

pp. 28–68, which counts Villeneuve-Bargemont among the precursors of "social Catholicism."

44. Villeneuve-Bargemont, *Traité*, II, 224; quoted from Duroselle, *Les débuts*, p. 64.

45. See Duroselle, *Les débuts*, pp. 218–227. For political reasons Tocqueville was not very active in these societies. Many of their members were taken in by Louis Napoleon, and Catholic support for the latter alienated Tocqueville.

46. His travel diaries show, however, that he had amassed a considerable volume of information; see Schleifer, *Making*, pp. 73–84. While writing volume II, Tocqueville kept careful track of the economic news; see OC, XI, 60, April 1838, for his interest in a new law relative to limited partnerships.

47. Certain of the letters had been published earlier in the *Journal des Débats*. We also know (thanks to Pierre-Marcel, *Essai politique*, p. 96) that before publishing *Democracy in America*, Tocqueville had read and summarized the work of Achille Murat, the son of the King of Naples, who had spent seven years living in the United States: *Exposition des principes du gouvernement républicain tel qu'il a été perfectionné en Amérique* (Paris, 1833).

48. Letter to Chabrol, 9 June 1831; unpublished but quoted by Redier, *Comme disait M. de Tocqueville*, p. 97. This was a relatively original idea at a time when many Frenchmen still thought of America as a virtuous Arcadia; see Rémond, *Les Etats-Unis*, III, 489–497.

49. See Yale archives, CV, h, notebook 3, 108–111, point 4.

50. See especially the conversations of 20 and 22 September 1831 with Josiah Quincy, president of Harvard, and Francis Lieber (OC, V, 1, 88–89 and 92–94) and the reflection of 30 November 1831 (OC, V, Diary E, 278), which contains the first use of the phrase "self-interest properly understood."

51. Condorcet, *Esquisse,*, p. 273; in his *Vie de Turgot* (1786), Condorcet also maintained that "the private interest of each tends naturally to merge with the common interest." Tocqueville never made such a statement without serious reservations.

52. Yale archives, CV, h, notebook 2, 103.

53. DA, II, B, 8, 129 and 128 (527 and 526).

54. DA, II, B, 8, 129–130 (527); Tocqueville is afraid that equality will establish "a sort of respectable materialism;" see DA, II, B, 11, 139 and OC, XIII, 1, 389, letter to Kergorlay, 15 August 1836; Mme de Staël had already denounced the risk of materialism in a politically lifeless liberal society; see Girard, *Le libéralisme*, pp. 62–63.

55. DA, II, B, 15, 151–152. Note that the argument of this chapter, like that of chap. 9 and of DA, II, A, 5, 33, does not refer to any particular religion; it simply implies belief in God and an immortal soul. See DA, I, B, 9, 310; DA, II, A, 9, 44; DA, II, B, 12, 140, and OC, XIII, 1, 388–389, letter to Kergorlay, 5 August 1836; Tocqueville was seeking "a middle path that mankind can follow, which leads neither to Heliogabalus nor to Saint Jerome."

56. DA, II, B, 9 (religion and self-interest, with a discussion of Pascal's wager); 5, 6, and 7 (associations); 4 (free institutions); see also Yale archives, CV, a, 7. In fact, the success of America in this realm is difficult to interpret. Arendt, in *On Revolution*, notes that the American Revolution did not settle the question of

whether the goal of government ought to be prosperity or liberty. D. Potter, *Les fils de l'abondance*, gives prominence to prosperity in his interpretation; Tocqueville gives prominence to liberty in his.

57. Yale archives, CV, d, 6–7; in addition, he sought to show that there is no incompatibility between self-interest and religion (DA, II, B, 9) or the disinterested search for the good (Yale archives, CV, k, notebook 1, 85). In Tocqueville's view, political freedom was a primary condition for true harmony to exist between private interests and the general interest. Economic liberty was a second condition, generally but not always useful and never sufficient.

58. See Chapter 2, third section.

59. *Esprit des lois*, book 21, chap. 20, p. 641.

60. Ibid., book 5, chap. 7.

61. Ibid., book 20, chap. 1: "It is almost a general rule that wherever manners are mild, there is commerce; and that wherever there is commerce, there are mild manners." On this question, see Albert Hirschman, *The Passions and the Interests* (Princeton: Princeton University Press, 1977), chaps. 1 and 8.

62. DA, II, B, 14, 146, second paragraph.

63. DA, II, B, 14, 147.

64. Ibid. Here is a similar, though later, passage from Rémusat, *Politique libérale* (Paris, 1860), p. 346: "I regard utility as the final arbiter in all questions of ethics, but utility understood in the broadest possible sense is based on the idea of man's enduring interests as a progressive being." On the question of individualism and the appetite for prosperity, Mill is content to summarize Tocqueville in his commentary without adding anything new (pp. xxi–xxxviii).

65. This is the most remarkable forecast but not the best-known; it is certainly less famous than the prophecy at the end of volume I concerning the future of the United States and Russia, destined to divide control of the world. René Rémond has shown that this same prophetic vision was expressed by a number of authors before Tocqueville, including Achille Murat and Michel Chevalier (see the latter's *Lettres sur l'Amérique du Nord*, letter 9, 24 April 1834). See also Rémond, *Les Etats-Unis*, I, pp. 378–379. Among Tocqueville's possible sources Rémond fails to mention Mme de Staël; yet in the sixth and last part of her *Considerations on the French Revolution*, she announced the supremacy of the United States and foretold the future of Russia.

66. DA, II, B, 14, 147–148; this text clearly reveals Tocqueville's hierarchy of values. He is a liberal rather than a conservative, and his liberalism is fundamentally political. See also Yale archives, CV, d, 11.

67. *Esprit des lois*, book 20, chap. 7.

68. See the travel diaries for England, which contain Tocqueville's first thoughts on this subject, dated July 1835, in OC, V, 2, 89–90 and 90–91.

69. DA, II, B, 16. Drescher, *Dilemmas of Democracy*, p. 69, notes that Tocqueville had in part anticipated Weber's notion of a relation between Protestantism and the spirit of capitalism. But Tocqueville is speaking of religion in general, not Protestantism, and the America that he knew was dominated not by Puritanism but by utilitarianism. Weber has analyzed the shift from Puritanism to utilitarianism, from the disciples of Calvin to those of Benjamin Franklin; Tocqueville analyzes the prevailing utilitarianism, taking account of the fact that religious

conviction has survived, but in severely limited form (DA, II, A, 5, 34). Weber was concerned with sects, but Tocqueville was interested in associations, a secularized form of the religious sect. Weber saw the sects as "one of the most important historical roots of modern individualism," whereas Tocqueville viewed associations as a remedy for individualism. In a rather Weberian spirit, however, Tocqueville did indicate that a religion-inspired restriction of material desires could contribute to prosperity. In my view, it is more accurate to compare Tocqueville with the Joseph Schumpeter of *Capitalism, Socialism, and Democracy* (New York: Harper, 1942), parts 2 and 4: the logic of utility, understood in a narrow, exclusive fashion, destroys the values on which capitalism and democracy are based, values partly inherited from the past and belonging to another social order.

70. Bertrand de Jouvenel, *De la souveraineté* (Paris: Librairie de Médicis, 1955), pp. 275–292, 293–312.

71. Chevalier, *Lettres sur l'Amérique du Nord*, letter 12; see also letters 16, 19, and 20 for further remarks on American industry.

72. OC, V, 2, 81; of Manchester he writes: "The immense palaces of industry . . . (and the poor houses all around) . . . here is the slave, there the master; there the riches of a few, here the misery of the greater number."

73. OC, V, 2, 78–84; on the differences between Manchester and Birmingham, see pp. 78–89.

74. Tocqueville made a distinction between the effects of mass production and large-scale industry and those of industry on a human scale. Similar ideas are expressed by Röpke, *La crise de notre temps* (Paris: Payot, n.d.), and, more generally, by the authors of the neoliberal school of Freiburg.

75. OC, V, 2, 78.

76. DA, I, B, 10, 421; Durkheim cites Tocqueville (DA, II, B, 20, 165) to illustrate the negative effects of an excessive division of labor: *La division du travail social* (Paris: Presses Universitaires de France, 1960), p. 6. But Jean-Baptiste Say, *Traité d'économie politique* (1803), book 1, chap. 8, and, even earlier, Adam Smith, *Wealth of Nations* (1776), book 5, chap. 1, had already pointed out drawbacks inherent in the division of labor.

77. DA, II, B, 20, 167 and 165. Poussin, *Considérations*, part 5, chap. 8, pp. 262–264, states that Tocqueville's concerns are ill founded in the case of the United States. It is true that the descriptions in DA, II, B, 20, are based on Tocqueville's observations in England.

78. DA, II, B, 20, 166; see also DA, II, C, 7, 199: "an exceptional fact, contrary to all that surrounds it."

79. DA, II, C, 7. It is unfortunate that Tocqueville chose not to treat economic questions in a sustained fashion. Chaps 5, 6, and 7 of part 3 logically should follow the end of part 2. He was perhaps daunted by the difficulty of the problem as well as by competition with Chevalier, and was probably reluctant to place together chapters as dissimilar as part 2, chap. 20, and part 3, chap. 7. In the margin of the chapter on wages in the Yale manuscripts we find this note: "This chapter suffers from setting forth today's largest question without even attempting to resolve it. The reader comes away from it disappointed."

80. Broadly speaking, prices also declined in this period. Between 1850 and 1856 both wages and prices rose sharply. From 1856 to the end of the century, wages

rose and prices fell. See Charles Morazé, *La France bourgeoise* (Paris: Armand Colin, 1952), pp. 132–134.

81. Duroselle, *Les débuts*, p. 68. In Villeneuve-Bargemont's writings we find phrases like "new feudalism" and "aristocracy of money and industry."

82. DA, II, D, 5, 316; earlier, in DA, II, B, 19, 160, he had noted that democracy causes the majority of men to develop a "distaste for agriculture" and that it "funnels them into commerce and industry."

83. Yale archives, CV, k, notebook 1, 12. In the margin we read: "To what I say about the master and the worker."

84. Is the analysis in volume I, based on the assumption of a basically agrarian and commercial society, still valid for an industrial society? Pierson, *Tocqueville and Beaumont*, and Pierre Birnbaum, *Sociologie de Tocqueville* (Paris: Puf, 1970), p. 101, have raised doubts in this regard. I am inclined to agree with Raymond Aron, *Dix-huit leçons sur les sociétés industrielles*, (Paris: Gallimard, 1962), who held that for the most part Tocqueville's analyses hold good for industrial societies.

85. Mill, "Commentary," p. xlii. Mill, pp. xlviii–xlix, agreed with Tocqueville that when the spirit of commerce and industry finally achieved dominance, an era of decline would begin.

86. Once again the imprecision of Tocqueville's vocabulary is unfortunate; he would have done better to speak of oligarchy.

87. DA, II, B, 3, 108 (509).

88. DA, II, B, 3, 107 (508). Yale archives, CV, a, 7: "This is a central idea. Feeling of independence which seizes a multitude of individuals for the first time and exalts them, so that selfishness is more apparent and less enlightened in a nation that is becoming democratic than in one that has been so for a long time."

89. OC, XI, 64. Note the phrase "stanches almost all the sources of enthusiasm" and compare it with Mme de Staël's definition of enthusiasm: "The Greek meaning of the word is its noblest definition: enthusiasm means *God in us*. Indeed, when man's existence is expansive, it has something of the divine about it. Almost anything that induces us to sacrifice prosperity or life is enthusiasm. The true course of selfish reason is to make oneself the goal of all one's efforts and to value in this world only health, money, and power." *De l'Allemagne* (1813), part 4. See DA, II, C, 21, 267.

90. OC, XI, 66, 21 July 1838.

91. *Esprit des lois*, XIX, 6, pp. 558–559; see also XIX, 27: "This nation, always overheated, would be easier to lead by its passions than by reason, which never has much effect on the minds of men, and it would be easy for those who govern it to engage it in enterprises contrary to its true interests." Tocqueville later recognized certain enduring elements of the French national character: see S, 89 and AR, I, 208 and 249–250.

92. OC, V, 1, 205–206 (notebooks 4 and 5, 14 January 1832); a similar text of the same date is in notebook E, pp. 256–257; OC, V, 1, 278, notebook E, 30 November 1831; DA, I, A, 2, 28; DA, I, A, 5, 59; DA, I, B, 8, 286; DA, I, B, 9, 318.

93. Yale archives, CV, a, 8. "All things considered, I do not believe that there is more selfishness in France than in America. The only difference is that in America it is enlightened, while in France it is not. The Americans know how to sacrifice some of their personal interests in order to save the rest. We want to hold

on to everything, and frequently we lose it all. Danger if conditions become equalized more quickly than enlightenment spreads." This text, which probably dates from August 1836, is, as far as I know, the first in which Tocqueville attempts to deal with both the role of enlightenment and the process of equalization.

94. DA, II, B, 3, 108 (509).

95. DA, II, D, 5, 316; it is unfortunate that Tocqueville did not revise part 2 accordingly.

96. AR, I, 208.

97. AR, I, book 2, chap. 8.

98. AR, I, 158.

99. AR, I, 167.

100. AR, I, 120.

101. AR, I, 159–167.

102. DA, II, B, 4, 112.

103. He was reading Plutarch as he wrote the final draft of volume II: see OC, XI, 60, letter to Royer-Collard, 6 April 1838.

104. Mill, in "Commentary," p. xxxix, slightly distorted Tocqueville's thought in summarizing it: he replaced the Tocquevillean notion of "political education" with the positivist one of "popular education."

105. Mill, "Commentary," pp. xlix–li.

106. DA, II, B, 4, and Yale archives, CV, g, notebook 1, 75: "I have shown that free institutions reduce selfishness; now it is a question of showing that they are necessary to the civilization of democratic peoples. Make no mistake: what is involved here is not only the heart but the future progress of the human spirit."

107. DA, II, B, 5, 116.

108. DA, II, B, 14, 148.

109. See the first section of the previous chapter.

110. *Esprit des lois*, book 19, chap. 4.

111. Ibid., chap. 27.

112. DA, II, B, 3, 108 (509).

113. OC, V, 1, 179.

8. Democracy or Revolution

1. DA, I, B, 9, 300.

2. DA, II, B, 14, 147.

3. There is nothing about England except for a brief allusion in chap. 5, p. 114. Note, however, that the contents of chaps. 19 and 20, in which England is not mentioned, are clearly based on observations that Tocqueville made in England.

4. Part 4 contains an important discussion of England: DA, II, D, 4, 304.

5. See esp. chaps 3 and 14.

6. DA, II, C, 2, 178.

7. See notes made on the Yale manuscript at the beginning of chap. C 16 and on the sleeve enclosing chap. C 12.

8. James Bryce, *The Predictions of Hamilton and Tocqueville* (Baltimore, 1887), p. 323.

9. Redier, *Comme disait M. de Tocqueville*, pp. 110–111. See also Pierre-Marcel, *Essai politique*, p. 95, and Boutmy, *Eléments*, p. 5.

10. See, for example, the review of *Democracy in America* in the *Journal des Débats*, 23 March and 2 May 1835.

11. See, for example, Jacquemont, *Correspondance inédite avec sa famille et ses amis, 1824–1832* (Paris, 1867), I, 142–143; Stendhal, *La Chartreuse de Parme* (Paris: Garnier, n.d.), p. 115 (the opinion of Sanseverina), and p. 416 (the judgment of Mosca).

12. See in particular DA, II, C, 14, esp. p. 226, where he alludes to the tradition of disparagement on the part of English travelers, apparently a swipe at Mrs. Trollope, whose book on the domestic habits of the Americans was translated into French in 1833.

13. DA, II, C, 1: "Mores become gentler as social conditions become more equal." Compare Chevalier, *Lettres sur l'Amérique du Nord*, chap. 31, esp. pp. 313–315, 318, 323–324, 326. Chevalier describes the violent disturbances and riots that broke out in many American cities in 1834 and 1835. Some of these scenes of violence, particularly an attack on an Ursuline convent in 1834, contributed to the shift in French opinion concerning American democracy. See Rémond, *Les Etats-Unis*, II, pp. 697–703.

14. AR, I, 65–66.

15. Constant, *Les réactions politiques*, cited from Bastid, *Benjamin Constant*, p. 706.

16. Aron, *Les étapes*, p. 245.

17. AR, I, book 1, chap. 5, p. 95.

18. OC, V, 2, 36 (7 September 1833); concerning the vote on the Reform Bill of 7 June 1832, see OC, V, 2, 68.

19. Arendt, *On Revolution*, pp. 55–56.

20. DA, I, A, 6, 114–115; even today it is obvious to the French that the French Revolution and the American Revolution are quite dissimilar: see Alain Clément, "Les Etats-Unis et la France, Révolution contre Révolution," *Le Débat*, no. 1 (May 1980), 39–48. For a Frenchman, the event in American history that most resembles the French Revolution is the Civil War.

21. Yale archives, c, I, d.

22. John Adams, *Defense of the American Constitution*; the letter to Mably is reproduced on p. 507 of the French translation (Paris: Buisson, 1792).

23. DA, I, A, 3, 45; see also Tocqueville's *Fragments inédits sur la Démocratie en Amérique*, p. 8.

24. Yale archives, CV, g, notebook 2, 108.

25. DA, II, D, 4, 305.

26. Yale archives, CV, h, notebook 5, 10; on the important role of the clergy and its sermons in the American Revolution, see Rossiter, *Political Thought*, pp. 7–10.

27. On the conservatism of the American Revolution, see Rossiter, *Political Thought*, p. 229; see also DA, I, A, 5, 70: "[The American Revolution] proceeded with love of order and legality."

28. For obvious political reasons Tocqueville preferred not to call attention to these characteristics of the American Revolution. In 1840 Guizot had made

Washington a symbol and model of the politics of the Party of Resistance (see his *Introduction sur le caractère de Washington*). In his *Mémoires* he again set forth his conservative interpretation of Washington and the American Revolution (IV, 315–319) and cited a letter from Louis-Philippe in support of his view (IV, 322).

29. DA, I, A, 5, 70.

30. DA, II, C, 21, 263.

31. DA, II, B, 3, 108.

32. DA, I, B, 10, 415.

33. DA, I, B, 5, 209.

34. OC, V, 1, 196, 8 January 1832.

35. DA, II, C, 21.

36. AR, I, 95.

37. AR, I, book 1, chap. 3.

38. AR, II, 131n.

39. AR, II, 132.

40. AR, I, 242, and AR, II, 334–335.

41. AR, I, 208, 230, 249–250; AR, II, 134, 281, 331–333, 415.

42. AR, I, book 1, chap. 2, and book 3, chap. 2.

43. AR, I, book 3, and AR, II, book 1.

44. AR, I, 208.

45. This has been observed by Lively, *Social and Political Thought*. chap. 8, esp. p. 204.

46. AR, I, 247; AR, II, 130–133, 174, 195, 198, 200.

47. AR, I, book 2, chaps. 2–6; see François Furet, *Penser la Révolution française* (Paris: Gallimard, 1978).

48. Following Condorcet, *Esquisse*, pp. 223–226, Tocqueville acknowledges that the American Revolution served as a signal to the Europeans: AR, I, 199, and AR, II, 44: "The voice of John crying in the wilderness that new times were near."

49. AR, II, 334.

50. Yale archives, CV, g, notebook 2, 173: "It is clear that, when examined closely, all the revolutions of our time were instigated by egalitarian and not libertarian passions. Liberty is a means of establishing equality." See also DA, II, C, 21, 259, first paragraph.

51. DA, II, C, 21, 258–269.

52. *Revue des Deux Mondes*, 22, no. 36 (14 April 1840), 322–334.

53. The château de Baugy, near Compiègne, belonged to Tocqueville's brother Edouard.

54. I have borrowed this title from Tocqueville for the title of the present section.

55. OC, V, 1, 196, 8 January 1832; see also DA, II, C, 17. In the Yale working manuscript (C, VI, a, vol. 3), we find this note added at the end of the chapter: "Note to place at the beginning of the chapter. The spirit of the chapter absolutely must conform . . . Equality induces man to make continual small changes and avoids great revolutions. That is the truth."

56. Yale archives, C, VI, a, vol. 3.

57. Faguet, *Politiques*, pp. 82–83. Faguet has ceased to observe the distinction between "great revolutions" and mere revolutions. In the margin of DA, II, D, 6,

in the Yale working manuscript, Tocqueville wrote: "Idea that revolutions and anarchy could be combined with this sort of administrative despotism. Days of anarchy in years of despotism. Revolutions always short and not very profound but perhaps frequent. Palace revolutions which I could easily distinguish from the general revolutions whose impossibility I described above." I shall have more to say about this question in chapter 9.

58. In AR, I, book 3, chap. 4, p. 225, Tocqueville shows how a maladroit pursuit of economic interests may lead to revolution; this contradicts the argument of DA, II, C, 21.

59. DA, II, C, 21, 259–263; when equality of conditions prevails, the risk of revolution is at a minimum. With his usual gift for prophecy, Tocqueville notes that the inequality of the races in the United States does pose a threat: "If the United States ever does experience a great revolution, it will be brought on by the presence of blacks on American soil; in other words, it will be due not to the equality of conditions, but to inequality."

60. See also Yale archives, CV, k, notebook 1, 4: what is to be feared in democracy is not great revolutionary passions which make men forget their duties but laxity in regard to public virtue—peaceful disorder—in other words, regularity and moderation amid pervasive vice, to which people give in without struggle or passion. See also DA, II, B, 11, 139; and letter to Kergorlay, 5 August 1836, OC, XIII, 1, 389.

61. Tocqueville uses this argument again in the second half of the chapter: DA, II, C, 21, 266–267. Note the repeated use of the word "enthusiasm," so characteristic of Mme de Staël's philosophical vocabulary.

62. See Hirschman, *Passions and Interests*, pp. xx; Andrew Ure published his *Philosophy of Manufacturing* in 1835.

63. Quoted from Hirschman, *Passions and Interests*, p. 119 (his translation altered).

64. See the unpublished texts I quoted in Chapter 1, fourth section .

65. Tocqueville clarified this idea in conversations with his brother Edouard. See Yale archives, C, vi, a, 3, last page: "Two remarks of Edouard's that I must take into account: (1) political revolutions: in aristocracies it is the majority which has an interest in revolution; in democracies, the minority. This is intimated several times; state it clearly; (2) intellectual revolutions . . ."

66. DA, II, C, 21, 263 (640).

67. DA, II, A, 2, 18-19; a note in the working manuscript underscores this relation and alludes to a plan different from the one finally adopted: "In the first chapter . . . communal beliefs, authority, in the second . . . intellectual revolutions." The second part of DA, II, C, 21 should logically have followed DA, II, A, 2. Tocqueville's notes reveal his doubts: "Before printing this part of the discussion, reread the things I say in the chap. on revolutions and weigh what I should leave there or move here."

68. Emphasis in the original.

69. DA, II, A, 1 and 2 present the first stages of this argument. The second half of DA, II, C, 21, is the third stage. Tocqueville decided to break up the presentation of the argument in this way for psychological reasons.

70. DA, II, C, 21, 265.

71. DA, II, C, 21, 265 (641).

72. Ibid. Tocqueville seems to attach particular importance to what Pareto would call the "second class of derivations." Indeed, in 1848 it was the authority of a name that won votes for Cavaignac and above all for Louis-Napoleon Bonaparte. Today, however, we know that ideologies are associated with all four classes of derivations in Pareto's typology.

73. Cf. AR, II, 167: "Only an absurdity can wrest such efforts from mankind."

74. AR, II, 268, especially the third paragraph.

75. Yale archives, CV, h, notebook 4, 65; compare with the text referenced in note 74.

76. Particularly important is the analysis of individualism; on the title page of DA, II, B, 3, in the working manuscript is this note: "Idea treated later in the political chapters that finish the title. Only after examining it in both places will I be in a position to see whether it should be eliminated in one or simply presented from a different angle."

77. DA, II, C, 21, 263; equality calms revolutionary passions, whereas revolution exacerbates egalitarian passions; see DA, II, B, 1, 103.

78. Tocqueville would make this point later; see AR, I, book 3, chap. 5, p. 231, and chap. 8, p. 246.

79. Compare, for example, DA, II, C, 21, 267, first paragraph, with AR, II, 131n.

80. Speech of 24 March 1836; a long excerpt from this speech was quoted in the second edition of this chapter.

81. Guizot, *Mémoires*, VIII, p. 521.

82. See S, 86: "To gently drown revolutionary passion in love of material pleasures: that was his lifelong idea."

83. I quoted an extensive excerpt from this assessment in Chapter 5, third section.

84. Quoted from Redier, *Comme disait M. de Tocqueville*, p. 48. Redier assigns the date November 1841 to this document.

85. Guizot, for his part, felt that the main reason for Tocqueville's opposition was Tocqueville's desire to be in his place. He maintained that the more moderate segment of the dynastic opposition was fundamentally in agreement with his politics. See *Mémoires*, VIII, 526.

86. Letter to Corcelle, 26 September 1840, OC, 1866 ed., VI, 101.

87. Yale archives, CV, k, notebook 1, 11; see also the beginning of the last chapter (conclusion).

88. DA, II, 348, note to text on p. 327 (DA, II, D, 6).

89. Seymour Drescher has forcefully underscored this difference between the two volumes of *Democracy in America* in his article "Tocqueville's Two Democracies." My own view is that the contrast between volumes I and II should not be overdrawn. What is involved is really a contrast between France and the United States; see DA, I, 93–94: "There are nations in Europe whose inhabitants think of themselves as a kind of colonist, indifferent to the fate of the place in which they happen to live. . . . In such places one still finds subjects but not citizens." This is an anticipation of DA, II, D, 6.

90. OC, 1866 ed., VII, 147. Letter of 27 January 1836.

91. *Esprit des lois*, book 2, chap. 3.

92. The first mention of the subject, as far as I know, occurs in a letter to Kergorlay dated 10 November 1836, OC, XIII, 1, 415, concerning apathy in philosophical and political thought. "This kind of unnatural horror of thought comes of the extreme fatigue produced by a long revolution."

93. OC, 1866 ed., IX, 4 and 10–11; see also letter to Royer-Collard, 15 September 1843, OC, XI, 115, last sentence.

94. AR, II, book 3, chap. 1, pp. 267–281, esp. 275–276 and 280.

95. Speech published in the *Moniteur Universel*, 18 January 1844.

96. Extensively quoted by Tocqueville himself at the beginning of S, 37–41.

97. In addition to the 1844 speech just quoted, see his *Entretiens avec Senior*, May 1850: "In the final years of his reign I never believed that a revolution could be avoided." And in Eichtal, *Alexis de Tocqueville*, p. 237, Mme de Tocqueville is quoted as saying: "You predicted it three years before it broke out."

98. The end of the Declaration of Brumaire says: "Citizens, the Revolution clings to the principles from which it sprang. It is over." The Constituent Assembly, too, thought that it had put an end to the Revolution in Year III, and others believed that it had ended even earlier, in 1791. Barnave had already formulated the following idea, destined to remain perpetually premature: "The Revolution is over." The phrase occurs in the political platform disclosed on 17 May by Adrien du Port: "The Revolution is over. We must consolidate and preserve it while combating its excesses. We must restrict equality, limit freedom, and settle public opinion. The government must be strong, solid, and stable." Quoted in Furet and Richet, *La Révolution française*, p. 138.

99. S, 35.

100. Ibid., p. 36. See also p. 30, as well as the letters to Stoffels dated 21 July 1848 and 28 April 1850, OC, 1866 ed., V, 456–461.

101. However superior Tocqueville may have been to Guizot as a philosopher, he was by no means a better judge of every political situation. Yet political involvement, and particularly experience in government, contributed a great deal to the political philosopher. In his response to the acceptance speech of Lacordaire, who succeeded Tocqueville in the French Academy, Guizot, at that time director of the Academy, stressed the superiority of *The Old Regime* over *Democracy in America*. Tocqueville had acquired "a better knowledge of the imperious conditions of liberty," according to Guizot, "through the difficult exercise of power and under the weight of responsibility." OC, 1866 ed., IX, 643.

102. DA, II, C, chaps. 19–26.

103. DA, II, C, 19, 252.

104. DA, II, C, 19, 253; the term "meritocracy" is of course not Tocqueville's, but he clearly had the idea, including emphasis on competitive examinations.

105. S, 54; AR, I, 164, and DA, II, C, 20. This chapter is typical of Tocqueville's manner: it is of general import and has great predictive value, yet at the same time it is rooted in the political problems of his time and recommends reforms. Bear in mind that at this time all public jobs, except in the army and the university, were awarded on the spoils system. Concerning the situation in 1839, Rémusat says: "Molé and Montalivet had exceeded all bounds in awarding jobs to their hirelings and secret funds to their newspapers." As examples he cites the purchase

of the *Revue des Deux Mondes* and various nominations, including that of Alfred de Musset as "librarian of the Ministry of the Interior, where there was no library." Rémusat then alludes to the calls for reform and the role of the deputies newly elected in 1839, including Tocqueville. See Rémusat *Mémoires*, III, 262–263.

106. DA, II, C, 19, 255.

107. DA, II, C, 19, 254; in Tocqueville's view, aristocracy is able to reconcile moderation with vastness of ambition, whereas democracy confounds moderation with mediocrity.

108. DA, II, C, 19, 254–255. The third-to-last paragraph on p. 254 anticipates, in just twelve lines, the portrait of Louis Napoleon in S, 211–213.

109. Yale archives, CV, f.

110. DA, II, C, 22, 270.

111. DA, II, C, 26.

112. AR, II, 248.

113. DA, II, C, 22, 273 and 346n.

114. Yale archives, CV, d, 3.

115. Yale archives, CV, d, 16.

116. DA, II, 347n, and Yale archives, CV, 1; also, CV, j, notebook 2, 9–12: "How democratic armies might cease to be warlike without ceasing to be troublesome."

117. In the preface to *The Old Regime* Tocqueville states which qualities of the men of the past he considered exemplary: "A true spirit of independence, an appetite for great things, faith in [themselves] and in a cause . . ." AR, I, 73.

118. See Chapter 3 on the primacy of law, and the question of "industrial aristocracy" in this chapter (Chapter 8).

119. DA, II, C, 19–26.

120. See this chapter, third section; see also Yale archives, CV, k, notebook 1, 46–52.

121. Yale archives, CV, k, notebook 1, 51; see this chapter, third section.

122. The only detailed outline of volume II in Tocqueville's hand ends with part 3.

123. Yale archives, CV, d, 30.

124. See, for example, AR, II, 247: "Audacity, violence, and imprudence are natural qualities in democratic governments, heightened when they are revolutionary—and, I would add, French."

125. Why did Tocqueville not complete his 1836 article? Because he could not answer a question he raised at the beginning: "What new divisions have replaced those that existed under the old monarchy? What new forms have aristocratic and democratic interests assumed?" AR, I, 66. Had he fully disclosed his thoughts about the French "middle classes," he would have been classed as an "aristocrat" and would have stood no chance of being elected to parliament. He wrote his *Souvenirs* in order to say all that he had been unable to say during his political career.

9. Servitude or Freedom

1. Yale archives, CV, d, 3.

2. It can be found, for instance, in the article "Revolution" written by

Rémusat for Block's dictionary (1st ed., 1863–1864). A few years earlier, Rémusat had published *Politique libérale* (1860), a work with a significant subtitle: *Fragments pour servir à la défense de la Révolution française* (Fragments to be used in defense of the French Revolution).

3. In Yale archives, CV, g, notebook 2, 17, we find this "general idea of the last chapter":

"1. Show how the human spirit in democratic peoples bends in every way toward unity and uniformity.

"2. Then show how this idea itself leads to administrative despotism.

"3. Need for sustaining human individuality.

"Union of liberty and equality, separation of the revolutionary element."

4. DA, I, A, 5, 86–98; see also Tocqueville's *Fragments sur la Démocratie*, pp. 5–6.

5. Sainte-Beuve, *Le Temps*, 7 April 1835; Faguet, *Politiques*, p. 66.

6. DA, I, A, 5, 95.

7. DA, I, A, 5, 97. In note K of the 1835 ed., p. 447, Tocqueville clarifies his thinking: the French Revolution, he says, perfected but did not create the centralization of the French administration. This note, which was reproduced in subsequent editions, anticipates ideas developed in book 2, chaps. 2–7, of *The Old Regime*.

8. Henrion de Pansey, *Du pouvoir municipal et de la police intérieure des communes* (Paris: Théophile Barrès et B. Duprat, 1820).

9. Ibid., p. 6 (I am quoting from the 3rd ed., 1833).

10. Ibid., p. 8.

11. Pierson, *Tocqueville and Beaumont*, esp. chap. 30; see also the travel diaries: OC, V, 1, 88–90 (Quincy, president of Harvard), 90 and 94 (Gray), 95–96 (Jared Sparks, author of *The Life of Gouverneur Morris*).

12. See Hervé de Tocqueville, "Coup d'oeil sur l'administration française," a 47-page ms., written at the behest of his son Alexis; Yale archives, C, III. Hervé writes: "Without the control that the king exercises over the administration, there would be no monarchy." Count Hervé passed for a decentralizer, but he was as cautious as one might expect a former prefect to be in that area. He had been a member of the commission charged with studying the possibility of decentralization at the end of Charles X's reign, and at the behest of Martignac he had written *La Charte provinciale*. He was chosen for these roles precisely because Martignac and Charles X knew that, although he favored decentralization, he was also cautious. The influence on Tocqueville of his father's ideas about decentralization should not be exaggerated.

13. The *département* was recognized as an entity and the offices of *conseiller général* and *conseiller d'arrondissement* became elective, but mayors and their assistants were appointed. The Republic of 1848 made the office of mayor elective, and the decree of March 1852 marked another step in progress toward decentralization. Later Broglie, Laboulaye, and Prévost-Paradol carried on Tocqueville's action in favor of decentralization.

14. OC, V, 2, 31–32 and 35.

15. OC, V, 2, 49 (see also 68–71).

16. OC, V, 2, 53–54.

17. Mill, *Autobiography* (London: Longmans, 1873).

18. OC, V, 2, 83–84, 89–90, and, on the "centralizing mania," 69.

19. Drescher, *Tocqueville and England*, (Cambridge, Mass.: Harvard University Press, 1964), chap. 5, pp. 74–104, and his *Dilemmas of Democracy*, pp. 35–38.

20. OC, 1866 ed., VII, 166–168, letter of 10 July 1838. The letter also tells us that at this point Tocqueville had decided to divide his "final chapter" into three parts: two chapters on "the general influence of the democratic ideas and sentiments, which the book has just examined, concerning the form of government," and a final chapter, quite brief, "a rhetorical summary of the various tendencies of equality and on the need not to combat equality but to turn it to advantage. This will be something that will link the end of the book to its introduction."

21. Montesquieu had already warned against the passion for uniformity: *Esprit des lois*, book 29, chap. 18.

22. Eichtal, *Alexis de Tocqueville*, p. 56.

23. That Tocqueville's fears were excessive is suggested, for instance, by this note, which identifies centralization with despotism: "General idea of the final chapter: How the ideas and mores that I have just described facilitate the establishment of despotism." Yale archives, CV, g, notebook 2, 16.

24. Yale archives, CV, k, notebook 1, 75; see also DA, II, D, 4, 305.

25. Here Tocqueville is following Montesquieu; by destroying the vitality of the intermediary bodies, administrative centralization had corrupted the principle of monarchy; see *Esprit des lois*, book 8, chap. 6. At bottom, it is the tendency of monarchy to abuse its power that leads to democracy.

26. AR, I, 55.

27. DA, II, D, 4, and on the centralizing role of revolutions, pp. 305–306 and 308–309. Though couched in general terms, the next-to-last paragraph on p. 309 actually deals quite specifically with the evolution of the July Monarchy. See also *Fragments inédits sur la Démocratie en Amérique*, pp. 4–5.

28. Yale archives, CV, k, notebook 1, 75–76.

29. AR, I, book 2, chaps. 2–7.

30. See especially AR, I, book 2, chap. 10, "The Crime of the Old Regime," p. 166.

31. The argument is worthy of Montesquieu and even of Henri de Boulainvilliers. The latter, in his *Histoire de l'ancien gouvernement de la France* (The Hague, 1727), wrote this about the intendants: "Only with great difficulty have I restrained my zeal against these oppressors of the fatherland, these vile adulators of a tyrannical power ... Therefore, when I dare to assert that the magistracy of the intendants ruined the ancient economy of the state and destroyed the sacred bonds of society, I appeal to the memory of centuries past, because it would require blindness for a reasonable monarchy to reject the methods that had sustained it for thirteen centuries in order to substitute others which do nothing but facilitate a despotic government better suited to the genius of the Persians, the Turks, and oriental peoples than to our constitution." Quoted in P. Pietri, *La réforme de l'Etat au XVIIIe siècle*.

32. AR, I, 216.

33. Letter to Grote, 27 February 1849, OC, 1866 ed., VI, p. 145; and S, 84. in

DA, II, D, 4, 307, he wrote that "extreme centralization of the government ultimately emasculates society . . . and weakens the government."

34. Faguet, *Politiques,* p. 92.

35. AR, I, introduction by Georges Lefebvre, p. 29.

36. AR, II, 200; see also AR, II, 343, and DA, II, D, 5, 320, last paragraph.

37. DA, I, B, IX, 319–323.

38. DA, II, D, 7, 333 (700); see also Yale archives, CV, g, notebook 3, 10.

39. Yale archives, CV, g, notebook 3, 16; compare Guizot's definition of the revolutionary spirit in his *Memoirs,* vol. II, chap. 9, pp. 21–22: "It imagines that its own ideas are complete and perfect and give it absolute power over all things, in the name of which it can, whatever the cost, destroy everything that is in order to remake it in the image of those ideas. This, in 1789, was France's capital error. In 1830 we attempted to relapse."

40. Cited in Pierre-Marcel, *Essai politique,* p. 338.

41. OC, V, 1, 202–203; the subject is first mentioned in this travel note from January 1832. In the margin of a draft to the introduction of DA, I, he wrote: "We are headed for a republic or for despotism or perhaps for an alternation between the two." Yale archives, CV, d, 28. See also DA, I, A, 5, 94, first paragraph: "Swinging between servitude and license."

42. OC, XI, 89–90. Letter to Royer-Collard, 15 August 1840.

43. Yale archives, CV, g, notebook 2, 188; see the similar passage in DA, II, D, 5, 320.

44. Yale archives, CV, k, notebook 2, 48–49; see also CV, k, notebook 2, 45: "days of anarchy in the midst of years of servitude."

45. See also Yale archives, CV, k, notebook 2, 45: "Centralization must increase because it is associated with immutable instincts . . . Anarchy is a passing symptom, centralization the disease itself."

46. Ibid., 48.

47. Yale archives, CV, k, notebook 2, 49; the same theme is broached in CV, g, notebook 2, 188, and CV, d, 17; an example of simultaneous anarchy and despotism is cited by Tocqueville in his chapter on the Directory: AR, II, book 3, chap. 1, pp. 269–281.

48. He used these notes in writing DA, II, D, 1 and 6, as well as the next-to-last paragraph of 4, 309, and 5, 321 and 319 (last paragraph).

49. DA, II, C, 14, 147 (end of last paragraph). Working manuscript of DA, II, D, 6, marginal note: "Our contemporaries are much more afraid of disorder than of servitude." Yale archives, CV, k, notebook 2, 53: "What you fear the most from the democratic social state is the political disturbance that it causes, while that is what I fear least. You are afraid of democratic freedom and I am afraid of democratic despotism."

50. Yale archives, CV, k, notebook 2, 48.

51. OC, XI, 79. Letter to Royer-Collard, 8 August 1839: "What I have seen of the political world from inside over the past few months has made me feel the need to revise certain parts of my work that I thought were finished."

52. The uprising of 12 May 1839, led by Blanqui and the Société des Saisons, drew only a few hundred participants and was quickly put down.

53. Anarchy is mentioned, however, in the final paragraphs of pp. 319 and

320. The possibility of anarchy as an end state is rejected in the penultimate paragraph of the chapter, on p. 321. The alternation idea recurs in S, 87, and in the conversations with Senior: see the conversation of 8 May 1851, cited by Eichtal, *Alexis de Tocqueville*, p. 307. The expression was also used by Guizot after 1848: "interminable and sterile alternations . . . anarchy or despotism." *De la démocratie en France* (1849), p. 155.

54. He noted these cycles much later on; see AR, II, 343: "Back-and-forth progress of our revolutions, which is misleading unless one looks closely. At the beginning, invariably a push toward decentralization: 1787, 1828, 1848. In the end, an extension of centralization. In the beginning people follow the logic of their principles; in the end they follow the logic of their habits and passions and those of the government."

55. DA, II, D, 5, 320.

56. Aron, *Les étapes*, pp. 260–261.

57. The final page of the next chapter's manuscript (chap. 6) contains this note concerning long-term tendencies: "A great political anarchy and an over-whelming administrative despotism."

58. DA, II, D, 5, 320–321; Tocqueville indicates that in France the two phases came very close together, almost simultaneously.

59. DA, II, D, 5, 320. See Yale archives, CV, g, notebook 2, 174: "The most original thing in my chapter is this still somewhat confused idea of two revolutions moving in almost opposite directions." See also CV, g, notebook 2, 187: "Clearly, these two very contrary revolutions are related; they both stem from the same cause and aid each other in their development."

60. DA, II, D, 5, 321.

61. See OC, V, 2, 53, for an analysis of these obstacles by John Stuart Mill.

62. Tocqueville's remarks on the alternation of anarchy and despotism do not apply to countries with a long-standing liberal tradition: he explicitly refers to countries "without established free institutions." Yale archives, CV, k, notebook 2, 48.

63. DA, II, B, 3, 108.

64. The cycle is attenuated, and revolutionary crises are avoided, as long as social mobility and democratic mores prevail, however.

65. Yale archives, CV, k, notebook 1, 39.

66. DA, II, D, 4: war, revolution, development of industry, and origins of the sovereign power.

67. This is perhaps a good place to respond to a criticism of Tocqueville by Thomas Molnar, *Le modèle défiguré: L 'Amérique de Tocqueville à Carter* (Paris: Presses Universitaires de France, 1978), pp. 140–141: "The crux of the problem is whether the logic of this ideology [of democracy] leads the country toward eventual submission to a tutelary state or toward a form of anarchy somehow vaguely contained by structures which are themselves defective. Tocqueville in-clines to accept the former alternative. The nature of this ideology, much more obvious today than it was in Tocqueville's time, leads me to think that the latter is more likely." But despotism was for Tocqueville only the most likely final outcome of a process much like the one that Molnar sees taking shape in the near future in America. Molnar is close to Tocqueville in his view of the dynamic; their only disagreement is over the final stable outcome.

68. DA, II, D, 8, 336.

69. DA, II, D, 6: "What Sort of Despotism Democratic Nations Have to Fear." Tocqueville at first refuses to name the phenomenon (DA, II, D, 6, 324). Then, on p. 325, he uses the expression "democratic despotism," which also occurs in a letter to his brother Edouard, 10 July 1838, OC, 1866 ed., VII, 167. Possible misunderstandings are eliminated by the statement that this is a new kind of despotism, different from the ancient and revolutionary forms. In a preliminary draft, Tocqueville casts about for a name for this new phenomenon: "I shall call it administrative despotism, for want of anything better." Yale archives, CV, g, notebook 2, 80. The expression also occurs in the published text, where one form of democratic despotism is characterized as "a compromise between administrative despotism and popular sovereignty" (p. 325).

70. DA, II, D, 6, 327.

71. Yale archives, CV, h, notebook 3, 21.

72. Ibid., 21 and 31: "This time the barbarians will not come from the frozen north; they will arise in the midst of our fields and cities."

73. Yale archives, CV, b, 32.

74. Tocqueville turned to the *Encyclopedia* for a definition of despotism: "Arbitrary and absolute tyrannical government by a single man." But he noted in the margin: "Must add: or by a single authority." A little further on he says: "This [definition] was written before I had seen the despotism of an assembly under the Republic." Yale archives, CV, g, notebook 2, 79.

75. See OC, VI, 1, 328, letter from Mill, 11 May 1840, as well as Mill's comments on I, xxviii, and II, vi–vii, of the Schocken edition.

76. Yale archives, CV, g, notebook 2, 79.

77. DA, II, C, 22, 273 (on the danger of military revolutions) and 24, 284 (on the prestige of the great military leader in a democracy). See also OC, V, 1, 186: "pernicious influence of military glory in republics."

78. OC, V, 1, 201–202, and AR, II, 29.

79. AR, II, 301.

80. DA, II, C, 19–26.

81. Yale archives, CV, j, notebook 2, 9.

82. Yale archives, CV, d, 3; see also pp. 4 and 16.

83. Yale archives, CV, i, and DA, II, 347n.

84. Yale archives, CV, j, notebook 2, 10 and 11.

85. DA, II, D, 6, 325.

86. DA, II, D, 7: "Continuation of the Preceding Chapters."

87. OC, XI, 79–83, letter to Royer-Collard, 8 August 1839, and Royer's response. See also Rémusat, *Mémoires*, III, 262–263, stating that Tocqueville and Beaumont came into parliament with exaggerated ideas about the gravity of the evil and with the noble plan of putting an end to it. Rémusat also shows that after Tocqueville became a member of the commission set up to investigate possible reforms, he adopted a much more prudent attitude. Finally, see OC, VIII, 1, 368–373.

88. There were also other revisions, which did not all result in important changes. A letter to J. J. Ampère, 17 September 1839, shows that Tocqueville revised DA, II, C, 5 (OC, XI, 128–130); a note dated 6 September 1839 indicates how he

wanted to correct DA, II, D, 4; see Yale archives, CV, k, notebook 1, 76 (quoted earlier in text). Not much seems to have come of this resolution, but it weighs in favor of my interpretation that Tocqueville's purpose was to distinguish between revolutionary and democratic causes of centralization.

89. Yale archives, CV, k, notebook 1, 21 and 22; CV, g, notebook 2, 18; CV, g, notebook 3, 9; CV, k, notebook 2, 50–51: "I do not believe that the government is organized ultimately for the benefit of the middle classes, and if I thought it possible, I would oppose it." See Chapter 1, fourth edition.

90. DA, II, D, 6.

91. For Tocqueville this was only a probability. A reawakening of liberty was always possible.

92. DA, II, D, 7, 333. See the second section of this chapter for a fuller treatment.

93. Guizot, *Histoire générale de la civilisation en France*, I, 243.

94. DA, II, D, 6, 323. This page links the theory of democratic despotism, which comes later, to the previous chapter (see p. 320, "two revolutions of contrary direction"), as well as to DA, II, D, 103, and DA, II, C, 21–26.

95. On the theme of equality and despotism, see also Montesquieu, *Esprit des lois*, book 19, chap. 3, p. 557, and book 6, chap. 4: "Men are all equals in republican government, and they are all equals in despotic government: in the former this is because they are everything; in the latter, because they are nothing."

96. *Esprit des lois,* book 19, chap. 27.

97. DA, II, D, 6, 324.

98. DA, II, D, 6, 324 (691–692).

99. See OC, 1866 ed., IX, 11, Tocqueville's acceptance speech to the French Academy: "It was to be feared that the government would finally dominate all [citizens], not because it had public opinion in its favor but because public opinion did not exist."

100. *Esprit des lois*, book 5, 14, p. 297; see DA, II, D, 2.

101. DA, II, D, 3, 303 (674).

102. The argument here extends certain reflections from volume I: see especially DA, I, B, 7, 266. Vauvenargues said of servitude that "it makes men so base as to make itself beloved."

103. On the relation between liberty and liberal sentiments, see Chapter 5, third section.

104. Raymond Aron, *Essai*, pp. 143–144.

105. Such a "mild" regime is the Swedish government. Roland Huntford, *The New Totalitarians* (New York: Stein and Day, 1972), goes too far, in my view, when he describes the "Swedish paradise" as a new totalitarianism. Huntford does not cite Tocqueville and obviously does not belong to the Tocquevillean tradition, but to that of Aldous Huxley's *Brave New World*.

106. Today's totalitarianism is not the same as democratic despotism. On this point I disagree with Giovanni Sartori, *Théorie de la démocratie* (Paris: Armand Colin, 1973), p. 121.

107. I cannot say as much for the judgment of Mayer, *Alexis de Tocqueville*, p. 60: "Thus, every nation will become a timid and hardworking flock, of which the government will be the shepherd. This is Aldous Huxley's 'brave new world.'

Some contemporary states resemble this portrait. Tocqueville's predictions have come true in less than a century."

108. See Paul Bénichou, *Le temps des prophètes* (Paris: Gallimard, 1977).

109. Aron, *Essai*, p. 143. Pierre-Marcel, *Essai politique*, pp. 228–229, has also noted the excessiveness of Tocqueville's fears of centralization.

110. See Chapter 6. In essence, the liberal state is a government of law. It coincided with the minimal state only in specific historical circumstances, as in the United States.

111. DA, II, D, 6, 325–326.

112. This is a classic theme of liberal thought, which has been treated by many writers, among them Bertrand de Jouvenel, *Les débuts de l'Etat moderne*, pp. 295–299, which contrasts what he calls "nomocracies" and "telocracies."

113. DA, II, D, 6, 327.

114. Robert A. Dahl, *After the Revolution?* (New Haven: Yale University Press, 1970): "I have tried to show why the exercise of popular sovereignty requires not one but several forms of delegated authority, certain of which are not democratic." It is not unreasonable to say that Tocqueville was the source of what is now called the theory of polyarchy. In order to see this, however, one must distinguish between the ideal type of democracy and the imperfect democracies of the transition period. The latter correspond quite closely to what are now called polyarchies, and the ideal type of democracy is the ideal toward which they converge.

115. Yale archives, CV, d, 11. After a revolution, liberty is even more frightening: "The same revolution which kills the appetite for liberty attracts men to equality." Yale archives, CV, d, 24. Recall that, according to DA, I, B, 1, 103, revolution exacerbates the passion for equality.

116. Yale archives, CV, k, notebook 2, 52.

117. DA, II, B, 1, and DA, II, D, 1, are particularly significant in this respect. Examination of the working notes suggests that both of these chapters stem from a single source; see Yale archives, CV, d, 23; CV, k, notebook 2, 14; CV, g, notebook 2, 16. In the working manuscript (CV, I, a) we find the text of DA, II, D, 1, but neither DA, II, B, 1, nor DA, II, D, 1, figures in the 1838 outline (CV, f). Both facts are further reasons to think that this chapter was originally part of DA, II, D, 1, and that Tocqueville belatedly added it to the beginning of part 2.

118. His chaps. 4, 5, and 7 are medium-range analyses, as is the end of chap. 6. The long-term analysis is found in chap. 8 and in the middle of chap. 6.

119. DA, II, D, 7, 333.

120. AR, I, book 2, chaps. 2–7, and book 3, chaps. 1 and 3–8.

121. Recall that part 2 of volume II was written in 1838 and revised in 1839, when Tocqueville's relations with Royer-Collard deteriorated as a result of certain disagreements; see Chapter 8.

122. DA, II, D, 8, 337.

123. DA, II, D, 7, 333.

124. Drescher, "Tocqueville's Two Democracies." Drescher himself stresses the fact that the most important innovation in volume II is to be found in part 4, in the theory of centralization. He sought to bring out the difference between volume I and volume II, whereas I am trying to indicate the most significant division in Tocqueville's work taken as a whole.

125. OC, XI, 307. Letter to J. J. Ampère, 1 February 1856.
126. S, 87.

Conclusion

1. Mill, *Auguste Comte and Positivism* (London: Routledge, 1908); the charge can be found on p. 149 of the French edition (Paris: Germer Baillière, 1868), trans. Georges Clemenceau.
2. S, 98.
3. S, 236.
4. DA, II, C, 19–26.
5. Mill, *Autobiography*, p. 193.
6. DA, I, B, 9.
7. DA, II, C, 21.
8. DA, II, B, 3, 108 (509).
9. DA, II, D, 7, 333 (700).
10. In 1838, while writing a preface for volume two, Tocqueville was prepared to recognize the error that he had made in volume one in predicting a weakening of the federal bond. See Yale archives, CV, k, notebook 1, 39.
11. DA, II, D, 6.
12. AR, I, book 2, chap. 10: "How the destruction of political liberty and the separation of classes caused almost all the ills of which the Old Regime died"; and AR, I, book 3, chap. 1: "How, toward the middle of the eighteenth century, men of letters became the country's leading political men, and the effects that resulted from this."
13. In the *Souvenirs* (p. 255), Tocqueville will again note this fact with admiration: "England, sheltered from the revolutionary malady by the wisdom of its laws and the strength of its ancient mores . . ."
14. OC, 1866 ed., VI, 227, 17 September 1853.
15. AR, I, 60–61.
16. See the final sentence of *Democracy in America*, DA, II, D, 8, 339 (705): "But it depends [on nations themselves] whether equality is to lead to servitude or freedom, knowledge or barbarism, prosperity or wretchedness."
17. See Chapter 6.
18. See Chapter 7.
19. *Social Contract*, book 2, chap. 12. Rousseau, as a disciple of Montesquieu, attempted to lay the foundations of a theory of democracy. He failed because his views were colored by the revolutionary spirit already forming within the bosom of the Old Regime, notably in the elaboration of a dogma of unlimited sovereignty.
20. Montesquieu, *Esprit des lois*, book 19, chap. 14.

Index